Ukraine's Unnamed War

The Russian invasion of Ukraine in 2022 has its roots in the events of 2013–2014. Russia cynically termed the seditionist conflict in Crimea and Eastern Donbas a "civil war" in order to claim non-involvement. This flies in the face of evidence, but the authors argue that the social science literature on civil wars can be used help understand why no political solution was found between 2015 and 2022. The book explains how Russia, after seizing Crimea, was reacting to events it could not control and sent troops only to areas of Ukraine where it knew it would face little resistance (Eastern Donbas). Kremlin decisionmakers misunderstood the attachment of the Russian-speaking population to the Ukrainian state and also failed to anticipate that their intervention would transform Ukraine into a more cohesively "Ukrainian" polity. Drawing on Ukrainian documentary sources, this concise book explains these important developments to a non-specialist readership.

DOMINIQUE AREL is Chair of Ukrainian Studies at the University of Ottawa. His publications include *Rebounding Identities: The Politics of Identity in Russia and Ukraine* (co-edited with Blair A. Ruble, 2006). He organizes the Annual Danyliw Research Seminar on Ukraine and is Director of the Annual ASN World Convention at Columbia University.

JESSE DRISCOLL is an associate professor of political science at the School of Global Policy and Strategy at the University of California San Diego. His publications include *Warlords and Coalition Politics in Post-Soviet States* (Cambridge, 2015) and *Doing Global Fieldwork* (2021).

Ukraine's Unnamed War

Before the Russian Invasion of 2022

DOMINIQUE AREL
University of Ottawa

JESSE DRISCOLL
University of California San Diego

CAMBRIDGE
UNIVERSITY PRESS

CAMBRIDGE
UNIVERSITY PRESS

Shaftesbury Road, Cambridge CB2 8EA, United Kingdom

One Liberty Plaza, 20th Floor, New York, NY 10006, USA

477 Williamstown Road, Port Melbourne, VIC 3207, Australia

314–321, 3rd Floor, Plot 3, Splendor Forum, Jasola District Centre,
New Delhi – 110025, India

103 Penang Road, #05–06/07, Visioncrest Commercial, Singapore 238467

Cambridge University Press is part of Cambridge University Press & Assessment,
a department of the University of Cambridge.

We share the University's mission to contribute to society through the pursuit of
education, learning and research at the highest international levels of excellence.

www.cambridge.org
Information on this title: www.cambridge.org/9781316511497

DOI: 10.1017/9781009052924

First published 2023

A catalogue record for this publication is available from the British Library.

ISBN 978-1-316-51149-7 Hardback
ISBN 978-1-009-05594-9 Paperback

Contents

Figures

Maps

Tables

Acknowledgments

Co-authoring is difficult. Our collegial relationship and our friendship, tested by the fire of war, is much stronger than it was before collaboration. We wrangled over every sentence, but the result is a book that we are both proud of, and that neither of us could have written alone. Lennon and McCartney.

The book would not have seen daylight without the valiant and dynamic assistance of a team of research assistants associated with the Chair of Ukrainian Studies at the University of Ottawa over many years. Oleksandr Melnyk (PhD, University of Toronto) was the main researcher during the Donbas war in 2014 until his return to Ukraine. (After four months under Russian occupation in Kherson oblast in 2022, he safely returned to Canada.) Chair doctoral students were central to the effort: Natalia Stepaniuk, who graduated in 2018, and the "new generation" of Alexandra Wishart, Bertrand de Franqueville, and Anna Vozna, from 2019 on. Iuliia Skubytska, who had taken part in a Ukraine Summer School co-sponsored by the Chair, became a key researcher from Kharkiv and Kyiv. Anastasia Llewellyn became our invaluable copy editor. On the Driscoll side, surveys with militia members and coding of social media data were facilitated by the extraordinary work of Ganna Grebennikova, who led a hardworking team comprised of Oleksandr Keniz, Alex Sabadan, Yulia Nagirniak, Iryna Sheremeta, Kateryna Zablotska, Olena Valsiuk, and Christinia Parandii. Iulia Wilson coded the birthplaces of Ukrainian martyrs used to produce Figure 6.1. We must also acknowledge the hard work of Alexandr Karkepov, whose nimble mind assisted in the initial translation/transliteration process for Twitter data coding in real time during the fall of 2014 – the work that generated the Danyliw paper which began the Driscoll–Arel collaboration.

We owe an incalculable gratitude to the numerous Ukrainian scholars, researchers, interviewees, subjects, and citizens who contributed to this book. Arel has been building ties with Ukraine for decades, in large part thanks to the networks developed through the Annual Danyliw Seminar held between 2005 and 2019 on the University of Ottawa campus (and resuming in 2022 after a COVID pause). He acquired more-than-a-lifetime of debts and acknowledgments, but a few names bear mention: Jars Balan, Anna Colin Lebedev, Mayhill Fowler, Alexandra Goujon, John Paul Himka, the late Valery Khmelko, Serhiy Kudelia, Daria Mattingly, Alti and Berel Rodal, Oxana Shevel, Ioulia Shukan, Lucan Way, and Yuri Zhukov. Driscoll visited Ukraine for the first time in 2014 and, with help from Arel, was lucky enough to make early contact with KIIS, a number of extraordinary Kyiv-Mohyla students, and especially Volodymyr Ishchenko, whose generosity and integrity continue to humble us.

Different chapters of the book benefitted from collegial feedback at the University of California San Diego – too many to list, but we will mention a few. Erik Gartzke, Jon Lindsay, Phil Roeder, and Rex Douglass were generous with supporting comments to an early paper (joint with Zachary Steinert-Threlkeld) analyzing Russian-language behaviors inside Ukraine, affirming that we were going after a big question with the right sample. Amelia Glaser and Peter Gourevitch assisted in hosting Slava Vakarchuk at UCSD midway through the book writing, providing a memorable morale boost. Nico Ravenilla, hearing this book's argument for the first time, pierced the conversation with the question "what institutions did Russian-speakers in Ukraine build to coordinate lobbying efforts and what happened to those institutions after Crimea" – an offhand clarifying comment that cemented our book's chapter structure two weeks later. We borrowed confidence from Craig McIntosh and Ron Suny (at Michigan) – exemplary empiricists from different disciplinary traditions – who saw maturing versions of the argument and assessed the big story as Russia's soft power weakness.

Barbara Walter and Roger Petersen are the two senior scholars that provided the most important mid-book encouragement. Walter's advice was that very few people want to read game theory. Petersen was forceful in his insistence that the theory chapter be written in plain language, taking aim at big questions and not allowing ourselves to get side-tracked with minutiae (whether game-theoretic or constructivist). Once the game theory was gated in the Appendix, we still spent months trying to get the presentation right in a way that might be pleasing to technical and nonspecialist audiences. In this we were steered in various ways by Renee Bowen ("I have a question"), Keith Darden ("...*really* complicated..."), and James Fearon ("Russia bad").

Arel had an opportunity to present earlier portions of the book to audiences at the Canadian Institute of Ukrainian Studies, the Harvard Ukrainian Research Institute, the Prairie Centre for the Study of Ukrainian Heritage, George Washington University (with Driscoll), Pennsylvania State University, and SciencesPo Paris. Driscoll presented at the Ohio State University, the College of William and Mary, the University of Chicago, George Washington University (PONARS), the University of Michigan, and Yale University.

Going back to his graduate days, a select number of scholars played a formative role in Arel's career: the late Bohdan Bociurkiw (who introduced him to Ukrainian studies), Roger Kanet, the late Jerry Hough, Thane Gustafson, Peter Solomon, David Kertzer, and Frank Sysyn.

Both Arel and Driscoll want to dedicate this book to David Laitin. We owe him an immense intellectual debt, as a mentor and inspiration. Most importantly for this book, David established a research agenda based on the coordination potential of the Russian-speaking population living outside of Russia's territory. A full generation has passed since he published *Identity in Formation* (Arel was the research assistant for Ukraine). This project studies some of the children, and grandchildren, of the research subjects whose experiences informed that book. Anyone who finishes this book and enjoyed it would do well to trace our academic lineage back to the root.

In the end, nothing is more foundational than emotional support. Arel owes everything to his beloved wife, Maria Salomon, a published scholar of medieval Russia, his parents, Lucienne and the late Gaston, and his daughter Clio. Max and Eleanor Driscoll, and their mother Emma Salustro, are excited to have their dad back with this book out of his head.

1 | *A War Within the "Russian World"*

For nearly twenty-five years after becoming an independent state in 1991, political order in Ukraine was based on a predictable East–West regional rotation of power.[1] Although there were moments of tension, periodic warnings that the state would "split in two" were at odds with Ukrainian political practice. The probability of political violence seemed remote. The Maidan protests, which occurred between November 2013 and February 2014, changed everything. Maidan introduced the use of politically driven violence by both state agents (the police) and protesters. A spike in lethal violence in February 2014 brought down a president, Viktor Yanukovych, with an electoral base in the East. Power shifted to an alliance of parties based in the West. For the first time, the East–West alternation of power took place outside the regular election cycle. Russia sent its military to annex Crimea. An armed conflict followed in the Donbas eastern region. The war had already claimed around 13,000 lives when Vladimir Putin made his historic decision, sometime in late 2021 or early 2022, to launch a full-scale military invasion to try to break Ukraine. This book is the story of Ukrainian politics during the 2013–2021 period, a period of adaptation to various "hybrid" Russian military interventions.

Summary of the Argument

The book considers the causes and consequences of the Donbas war of 2014–2021. In these pages, we provide empirical evidence supporting three analytical arguments. The first deals with how the war started. The

---

[1] In public and academic discourse, Ukraine's twenty-five *oblasts* (provinces) are generally divided into four broad regions: East, South, Center, and West. For simplicity's sake, and unless otherwise indicated, we will refer to East (East and South) and West (Center and West). The regional rotation had occurred three times in presidential elections since independence – with the election of Leonid Kuchma in 1994 (Eastern electoral base), Viktor Yushchenko in 2004 (Western electoral base), and Viktor Yanukovych in 2010 (Eastern electoral base). After 2014, both presidents (Poroshenko and Zelensky) obtained a nationwide mandate.

second relates to how the war has been fought. The third concerns why the war was so difficult to end. We argue that the dynamics of the armed conflict in Donbas were initially consistent with those of a civil war in the social science meaning of the term – not in how Russia used the term in its state propaganda – and that considering the Eastern Donbas conflict as a civil war had analytical utility in the pre-2022 war period.

Our first argument involves the proximate causes of Ukraine's war in Donbas. Our theoretical contribution is an explanation of what happens to individuals and a society in the months just before a war breaks out. The empirical contribution methodically traces the origins of the war from the violent protests on Maidan to an insurgency in Donbas that was galvanized by the Russian intervention in Crimea.

The deadly violence on Maidan caused the collapse of the central government, but not of the central levers of state power. After the president was removed by parliament, the security institutions housed in Kyiv – army and police – immediately recognized the new authorities that had backed Maidan as legitimate claimants to political power. Outside of the capital, however, the loyalty of security officers varied according to regions. State capacity had faltered in the Ukrainian West prior to the resolution of Maidan, when protesters stormed police stations and established impromptu checkpoints, but order was quickly restored after the regime change. The situation was ominously different in the East, the electoral base of the ousted regime.

In the Crimean peninsula, local elites quickly coordinated on sedition, mediated and facilitated by prewar state institutions. More than two-thirds of government officials, civil servants, security officers, and army personnel defected to the Russian state. As a result, Russia captured an entire state apparatus through the surgical use of coercive tools. A mere two deaths were reported. In the continental East, however, the streets largely determined the political fate of key oblasts. Over a period of two months, clashes frequently occurred between anti-Maidan and pro-Maidan groups across the East, with little police intervention. Pro-Ukrainian forces ultimately prevailed, except in Donbas. The Ukrainian state proved sturdier in areas where ethnic Ukrainians formed a strong majority compared to areas of ethnic Russian concentration, but our story emphasizes the agency of actors and communities over structures. Demographics were not destiny.[2]

---

[2] In the last Ukrainian census, carried out in 2001, ethnic Russians formed approximately 60 percent of the population in Crimea (70 percent in the port

In Eastern Donbas, the urban and industrial core of the region, state institutions imploded chaotically. Armed men seized buildings. The regional and local administration gradually ceased to function. Few government officials defected as antistate forces came out of the woodwork and haphazardly established parallel institutions. Indigenous actors likely had some assistance from Russia, but the extent of Moscow's influence in these early months is contested and will likely remain so. Importantly, Ukrainian state weakness in Crimea and Eastern Donbas was contrasted with institutional resilience most everywhere else. Despite street pressure, most state officials remained in their posts. The Ukrainian West massively supported the abrupt regime change. The residual capacity of state institutions to endure in Ukraine's East could not have been confidently predicted in advance.

Our second argument emphasizes Ukrainian political agency during what came to be known in the Russian media as the "Russian Spring," that is, the anti-Maidan demonstrations in the East in March–May 2014. The evidence of unified Russian command and control over local actors in Ukraine's East is clearest in Crimea. In Chapter 5, we document the use of Russian special forces to seize the levers of state power. Evidence of similar activities occurring elsewhere is sparse. In retrospect, it seems to us that Russia deployed so-called Little Green Men (unmarked Russian soldiers) conservatively, sending them only to areas of Ukraine where they knew they would be able to operate in safety. In Donbas, Putin held back for months before ordering the military to intervene in order to stabilize the front lines, not to pacify additional territory.

The purpose of this distinction is not to absolve the Kremlin of blame for the violence or downplay Russia's role. Russia initiated the armed conflict by seizing Crimea. The sequence in the Donbas is less clear. On the one hand, Russian public diplomacy and television – what might be called information warfare – spared no effort to delegitimize the post-Maidan Ukrainian state. On the other, Ukrainian protagonists had a decisive impact shaping the 2022 war map.[3] After Crimea, Russian

city of Sevastopol), and just under 40 percent in the two Donbas provinces of Donetsk and Luhansk (Rowland 2004, 502). In the Donbas areas where the insurgency had stabilized after September 2014, ethnic Russians were close to, or exceeded, 50 percent of the population. In no other Eastern oblast was the figure higher than 26 percent.

[3] Ukrainian in the territorial citizenship sense (resident of Ukraine prior to the conflict). Many protagonists defined themselves as political Russians in February 2014. Many surely still do.

involvement was reactive. This book documents a largely ineffectual quest by the Kremlin, beginning in 2013 and persisting until 2022, to find reliable Russian political surrogates in Ukraine.

The Donbas rebellion turned into an actual war, a military conflict, when a commando headed by Russian citizen Igor Girkin, also known by his *nom de guerre* Strelkov, seized Sloviansk (Donetsk oblast) in April 2014. The Ukrainian government reacted by sending the army to besiege the town. In the Ukrainian narrative, Strelkov was an agent taking orders from the Kremlin. The war, in this narrative, was thus clearly initiated *externally*. The optics at the time certainly reinforced the impression. The Girkin men looked like the Crimean Little Green Men and arrived from Crimea. Yet available evidence suggests that Strelkov was a freelancer, someone tolerated (but mistrusted) by Russian authorities, who hoped to incite a local uprising. Whether Moscow *ever* had direct control over Strelkov remains disputed. His departure from Donbas appeared to have been a condition for Russia to intervene militarily in August. It is plausible to us that Sloviansk marked the beginnings of a Russian policy of encouraging volunteers to go and fight in Donbas, hoping that the contagion would spread to destabilize the rest of Russian-speaking Eastern Ukraine.[4]

The point here is not to deny that Russia had military intelligence personnel, perhaps even special forces, in operation in Donbas in the four months before Russian soldiers were sent in. It is rather to assert that there is no compelling evidence that these Russian actors *controlled* events on the ground until August. Even less convincing is the notion that Russia activated an existing pro-Russian network of agents in Donbas. On the contrary, available evidence suggests that Russia spent months seeking local agents of influence. Unlike in Crimea, in Donbas, Russia was forced to reach outside the existing (and fast imploding) power structure, leaving behind as potential partners for the Kremlin only a smattering of former police officers, fringe Russian nationalists, street hooligans, and individuals from the lower rungs of the Party of Regions.[5]

---

[4] In the months preceding Russian military intervention, thousands of volunteers from Russia joined anti-Kyiv battalions in Donbas. These men received logistical assistance from the Russian military to cross the border but were not in service (contra the soldiers sent later that summer).

[5] We agree with Hauter (2021b, 222), who takes several authors to task for a tendency to "assume rather than prove causality" when it comes to Russia's role as an instigator. We understand our project as an answer to Hauter's call for careful causal process tracing.

The Kremlin was clearly reticent to act if there was a legal discontinuity in the establishment of anti-Kyiv governments, as was the case with the proclamation of Donetsk and Luhansk "people's republics" (known by their Russian acronyms DNR [Donetsk People's Republic] and LNR [Luhansk People's Republic]) in May 2014. In areas where insurgents were forced to improvise the creation of new parallel state institutions from scratch, they received less Russian support. If quickly coordinated locals could retain control of existing institutions, the Kremlin was more willing to act. The failure of Eastern Ukrainian elites to coordinate outside of Crimea meant there was no "legitimate" institutional face of insurgency for Russia to support. Many abortive uprisings took place nonetheless. The hope that Russian support was just over the horizon motivated thousands. Statements of Kremlin officials, very large Russian military troop movements at the Ukrainian border, and other signals led insurgents in Donbas to believe the Russian military was about to arrive.

Our third argument is that ignoring the local roots of the conflict in Donbas generated the wrong policy prescriptions during much of the 2015–2021 period. This is not to relativize the Russian violations of the territorial integrity of Ukraine, and especially not to link Ukrainian or Western behavior to the unprovoked Russian invasion of 2022. Our more modest goal is to explain why some opportunities for resolution were rejected by political actors in Kyiv and Moscow. The narrative that Russia had engineered the war from the start pointed Ukrainian actors toward a "No to Capitulation" position that only unconditional withdrawal of Russian forces could yield lasting conflict resolution. The Minsk Agreement implicitly acknowledged that for the conflict to be resolved, the political grievances of Donbas actors had to be addressed first (through elections and what amounted to autonomy over language, police, and trade) before Russian forces withdrew (with Ukraine resuming control of the border). The very notion that Donbas warlords could acquire internationally validated electoral legitimacy and a special status for their territory was considered anathema in Ukrainian political discourse, a "red line" that could not be crossed. This book explains how that impasse came to be constructed as natural and hegemonic by Ukrainians. In January–February 2022, despite the threat of a military invasion and the request by France and Germany to revisit its positions (Sorokin 2022), the Ukrainian government would not budge on Minsk.

The Concept of Civil War

The seemingly simple matter of *naming* the war in Donbas was extremely controversial. In Ukraine, the term civil war remains politically radioactive. This is because Russia appropriated the term from the 2014 outset to assert that the conflict was entirely between Ukrainians – between citizens of Ukraine – and that Russia's only involvement was humanitarian in nature. In fact, Russia sent heavy weapons to Donbas fighters, shelled Ukrainian positions, stealthily dispatched regular troops to support an insurgent offensive, and eventually integrated Eastern Donbas battalions into the Russian military chain of command. In that sense, *civil war* in its political use by the Russian state was wrong and offensive. Political and academic discourse sympathetic to Ukraine rejected the term out of hand, which precluded any meaningful discussion about its validity.

Names, however, serve a different purpose in scholarly research than in public discourse. As an analytical tool, the concept of civil war applies to an observable situation wherein a critical mass of individuals, who belong to the same polity (state), fight each other beyond a minimal threshold of deaths (Kalyvas 2006, 17).[6] This does not preclude the presence of foreign actors on the theater of operation. As a matter of fact, foreign intrusion in civil wars is quite frequent, closer to the norm than the exception. Civil wars since 1945 have often featured an international component – not just direct foreign intervention, but also diaspora mobilization, the use of mercenaries and freelancers, arms sales, intelligence sharing, and information warfare.[7]

As already mentioned, a number of Russian military intelligence agents were probably active early on, and likely increasing in number before the Russian army sent weapons, and then soldiers, to Donbas. But with the exception of the Strelkov commando unit (of sixty men) and of the thousands of Russian volunteers pouring in, the great majority of fighters joining improvised militias and battalions were locals. This was

---

[6] A common coding rule for empirical political scientists using cross-national data is a violent event that leaves 1,000 citizens dead, including at least 100 on the government side, following Fearon and Laitin (2003) and Sambanis (2004).

[7] A large body of scholarly work challenges the black-and-white typology of civil vs. interstate wars, including Salehyan, Gleditsch, and Cunningham (2011) and Gleditsch (2007). Cunningham, Gleditsch, and Salehyan (2009) estimate that about 45 percent of rebel groups receive explicit support from

recognized by the Ukrainian army at the onset of hostilities. Military commanders and soldiers were reluctant to fight what they thought was a domestic insurgency (Bukkvoll 2019, 299). The war began as an armed rebellion goaded a state overreaction. The rebel insurgents were people who lived in Ukraine before the hostilities. Russia directly intervened later on, making the war both internal and external, a civil war and an interstate war. Russia would never officially acknowledge its military presence and intervention in Donbas. The Ukrainian government considered it a war of aggression from the very outset.

International humanitarian organizations, which had personnel on the ground in Donbas, also emphasized the internal nature of the conflict. In summer 2014, when the military clashes escalated, the Red Cross and other prominent nongovernmental organizations (NGOs) made the determination that the violence had now become a *noninternational armed conflict*, which is to humanitarian law what civil war is to political science (International Committee of the Red Cross 2014; Williamson 2014). After the Russian army directly intervened in late August 2014, *international armed conflict*, the equivalent of an interstate war in the social science lexicon, was added to – but generally did not replace – the noninternational categorization of the conflict.[8]

The war in Donbas was thus a civil war at its root. The warfighting technology of the Donbas war was unusual in that the conflict developed fairly rapidly into a highly conventional civil war. After being initially fought on both sides by irregular formations (improvised volunteer battalions that sometimes intermingled with the civilian populations), pro-Ukraine and anti-Ukraine forces resorted to heavy

a foreign government. Other recent high-profile studies on the effects of third parties on civil war processes, all of which assume that foreign intervention is ubiquitous, include Balch-Lindsay, Enterline, and Joyce (2008), Popovic (2017), and Lee (2018). Research programs on proxy warfare (Berman and Lake 2019), cross-domain deterrence (Gartzke and Lindsay 2019), and nonstate warfare (Biddle 2021) all intentionally blur the comfortable subdisciplinary distinctions between intrastate and interstate conflict.

[8] In September 2014, Amnesty International announced that the armed conflict was now "international" (Amnesty International 2014). Other major NGOs were more nuanced. Human Rights Watch (2016) said the conflict remained "primarily non-international." The Moscow-based NGO Memorial called it both internal and international (Pravozashchytnyi tsentr Memorial 2015). The Kharkiv-based NGO Human Rights in Ukraine said that it "may qualify" as international (International Partnership for Human Rights 2016). All these NGOs seemingly agree that the war began as an internal (noninternational) conflict.

weaponry characteristic of interstate warfare, complete with trenches, artillery battles, mines, and snipers.[9] This explains one comparatively unusual aspect of Ukraine's civil war: the relatively low civilian death count between 2015 and 2022. The estimates of at least 3,000 deaths in Ukraine paled in comparison to 50,000 in Bosnia, or over 100,000 in Syria (Seybolt, Aronson, and Fischhoff 2013, 5; Guha-Sapir et al. 2018). The proportion of civilian to combatant deaths was also much lower in Donbas (over 25 percent) than in Bosnia (over 50 percent) or Syria (over 70 percent).

This is because – like most conventional interstate wars since the nuclear revolution – two armies eventually settled into clashing with each other across a contested line of control. Both sides were supported by civilian populations, but both sides also held back from total war, so civilians could gradually remove themselves from lines of fire. Ukraine's violence never felt like 1990s Bosnia. There were no roving bands of predatory militias, no mass graves, no mass rapes. As the security levers of the Ukrainian state collapsed in a large area of Donbas, most of the early combatants on both sides had little military training. Still, most military encounters gradually took on a conventional guise, as if theatrically recreating World War I tactics.

If irregular warfare had spread across the country, or if Ukrainian volunteer battalions had tried to occupy hostile urban centers, or if Russia had used its military much earlier instead of just threatening to do so, civilian victimization could have been far more widespread, brutal, and atrocious.[10] Until 2022 Ukraine's war was fought like an interstate war, but it was largely a conflict where Ukrainians (in the territorial sense) shot at other Ukrainians.

Our argument is that the concept of *civil war* is analytically useful for scholars and also instrumentally useful for policymakers trying to

---

[9] One striking difference between Donbas and other intrastate battlefields is that aerial bombing was used only intermittently for most of the period covered in our study.

[10] Our point is that *systematic* attacks on civilians did not occur as part of armed encounters, contra Syria, Yemen, or numerous other civil wars ongoing in 2014. For evidence that civilian victimization tends to be higher if a style of warfare closer to the irregular ideal-type is employed, see Kalyvas and Balcells (2010; 2014). Following Biddle (2021, 9), our analysis of military matters in this book shoulders "the social science challenge of understanding actors' internal political dynamics rather than the traditional military task of counting weapons or assessing technology per se."

understand the roots of one of the most important conflicts of the early twenty-first century. The DNR/LNR came into being because of the breakdown of the inherited post-Soviet political institutions that had managed high-stakes bargaining between social forces until 2014. The story of "Ukraine fighting off an invasion" in 2022 has quite naturally crowded out the story of "Kyiv bargaining with its Russian-speaking periphery." Our aim is to gently correct the shift in language for the historical record. We suspect many Russian-speaking communities living in Ukraine's East would recognize themselves in the story we present prior to the 2022 war. Naming the Donbas war 2014–2021 a civil war was controversial from a policy perspective, admittedly, since it drew attention to and placed causal weight on domestic factors in Ukrainian politics. This could be caricatured as "blaming the victim." In our view, however, domestic Ukrainian politics *were* root causes of the war in 2014.

The decision by Putin in 2022 to unleash a full-scale war of aggression on Ukraine is not the subject of this book. The war was unprovoked. The claim that the Donbas population had to be protected from "genocide" is an absolute fabrication. In fact, after a violent spike in summer 2014–2015 (see Chapter 7), civilian casualties had remained low between March 2015 and February 2022 (see Chapter 8). Static trench warfare dividing two competing, but consolidating, state projects – one recognized by most of the international community (based in Kyiv) and the other basically kept on life support by Russia. But the population supplying the foot soldiers for the anti-Kyiv side had lived in Ukraine before 2014. The Russian language was hegemonic on their side of the line of control, too – but also spoken quite a bit on the Kyiv side.

Prior to the pre-February 2022 war, then, violent and competitive political processes pitted Eastern Ukrainians against each other. If one were willing to adapt Russian terminology, what was occurring was the first *intra-Russkii mir* (Russian World) civil war in nearly a century.[11]

---

[11] *Russkii mir* is a construct premised on the idea that Russian language, culture, and politics are one, and aiming to validate Russian intervention abroad (Toal 2017, 70–91, 204–5, 237–44). After the 1917 Bolshevik Revolution, Ukraine was the principal terrain of a devastating civil war that initially opposed monarchists ("Whites") and revolutionaries ("Reds"), most of whom saw themselves as Russians. The war later involved Ukrainian nationalists and peasant-anarchists.

Since Ukrainian independence, the loyalty of Russian-speakers in the East toward the Ukrainian state had never been tested as it was in 2014.[12] Fighters on both sides were motivated by perceptions of political equality and cultural security. Some feared domination by a Ukrainian-speaking center. Some feared domination by Putin and Moscow. Russian-speakers outside Donbas, imagined by Russia to belong to this Russian World, on the whole remained loyal to a Ukrainian state in 2014. They did so again in 2022, with far greater unity, since the first cities to be bombed indiscriminately were Eastern Ukrainian Russian-speaking majority cities. Our story emphasizes the initial division *among* Russian-speakers, between a Donbas constituency and the rest of the East.

A War of Narratives

The war in Donbas is about territorial control, but, as is always the case with violent internal conflicts, it originates in disputes over political legitimacy. There are two polarized views on how to describe Maidan and the Donbas war. In both versions, the two events are causally connected. The war of narratives presents Maidan as either a protest against state violence (a "Revolution of Dignity") or a coup. The Donbas war is described as either a war of aggression or a civil war.

On Maidan, the divide is over the interpretation of violence. Violence was first used by the police against peaceful protesters in late November 2013. Groups of protesters resorted to violence against the police on the following day, but were disavowed by Maidan leaders. In January–February 2014, these groups used violence against the police in order to break a political impasse. Violence by protesters was now framed as self-defense, and therefore legitimate, in the pro-Maidan narrative. The disproportionate use of counterforce by the police, which culminated in a sniper massacre, brought down the government, and the president was removed.

The counternarrative is that Maidan produced a coup, or *coup d'état* (*perevorot*, in Russian). The image of protesters firing at the

---

[12] Russian-speaker is defined here as the *preference* to speak Russian, not the ability to speak it (see Chapter 3). By that criteria, surveys show that most people in Ukraine's East are Russian-speakers, and most in the West are Ukrainian-speakers, that is, prefer to speak Ukrainian.

police, and of the government falling shortly thereafter, lent credence in some quarters to the idea that a coup – understood here as the use of violence to bring about a change in power – had taken place.

Narratives of legitimacy are selective: the self-defense of protesters in one is overshadowed by the self-defense of state agents (the police) in another. In political discourse, Revolution of Dignity or coup are used normatively to legitimize or delegitimize a political outcome. In our book, our interest is more analytical than normative. We hope that readers will come to understand the logic of violence and its political consequences. The police used what certainly appeared to be disproportionate force, particularly at the very beginning and the very end. Frontline protesters used violence strategically in order to provoke a political change.

The Dominant Policy Alternative: Hybrid Warfare

There is an alternative way of viewing the conflict that puts the locus of blame on great power politics. In this account, Ukraine is being fought over by Russia and the West. When Russian policy elites felt they were losing the tug of war, they decided to punish Ukrainians by unleashing new "hybrid warfare" techniques. This is not our argument, but we acknowledge that it has more than a grain of truth to it.

The standard account of the war in Ukraine begins with geography. Ukraine is located between Russia and the West (or the Western Security Community). Realist considerations drive decision-making at the highest levels in the Kremlin and in NATO capitals, and this is not lost on Ukrainian political elites. Their country is a buffer between great powers. Just as the United States would not allow Mexico to join a mutual defensive security alliance with China, the prospect of Ukraine joining NATO is anathema to Russia.

For many decades, balancing these interests was possible. In the early 1990s, against the backdrop of the breakup of the Soviet Union and the August 1991 failed coup, the United States and Russia bargained and compromised. As a sovereign nonnuclear Ukraine emerged, the West was sensitive to the need to help moderate forces in Russia consolidate power. This meant treading lightly, since nothing in the post-Soviet periphery was seen as worth the risk of trading Russian President Boris Yeltsin for someone like Gennady Zyuganov (Yeltsin's Communist opponent) or Alexander Lebed (a Russian general who had acted as a free agent in the 1992 war in Moldova). Russian diplomats failed to secure a written commitment that NATO would not expand eastward, it seems, because they did not think that they had to.[13] There is scant evidence that NATO expansion to Ukraine was considered or even discussed in the early 1990s (Krawchenko 1993, 83–4, 90–5). Ukraine was understood to represent a vital Russian interest.

Another aspect of the compromise was that Ukraine would have the diplomatic support of Western powers, so long as it relinquished its nuclear weapons (a gamble eased by the recent experience of the Chernobyl disaster). Ukraine agreed to comply under the framework of the 1994 Budapest Memorandum in which the United States volunteered security "assurances" that fell conspicuously short of a commitment to use force to uphold the territorial integrity of Ukraine (Pifer 2017, 49).[14] In the following decade, Ukraine sought to balance Russian and Western geopolitical interests in a pragmatic "multi-vector" foreign policy (D'Anieri 2019b, 73–8).

---

[13] Following Sarotte (2014) and Itzkowitz Shifrinson (2016), we are intrigued by the historical counterfactuals. What might have been had Russian elites in 1990 not been so internally divided, so optimistic about Russia's ability to join the West, and so myopic about the temporary leverage that they had? Russia might, for instance, have demanded that the United States sign a simple, clear, unambiguous promise never to expand NATO into former Soviet-dominated territory. Russian diplomats could have bundled these kinds of "concessions" (which at the time might not have seen as concessions at all, but simply formalization of mutually shared understandings at the highest levels) with the resolution of the German question, or traded them for authorization by the UN Security Council to use force in the First Gulf War against Iraq. Our point is not to advocate for these kinds of positions, nor to argue that they would have been enforceable, but simply to note that alternative arrangements for Ukraine from the 2000s–2010s onwards might have been feasible if Russian elites had behaved differently than they did in the early 1990s.

[14] Western governments made economic and geopolitical support for Ukraine contingent on the removal of nuclear weapons (Cohen 2017). In hindsight, Ukrainian nuclear disarmament can be seen as overdetermined by the fact that the state was too poor to pay for its maintenance and would have been barred from legally acquiring necessary components from abroad (Rublee 2015, 145–7). At the time there were grave concerns that economic pressures might tempt Ukraine to follow North Korea's example, and export weapons or technical expertise (Jones et al. 1998, 93–6). Mearsheimer (1993) and Posen (1993, 44–5) warned that unilateral nuclear disarmament would give Russian nationalists more freedom of action, raising conflict risks. Stone (2002, 184) notes that as part of the package deal of abandoning nuclear weapons Ukraine became, for a time, the third-largest recipient of all US foreign aid.

Russian–Western relations declined gradually.[15] The United States opened diplomatic and economic relations with all of the post-Soviet republics, and NATO expanded into Central Europe despite Russia's objections (Charap and Colton 2017, 30–94). NATO fought an air war against Serbia in 1999, which eventually yielded independence for Kosovo in 2008, despite Russian opposition. Russian diplomatic concerns about "encirclement by NATO" were dismissed as rhetorical exaggerations. At the Bucharest Summit in 2008, NATO declared that Ukraine and Georgia "will become members" (NATO 2008).[16] Russian calls for a geopolitical sphere of influence that would be analogous to the US Monroe Doctrine in the Western Hemisphere were rebuffed with the claim that sovereign countries should be able to choose which international agreements they wish to join. Russian military power had started to rebound in the first decade of the twenty-first century as well.[17] The 2014 Winter Olympics, hosted by Russia, were its best foot forward in terms of soft-power production.

Against this background, things came to a head. Late in 2013, Ukrainian President Yanukovych's abrupt decision to forego a free trade deal with the EU signaled intent to explore membership in the Eurasian Economic Union, Russia's proposed geoeconomic competitor to the EU. In Ukraine, the proposed Economic Union was more popular in the East than the West. Western-oriented Ukrainians took to the

---

[15] Whether the increased antagonism was due to changes in Western values and policy, changes in Russian values or policy, both, or neither, is a fount of academic dispute. For an argument that the choices made by Russia are dependent on its type of regime, see McFaul (2020). For an argument that a different Russian leader or regime might have made similar choices under a similar international environment, see D'Anieri (2019b, 18).

[16] The West saw the statement of intent as a compromise, since no membership path was offered, as had initially been envisaged (D'Anieri 2019b, 163). Russia saw it as a threat and a slap in the face (Freedman 2019, 58), and signaled its displeasure with a small, ugly war in Georgia a few months later. NATO expansion was also accompanied by EU expansion, with eight Central European states joining the EU in 2004 (including the three former Soviet Baltic republics of Estonia, Latvia, and Lithuania), and two more in 2007.

[17] Contextualizing Russia's temporary/local strength with cutting observations of its long-term decline as a society, and a global power (vis-à-vis China and its neighbors), was common in the West after the Cold War. By the time of the events of Chapter 4, the balance of power between Russia and the United States had favored the NATO alliance member states for a generation (Wohlforth 1994, 102–15). The gap is starker if US power is added to that of its allies and Russian power is added to its impoverished dependents (Kotkin 2008, 24).

streets and did not disperse. In the Russian version of this conflict, external enemies choreographed mass protests in Maidan – part of a longer-term pattern. The nonviolent 2004 Orange Revolution was bankrolled by Western NGOs, they argued, and the violent 2014 Maidan militants were trained by Western security services (Wilson 2005, 183–8; Ernst 2015). In the Western version, the Kremlin responded by testing its new *hybrid warfare* techniques in Crimea and Donbas.

What is hybrid warfare? It is an umbrella term for military coercion steeped in plausible deniability. The strategic goal is to send a threatening signal, avoid escalation, and impose costs on another state.[18] Hybrid warfare methods include various kinds of disruption using clandestine agents, disinformation and media manipulation, social media trolling, covert funding for political parties, economic tools (like sanctions and parastatal companies), spycraft, and the use of soldiers without insignias trying to pass as civilians (Reisinger and Golts 2014; Charap 2015; Van Herpen 2015; Conley et al. 2016; Kier 2016; Chivvis 2017). The extent to which any of this was actually new is disputed (Galeotti 2019).[19] Whether Russia or the West is responsible for initiating hybrid hostilities is also open for debate.[20] The important escalation was that Russia sent troops into Ukraine while claiming that it was not, violating a commitment to respect borders made in a 1994 multilateral memorandum (when Ukraine agreed to give up nuclear weapons) and a 1997 bilateral

---

[18] Another term of art in US military circles is "gray zone" conflict (Schram 2021).

[19] New frontier technology applied to warfare may be leveling the playing field between weak and strong nonstate and state military actors (Biddle 2021, 8). Cell phones, for example, interact with the "Web 2.0" leading to the production of high-quality content at low cost, and the dissemination of the content quickly, semi-anonymously, and independently (Walter 2017; Pomerantsev 2019, 85–97). Speculative scholarly efforts to document "hybrid war" techniques in Ukraine as a window into the future of war include efforts to evaluate the efficacy of cyberattacks (Kostyuk and Zhukov 2019), the potential to repurpose patterns of social media for military intelligence (Driscoll and Steinert-Threlkeld 2020).

[20] Orenstein (2019, 11–17) astutely notes that this question, asked in this way, really has no answer, since the West and Russia are in a security dilemma. Galeotti (2019, 1) points out that "Moscow considers itself rather a *target* of Western hybrid aggression." Consider a famous 2013 speech by Valery Gerasimov, often referenced as the authoritative description of Russia's "new" strategy, with ample references to "the broad use of political, economic, informational, humanitarian and other non-military measures" and "concealed" fifth-column armed forces. Gerasimov, in context, is reflecting on *American* military practices of war (Freedman 2019, 174–5).

treaty with Ukraine. Few analysts are tempted to call the flagrant violations of those same commitments in 2022 "hybrid warfare" for many reasons, but one of them is that Russia openly announced it was sending its military (while avoiding full mobilization and not calling it a "war").

In the Western policy-shorthand version of this conflict (among most NATO military professionals), the Donbas militants were, and are still, directed by Russia. Pro-Russian rebels took over government buildings in Kharkiv or Donetsk in the spring of 2014 because Russia told them to (Umland 2016). This caused anxiety in the NATO alliance. How would its member states respond if the same sort of thing occurred in Latvia, Lithuania, or Estonia? A host of seemingly technical questions, such as how to precisely define aggression in the cyberrealm, gained new salience to war planners. Since Ukraine was not yet a NATO member state, a contained hybrid war served a theatrical purpose. Russians, Americans, and others could observe each other play war games, update public statements, and begin to signal what they would be willing to risk in the event of a more severe clash of interests in Eastern Europe (Shaplak and Johnson 2016).

Zones of fighting ossified into stable front lines in late summer 2014 and winter 2015, after Russia overtly sent regular troops to tip the scales at two critical junctures, the Battles of Ilovaisk and Debaltseve. Until February 24, 2022, territory had barely changed hands since those battles. As the war conventionalized along a frozen and fixed line of contact, the number of deaths dropped considerably.

The great powers began to circle their wagons for a long game of trying to wait out the other. The optimism in the West depended on a theory of soft power, the optimism in Russia rested on a theory of hard power. Many social forces within Ukraine saw NATO, the EU, and the West as Ukraine's future. They argued that Russia has shown it cannot win – or even compete – in what Gramsci (1987) would have called a global *war of position* over interpretation of the war. Most members of the United Nations rejected Russia's interpretation of the Crimea events. The Ukraine conflict exposed Russian soft power as much weaker than had been previously assumed, and "increased American power and European influence in Russia's western borderlands."[21]

---

[21] This is the analytic conclusion of Kivelson and Suny (2017, 392), who take a historical view of Russian cultural ("soft") power projection. For historical retrospectives on soft power in the Cold War period, see Selznick (1952,

The Kremlin, for its part, was also comfortable imagining a long game in which geography and demography are destiny. In this view of hard power, a protracted war, fought over a part of the planet that Russia cares about much more than any other great power, is not going to go on forever. When it ends, a war on Russia's border is likely to end on Russia's terms. Due to geography and history, Russia cannot "leave" Ukraine. The Kremlin has military leverage. It will enjoy political influence post-settlement.

Distilling Ukraine's conflict down to a contest between Russian hybrid warfare and Western soft power is appealing for many reasons. It is simple (see Appendix B), teachable, and prescriptive for military planners. It leaves out a great deal, however.

The Policy Implications of Academic Language Choice

This book is a reaction to many descriptions of the Russia–Ukraine conflict between 2016 and 2021. It frustrated us that the dominant frames in Western policy circles so quickly calcified into morality tales of Russian aggression, where Ukraine was abstracted as a helpless victim. Even those inclined to locate all the blame on Kremlin policy had to admit that some changes had taken place in Ukrainian society since March 2014 that Putin probably did not anticipate or engineer.

To put a fine point on it: In Western policymaking circles, the language of hybrid warfare conflated "Eastern Ukrainian" with "Russian" interests and "Western Ukrainian" with "Western" interests. While it was clear that Russian military intervention in Crimea and Donbas was not supported throughout Eastern Ukraine, public opinion in the Russian-speaking East remained divided on assuming responsibility in triggering the conflict.[22] This blurring was common

---

48–70) and Barghoorn (1964). In retrospect, the United States had a clear comparative advantage in soft power throughout the Cold War: "American music and films leaked into the Soviet Union with profound effects, but indigenous Soviet products never found an overseas market. There was no socialist Elvis" (Nye 2004, 74). Recent observational (Avgerinos 2009; Gentile 2020) and experimental (Fisher 2020) studies conclude that Russia still competes at a relative disadvantage in the production of credible news.

[22] In a 2019 survey, while 45 percent of the entire population saw the Donbas conflict as "Russian aggression," the proportion fell to 22–24 percent in the Southeast, while 21–22 percent saw it as a "purely internal civil conflict" (Fond demokratychni initsiatyvy 2019).

in Ukrainian policy debates for historical reasons, as well. What made the "hybrid warfare" language such an impediment to creative discussions on the specifics of conflict resolution was its interaction with US domestic politics in the 2016–2020 period, when Democrats blamed Russian policy for the election of Donald Trump to the presidency. Meanwhile, the Ukrainian government – increasingly aligned with the "No to Capitulation Front" that we will discuss in Chapter 8 – staked out policy positions on language, historical memory, and the implementation of the Minsk accords that were more popular in the Ukrainian West than the Ukrainian East.

One effect of this was the sidelining of anyone willing to challenging the narrative that the Donbas war had been, at its roots, a war of Russian aggression. In Ukraine, this had the practical effect of marginalizing the views of an important constituency of Eastern voters. This, in turn, as we shall see in Chapter 8, had implications for the status of contested territory in Donbas, for the status of the Russian language in secondary school curricula throughout Ukraine, for the Ukrainian Orthodox Church Moscow Patriarchate, and much more. Criticism of state policy over any of these issues became associated with an indefensible pro-Russian position. The Russian army had seized Ukrainian territory, and Russia needed to leave. The hard truth is that in August–September 2014, and again in February 2015, the Ukrainian army could not fight the Russian army. Kyiv was forced to commit internationally to the principle of granting some kind of de jure autonomy to the two Donbas territories that it no longer de facto controlled. These political conditions proved politically impossible to implement. The de facto policy was to interpret the Minsk Protocol to mean that Russia had to withdraw its military completely before political steps could be taken.

We wrote our book in an effort to add nuance to the analysis of the Ukrainian political landscape between 2013 and 2021, before the Russian invasion of 2022. Our strategy for accomplishing this is an analytic narrative. Our aim is to challenge the notion that there was a hegemonic view in Ukraine on how to assess the origins of the war in Donbas and how to devise a political solution. This is not about whether Ukrainians, whatever language they speak at home, believed in the territorial integrity of Ukraine. A majority of Eastern Ukrainians identified with the Ukrainian state in 2014 and rejection of the Russian invasion of 2022 became nearly hegemonic quite early on

(Reiting 2022). Our goal, for historians interested in more nuance, is to analyze how Ukrainian politics actually operated before this invasion. Eastern Ukrainian opinion, parties, and elites could not be easily reduced to a "pro-Russian" position. For instance, an important strand in our narrative shows how even the Party of Regions, portrayed as aligned with Russian interests, was mistrusted by Russian officials and ultimately failed to accomplish what Putin expected.

A second problem with the language of "hybrid warfare" is that it functionally loaded the US conversation in favor of particular policy response: demonstrating resolve to Russia. This ignored a serious realist counter, which is that Western policy may have played a role in provoking the 2014 conflict – more than Western government agents can easily admit because of the nature of the security dilemma.[23] In practice, "hybrid warfare" conversations invited scholars to weigh in on an ongoing policy conversation asking, "What else can we do to assure our Ukrainian security partners and deter Russians from engaging in new styles of aggression?" For restrainers in the realist school, a prior question may be what US interests are in Europe and whether the generous support to European allies and partners actually serves those interests or can have unintended consequences.[24]

As social scientists interested in curating the historical record, we feel that ignoring Ukraine-specific details in favor of crude geopolitical plate tectonics misses many important stories. Filtering all incoming information about the 2014–2020 war through a top-down international relations (IR) lens obscured the agency of Ukrainian actors, effectively silencing the voices of millions of Russian-speaking Ukrainians. This is important because a theoretically informed understanding of how the conflict broke out in 2014–2015 is necessary to imagine an eventual final settlement. Specific policy-relevant questions include: Why did the Kremlin send troops to some places and not others? Why did the conflict zone have the geographical boundaries that it did in 2022, when Putin recognized the DNR/LNR and invaded?

---

[23] This is not our book's position, but neither was it a "fringe" position in 2014–2015. See, for example, Mearsheimer (2014), Walt (2014, 2015), Posen (2016), and Charap and Colton (2017).

[24] Posen (2014) ably summarizes the restraint position. His view of European security (including Ukraine) is informed by his study of the pathways to inadvertent nuclear use by Russian and NATO war planners (Posen [1991], especially 21–3, 45–7, 60–7, 146–58).

Why was Ukraine more cohesively "Ukrainian" (distinct from geopolitically "Western") seven years after Crimea? Why was settling the conflict in the Donbas so difficult?

These are not simply rhetorical questions. Our book provides clear answers.

1. The Kremlin sent troops where it did after observing the strategies of Russian-speaking communities within Ukraine.[25] Such communities directly adjoining Russia's border (Kharkiv and Donbas), and Russia's redefined border post-Crimea (such as the Donbas city of Mariupol and the oblasts of Kherson and Odesa – close to Transnistria and the ocean) acted with a higher chance of successful separation compared to the heartland areas of Dnipro, Zaporizhzhia, or Mykolaïv. The Kremlin waited for either local allies to obtain the backing of the regional parliament or for local armed allies to secure territory first. Russia was responsive and opportunistic.

2. The conflict had the geography it did because of choices made by Russian-speaking elites. Russian machinations shaped the information environment, but the choice between sedition or loyalty to the post-Maidan Ukrainian political order was made within Russian-speaking communities. A tip toward sedition proved arduous, and despite a great deal of jockeying on the streets, most communities did not tip or come close. As elites worried their neighbors were approaching a tip, one response was violent threats against elites considering *sedition*. The only part of Ukraine with no antisecession vigilantes, Crimea, tipped in days. In the industrial core of Donbas, elites were pushed aside by angry mobs and anti-institutional newcomers in the space of a few dramatic weeks. Outside these towns, no other communities tipped.

3. Since 2014, Ukrainian political identity has come into its own as a "new" ethnic supermajority due to two processes. First, after the de facto border change in Crimea, the demographics and politics of Ukraine changed. This left the government in Kyiv more willing

---

[25] The concept of *community* is integral to the theoretical model that we are presenting in Chapter 2. We define community using the Taylor (1982) criteria: Direct face-to-face relations between members, many-sided relations, reciprocity, rough equality of material conditions, and common sets of beliefs and values.

to pay costs in blood in order not to cede territory. Second, the crisis altered perceptions of Russian military intentions. As a result of watching where Russia did – and did not – send its military, beliefs about the probability of Russian military intervention were revised downward. (These beliefs turned out to be false in 2022, but they existed until the very last minute.) Our prediction is fewer cultural concessions to Russian-speaking communities under these circumstances.

4. Settling was difficult for two reasons. First, the collapse of political institutions in 2014 made it impossible a return to the old social contract due to commitment problems. The relevant actors feared that the other side would renege on what they committed to if they moved first. Second, a narrative of the conflict has taken root within Eastern Donbas that sedition was legitimate. Social policies chosen in Kyiv reinforced the view that the Donbas population would be treated as second-class citizens if Ukraine ever reclaimed the territory.

Where Is this Book Going?

Employing the language of *civil war* violated a taboo in Western foreign policy circles throughout 2014–2021. Since Russia called the war in Ukraine a *civil war*, Western officials had to call it something else. Since both sides were sending costly signals of their intent to wait the other out, adopting the language of the enemy felt like a tactical concession.[26] With Putin's decision to escalate the conflict over Ukraine with a full-scale invasion, as well as repeated nuclear threats, this taboo has outlived its utility. If Western policymakers revisit this period critically, and describe this as an *intra-Russkii Mir* civil war, the shoe is suddenly on the other foot. The civil war that we describe in this book is not the civil war Putin imagines it to be. There is no war pitting "real" Ukrainians (the belief that Ukrainians are a subset of Russians) against "nationalist" Ukrainians (the belief that the Ukrainian nation is an artificial creation of foreigners and a threat

---

[26] For readers unfamiliar with the reference to "costly signaling," a common vein of argument is that professional diplomats engage in regular "cheap talk" performances (colloquially: diplomats lie). To show they mean business, sometimes states have to incur costs, like putting soldiers' lives at risk and running risks of escalation/war, in order to communicate with each other.

to Russia). This is rather a war that always divided a narrow sub-set of Eastern Ukrainians, mostly concentrated in Donbas, against the majority of Eastern Ukrainians, Donbas included (who were ambivalent on Maidan and on the sources of the conflict, but opposed Russian military intervention). In our historical and analytic narrative, we believe that reclaiming the language of civil war has the potential to do three things.

First, the grains of truth in the Russian version of events can be plucked from state propaganda (Radnitz 2021: 44–9, 119–28). What emerges is a bottom-up story, emphasizing that the genesis of the war in Ukraine came from choices made on Ukrainian territory. In the language of our model, critical first- and second-movers thought of themselves as political Russians defending their homes.

Second, employing the language of civil war to approach the 2014 origins of the Donbas war clarifies how different this part of Donbas was, and arguably remains, from the rest of Eastern Ukraine. Putin identifies *Russkii mir* with Russian-speakers and expected Ukraine to collapse over all of Eastern Ukraine in 2014. The problem is that *Russkii mir* failed everywhere, except parts of the industrial core of Eastern Donbas, where Kyiv lost control of security institutions well before Russia sent troops. The 2014 war mostly opposed pro-Ukraine Ukraine-born combatants to anti-Kyiv Ukraine-born combatants.[27]

Third, reclaiming the language of civil war highlights the argument for more serious conversations within foreign policy circles, especially in NATO capitals, about what it is reasonable to expect from a post-war Ukrainian polity. Policymakers hoping to educate themselves on the war that preceded the Russian invasion of 2022 will find answers to many of their factual questions in the pages of this book.

In Chapter 2 we present our theory in normal language and describe the analytic narrative approach we will use in data presentation for the remaining chapters.

In Chapter 3 we present a gloss on Ukrainian political history in order to introduce key insights on Ukrainian identity, regional and memory politics, and demonstrate the plausibility of model assumptions.

---

[27] To clarify: We are not claiming that Russian-speaking Ukrainians see themselves as part of *Russkii mir*, but rather that a critical mass demonstrated in 2014 that it does *not*. It is only from the perspective of the talking points of the Russian state that the *Russkii mir* is at war with itself.

In Chapter 4 we describe the critical juncture of the Maidan protests (November 2013–February 2014) with a focus on the logic and consequences of political violence.

In Chapter 5 we describe the political aftermath of the Maidan events in Crimea. This chapter explains why the secession of Crimea did not result in very much violence.

In Chapter 6 we describe the political aftermath of the Maidan events in Eastern and Southern Ukraine (outside Crimea and the Eastern Donbas). An Eastern Ukrainian political rebellion, expected by Russia, did not happen and the street turned pro-Ukrainian.

In Chapter 7 we describe the political aftermath of the Maidan events in the Eastern Donbas region. This chapter explains the outbreak of Ukraine's war.

In Chapter 8 we describe the international diplomatic stalemate on settling Ukraine's unnamed war, the effects of the war on Ukrainian society, and briefly comment on Russia's decision to engage in a full-scale war of aggression reminiscent of World War II.

2 | A Theory of War Onset in Post-Soviet Eurasia

Since so many of the structural features of the Ukraine–Russia relationship did not change from 1993 to 2013, the timing of the outbreak of violence in Ukraine is puzzling. Something about the specific nature of the crisis of 2013–2014, and the contested information environment in subsequent years, led to Ukraine's unnamed war of 2014–2022. The failure to settle this war diplomatically created the conditions for the Russian invasion in February 2022. Can we be more specific about causal processes? What happens to citizens that sometimes causes many of them to turn violent?

Hobbes (1651) noted the ability of modern territorial states to prevent citizens from becoming violent most of the time. The state benefits from what Hobbes called *awe*: a widely shared assumption of an overwhelming comparative advantage in the production of violence and justice. Most of the time, most people moderate their behaviors due to deterrence or socialization. This vein of social theory taps into a lineage in political science stretching back to Max Weber by way of Huntington (1968). When civil wars reoccur in the same territory over and over again, we say a state is illegitimate or weak.

Why are some states more prone to bouts of large-scale violence than others? Empirical researchers have tried to address this question by investigating the structural features that put some countries at higher risk than others for onset of civil war. These scholars have found that, even for the poorest states in the international system, governments can usually adapt to crises or deescalate domestic unrest before it gets anywhere close to becoming a civil war.[1] Most citizens most of the time know this, so they can anticipate what behaviors state agents will tolerate and what they will not. Since the rules

[1] As explained in Chapter 1, scholars define a civil war using two empirical criteria: citizenship (most combatants on either side being citizens of the state prior to hostilities) and threshold of fatalities (a death count of at least 1,000, with at least 100 among government forces).

undergirding social order are common knowledge, violence needs only to lurk in the background to hold order in place. States must be able to repress effectively, however. Repression requires a certain kind of state capacity – competent intelligence gathering, paired with professional domestic security forces and an effective chain of command.

Citizens must believe other people share their own assessments of the strength of the state. Government-funded rituals can reduce uncertainty on this point: military parades, high-profile televised criminal trials, and the like. Citizens also make inferences about their state capacity by observing how the state responds to crises, such as mass demonstrations, street violence, terrorism, insurrections, or wars. When the state certainty of its control of repression falters, or many citizens begin to doubt the legitimacy of the state's repressive capacity, or both, there is a higher risk that domestic order falls apart. This sometimes even yields civil war.

Civil wars are very rare events, however. A more common outcome is gradual deescalation. Usually, social groups and state actors can demonstrate power and resolve to each other with vote counts and nonviolent civil resistance, reaching a cooperative outcome that maintains social order and avoids of large-scale societal breakdown.[2] States or citizens sometimes miscalculate in a way that spirals to sustained violence, however, due to a combination of information failures, emotional decision-making, and the inherent difficulties associated with policing and counterinsurgency. While we will discuss each in turn, information failure is at the heart of our theory. We see peace and order as an *equilibrium* (in rational choice jargon) held in place by an expectation of violence if anyone changes their strategies. When a crisis introduces uncertainty and forces armed actors to second-guess each other's strategies, the result can be deadly.

The Strategic Setting: Post-Soviet Eurasia

Because we are interested in state–society relations and how they sometimes break down, defining the relevant strategic players and the order of interaction requires transitioning from general political theory to a more locally scoped model of Eurasian political order. The context of

---

[2] For arguments about the general efficacy of *nonviolent* tactics as an optimal bargaining instrument for groups seeking to affect change, see Stephan and Chenoweth (2008) and Chenoweth (2021). For theoretical works on bargaining, see Elster (1989, 135–46), Fearon (1995b, 1998), and Wagner (2000).

bargaining is different for post-Soviet states than for states in central Africa. For one thing, all of the states that emerged from the breakup of the Soviet Union were "born strong," inheriting a panoply of "strong state" institutions, such as a party network, centralized media, delineated borders (between republics), administrative units, high rates of literacy, and a secret police (Driscoll 2015: 4, 125). This basic fact goes a long way toward explaining why interethnic warfare was so rare during the breakup of the Soviet Union and why wars, when they did occur, ended so fast. Post-Soviet states have been able to control most of their people, most of the time, by channeling violence through institutions.

The relevant feature of post-Soviet states is that political games are played against the backdrop of inherited Soviet demography and interstate borders born from what were once ethno-federally demarcated territorial units. Across Eurasia, many communities contain a critical mass of people who prefer to speak Russian and/or self-identify as Russian. After the Soviet collapse, millions found themselves living outside the borders of Russia. They had to decide whether to organize as political Russians, encourage their children to assimilate (by acquiring fluency in the language of their new state), or emigrate to Russia (where most had never lived) (Laitin 1998, 2018).[3]

We are defining state capacity as the state's ability to cauterize violent challengers before they reach the boiling point of civil war. Eurasian demography relates to state capacity in two ways. The first involves facets of distributional politics that intersects with ethnic polarization to produce a feeling of zero-sum tradeoffs. Since the break-up of the Soviet Union, there has been more-than-occasional push-and-pull between (1) communities defining themselves politically as Russian, (2) Russian-*speaking* communities sharing common interests with political Russians, (3) communities identifying with the majority (titular) nationality of the state, and (4) communities neither Russian nor titular. *Intrastate* bargaining over issues of autonomy and

---

[3] Laitin was inspired by the triadic model of Hirschman (1970): exit (immigration), voice (organization), and loyalty (assimilation). He named the emergent social category that faced this choice set the Russian "beached diaspora." In post-independence Ukraine, all three avenues were pursued by the beached diaspora, as we shall see. The Party of Regions aggregated the preferences of Russian-speakers throughout the East. The great majority of children in East (outside of Donbas and Crimea) were sent to Ukrainian schools. The 2001 census registered 3 million less Russians than 1989, either due to ethnic reidentification on census forms or to migration (mainly to Russia).

assimilation involve periodic flare-ups (at soccer games or bar fights) and can sometimes gin up votes. There can be salient differences between the preferences of peripheral Russian or Russian-speaking community elites and state elites when it comes to elementary educational curricula, language of primary school instruction, composition of police and border units, the language of bureaucracy, names on street signs, recognized holidays, regional public sector subsidies, monuments, sports mascots, flags, and more (Jenne 2004, 732–3).

The second, relatedly, is the *interstate* dimension: the shadow of Russian military intervention into domestic politics. Russia is enormous. Russians are more numerous than most any other Eurasian ethnic group. For the many independent post-Soviet states that share a border with Russia, this introduces a practical problem: When non-Russian capitals threaten elites that can claim to speak on behalf of communities that Russia sees as Russians, those elites can call for help from the Kremlin. A knife-edged interethnic peace based on deterrence hangs over the post-Soviet space. As we saw in 2022, Moscow may even opt to fabricate crimes against "its people" in order justify wars of aggression. The larger point is that in Eurasia everyone can calculate that if social order were to collapse, potential insurgents might incorporate into their calculations the possibility that Russia will launch a "rescue" operation on their behalf. This threat of great power intervention is simply not as acute or predictable in other parts of the globe.

Actors, Choices, and Order of Play

Domestic order in post-Soviet Eurasia is held in place by three kinds of players anticipating each other's strategies: (1) central political elites in Russia, (2) central political elites in the neighboring state, and (3) community-level elites in the periphery of that state. This *triadic relationship* is a defining feature of post-Soviet politics, since Russia has the potential to "insert itself" into bargaining between "its" communities and titular capitals (Brubaker 1995, 1996, 55–76).[4] There are three

---

[4] Brubaker's triadic configuration also inspired Laitin (1998), Van Houten (1998), Cetinyan (2002), and Jenne (2004). Sambanis, Skaderpas, and Wohlforth (2020) analyze a dynamic model in a triadic setting that explicitly endogenizes polarization of ethnic identities with third-party (Russian) intervention, and lean heavily on Russian intervention into Ukraine to illustrate the plausibility of their model's assumptions.

distinct locations of strategizing, all of which are watching the others for information that might provide clues about shifts in strategy.

During a crisis, the first locus of action is inside Russia-speaking communities. As individuals in these communities observe that normal constraints are breaking down, they look for information on television, on the Internet, and by listening to community elites. A few talented people, if they are centrally located in social networks and capable of linking diverse constituencies, can potentially induce many others to flip their stance or political identity (Popkin 1979; Petersen 2001). We call this producing a cascade to a social tip within a community. These elites, if they coordinate, can use their influence to capture local institutions and make it clear that street power will be allowed to "take off." These cascades can have outsized political effects and allow social actors that are normally on the fringe to enter politics.

The first major question on the slide to civil war, then, is whether or not there is coordination on the desirability of sedition – defined as insurrection against the state – by high-status members of these communities. We have in mind oligarchs, respected religious figures, high-status teachers, and the like. If *coordinated sedition* fails to emerge, there are no high-status brokers between the state and the street, so the crisis passes. If elites coordinate, and decide that their community needs to "bargain hard," they lay claim to the authority of precrisis institutions, including the police. This allows "the community" to speak with one voice. The community coordinates on a bargaining position, and makes it clear that they will activate a plan to secede from the polity if their demand is not met. We call this *coordinated sedition*: an entire Russian-speaking community uniting and constructing their identities politically as Russian, and demanding recognition of their rights as such.

Some communities are better positioned than others to make good on the threat to exit the polity. Geographic proximity to the inter-state border is a factor. Elites in densely packed communities close to Russia's border are relatively well positioned to secede if they have to.[5] Important variables in determining what a community can expect to happen in a war include population density, demographics, terrain, and

---

[5] In Appendix A, parameter p is meant to capture many factors salient in the literature, such as proximity to an interstate border (Treisman 1997, 2001), as well as factors such as demographic concentration (Toft 2003; Lacina 2017), substate institutions (Roeder 2009), sacred land (Hassner 2007), foreign religious support (Toft and Zhukov 2015), physical geography (Fearon and

perhaps other things that local elites have a comparative advantage in assessing (such as the private beliefs of nonvoting citizens, intra- and interfamily social status hierarchies, etc.).

The demand shifts the locus of decision to a second class of actors: elites in the capital city. They face a critical decision point: They must either "buy off" the Russian-speaking communities with policy concessions to deescalate the crisis nonviolently, or try to arrest the ringleaders and restore order coercively. If repression is chosen, however, the risk is that Russia may intervene with disproportionate violence.[6]

State elites and peripheral elites should be able to compromise and avoid a clash of values that ends in violence and counterinsurgency. So long as every actor plays strategically, and since communities want to avoid police actions, elites coordinate to make a demand to elites in the capital that they expect will be actually accepted.

The key to an orderly, brokered equilibrium is common knowledge. There must be a reasonable expectation by all of the players that they are all correctly assessing facts the same way and that they understand the incentives and strategies of the other players. Most of the time, community elites are deterred from making excessive demands because it is risky to face off against a high-capacity state. Most of the time, elites in the capital hesitate before sending police to arrest community leaders, trying to anticipate how the Russian government might respond.[7] Most of the time, elites' broker deals and violent threats are not even articulated. In fact, though it is beyond the scope of the simple model we analyze in Appendix A, it is not difficult to see the advantage of coordination pooled across Russian-speaking elites in many communities. An orderly aggregation of preferences by voters transforms "seditionist" dissident politics into normalized special interest group politics: cohesively organized constituent demands. This

Laitin 2003), social structure (Petersen 2001; Parkinson 2013; Lewis 2020), or group socioeconomic characteristics (Alesina and Spolaore 2003; Cederman, Weidmann, and Gleditsch 2011; Zhukov 2016).

[6] Russia may also intervene anyway for reasons that have nothing to do with protecting the rights of Russian-speakers while cynically *claiming* to be intervening to protect Russians. That possibility was outside the scope of our analysis in this model, but we thank Tymofiy Mylovanov especially for continuously pushing us on this point.

[7] In the model, the costs incurred by community leaders in facing the center are identified as c (lowercase) and the costs facing the center in anticipation of Russian behavior C (uppercase).

describes well how the Party of Regions functioned before Maidan (as we will describe shortly, in Chapter 3).

When these normal institutions disappear, however, community elites face a terrible dilemma. They are forced to make choices without enough information, and are not able to anticipate correctly knowing how the crisis will unfold in the end. Because of the order of moves, only by going through with a rebellion can peripheral community elites collect information on Russia's true intentions. This entails dangerous risks. If only some elites attempt sedition, but not enough of them, there is no safety in numbers. First-movers, and their families, will be identified and subject to threats.[8]

The slide toward civil war begins with a crisis that raises the stakes of politics. Various players have to reassess each other's intentions. The crisis itself is an unanticipated event – an earthquake, an invasion, a currency collapse, or an irregular leadership change. The loyalty of a military is rarely tested as it is after an authoritarian leader dies unexpectedly or after an extra-constitutional change of power. The crisis is more dangerous if it provides new information revealing an absence of state capacity. All states benefit from *awe*, but this reverence can be rendered ineffective. If government buildings are obliterated by a natural disaster, and then a state cannot organize a response to search the rubble for survivors, citizens learn state capacity is weaker than previously believed. As *awe* disappears, anarchy can become more frightening. Time can seem to be moving faster as powerful emotions shape perceptions of events.

Common knowledge of rules and expectations of law enforcement can also be undercut by political crises. Citizens can gather information during extended standoffs between protesters and police. Say protesters converge in, and refuse to disperse from, the main square of the capital. Say that days turn into months. Say that clashes with riot police are indecisive. Clearly the capacity of the state to coerce and deter was never as absolute as had been assumed. One might infer that the state's coercive capacity was weaker than previously assumed. And if the state cannot even control its own capital, where the state can easily deploy elite troops, how could it possibly have eyes everywhere in the periphery (where the state may be unable to dispatch elite troops)? If seditionist leaders organize publicly using social media, and they are

---

[8] Formally, we call this intra-community risk of punishment μ.

not silenced, jailed, or sent to psychiatric prisons, this reveals information about the state's capacity to selectively punish dissident thinkers.

A crisis is especially dangerous if it results from the unexpected success of large-scale, steadily growing, self-declared "revolutionary" political processes that promise fundamental changes to the social structure or the country's geopolitical orientation. A literal act of nature (an earthquake or a stroke affecting the leader) may reveal a lack of state capacity. When a social movement can harness energy from grievances that have been "pent up" for a long time and challenge the state directly, it almost always reveals a lack of state capacity (since it begs the question of how the regime leadership allowed things to get so out of hand).[9] Political earthquakes are especially high stakes because they promise to change the institutional rules of the future: whose children are more likely to be rich and whose are more likely to be poor, who may have an edge in accessing state jobs or resources, who will be eligible to vote or access power.

To summarize: The crisis initiates a one-shot, high-stakes game. The primary actors are elites.[10] The path of play is the following: (1) Russian-speaking community elites either coordinate on sedition or do not; (2a) if elites coordinate, they articulate a demand and threaten to secede if their demand is not met; the state elites either accept the demand or opt to repress; (2b) if elites do not coordinate, state elites set the autonomy agenda, making a take-it-or-leave-it offer to the community; each elite within the community evaluates the offer and can either accept it or refuse (which amounts to sedition and invites targeted repression); and (3) if there is repression, the Kremlin decides whether to intervene militarily on behalf of seditious elites.

The Onset of War in Ukraine

The puzzle of war initiation can now be framed more sharply: Why did some Russian-speaking communities persistently issue demands so

---

[9] Fearon (2004, especially 406–12) argues that domestic social crises based on pent-up self-determination claims (e.g., an identity group instigating a domestic crisis to "call for external help," organizing with a terminal goal of partition, annexation, or alteration of interstate borders) are especially dangerous in the modern interstate system.

[10] This simple account of community-level politics does not distinguish between different types of elites. In our empirical chapters on politics in Ukraine's East, we often describe situations in which well-established institutional elites found

much higher than the post-Maidan government in Kyiv could accept? Our answer, clearer in 2022 than it could have been in 2014, is that both Donbas actors and Kyiv elites miscalculated Kremlin intent.

Before 2013, Russian-speaking community elites in Donbas had taken over much of the Ukrainian state through electoral means. They were ruthless and well organized, but they relied on elections and were nonviolent. Taking up arms against the state was not a "real" political strategy considered by most Donbas voters, most of the time.[11] The crisis that started on Maidan in the fall of 2013 gradually changed this. By January 2014, it became clear that the Ukrainian state lacked the capacity to stop protesters. This was partly because the state was not ruthless enough, partly because its tactics backfired in the social imagination, and partly because the cause being demonstrated for had huge support. This support came from the Ukrainian West, perennially unhappy with the political weight of Russian-speakers further East, and also from a variety of liberal constituencies with allies in Western Europe and North America. By the time the state began to rely on mass indiscriminate repression, rebellion had spread well beyond Kyiv, paralyzing the Ukrainian West.[12]

Rapid political change can create waves of destabilizing uncertainty. The decision by Ukrainian President Yanukovych to flee the capital on February 21, 2014 was shocking. His majority in parliament collapsed. It was a de facto regime change. The state security service members that had been fighting to preserve the old order, humiliated and demoralized, gave up. Russia called it a coup by fascists. In the next few days, Russian television selectively amplified and distorted incidents to stoke fears within Russian-speaking communities. The Kremlin sent troops to facilitate the rapid exit of Crimea from the polity. The Russian army entered Crimea, and it suddenly became possible that the same *might* happen elsewhere – which altered local calculations in Donbas,

themselves challenged by new entrants into the political arena coming out of the woodwork or emerging from the street. In our stylization, these "new elites" were always present in communities, just not visible until the crisis occurred.

[11] For the most part, the claims by fringe groups failed to cross (or even approach) what Lustick (1993, 42) calls an "ideological hegemony" threshold of political contestation, which is to say that the ideas did not pose threats to regime integrity. Chapter 3 discusses a few exceptions.

[12] Had there not been a regime change at the center, it seems probable to us that there would have been an antistate insurgency centered on Lviv (and possibly even a civil war – though we see this as unlikely).

Kharkiv, and Odesa. Ukraine was, in important respects, a completely different country by March 22, 2014 than one month before. No one knew where the territorial changes would end.

Observing this, other would-be seditious elites in Russian-speaking communities were forced to make agonizing decisions without enough trustworthy information. Could they replicate Crimea's success? How would they be treated if they tried and failed? Maidan was revolutionary change – but how would their families fare in the new social contract, which promised sweeping implications for political and property rights? If the Party of Regions had not been so internally divided and delegitimized by the Maidan events, it is likely that more communities would have coordinated, with more coherent demands leveraged on the capital – but the Party of Regions was gone.

The temporary breakdown of *awe* also introduced new political actors, as community elites found themselves pressured by street actors (both pro- and anti-Maidan) that they had no ability unable to control. All of the Russian-speaking communities contain large numbers of unemployed men, marginally employed youth, religio-charismatic anarchists, football hooligans, and fringe political activists. Instead of elites being drawn from the "normal" pool of union bosses, party organizers, teachers, elders, or oligarchs within the community, in some cases charismatic people emerged from the former group and proved effective at organizing, convincing others to accept risks, and using their social location to form network linkages and try to "push" their communities toward a cascade.

Russia plays a destabilizing role in our account, but ours is not a theory of seditious plots conceived, organized, or controlled from Moscow. Russian-speaking community elites were the primary agents, bargaining with central elites while being pressured by the street. War is the result of bad guesswork during a crisis. Elites are acting with incomplete information. Agreeing on a compromise is difficult since the crisis has thrown some of the model parameters into dispute. Estimations might change not only as a result of the crisis that begins the game, but also because of interactions that are haphazard, because elites are watching misleading television statements or observing troop movements and drawing the wrong inferences. More specifically, according to our model, war occurs because Donbas elites asked for too much (anticipating Russian intervention), yielding a domestic police action (because Kyiv did *not* anticipate a Russian intervention would take the form it did). In the end, Russia intervened.[13] This only happened after many missed signals and off-ramps that might have avoided war.

To scaffold our theory of civil war outbreak, we wish to emphasize two salient findings from the civil war literature: (1) the causal role of emotions unleashed by a threat of group-status-hierarchy reversals, and (2) the military challenge of urban pacification by armies equipped with heavy weapons but no training in counterinsurgency operations.

The internal collapse of the Party of Regions and the triumphant success of demonstrators at Maidan altered the balance of power between the Ukrainian East and West. The monumental decision by the legislature to repeal the official status of the Russian language as their first order of business after President Yanukovych was removed was probably driven by emotion, not calculation. Among ourselves, we see a decision driven largely by spite, efforts to reverse humiliation, and desire for symbolic payback – not the sort of cold, forward-looking calculation that our model assumes.[14]

The repeal of the language law was just one of many examples in this book of an emotional decision that was not very well thought out. Following Petersen (2002, 2017), we recognize that emotions can change how information is processed and what beliefs and preferences are formed in the minds of participants. Emotion is not synonymous with irrationality. Emotions have cognitive antecedents that can be studied. When citizens notice that more and more of their neighbors are attending rallies for far-right parties that would have been "fringe" before the crisis, it is a reminder that the politics of antiliberal exclusion was always possible – just not a strategic choice under prior constraints.[15] As it becomes increasingly clear that those constraints are

---

[13] In any setting in which actors may not assess the strategic parameters in the same way, they are potentially susceptible to bluffing. If gains can be extracted by strategic dissimulation (bluffing, or theatrical sedition), then, as in poker, eventually someone has to "call" (Gartzke 1999). In the higher-stakes context we are describing, the analogy to "calling" is state-initiated militarized repression.

[14] For descriptions of spite, malice, and envy, see Elster (1999, 62, 68–70, 164–203). Chapters 3, 4, and 6 will discuss this law further. The practical effect of the repeal was to restore the pre-2012 status quo (no official status for Russian, though with Russian used as the language of regional administration), but the symbolism of "banning" Russian was quite potent, as we shall see.

[15] De Figueiredo and Weingast (1999) argue that in these settings, even small probabilities of outcomes can trigger rationalizable defensive reactions.

disappearing, the possibility of terrible outcomes becomes more real, and thus more emotionally salient.

Often the assumption in conflict studies is that a descent into anarchy amplifies the emotion of *fear*. Citizens come to be afraid of each other, or afraid of state security services, or both, and often reasonably so.[16]

Another distinctive emotion is *resentment* – usually triggered by an expectation or realization of group status reversals. The prospect that sudden political change might lead to institutionalized subordination, below a group previously lower in the status hierarchy, can be a motivator to violent action.[17] The highest risks involve explicit ethnicized discrimination – the prospect of a group being thrown out of power, and the institutional rules changed to make this subordination of status permanent.[18] Having the rules changed, as a result of the irregular transfer of power, in a way that limits your (or your children's) ability to ever return to power elicits an emotional response distinct from fear. The prospect that new elites (and their children) may benefit from the new social order at the expense of old elites (and their children) can unleash massive energy.[19]

---

[16] Posen (1993, 32) identifies indefensible pockets ("islands") of ethnic groups as a special risk for defensive mobilization spirals of this sort (magnified by the impossibility of distinguishing offensive from defensive intentions by weapon type). When citizens notice that violent, antisocial groups are self-organizing into citizens' self-defense militias, and that these irregular infantry units can just as easily go on the offense as hold neighborhoods defensively, it can yield arms racing.

[17] Petersen (2002: 40) defines *resentment* as caused by "the perception that one's group is located in an unwarranted subordinate position on a status hierarchy." Coding criteria for identifying ethnic status hierarchies in multiethnic societies can be found in Petersen (2011, 142). If subordination in a status hierarchy is foreseeable below a group that is not only resented, but also *hated*, the risks of violence are even higher for a variety of reasons discussed in Petersen (2002, 62–8) and Elster (1999, 64–8).

[18] For a treatment of the sources of fear, see Fearon (1995a, 1998). In Ukraine, status competition described in Chapter 3 is (we argue) not so much ethnic, as intra-ethnic: the fear that Eastern Ukrainians would be subordinated to Western Ukrainians.

[19] Empirics are contested, but studies suggesting a link between institutionalized ethnic discrimination and civil war include Davenport (2000), Wimmer, Cederman, and Min (2009), and Cederman, Wimmer, and Min (2010). The review in Davenport, Melander, and Reagan (2018) on how this point is treated in the "peace studies" literature (with a general focus on outbreak and termination, at the expense of the quality of peace) is highly valuable and complements our bottom-line prescriptions.

The second salient finding in the civil war literature pertains to the correlation between the kinds of military operations employed by armies and overall levels of civilian victimization. Insurgents sometimes employ asymmetric strategies against state military opponents, interspersing themselves among civilians, using human shields, and daring militaries to strike back with indiscriminate force. Against an insurgent army employing these tactics, only unusually disciplined forces with special training can avoid inflicting high civilian casualties as they pacify the enemy.

When they were tasked with fighting the "terrorists" emerging in a few Eastern Russian-speaking communities, the Ukrainian military was not initially prepared for urban counterinsurgency operations. Assaults were spearheaded by volunteer battalions. These soldiers lacked training for complex urban operations. Both sides in the Donbas war used weapons that could not discriminate between civilian and military targets. What temporarily introduced conventional military symmetry to the conflict, and reduced overall levels of civilian victimization, was the stabilization of the front lines resulting from the arrival of Russian regular troops in late summer 2014.[20] In 2022, the Russian regular troops altered their mission, moved the line of control, and began attacking population centers (events summarized in Chapter 8, ending our book).

Toward an Analytic Narrative

Beginning in the fall of 2013, coordinated street protests raised the political stakes in Ukraine. The formation of self-defense militias, protest violence, the seizure of government buildings, attacks on police stations, the establishment of checkpoints on roads leading to the capital – all of this was unprecedented. This escalation in the contentious political repertoire, and the abrupt fall of a Russia-oriented Ukrainian president and government, paved the way for Russia to seize Crimea with minimal resistance. Seditionist militants in the East began to imagine the Russian military would help them, as well. In Donbas, after a month of unrest, government buildings were seized. War followed.

---

[20] This point applies largely to the period following the second Minsk Accords in February 2015. After a four-month lull, indiscriminate shelling resumed in January–February 2015, mostly from Russia-backed forces, causing a spike in civilian deaths.

We describe these events using an analytic narrative approach.[21] Analytic narratives are tools for disciplining empirical description without sacrificing richness of contextual detail.[22] The modeling enterprise forces scholars to "reconsider the narrative and then to re-evaluate the extent to which key elements of the narrative lie outside the proposed theory" (Bates et al. 2000, 687). Formalization also provides a measure of confidence that analytical rigor is being maintained without forcing readers to break narrative prose for clunky hypothesis testing (Bates 1998). Deductive rigor disciplines the narrative. Reductionism commits us to a single "fundamental utility," or the main benefit pursued by actors, for our study. As Levi (1999, 155–6) puts it, "the assumption of a fundamental utility radically simplifies the world and the people within it, but, if done with attention to the problem, it simplifies the world realistically and usefully."[23]

In our theory, actors are trying to maximize *security* in an uncertain environment. Individuals and groups are potentially threatened, have access to arms, and are considering taking steps to defend themselves. Security calculations are magnified by rapid and unexpected institutional breakdown. Security in our study refers to both *securing physical safety* as state institutions weaken, and also to *securing cultural preservation* for a minority community from a hostile majority.

The members of the Eastern Ukrainian communities in our analytic narrative have complex identity repertoires. In censuses and surveys,

---

[21] The theory generation process began inductively, with observation of Ukrainian politics during the 2014–2015 period after Maidan. The initial draft of the narrative – material that would become Chapters 6 and 7 – was written prior to any mathematical formalization, and intentionally leaned heavily on sources from Ukraine to maximize local validity. We decided, as a guiding principle, that action emerging from within what we call Russian-speaking communities was the most critical, and so our formal utility assumptions, and the analytic narrative in this book, will try to capture the perspective of these elites as much as possible.

[22] Identifying actors, defining a sequence of strategic interactions among them, reducing the choice set available to these actors to something manageable, specifying the structure of information (e.g., signals actors send each other to inform others of their beliefs), and the payoffs to actors for choosing different strategies – some find this reductive exercise plodding and tedious, but others find formalization makes it easier to generalize from one case to another.

[23] Levi cites Scharpf (1990, 484–5) on this point. If an economist investigates market behaviors with a simplifying assumption that all firms are trying to maximize wealth, it leaves out a lot, but the body of conclusions flows from a conversation bounded by similar premises.

asked to define themselves in terms of a nationality (ethnic belonging) and a language of origin (*ridna mova/rodnoi yazyk*, generally, if misleadingly, translated as mother tongue), respondents in Eastern Ukraine often chafe at the attempts to impose classification categories. Ukrainian-speakers live close by Russian-speakers. One complication is that many self-identified Ukrainians claim Russian as their language of origin. Even more prefer to use Russian in their daily interactions. The Ukrainian dominant narrative presumes that a self-defined Ukrainian identifies with the Ukrainian state irrespective of language spoken. The Russian dominant narrative (Putin's so-called *Russkii mir*) presumes a Russian-speaker identifies with the Russian nation – and, by extension, the current Russian nation-state.

Our model assumes that identity can be reconfigured by strategic behavior. In the post-Maidan uncertainty, the main actors – elites and street militants – revealed themselves as either political Ukrainians or political Russians by taking actions oriented toward defending the Ukrainian state or embracing Russian irredentist policy.[24] Since the identity markers distinguishing Ukrainians from Russians are more political than cultural, we approach the concept of minority through a constructivist lens, as well. To say that Russian-speakers form a minority does not mean they were a numerical/demographic minority, but that they found themselves in the *political* minority. After Maidan, some feared a minority status was being institutionalized.

We describe Russian-speaking communities with nationalists on both sides itching for a fight – activating a Russian or Ukrainian political identity by flying flags, firing guns, saying prayers, and getting tattoos. Many high-risk actions were attempts to signal to other community members that a social "tip" was imminent or underway. Outside Crimea, most Russian-speaking communities "tipped back" toward loyalty to Kyiv.

Importantly, we posit no theory of Kremlin decision-making processes. We do not need to psychologize Putin to tell our story. We have little reliable information on his thought processes. For our argument

---

[24] On the rise of political identities in a complex identity environment during a conflict, see Dragojević (2019). The core members of the leading Ukrainian volunteer battalions in 2014 were Russian-speakers from the East. They may have been culturally indistinguishable from the political Russians they were fighting against, but they acted as political Ukrainians and radical Ukrainian nationalists.

to cohere, all that is necessary is to notice that Ukrainian political elites in the spring of 2014, at the center or the periphery, did not have reliable information, either. It is unrealistic to assume that local actors within Ukraine could correctly make inferences about Russian behavior and then backward induct. Uncertainty about Russian policy objectives and military designs is critical to our account. The question of "what the Kremlin is signaling" with a military action can be an endless font of speculation.[25] In this book we focus instead on choices and calculations within Eastern Ukrainian communities regarding Russia's intentions, since these matters can be assessed with empirical data.

Complete analysis of a simple multistage game can be found in Appendix A. The purpose of the model is to reduce from local complexity, highlight essentials, and ease comparisons to other cases. While many Ukrainians remember Maidan, the invasion of Crimea, and the war in Donbas as a chain of unique historical events, we see them as an example of something that occurs at unpredictable intervals in many societies: *temporary* weakness of state institutions, with expectations that strong state institutions will endure. Status hierarchies in the reformed state become salient.

There are just a few parts of Ukraine with critical masses of ethnic Russian minorities sufficiently close to the Russian border to have a reasonable chance at successful secession (high p). In our account there was a military intervention, but little killing in Crimea. War broke out only in the Donbas region. We attribute this to an unusual cascade of events with local roots. Everywhere in the East, one mainly observed thousands of mostly anti-Kremlin Russian-speakers taking up arms in militias to control the streets. At times they clashed with pro-Russia militias, defending their cities against a perceived Russian invasion. At other times, elites stayed safely indoors.

In our chapters we compare outcomes across many different Russian-speaking communities. Table 2.1 summarizes our book's

---

[25] Why didn't the Russian army intervene in Donbas in April/May 2014? When it did in August 2014, why did it "stop pushing" at the line of control – but then move that line in 2022? Were threats of retaliatory punishment (economic sanctions) from other great powers a deterrent? Were the costs of occupying a territory housing a hostile Russian-speaking population salient? Were Kremlin elites acting emotionally? Improvising? Miscalculating? Acting on incomplete intelligence? We can speculate, but no better than others.

Table 2.1 *Analytic narrative structure*

	Physical site of contestation	Key parameter values	Coordination mechanism	Response from Kyiv to autonomy demands	Russian-speaking community payoffs (often x^*)
Before Maidan (Ch. 3)	Entire country. Focal point in capital city K	p = variable by [geo/demo]graphy a = low, but > 0 μ = low	Party of Regions (succeeds)	**Accept:** Brokered autonomy + expectation that power will rotate	Brokered autonomy (x^*)
Irredentist Annexation (Ch. 5)	Urban centers in Crimea	p = very high a = 1 μ = zero	Little Green Men + Rump Party of Regions (succeeds)	**Concede:** Unchallenged secession of Crimea	Best: Bloodless homecoming ($x^*=1$)
The "Russian Spring" (Ch. 6)	East/Southern Russian-speaking communities	p = variable by [geo/demo]graphy a = nonzero μ = high	Russian television (fails)	**N/A:** No offer, no coordination. (Terminal payoff: enforced assimilation)	Coordination fails + vigilantism ($p-c+\varepsilon-\mu$)
The Donbas War (Ch. 7)	Communities in Donbas region, including DNR/LNR	p = fairly high a = high, but signals mixed μ = nonzero	Street power overwhelms old Party of Regions elites	**Offer rejected:** Domestic police action → internationalized conflict	Worst: Conventional war ($p-c$, high c)
The War: 2015–2022 (Ch. 8)	Entire country, but changed de facto borders. Focal point in capital city K	p = variable by [geo/demo]graphy a = nonzero, raised starting fall 2021 μ = moderate	Russia's military presence in DNR/LNR	**Reject:** Frozen conflict in DNR/LNR, enforced assimilation elsewhere	x^*< in Ch. 3 due to absence of Party of Region voters, Crimea & DNR/LNR. High C starting 2022.

empirical strategy. The parameters that matter the most in our causal narrative are: (1) the probability of successful insurgent secession (p), (2) the probability Russia would intervene militarily in a police action (a, a source of uncertainty), and (3) the local risk of antisedition vigilante violence in a community (μ).

Chapter 3 provides background on Ukraine since independence. One of the most important points of departure between our book and others in this space is the decision to take seriously the *choice* of political identity – in this case Russian. A political identity is the output of a bargaining process, not a culturally driven (let alone primordial) outcome within communities. This is an assumption that allows us to analyze seditious community politics as sometimes being theatrical. This more malleable, constructivist language, in the shadow of Brubaker's (1996) triadic configuration, also draws attention to something obvious, but uncomfortable, to many Ukrainians: between 1991 and 2014, Russian-speaking communities have been able to subtly and indirectly extort the Ukrainian center with the implied threat of renegotiating the border with Russia.[26] *Coordinated sedition* in the model occurs when a critical threshold of high-status community members embraced the Russian narrative with the intent of destabilizing Ukrainian national politics – "shaking up the center" to maximize their leverage. To do so, they become politically "Russian" in order to bargain. In a simple setting which reduces the choice set to a simple binary, the performances of a few elites "activating" their "latent" Russian identity can potentially tip a community.

Though it has become common shorthand to describe the Party of Regions as a "Russian Party" or nefarious conduit for Kremlin influence, we believe it is more analytically useful to imagine it as a machine for aggregating preferences across multiple constituencies. Coordination is achieved most efficiently through institutions (Weingast 1997; Roemer 2019, 11) and the Party of Regions, which largely carried the Eastern Ukrainian vote in elections between 2002 and 2012, served that coordination function within Russian-speaking communities.[27] Even though the Russian language was nearly hegemonic in urban centers of the

---

[26] We are not originators of this point. Van Evera (1997, 40–1), though often tagged with primordialism, made a very similar argument, as did Van Houten (1998).

[27] Tsebelis (1990, 38) argues that iterative institutionalized settings are the most appropriate for rational choice approaches.

East, many Russian-speakers were anxious about the political dominance of Ukrainian-speakers at the center. The Party of Regions – and in the 1990s, the Communist Party and other Eastern-based parties – made political capital out of these concerns. Compromises were struck among elites (until a Donbas-driven language law in 2012 severed the political equilibrium). In the one instance where *ethnic* Russians formed a majority of the population, the peninsula of Crimea, additional autonomy protections were brokered. Eastern Ukrainian community elites had bargained by provoking crises at the center more than once, with Russia casting a shadow over regional bargaining within Ukraine.

Since the sequencing of actions is important for model predictions, we provide evidence that demands for autonomy were often initiated in the periphery (through community-level mobilization, sometimes backed by an overt threat of secession), and foisted on the center as take-it-or-leave-it offers.

Chapter 4 describes the crisis – the Maidan events – which collapsed the Party of Regions, initiated the game, and, in our causal narrative, started the war. Maidan symbolized the rejection – by a mostly Western Ukrainian constituency with a high potential for mobilization – of the explicit pro-Russia reorientation of the Yanukovych government (the abrupt decision to drop an EU trade agreement) after decades of balancing Western and Russian interests. It also marked the first time since independence that state agents – an elite police unit – used excessive force against protesters. This prompted a radical wing of protesters to use violence against the police as a strategic response to break a political impasse. The escalation of violence ultimately impelled Party of Regions MPs to defect and officials to flee, ending the Yanukovych government. The irregular (extra-electoral) transfer of power to a coalition of opposition parties was a source of anxiety, heightened by a symbolic vote to repeal the 2012 language law that had granted official status to Russian in Eastern Ukraine.

All of this created two high-powered geopolitical narratives, one espoused by Western officials and the other by Russian officials, which persist to this day. In the first, the illegitimate violence against protesters finished the regime. In the second, the illegitimate violence against the police overthrew the government. Fears of status reversals became salient. Some anti-Maidan protesters who began to organize in Crimea, Donbas, and elsewhere in Eastern Ukraine formed militias, acting on the second narrative. In that sense, the roots of Ukraine's civil war can be traced back to the square. The question was whether elites in periph-eral communities would accept the first storyline or accept the second storyline and opt for *sedition*.

Chapter 5 describes the rapid coordination by elites in Crimea on sedi-tion. Crimea distinguished itself from the rest of Ukraine by the speed of coordination; the drama played out over days, not months. There was also never a pro-Ukraine self-defense group attempting to con-trol the streets, due to the presence of Soviet veterans, Russian military units based in Sevastopol, and – just days into the crisis – the arrival of Russian soldiers in the capital. It seems to us that the Kremlin's preferred sequence would have been for the local parliament to signal its intent to separate through a referendum and then invite Russian troops for pro-tection. When a massive pro-Ukraine demonstration by Crimean Tatars prevented parliament from voting, however, Russian soldiers were sent in to seize parliament (and government buildings) and the vote took place. In the language of our model, prior to the arrival of Russian soldiers, on February 26, Tatar demonstrations and fear of retribution from Kyiv inhibited coordination. With Russia's arrival, the fear subsided ($\mu = 0$). This did not guarantee the outcome, but choosing the higher-payoff equilibrium in a lower-risk social environment made elites' coordination easier. By March 1, *coordinated sedition* was a fait accompli.

Why did Russia intervene in Crimea so rapidly? We believe that despite the uncertainty over the degree of Crimean Tatar resistance and the loyalty of local elites, the extremely high value that the Russian military put on maintaining access for its Black Sea Fleet to the deep-water port at Sevastopol was probably the deciding factor. The Party of Regions networks served a coordinating function, repurposing state institutions to legitimize the Russian presence and ensuring insti-tutional continuity. Crimeans voted to leave Ukraine, the Kremlin argued it was a victory for self-determination, the new government in Kyiv was checkmated, and an orderly evacuation of rump Ukrainian military units occurred. *Coordinated sedition*, however, would not unfold so neatly in Donbas, Kharkiv, Odesa, or anywhere else.

Chapter 6 describes the chaotic "Russian Spring." As everyone watched Russia's de facto borders expanding and Ukraine's contract-ing with the annexation of Crimea, the existential question was whether the Ukrainian state was in danger elsewhere in Eastern Ukraine. Since the Party of Regions had imploded at the center, dozens of Russian-speaking communities each had to extemporaneously decide whether sedition or loyalty to Kyiv would prevail. Once the mechanism of Party of Regions cross-oblast aggregation broke down, in the 24–48 hours after the Kharkiv Congress on February 22 (the day that President Yanukovych was removed), peripheral elites were on their own. We describe elites in different communities trying to second-guess the center and keep a lid on the explosive energy erupting from the streets, as anti-Maidan protests became a regular feature in several Eastern oblasts. Russian television provided a script that delegitimized the Ukrainian state and amplified a threat of domination by "fascists," magnifying both the threat of physical risks for those considering sedition (μ) and the political risks of inaction. But who would act out this script?

Most elites were cautious of overt sedition. Russia attempted, but failed, to recruit established Russian-language-speaking community elites in Ukraine's South and East, and secessionist uprisings were not attempted in most Russian-speaking communities. An abortive uprising in Kharkiv was put down through improvisation. For a four-month period, between February and May, elites carefully weighed their options. Finally, after a fire in Odesa killed nearly fifty pro-Russia militants, anti-Kyiv protests died down virtually everywhere – except in Donbas.

Why? The standard answer is that Russian-speaking Ukrainian elites did not *believe* in a map revision based on *Russkii mir* (or its related construct of *Novorossiya*, Russian territorial claims going back to the era of Catherine the Great) as a viable focal point for *seditious* social coordination (Roeder 2018, 94–5). Surveys conducted in Ukraine's East (excluding Donbas and Crimea) showed that only 15 percent of respondents supported *Novorossiya* as a basis for separation from Ukraine (O'Loughlin, Toal, and Kolosov 2017, 33). Survey behaviors can be imperfect gauges of sentiment, but it is reasonable to assume that most people did not believe in the legitimacy of Putin's project. It could also be that overt behavior challenging the Ukrainian state after Maidan was too risky with guns on the street. Russian-speaking elites may have feared vigilante violence, which became indistinguishable from state repression once the government legitimized volunteer battalions to go and fight in Donbas. The fear was amplified by the narrative on Russian television. Separately, elites might have intuited that bargaining and escalation processes might get out of hand – especially in communities close to the Russian border, and particularly by late May 2014, when it had become clear that Kyiv's policy response to sedition would be fully militarized (e.g., artillery shelling).

What did failed or partially-successful community-level attempts at seditious coordination actually look like, in practice? They were very messy. In the end, very few communities tipped toward sedition. The chapter describes street crowds pushing each other, elites making speeches to empty rooms, keyboard warriors fact-checking each other's assertions or spreading disinformation as fast as they could, and Russian flags being raised over buildings only to be taken down overnight. Diverse social actors were anxiously searching for information and trying to update their strategies. Elites in Kyiv had to choose to engage in a police action without certain knowledge of whether Russia would come to the aid of rebels – and indeed, whether it already had. Confusion about whether enemies were local militias or cross-border Russians was a defining feature of what Kyiv called an "antiterrorist operation" (ATO).

Chapter 7 describes the collapse of social order in Eastern Donbas. A population, which featured a plurality or near majority of self-described ethnic Russians, turned in on itself, then rejected Maidan completely. New social actors emerged and new militias found themselves in control of the territory, organized voting exercises (in an attempt to ape Crimea), and refused to recognize the legitimacy of the central government. The Donetsk People's Republic (DNR) and the Luhansk People's Republic (LNR) emerged on maps. Military miscalculation occurred at many stages on the escalation ladder. Seizing government buildings and hoping Russian assistance would arrive to bail them out (with brokered amnesty) may have been a bad bet, but militia leaders in the Donbas were not gambling irrationally. The confused sequencing of moves and countermoves on the part of local commanders, and the emergence of social actors from the streets (bypassing community elites) is discussed. Consistent with our model, even at the peak of conventional momentum in August 2014, it was not obvious to anyone whether Russia would actually send troops into Eastern Ukraine to assert control. Actors in Donbas overplayed their hand. Russia's presence has internationalized the conflict, and quietly facilitated coordination since 2015.

Prior to Russia's military arrival, we describe how "tidal" political processes on the streets quickly hardened what were previously fluid identity choices.[28] The Luhansk Council, in Donbas, was the only

---

[28] With the breakdown of institutions, in our narrative the relevant process-based mechanisms of coordination on *sedition* strategies, where they occurred, were informational cascades (Lohmann 1994), herd behaviors (Banerjee 1992; Bikhchandani, Hirshleifer, and Welch 1992), and likely various kinds of norms (family/clan and honor-based ties, reciprocity-based communal ties) (Petersen 2001).

regional parliament in the Southeast to issue a direct challenge to the post-Maidan government in Kyiv in the Crimea model. The far more significant Donetsk Council did not follow suit. What occurred, instead, was a process whereby the street overwhelmed old institutions as it became obvious that coordination by elites was not emergent. (Even in Luhansk, the council stopped functioning.) In the language of the model, we would say that there was no coordination in the first period, a hastily improvised autonomy offer from K (sending police but ordering them not to fire), and rejection of the offer by new elites who came out of the woodwork. The realization that no law enforcement body was consistently making arrests emboldened some groups. The emergence of new local players who dragged their communities into sustained *sedition* is critical to our narrative. In any event, miscalculation occurred. It was common for anti-Maidan protesters across the East to take to the streets armed and prepare to face-off against pro-Maidan protesters (μ), with hopes Russia might intervene to alter the momentum of events (a). In the Donbas, eventually, Russian troops did arrive. When they did, they inflicted huge costs on the Ukrainian government (C) in defense of "their people" living in this territory, but only after local volunteers demonstrated an ability to hold buildings for weeks (p).

Chapter 8 stands apart from the rest of the book. First it describes the aftermath of the Russian military arrival: "frozen conflicts" in Crimea and the DNR/LNR. The geopolitical status quo had not changed between 2015 and 2021. In Ukrainian-controlled territories, however, there were substantial social changes. Consistent with model predictions, the diminishing bargaining power of Russian-speaking community elites amplified the policy preferences of the Ukrainian West. Ukrainian language policy removed the teaching of Russian as a first language from high schools and memory politics emphasized the historical break with Russia and the Soviet Union. The failure to reconstitute anything like the Party of Regions that might allow Russian-speaking communities in Ukraine to coordinate efficiently facilitated these policy changes. In the language of the model, a *brokered autonomy* equilibrium was replaced by an *enforced assimilation* equilibrium. The second part of the chapter describes the barriers to conflict-resolution sequencing, demobilization, and reconstruction that prevailed in 2015–2021. Sequencing was difficult because of commitment problems in settlement, that is, the fear that the other party might renege. Finally, we describe Putin's 2022 decision to considerably escalate the interstate war, raising costs C.

3 | *Before Maidan*

This chapter has two purposes. The first is to provide some essential background on Ukraine for the general reader. In independent Ukraine, pre-2022, the politics of regional autonomy in Ukraine continued to be constructed as zero-sum. A gain for the center was almost always framed as a loss for the regions. This is a key assumption of our model that requires local empirical validation. The second aim is to describe the brokerage that – for twenty-five years of independence until Maidan – kept Ukraine's zero-sum conflict from turning violent. Crises deescalated and bargains were institutionalized.

The first part of the chapter will introduce a discussion of two clashing master narratives of Ukrainian history. For ease of reference, we will refer to one as a *Russian narrative* and the other as a *Ukrainian narrative*.[1] These should not be confused with a term we employ elsewhere in the book, *analytic narrative*, a style of presentation designed to test a formal model. Memory politics are politically salient as a result of the 2014–2021 war, amplified further since Russia's invasion of 2022. We shall show how the forced choice between master narratives divided Ukrainians. The gruesome bombing of Eastern Ukrainian cities in early 2022 discredited the Russian narrative most everywhere in the West and throughout Ukraine, but prewar these clashing narratives reflected elemental normative and geopolitical questions. The Russian narrative emphasized the shared history, and suffering, of Russians and Ukrainians. The Ukrainian narrative emphasized their distinct history and the violence perpetrated by a Moscow-rule state toward Ukraine. These positions were very hard to reconcile. They could quite easily be made to feel zero-sum.

In the second part of this chapter, we resume the use of the language of analytic narrative and present Ukrainian historical data in order to

---

[1] The use of the concept "narratives" is standard in memory studies. See, e.g., Galai (2022)

evaluate their congruence with our model. The Ukrainian political system was tested at three critical junctures: 1991–1992 (independence and Crimean autonomy), 1993–1994 (Donbas strike and Crimean secessionism), and 2004 (Orange Revolution). In each case, there was a crisis in Kyiv, followed by coordinated mobilization in demographically concentrated Russian-speaking communities in the Eastern provinces. In all three crises, the bargain that established or restored state legitimacy involved the Ukrainian center acceding to demands for political power initiated in the periphery. This is consistent with our model's sequencing of actions. In the calculation of what offers might diffuse the crises, in the background were questions about how the Kremlin would respond to unrest.

Historical Background

The history of Ukraine is intertwined with the history of empires. Most of its territories have been part of the Russian political space for centuries. The territorial core of Central Ukraine belonged to Poland, known as the Polish–Lithuanian Commonwealth in the premodern period, until the mid-seventeenth century, when Muscovy, the pre-Imperial Russian state, annexed its Left Bank – essentially Kyiv and the provinces of the Northeast, all the way to Kharkiv. (Moscow added the territories of the Right Bank, west of Kyiv, a century later when the Polish state was partitioned.) This incorporation is presented as a "reunification" in the Russian historical narrative, on the claim that the medieval state of Kyivan Rus' (ninth–thirteenth century) was Russia's ancestral state. The Ukrainian national narrative, in contrast, presents Kyivan Rus' as a proto-Ukrainian state and the subordination of Ukraine to Russia as a betrayal of the terms of a treaty signed in 1654. This constitutes the fundamental Russian–Ukrainian clash over the national myths of origins.

At the end of the eighteenth century, the defeat of the Crimean Khanate, an Ottoman protectorate, opened up the Ukrainian Southeast to permanent Slavic settlement. By the second half of the nineteenth century, the Donbas region became the first site of mass industrialization in Imperial Russia, attracting a significant labor force. The Russian narrative dubbed this new population zone from Odesa to Donetsk "New Russia" (*Novorossiya*), whereas the Ukrainian narrative stressed that most settlers were ethnic Ukrainians migrating south.

This set up the second national narrative clash, between a territorial criterion ("the Russian government settled ..."), and an ethnographic one ("the Ukrainian people settled ...").

Two critical regions became part of a territorially unified Ukraine only in the twentieth century. Galicia, nestled in the far West, is the cradle of Ukrainian political nationalism.[2] This region was annexed by the Soviet Union in 1939 following a secret clause of the Molotov-Ribbentrop Pact.[3] Occupied by Germany in 1941, Galicia became the site of what became arguably the largest insurgency in Europe – by the Organization of Ukrainian Nationalists (Orhanizatsiia ukraïns'kykh natsionalistiv, or OUN) and its underground army the Ukrainian Insurgent Army (Ukraïns'ka povstans'ka armiia, or UPA) – against the reestablishment of Soviet power. In contrast to most of Central, Southern, and Eastern Ukraine, Western Ukraine's experience of rule by Moscow began in World War II.[4]

The second relative latecomer was Crimea. Attached to Russia at the formation of the Soviet Union in the early 1920s, Crimea was "gifted" to Soviet Ukraine in 1954 – symbolically, in the year marking the 300th anniversary of the "reunification" of Ukraine with Russia, when the Left Bank came under Moscow rule.[5] Crimea is important to Russian identity. The port city of Sevastopol, home to the Black

[2] While the idea of the Ukrainian nation originated in Central Ukraine, in Imperial Russia, around the mythic figure of the poet Taras Shevchenko (Grabowicz 2014), Ukrainian nationalism as a mass movement first developed in Galicia, which belonged to the Austrian Empire under a Polish administration (Himka 2006). Religiously, Galicia is more likely to be associated with Byzantine Catholic heritage than the rest of Ukraine.

[3] In the Pact, named after their foreign ministers, the Soviet Union and Nazi Germany pledged nonaggression toward each other. The secret clause allowed the Soviet Union to annex the Baltic states and two territories that had belonged to Poland in the interwar period: Western Ukraine (Galicia and Volhynia) and Western Belorussia (now known as Belarus).

[4] For a short period during World War I, parts of Western Ukraine were under Imperial Russian military occupation (Bartov 2018, 38). Most of the "action" in our model (elite coordination) takes place in the Ukrainian East (Southern and Eastern), where Russian-speaking communities are concentrated. This chapter, however, emphasizes the historical distinctiveness of Western Ukraine, the westernmost territories of the Ukrainian West (Western, Central).

[5] In the Soviet period, Russia was known as the Russian Soviet Federative Socialist Republic (RSFSR) and Ukraine as the Ukrainian Soviet Socialist Republic. "Russia" and "Ukraine" are used here as shorthand. While the reunification trope received extensive coverage in the Soviet press at the time, Crimea was curiously absent from the script (Sasse 2007, 101).

Sea Fleet, held great significance in the Russian memory narrative that had developed since the 1853–1856 Crimean War (Plokhy 2000). The baptism of Prince Volodymyr in the tenth century, which occurred near present-day Sevastopol, is also a seminal moment in the history of the Russian Orthodox Church.[6]

Prior to World War II, several other ethnic groups called the Ukrainian territories home. After the Holocaust of Jews, and the mass deportation of Poles and Crimean Tatars, the two dominant nationalities left in Ukraine were Ukrainians and Russians.[7] In 1989, the last census of the Soviet Union, the ratio was 73 percent Ukrainian to 22 percent Russian.

Then the Soviet experiment ended. Twenty-five million ethnic Russians awoke to discover themselves living in new states. About half of this number resided in Ukraine. In the 2001 census, the only one conducted in post-Soviet Ukraine, the ratio was 78 percent Ukrainian to 17 percent Russian. One reason for the decline is emigration. Another is that the identity boundary of "beached diaspora" Russians (Laitin 1998) remains fluid. An ambiguous relationship between language and nationality allows individual redefinition.

This was not always the case. In the Soviet tradition, in line with nineteenth-century practice in East Central Europe, language defined nationality. The nation was a line on every person's passport. For a nationality to be recognized, it had to be based on what the state considered a distinct language (Arel 2002b). In the 1897 census, the first to be conducted in Imperial Russia, language was used as a proxy for nationality. The state recorded the *rodnoi yazyk* (language of origin) of individuals. This was interpreted as nationality data.[8] Importantly, the Imperial state did not categorize Ukrainian as distinct from Russian. Russians were known as Great Russians and the Ukrainians as Little

---

[6] The main text includes the Ukrainian spelling; the Russian spelling is Vladimir. Some argue that this event makes the peninsula also, by extension, a site of dispute over the meaning of Orthodoxy in Russian and Ukrainian national identity (Griffin 2021). As we will see in Chapter 8, the status of the Ukrainian Orthodox Church – whether or not it should be subordinated to the Moscow Patriarchate – is a recent field of contestation.

[7] There are other groups, too, such as two concentrated pockets of rural Hungarians and Romanians straddling the interstate border of two oblasts.

[8] "Language of origin" is a more accurate translation than the commonly used "native language." *Rodnoi* implies an identification with the group (nationality), not necessarily the first language spoken, the usual connotation of "native" or "mother" tongue (Arel 2002a).

Russians. The Imperial census tabulated speakers of "Little Russian" (the Ukrainian idiom) as a subset of Russians.

The Soviets innovated on this structure. Soviet leaders recognized Ukrainian as a separate language and thus a distinct nationality, taking its place alongside many non-Russian nationalities. Soviet authorities separately solicited language of origin and nationality on the 1926 census, making it possible for a respondent to claim Russian as a language of origin and a nationality other than Russian. Outside of Russia, Ukraine was the area where split responses were recorded most often. Over time, the proportion of self-declared Ukrainians who claimed Russian as *rodnoi* (*ridna* in Ukrainian) grew, reaching 15 percent in 2001 (Arel 2002a). This is the standard understanding of "Russian-speakers": those Ukrainian by nationality whose *rodnoi yazyk/ridna mova* is Russian.

Both ethnic Russians and Russian-speaking Ukrainians are concentrated in the Ukrainian East (Eastern and Southern). So while in the 2001 census Eastern Ukraine was 63 percent Ukrainian and 30 percent Russian by nationality, this understates the cultural influence of Russian in the East. Since almost all ethnic Russians and one third of Ukrainians claimed Russian as *rodnoi* in the East, this meant that roughly half of the entire population of Eastern Ukraine (51 percent) was Russian-speaking using census categories. In the Donbas and Crimea, the proportion of residents identifying with the Russian language was higher than 67 percent.[9]

In 2013, on the eve of the complex events described in Chapter 4, a foreigner visiting an urban center in the East would have been struck by the near hegemony of spoken Russian in the streets. An expert on social policy or children's education might be aware that most schools had switched to Ukrainian as the main language of instruction (Moser 2013, 53), and advertisers pushing countrywide campaigns would have been encouraged by law (and market demands) to use Ukrainian, but the great majority of people going about their everyday lives preferred to speak Russian given the opportunity. Waves of Ukrainian sociological surveys confirm the language of preference in Eastern Ukraine was Russian for more than 90 percent of residents.[10]

---

[9] Figures calculated from oblast-level 2001 census data.

[10] An aggregation of twenty-two surveys conducted in the electoral year 2004 by the Kyiv International Institute of Sociology had the proportion of Russian-speakers in the East at 94 percent. If the option "a mixture of Russian and Ukrainian" was given, it went down to 88 percent (Arel and Khmelko 2005).

In this book "Russian-speaker" is not meant to suggest mere bilingualism, or the ability to speak Russian in addition to Ukrainian. The vast majority of ethnic Ukrainians are fluent in Russian. That does not make them "Russian-speakers" in our usage of the term. "Russian-speaking" denotes preference, not ability. The same is true for "Ukrainian-speakers," since most Russians from Ukraine can speak at least basic Ukrainian (and virtually all understand it well enough to get by). With most people passively bilingual, language politics in Ukraine are not about whether everyone should *learn* Ukrainian per se, but whether everyone should *have to* use Ukrainian in certain formal settings. The high-stakes question is whether Ukrainian should be the privileged language of social mobility in Ukraine – for passing tests to enter school, for getting a good job with a pension, for making a career in politics, and more.

Zero-Sum Bargaining: Language, Symbolic Politics, and Geopolitics

The central tenet of the Ukrainian national narrative is that Ukrainians form a distinct nation because they speak a distinct language. The public use of the Ukrainian language is the core of Ukrainian nationalism since their language is the central warrant for the claim they are not "actually just" Russians that had forgotten their past.[11] In Imperial Russia and with a few exceptions in the Soviet Union, the language of the state on the territory that is now Ukraine was Russian.[12] Russian was the Soviet language of high culture and social mobility. In 1989, following the Baltic republics, the parliament in Kyiv passed a law

---

[11] The Austrian Empire pioneered the recognition of nationalities (ethnic groups) in schools, public administration, and on the census. The Ukrainians of Galicia were one of the beneficiaries, which led to this persistent belief, famously expressed by the writer Alexander Solzhenitsyn (1991), that Ukrainian nationalism is an artificial creation to undermine Russia.

[12] The Ukrainian ("Little Russian") language was banned in the last decades of the Russian Empire (Remy 2016, 157–232). The Soviet Union initially promoted the use of Ukrainian in state institutions and in schools as part of a policy known as indigenization (*korenizatsiia*)(Liber 1992; Pauly 2014). This was quashed in the 1930s, and Ukrainian schools disappeared from cities by the 1950s, but the "affirmative action" policy of promoting ethnic Ukrainians to state and party posts remained (Martin 2001). The exception is that Ukrainian remained broadly used in the Western Ukrainian provinces annexed during World War II.

making Ukrainian the state language (*derzhavna mova*). Until 2012, this law was neither amended nor replaced, and the 1996 Constitution enshrined Ukrainian as the sole state language.

Ukrainian increasingly became the language of power at the national level. Russian remained predominant in Eastern Ukraine, but there was recognition that one could not aspire to a career in Kyiv without fluent Ukrainian. There was a certain apprehension that Russian-speakers in the East would someday day be forced to use Ukrainian locally, as evidenced by the fact that, from the 2000s, the Party of Regions (and, before that, the Communist Party and a few smaller Eastern Ukrainian parties) wrote platforms demanding official status for Russian in the East. With one exception, every election cycle featured a demand, supported by millions of voters, to give an official status to Russian (Arel 2017). In three of the four presidential elections between 1994 and 2010, the candidate from the East (Leonid Kuchma, and twice Viktor Yanukovych) carried all Eastern oblasts with huge majorities, while the candidate from the West (Leonid Kravchuk, Viktor Yushchenko, Yulia Tymoshenko) won almost all Western oblasts.[13] Individual beliefs about making Russian an official language were among the most important predictors of voter preferences (Arel and Khmelko 1996, 2005).

In 2012, after securing the presidency for the first time, the Party of Regions broke the language policy status quo by adopting a law giving official status to Russian – making it a "regional" language. The status applied in oblasts with at least 10 percent of the population declaring Russian as a language of origin (the entire East). The law aroused great controversy among Ukrainian-speakers because of the symbolism of Russian sharing the same status as Ukrainian. Moreover, the law allowed Russian to be used in all situations, even at the center, thus negating the objective of Ukrainian becoming the main language of public life (Arel 2014). For its proponents, the law was necessary to arrest the drive by the Ukrainian-speaking West to culturally dominate

---

[13] Kravchuk was elected the first president of Ukraine in 1991 with pan-regional support, except in Galicia. By 1994, however, his electoral base became limited to most of the Ukrainian West, and Kuchma was elected mostly thanks to Eastern Ukraine. In 2004, Yushchenko defeated Yanukovych by carrying the West. Regional polarization was maintained in 2010, except that turnout went down in the West and Tymoshenko lost. Similar regional trends were maintained in parliamentary elections after partial proportional representation was adopted in 1998.

the Russian-speaking East. This was clearly a zero-sum political issue. Both sides championed policies premised on the idea that their language was threatened by the creeping advance of the other.

As we have hinted, language politics is so politically potent because it crystalizes and symbolizes the two main competing tropes of common destiny. The Russian narrative claims that Russians and Ukrainians share a common past, and therefore a common future. The Ukrainian narrative emphasizes their distinct origins, and therefore their distinct futures. The future revolves around the legitimacy of statehood, or how truly independent a Ukrainian state can be vis-à-vis the Russian state. Since, in the Ukrainian narrative, language is the historical marker that distinguishes Ukrainians from Russians, a Ukrainian state must symbolically express itself in Ukrainian. It quickly follows that the political status of Ukrainian must be higher than Russian, so granting equal status to Russian is tantamount to subordination of Ukraine to Russia. The Russian narrative sees Ukraine as the historical land of both Ukrainians and Russians. Russian-speakers ought to have equal linguistic rights alongside Ukrainian-speakers.

Battles over whether or not Russians and Ukrainians share a common destiny are also expressed through contested national symbols. Memory narratives are always and necessarily selective. Three events occupied center stage in memory wars in Ukraine and between Russia and Ukraine: the anti-Soviet insurgency in Western Ukraine during World War II, the 1932–1933 Ukrainian famine (Holodomor), and the violence of the Soviet past (Stalinism in particular).[14] In the Ukrainian narrative, the insurgents fought for Ukrainian independence, the famine was a targeted genocide, and the Soviet Union was a criminal state. In the Russian narrative, the insurgents were fascists, the famine hurt everyone and did not specifically target Ukraine, and Stalin's harsh policies were necessary to industrialize quickly and win the most important war in recorded history.

---

[14] The insurgency was led by the OUN. The OUN was created in 1929 at a time when Western Ukraine was under Polish rule. It split in 1940 with Stepan Bandera leading a faction that attracted the youth. After the Soviet Union incorporated Western Ukraine in 1939, Moscow had become the main enemy and the OUN-Bandera began to work with German military intelligence. When the German army invaded Galicia in 1941, it arrived with an advanced Ukrainian battalion led by an OUN officer. For a synthetic treatment of Ukrainian memory wars, see Wylegala (2017) and Wylegala and Glowacka-Grajper (2020).

A few points bear emphasis for novices to this part of the world. First, the sheer numbers involved are staggering. The Soviet secret police killed nearly 10,000 political prisoners (mostly Ukrainians) in Western Ukraine 1941 before fleeing the German advance (Motyl and Kiebuzinski 2016; Bartov 2018, 338). As part of its counterinsurgency in 1944 and after, the Soviet Union killed more than 75,000 unarmed insurgents, and deported more than 200,000 family members deemed collectively responsible for the rebellion (Weiner 2001, 173; Zhukov 2015, 1165). Demographers estimate that the 1932–1933 famine caused 3.9 million "excess deaths" (Rudnytskyi et al. 2015, 64).

Second, much of this victimization was officially denied for fifty years during the Soviet era and is still largely absent from public discourse and historical research in Russia. The magnitude of these traumatic events left scars still easily visible in the demographic map of Ukraine today (Rozenas and Zhukov 2019), but it was dangerous (even suicidal) to publicly invoke these events until Ukrainian independence. Before 2022, Eastern and Western Ukrainian voters remained divided on what to make of these traumatic events. Statues of Bandera, the OUN leader, proliferated only in the West. Statues of Lenin, the Soviet leader, were maintained primarily in the East (Shevel 2011; Portnov 2013). When the Ukrainian parliament, at the initiative of President Yushchenko, adopted a law proclaiming the Holodomor a genocide, it passed by a bare majority. All but two MPs from the Party of Regions symbolically abstained from this vote (Maksymiuk 2006). After Yanukovych was elected in 2010, he made a point of publicly expressing his opinion that the Holodomor was tragic but not a genocide (RIA Novosti 2010).

Third, the past is not past. The grammar of the ongoing conflict between Russia and the West recycles these tropes. Russian media routinely hurls the epithet of "fascists": at Maidan protesters, at volunteer battalions in the East, at the democratically elected of Ukraine and its armed forces in 2022. It is an epithet with special political meaning in Russia.[15] Its frequent use reveals how the memory of World War II permeates contemporary discourse. The theatrical invocation imagery goes both ways. Ukrainian radical nationalist groups

---

[15] The Russian narrative, in line with the postwar Soviet narrative, refers to German occupiers exclusively as "fascists," never as "Germans." Since more than 10 million civilians were killed in Soviet territory occupied by Germans, "fascist" is associated with the worst atrocities committed during World War II.

speak for just a tiny minority of Ukrainian voters, but they *do* proudly embrace a lineage that runs directly to the OUN and Bandera. The Russian narrative calls the OUN fascist because it collaborated with Germany. The accusation goes deeper. Since the OUN's first act after the German arrival in Lviv was to proclaim Ukrainian independence, and since OUN members called themselves "nationalists," the Russian narrative implies that Ukrainian nationalism is tainted with fascism. This delegitimizes the very idea that Ukrainians should have their own state (separate from Russia) and nests normatively with claims that Ukrainian nationalism is artificial, that Russians and Ukrainians are "essentially one people," and the more extreme claim that Ukraine is "not even a state" (Allenova, Geda, and Novikov 2008).

These views are quite prevalent in Russia (Trenin 2017). The quote at the end of the last paragraph is attributed to Vladimir Putin, at the 2008 NATO Summit in Bucharest. In 2022, that view became Russian official policy. The shift had been telegraphed months earlier. In 2021, in a long published essay on history, Putin explicitly called Russians and Ukrainians "one people" (*odin narod*), part of "what is essentially the same historical and spiritual space," claiming that there is no "historical basis" to the notion that Ukrainians and Russians form two separate nations (the premise of Ukrainian nationalism) and that in creating nationality-defined republics such as Ukraine, Russia was "robbed" and the victim of a "crime" by the Bolsheviks (Putin 2021a, 2021b). While each of these assertions have formed the basis of Russian nationalism vis-à-vis Ukraine for over a century, they were striking as a renewed challenge on the territorial integrity of the Ukrainian state.

These bold and entrenched views in Russia also explains why many Ukrainians, far exceeding the ranks of the Ukrainian radical right, tend to see the OUN primarily as a historical vehicle of resistance to Russian domination (particularly since the OUN was fighting in an area that had historically never been under Russian rule; see Kulyk 2010). This symbolic polarization – the OUN and 2014 radical militants as either fascists or fighters for Ukrainian statehood – lies at the core of the clash of narratives over common destiny. In one trope, Russians and Ukrainians fought – and are fighting – together against fascists (which include Ukrainian nationalists). In the other, Ukrainians have fought – and are fighting – subjugation by Russia.

Zero-sum identity politics, like religious schisms, can be weaponized by entrepreneurs to appear existential and irreconcilable. In fact, practical compromises on identity issues emerge out of political necessity in every diverse society (Fearon and Laitin 1996; Cetinyan 2002, 647, fn. 12). Zero-sum issues do not preclude pragmatic compromises. A concrete example may help illustrate what we mean.

Post-Soviet Ukraine experienced a volatile crisis, resolved by quiet compromise, over one of the most important national symbols: the flag. When the Ukrainian nationalist movement Rukh was founded in 1989, the blue and yellow national flag, which had long been banned, reappeared.[16] As recently as 1991, the ruling Ukrainian Communist Party continued to resist its use. After Ukrainian independence in December 1991, the situation became urgent. Soviet Ukraine was no more and the new state needed a flag. The ex-Communists lacked a concrete alternative, yet remained reluctant. Since a majority could not be achieved to amend the constitution, the law on state symbols passed with a simple majority. The initial compromise was to temporarily accept this violation of parliamentary protocol and adopt the blue and yellow flag (Wolczuk 2001, 90). When a new constitution was adopted in 1996, a more comprehensive compromise was reached with MPs representing Eastern Ukraine. This somewhat contentious state symbol would be enshrined in the constitution in return for a constitutional acknowledgment of Crimean autonomy and a promise that the Russian language would be protected.[17]

On foreign policy issues, however, the symbolic battle over common destiny tended to have a polarizing effect in the Ukrainian electorate. The main issue was whether Ukraine should orient itself toward Russia, toward the West, or try to steer a middle ground. In the 1994 and 2004 presidential elections, surveys suggested correlations between language status, foreign policy orientation, region of

[16] The flag had first been used by the Ukrainian People's Republic (UPR), proclaimed in 1917 after the October Revolution, and overrun by the Bolshevik Red Army in 1919. It flew in 1941 when the OUN, on the first day of the German invasion, proclaimed the "restoration" of Ukrainian state independence in Lviv. The flag was therefore banned in the Soviet Union.

[17] These compromises rested on creative ambiguity and promises ("guarantee") were renegotiated. Ukrainian is the state language, while Russian is "protected" but without an official status. Ukraine is a unitary state, but Crimea is autonomous. Ukraine rests on the right to self-determination of the "Ukrainian nation" but also of "all the Ukrainian people" (all nationalities). See Wolczuk (2001, 228–32) and the stenographic reports of parliamentary debates (June 1996).

residence (East vs. West), and electoral preference. For more than a decade, however, Ukrainian governments had defused this latent conflict. This was true regardless of whether the ruling party had a Western (Kravchuk 1991–1994) or Eastern (Kuchma 1994–2004) electoral base. A "multi-vectoral" dance involved curating political and economic links with the West without alienating Russia. The game changed after the election of Viktor Yushchenko in 2005, as he later campaigned to have Ukraine join NATO. Since Russia was not invited to join NATO, international organizational membership for Ukraine was seen as zero-sum by Russia.[18]

This geopolitical question divided Ukrainians along a predictable East/West axis. When Viktor Yanukovych was elected with an Eastern Ukrainian base in 2010, he quickly concluded an agreement for a twenty-year renewal of the Russian lease of Sevastopol for its Black Sea Fleet. This was interpreted as a symbolic bulwark against NATO expansion – popular with Eastern voters, antagonizing the West (Marson and Boudreaux 2010). On the eve of Maidan in November 2013, Western Ukrainians supported joining the EU roughly in a proportion of two to one. East Ukrainians were Euroskeptics in roughly in the same proportion (Kyiv International Institute of Sociology 2013b).[19] Support for joining NATO was never high, but below 10 percent in Eastern Ukraine in 2012, closer to 25 percent in Western Ukraine, a bit higher in Galicia (Haran and Zolkina 2017).

Analytic Narrative

We model zero-sum bargaining that took place between Ukrainian domestic forces. The critical inputs to the model are raw power: variables allowing Russian-speaking communities to threaten secession to get their way. The model assumes a bargaining sequence in which challenges are initiated in the periphery and "bought off" by the center most of the time. There is always the option of a peaceful bargain. The empirical question is how Ukrainian political elites found their way to the bargain that they did.

---

[18] Kupchan (2010) was a rare, isolated voice arguing that NATO was making a strategic mistake in not inviting Russia to join. Writing in 2022 the idea of Russia in NATO is politically impossible.

[19] The "undecided" survey respondents are excluded here. Ratios are still informative.

Threats by peripheral Russian-speaking community elites to yoke
the anger and strength of their aggrieved constituents, mobilize votes,
engage in parallel institution-building, and flirt with sedition have
been driving forces in Ukrainian politics.[20] Time and again, the center
"bought off" the periphery. Elites in the periphery came to anticipate
this. In the language of the model, they benefit from their first-mover
position in the bargaining structure, pocketing the "lost utility" of
threatened secession as normal corruption (political graft, closed-bid
contracts, jobs for family members). Elections are headcounts for
coordination used to distribute power by simulating approximate
political strength. Kyiv would have to give relatively more autonomy
to "buy off" a densely packed ethnic Russian stronghold featuring a
Russian military base.

Finally, uncertainty about Russian behavior has also been incorporated into Ukrainian calculations as Kyiv extends cultural rights to
Russian-speaking communities. The question of "what will Russia's
military do?" loomed ominously in the background of each of the following three critical junctures.[21]

Crimea: 1991–1994

The Crimean Peninsula has always been a special case in Ukraine.
Unlike any other province, it had previously belonged to Soviet Russia.
Crimea originally received the status of an "autonomous republic"
within Russia, due to the presence of a Crimean Tatar minority.[22]
After the mass deportation of Crimean Tatars in 1944, Crimea became
a simple oblast, a status which it kept after it was transferred to Soviet

---

[20] Secession may not have been explicitly conceptualized as civil war; the thought
   experiment was surely something more analogous to the Czech–Slovak story
   for many participants.

[21] This is parameter *a* in our model.

[22] In the logic of Soviet administrative borders, territories identified with an
   "indigenous" (*korennoi*) nationality were given the status of either a republic,
   or of an autonomous republic (or autonomous oblast) within a Union
   republic. Indigenous referred to nationalities (ethnic groups), as opposed to
   First Nations, who were categorized separately as "small-number peoples"
   (*malochislennye narody*). Indigenous groups did not have to form a majority
   for the principle to apply, and only one quarter of the population of the
   Crimean Autonomous Republic identified as Crimean Tatar in the 1926 Soviet
   census. Breaking with the norm, however, the autonomous territory was not
   named after the titular group (Crimean Tatar), but the region (Crimea).

Ukraine in 1954.[23] In the late Soviet era, Crimea was the only territory of Ukraine with a clear ethnic Russian majority (67 percent in the last Soviet census of 1989).

In 1991, Crimea became anew an "Autonomous Republic," this time within Ukraine, a status that was codified in legislation the following year. Its unique arrangement reflected the outsized bargaining strength of this constituency (a high p). Crimea received its autonomous status within Ukraine by threatening exit. In 1990, the Russian parliament, led by its chairman Boris Yeltsin, declared "sovereignty" from the Soviet central state, under its president Mikhail Gorbachev. The application of "sovereign" powers was unclear, but it signaled a weakening of central control, and unleashed a wave of similar declarations (a "parade of sovereignties") throughout the republics and autonomous areas of the Soviet Union (Kahn 2000). Within a month, Ukraine issued its own Declaration of State Sovereignty. Six months later, in January 1991, Crimean authorities organized a referendum on the "restoration" of Crimean autonomy (93 percent were in favor; see Sasse 2007, 138). To avoid confrontation, the Soviet Ukrainian parliament granted Crimea *samostiinist'* ("self-rule") (Holovatyi 1992). An agreement on the substance of autonomy required additional negotiation.

Crisis was finally averted when Kyiv acceded to Crimean demands, and the Ukrainian constitution was amended to clarify Crimean autonomy. In 1991–1992, the Crimean political Russians saw themselves (not the Tatars) as the politically relevant minority within a Ukrainian-majority Ukraine demanding special status, though neither side could openly acknowledge that the autonomy compromise had been made to satisfy the Crimean Russian majority. A Crimean Russian majority was a social fact, but Ukrainian nationalists argued (following Soviet practice) that autonomy could only be given to nationalities indigenous (*korinne*) to the land, such as Crimean Tatars – and, of course Ukrainians. Already the argument was made openly that Russians were only indigenous to Russia proper (*Biuleten'* 11 1991; Holovatyi 1992).[24]

---

[23] The Crimean Tatars were one of a dozen ethnic minorities collectively accused of collaboration with Nazi occupiers during World War II and deported to Central Asia (Polian 2004; Uehling 2004). They were only allowed to return to Crimea in the late 1980s.

[24] Thirty years later, the Ukrainian parliament passed a law making Crimean Tatars (and the very small numbers of Karaims and Krymchaks) the only "indigenous peoples" (*korinne narody*) in Ukraine (all of them concentrated

Two years later a Russian nationalist, Yuri Meshkov, was elected president of Crimea. Meshkov's party, the Russkii blok (Russian Bloc) obtained a majority in the Crimean parliament as well. Meshkov believed he had the leverage to renege on the 1992 autonomy agreement, demanding control over police and the stationing of Crimean army conscripts (Sasse 2007, 165). This was a bridge too far for Kyiv, and a special detachment of the Ukrainian Ministry of the Interior took direct control of its Crimean branch. The police did not defect and Meshkov (contrary to 2014, as we will see) did not have paramilitary elements to claim the streets. The political impasse lasted for months and was defused by the election of a pro-Russian Ukrainian president, Leonid Kuchma, in July 1994. Meshkov lost the support of his own parliament. Crucially, it was acknowledged at the time that the Yeltsin government in Russia had no interest in redrawing the map or undermining the territorial integrity of the Ukrainian state (Ozhiganov 1997, 127).[25] Kyiv maintained control of security forces in Crimea, and abolished the Crimean presidency to prevent the same sort of thing from happening again. Meshkov left the peninsula in disgrace. The old Crimean elite stayed in power and the basic terms of the initial autonomy remained with minor modifications. Autonomy was enshrined in the Ukrainian constitution two years later.

The sequence of Crimea's bargaining for autonomy fits the model quite closely. The challenge was initiated by elites in a well-organized, demographically concentrated Russian-speaking community. These elites threatened separation. Russia remained distant. We will never know what pressure Yeltsin might have come under to intervene if local security forces had split or defected. Given the geography, and the presence of a Russian naval base, the outcome of a secessionist war

in Crimea), depriving Russians of this status (Verkhovna Rada Ukraïny 2021). The law plays on semantic ambiguity. On the one hand, it adopts the international understanding of "indigenous," as in First Nations in Canada. On the other, *korinni* (*korenoi* in Russian), stemming from the Soviet experience, refers to nationalities (ethnic groups) "titular" to the land (i.e., having the right of self-rule on their historic territory). This is why the campaign to have nationalities better represented in their Soviet republics in the 1920s was called *korenizatsiia* (indigenization). The upshot is that Ukrainians (everywhere in Ukraine) and Crimean Tatars (in Crimea) are indigenous – not Russians.

[25] Meshkov had a far more receptive audience in the Russian parliament, but at the time parliament remained powerless on foreign policy, and Yeltsin was still chasing alignment with the West.

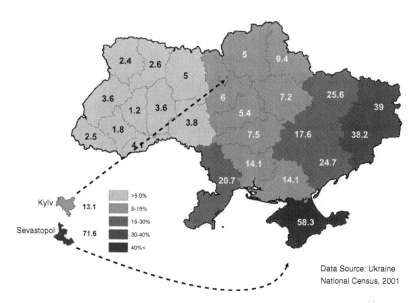

Map 3.1 Self-identified Russians as a percentage of *oblast* population

would likely have been favorable. In the end, an autonomy bargain was reached that functionally defused support for separation (and/or reunification with Russia) for two decades.

Note that our approach treats Russian political identity as an *output* of bargaining processes – a constructivist assumption, not simple primordialism. Embracing the Russian narrative allows one to become politically "Russian" in order to vote in a coordinated bloc. That bloc gets institutional protections which can be used to reproduce identity categories. Map 3.1 shows the results. The number of self-identifying Russians in Crimea in the 2001 census compared to everywhere else in Ukraine remained very high. Roeder (2018, 95) sees the 1994 events as a dress rehearsal for 2014: "the Crimea campaign had coordinated expectations in its platform [titular] population that could be mobilized quickly in surges when opportunities arose."

The Donbas: 1993

Ukraine experienced a parallel regional challenge in the industrial backbone of Ukraine. In the Soviet era, even though the Donbas was part of Soviet Ukraine, its huge industrial sector was administered by central ministries, while political elites in Kyiv came from either Dnipropetrovsk or Kharkiv.[26] In the ultra-centralized Soviet system, the Donbas – a conspicuous hub of railroads and highways on Eurasian infrastructure maps – operated as an enclave reporting directly to Moscow. Ukrainian independence had functionally severed links with Moscow. Donbas elites realized they were at risk of being dealt out of the real power, now Kyiv. A new political bargain would be necessary.

In 1993 a general strike in the Donbas held Ukraine's economy hostage. This was the second major Donbas strike in four years. In 1989, Donbas miners had joined their brethren in Russia (from the Kuzbass region) to protest appalling working conditions (Friedgut and Siegelbaum 1990). In 1993, the context was a catastrophic economic crisis characterized by hyperinflation. Factory directors and local elites sided with the strikers on the streets, united their voices to challenge Kyiv. In contrast to 1989, the endgame was overtly political. The strike resolved with the promise of a vote of no confidence against the Ukrainian president. Months later, it was decided instead to hold early parliamentary and presidential elections, two years before the end of President Leonid Kravchuk's scheduled five-year term (Crowley 1994).

Donbas elites used this strike to secure a stable foothold in the capital. A short-term result was the appointment of the mayor of Donetsk and former factory director Yefym Zviahils'kyi as interim prime minister, along with another Donetsk official, Valentyn Landyk, as deputy. A more lasting impact was the coordination of a reconstituted Communist Party of Ukraine to gain electoral power in much of Donbas during the 1994 parliamentary election. These elites would emerge as the core group of a larger coalition of Russian-speaking MPs from Eastern Ukraine that would coordinate on policy.

The standard Donbas grievances crystallized during the electoral campaign: demands for the recognition of Russian as a second state language, autonomy for Donbas (using the code words of "federalism" and "economic independence"), and nurturing geopolitical links with Russia. A local referendum held during the elections carried huge majorities for each of these demands (Arel and Wilson 1994; Kovaleva 2007). In the 1994 presidential election, Leonid Kuchma, a former

---

[26] Kharkiv was the capital of Soviet Ukraine until 1933. Dnipropetrovsk native Volodymyr Scherbytskyi ruled over Soviet Ukraine for seventeen years until 1989, when he was replaced by the Kharkiv party boss Volodymyr Ivashko.

prime minister of Ukraine who had been in charge of a rocket factory in Dnipropetrovsk for twenty-five years, took his cue from their electoral platforms and campaigned for making Russian a second state language. He carried the Donbas and the East, and unseated Kravchuk.[27] This took the foot off of the gas of Donbas politics for a bit, since the elevation of a Russian-speaker (Kuchma) over a Ukrainian-speaker (Kravchuk) represented a fundamental social realignment.[28]

For the next decade, Eastern Ukrainian MPs broadly supported Kuchma, but without the discipline of an organized political formation. Kuchma was not affiliated with any party, lending a certain instability to parliamentary coalition politics.[29] In time, as privatization gradually changed the economic landscape, the Communist Party lost zeal and appeal. By the early 2000s, Donbas elites began to shift their allegiance to a new party which appealed to the largely Russian-speaking East. They called themselves the Party of Regions.

The new party ran under a larger Eastern Ukrainian umbrella bloc in the 2002 parliamentary election, and its leader, Viktor Yanukovych, was appointed prime minister. By the 2004 presidential election and the 2006 parliamentary election, the Party of Regions had emerged as the main vote aggregator of Eastern Russian-speaking communities, eclipsing the Communist Party. The Party of Regions between 2000s and 2010 was often depicted in policy as an agent of Russian political interests within Ukraine. This was partly true. Eastern elites sought to protect their economic interests which were often co-aligned vis-à-vis Russian interests, but it was not a Russian nationalist party, despite being popular in parts of Ukraine with the highest ethnic Russian concentration. The Party of Regions appealed to a wider Russian-speaking demographic receptive to the narrative of a common destiny with Russia, translating into a pro-Russian agenda for language, foreign policy, and memory politics.

[27] Kuchma then forgot about his language promise, since he needed Western Ukrainian support to push through his economic reforms

[28] Kravchuk was from Western Ukraine (Volhynia) but made a name for himself as ideological secretary in the Ukrainian Politburo. He was elected president in 1991, carrying all oblasts except in Galicia (Western Ukraine). In the three years of his presidency, his electoral support shifted to the Ukrainian West and his defeat was viewed in the East as a symbolic victory.

[29] In 2003, Kuchma came a few votes short in an attempt to amend the constitution and diminish the power of the presidency (anticipating that a candidate from Eastern Ukraine might lose the 2004 election).

A vote for the Party of Regions was not usually a vote threatening secession. It is nonetheless useful to view the Party of Regions through a model of center–periphery bargaining. Ukraine contains hundreds of demographically dispersed pockets of Russian-speakers who have no chance at all of seceding ($p = 0$). The Party of Regions made them the promise of coordinating across communities, pooling bargaining strength from many regional minorities to extract cultural concessions from the center greater than the sum of their parts.[30] Our argument is not that the Party of Regions was an organized platform for a secessionist/irredentist movement, but rather that the potent emotions unleashed by Russian identity politics reliably mobilized millions of voters.

Orange Revolution: 2004

A lesser-known instance of coordinated sedition took place in 2004. Yanukovych, the prime minister and leader of the Party of Regions, was the Eastern candidate. He went head to head against Viktor Yushchenko, the Western candidate and a former prime minister. In the runoff, the Party of Regions fabricated 750,000 votes in Donetsk to put Yanukovych in the majority (Myagkov, Ordeshook, and Shakin 2009). Mass protests erupted for weeks on Maidan Square in Kyiv.

Sensing that its hold on power might be slipping, the Party of Regions held a special meeting in the Donbas town of Severodonetsk, threatening to call a referendum on "possible changes in the administrative-territorial structure of Ukraine." The threat was to empower regions to disregard orders from the center in the event of the defeat of Yanukovych (*Ukrains'ka pravda* 2004). The governors of Kharkiv and Luhansk, as well as the head of the Donetsk regional parliament, called for the creation of a "South-Eastern Autonomous Republic." The Kharkiv governor explicitly threatened to call for Russian military intervention (Skorkin 2016).

A week later, the Ukrainian Supreme Court ruled the election invalid due to voting irregularities, ordering a third round. Yushchenko needed a new electoral law preventing fraud, but the law would have

---

[30] Our intuition is that, assisted by forward-looking programmatic party institutions (Roeder 2018, 46–66), thirty different well-placed Russian-speaking communities, each of which have $p = .001$, could sometimes coordinate to vote strategically and achieve legislative bargaining outcomes more like $p = .15$ than $p = .03$.

to be passed by a parliament controlled by Yanukovych. The compromise was ultimately to have Yushchenko agree to diminish the powers of the presidency (through constitutional amendments that would eliminate the presidential power to dismiss the prime minister) in exchange for a new electoral law (Kudelia 2010).[31] The compromise ensured that Donbas elites were not excluded from central power, since they could potentially join an emergent parliamentary voting bloc against the Western-backed president. This is essentially what then happened in 2007 when Yushchenko was forced to accept the nomination of Yanukovych as prime minister. The coalition proved unstable. Yanukovych lost the post of prime minister again in 2008, though his loss set the stage for his future rise to head of state.

Again, this tracks the model quite closely. A crisis in the center (massive voter fraud occurred in the periphery, but the crisis was in Kyiv) began the game. The response of the Party of Regions was to consider a proposal that would amount to unified sedition in an attempt to crack the polity. Yanukovych and his party ultimately accepted a deal that spared their core constituents the costs of a constitutional crisis that could have degenerated into violence. This is consistent with a brokerage account. The sequencing of play – first coordination (or not), then proposals for autonomy backed by threats initiated in the periphery foisted on to the new coalition in the center – is also consistent with the model.

To deliver the reader to the beginning of the analytic narrative, suffice to say that under Yushchenko the Western coalition fractured while the East coordinated in more reliable lockstep. The relationship between the two factions became so destructive that it deflated turnout in the West at the 2010 presidential election, when Yanukovych defeated Tymoshenko, this time without fraud (Yushchenko did not survive the first round). This was the first time that Donbas elites took control of the executive branch. The Yanukovych faction presented itself as the party of all the regions of Eastern Ukraine, but most of its top names on the party list were from the Donbas (even more

---

[31] A useful simplification would be to say that Kravchuk, ostensibly from the West but juggling the chaos of transition to independence, did not really have that much power vis-à-vis parliament. When a new constitution was adopted in 1996, Kuchma obtained a clarification of his (substantial) powers. The trend was toward a stronger president when the incumbent was from the East, and a weaker president when the office was filled by someone from the West.

specifically, from the city of Donetsk).[32] Almost all "power" ministries were now directed by Donetsk – 42 percent of all ministerial-level appointees by some estimations (Darden 2014).

Conclusion

Ukrainian domestic distributional politics had a tendency to pit the interests of the East against the interest of the West. Russian involvement prior to 2014 was indirect. Some political actors from the Ukrainian West benefited domestically by acting as if all Eastern politicians were de facto Kremlin proxies; some Russian political elites in Moscow acted as if they actually believe their skewed version of history is destined to become automatically hegemonic in the *Russkii mir*. Neither is accurate. Eastern Ukrainians have been pragmatic. Some have switched parties adaptively, traded votes, compromised on some identity politics some of the time in order to maximize situational bargaining leverage.

In all three of the crises we describe, cultural and national symbolic issues mobilized voter energy allowing the periphery to make a power grab at the center. Kyiv was forced, as a result of the compromises that defused these crises, to direct policy toward the Russian-language-speaking East. The policy shift, in all of the cases, was launched from an organized (and fairly militant) base in Donbas and Crimea, the two parts of Ukraine where density of ethnic Russians is highest. What we will describe in Chapter 4 is something a bit different: a policy shift – indeed a full-blown regime change – launched by an organized (and fairly militant) base in the Ukrainian West. Winding the clock back to the fall of 2013, we find intense energies unleashed by seemingly mundane politics of international trade policy negotiations. By February 2014, the outcome had acquired near-existential stakes in the minds of many who feared foreign domination.

---

[32] For readers unfamiliar with the notion of a "party list," Ukraine uses a split system with proportional representation (PR) apportioning half of the deputies.

4 | *Regime Change (Maidan)*

The game begins with a crisis that delegitimizes state institutions and initiates zero-sum bargaining between social forces. The purpose of this chapter is to describe the abrupt and unexpected collapse of the Party of Regions in February 2014. Our account leans heavily on Ukrainian primary sources and first-person observations.

After months of gradual escalating tactics, from November 2013, and in the wake of violence that had killed more than thirty protesters and policemen in mid-February 2014, the government announced an "anti-terrorist operation" (ATO) to deal with what it called a violent threat to state order. A few days later, institutional support for the regime evaporated, the head of state was on the run, the constitution was amended to reempower parliament, and the language law giving official status to Russian was repealed. The opposition achieved a total political victory, reversing the East–West balance of power. In the view of Washington and Brussels, the "Revolution of Dignity" had triumphed. In the view of Moscow, fascists assisted by Western intelligence agents and diplomats had staged a coup. Across this chasm, one of the few points of agreement is that Ukraine's war began in the square.

An Elusive Trade Deal

There is consensus on the sequence of events that triggered the Maidan events. Ukraine had been expected to reach a trade deal with the EU at an EU Summit in Vilnius, Lithuania. This deal was the central part of a Ukraine–EU Association Agreement that came out of an Eastern Partnership initiative.[1] A week before the summit, on November 21, the

---

[1] In 2011, the EU launched a Partnership aimed at six former Soviet states not on track for EU membership. As a result, Association Agreements with three countries (Ukraine, Moldova, and Georgia) – covering political, economic, and judicial matters – were scheduled to be concluded in Vilnius. In each case, a trade treaty, known as a Deep and Comprehensive Free Trade Area (DCFTA), constituted the keystone of the accord.

Ukrainian government suddenly announced the suspension of plans to sign. Heeding an appeal on social media by journalist Mustafa Nayyem, thousands of protesters converged on the centrally located Maidan Nezaleshnosti (Independence Square) in downtown Kyiv (Nayyem 2014; Amosov 2018). Following the script of the Orange Revolution, also held on Maidan, demonstrators began a round-the-clock vigil. Tens of thousands of supporters attended the following Sunday (Herszenhorn 2013).[2] Street protests initially had little effect. Ukrainian President Yanukovych went to the Vilnius Summit, but his position did not budge.

What was the controversy? The Agreement was the next step in bringing Ukraine into the EU free trade zone, eliminating almost all tariffs and standardizing product definitions. Euro-optimists argued that such reforms would attract foreign investment, modernize the economic infrastructure, and stimulate growth in Ukraine (Zanuda 2013; Aslund 2015, 47). Euro-pessimists claimed the Agreement would neither compensate Ukrainian enterprises vulnerable to stronger European competition nor allow Ukraine to retrain industrial workers affected by austerity measures (Bruszt and Langbein 2017, 307–8), leaving the Ukrainian economy at the mercy of fluctuations in transnational capital, without securing European commitments on labor mobility (Böröcz 2013).

In 2011, after the EU set in motion its Eastern Partnership program, Russia unveiled its version of a geoeconomic counterweight, the Eurasian Economic Union.[3] The Union aimed at lowering trade barriers, integrating legal systems, and even strengthening military capabilities (Freedman 2019, 67). Due to its geography, population, and centrality in Russian historical narratives, Ukraine became the main theater of contention for the rival alliance projects. It became clear that the Kremlin saw the EU Agreement as a competitor to – and thus fundamentally incompatible with – its newly created customs union.[4]

There was strikingly little public debate within Ukraine about the economic merits of the Ukraine–EU Association Agreement (Dragneva

---

[2] Concurrent protests initially took place in Independence Square and European Square, a few hundred meters apart, before converging on the former, simply known as "Maidan."

[3] The original name of the pact was the Eurasian Customs Union.

[4] Ukraine had joined a Common Economic Space with Russia, Kazakhstan, and Belarus in 2003, but that largely declarative agreement neither eliminated tariffs nor prevented Ukraine from negotiating for economic integration with the EU (Dragneva and Wolczuk 2014, 226–7). In 2011, Russia clarified what

and Wolczuk 2014, 224). Negotiations over the economic components of the Agreement were held behind closed doors. Public statements by EU and Ukrainian government officials were vague and symbolic. Yanukovych had initialed the Agreement in 2012, but splits between backroom power brokers with ties to industry (colloquially "oligarchs") reflected divergent economic interests.[5]

The public debate was over political conditions attached to the EU trade deal. Association Agreements were officially justified in Europe as positive incentives for states showing progress on democratic indicators. Since the election of Yanukovych in 2010, however, most observers of the Ukrainian political system were anxious about authoritarian backsliding.[6] A glaring expression of this trend was the imprisonment of Yulia Tymoshenko after a politically driven trial (Popova 2013). A two-time prime minister between 2005 and 2010, Tymoshenko barely lost the 2010 presidential election. Yanukovych's brazen criminalizing of the opposition tempered European enthusiasm for an agreement his government could claim as a victory.

The Yanukovych government initially showed little interest in joining the Eurasian Economic Union. The economic benefits to Ukrainians were uncertain and the geopolitical symbolism was troubling. The Union was envisaged by the Kremlin as a mechanism of subordination reminiscent of the Soviet Union's dominance over Ukraine, whereby Ukraine would first integrate with the Russia-dominated Union, and

---

it saw as the incompatibility of the EU and Eurasian Economic Union. In an amended multilateral Free Trade Zone Agreement (Dogovor o zone svobodnoi torgovli) with a group of post-Soviet states that included Ukraine, Russia introduced a clause giving itself the unilateral right to impose higher tariffs "if a signatory state concluded an agreement which resulted in higher volumes of imports from that country to an extent that caused harm or the danger of harm to an industry" in Russia (Dragneva and Wolczuk 2015, 76).

[5] In a nutshell: mining was heavily subsidized, machine-building relied on a declining Russian market, while metallurgy was part of an expanding world market. Skilled Ukrainian laborers often sought a right to work in both Europe *and* Russia.

[6] For these critics, the turning point was his ability to compromise the Constitutional Court. In 2010, shortly after his election and at his behest, the Court overturned constitutional amendments in force since 2005 that had shifted power away from the presidency toward parliament (Koliushko and Zhurba 2011). What Yanukovych got back was the right to dismiss parliament and control power ministries. Fraud in the 2012 parliamentary elections (Kovalov 2014), and efforts to stifle independent media (Leshchenko 2013) were aggravating factors.

then negotiate trade with the EU only through Moscow (Dragneva and Wolczuk 2015, 69; Zhukov 2016, 4). So long as the details of these issues were not much discussed publicly, Yanukovych could try to have it both ways, simultaneously pursuing the EU Association Agreement and separate trade agreements with Russia.

The official Russian line was that the Agreement would flood the Russian market with EU goods, and hurt local entrepreneurs. On its technical merits, at least in the immediate short term, the concern appears specious, since customs officials, through "rules of origin" could presumably have detected EU-produced goods entering Russia from Ukraine (Charap and Colton 2017, 119). In the long run, however, the geoeconomic fear in Russia was that that European investment capital would seep into Ukraine by way of joint ventures that would gradually render the distinction between "Ukrainian" and "European" exports to Russia moot.

Starting in spring 2013, therefore, Russia began to signal intent to push back forcefully. From the beginning, the EU had linked the Association Agreement to a political condition: the liberation of former presidential candidate Yulia Tymoshenko. Putin was apparently convinced that Yanukovych would never allow Tymoshenko's release, which would stall EU expansion and allow the Eurasian Economic Union to gain momentum. In early summer 2013, however, the Russian authorities learned that German chancellor Angela Merkel was willing to drop the condition (Hosaka 2018, 329). The November EU Summit for the first time established a concrete deadline.

The official statements of the Russian government abruptly changed. The Ukraine–EU Agreement was now framed as a security threat. In the recent past, most states which signed an Association Agreement were later admitted into the EU and, eventually, NATO (Hahn 2018, 64). By late summer 2013, Russian coercive bargaining intensified. Customs checks on shipments from Ukraine disrupted supply chains (Popescu 2013).[7] Putin hinted that the Ukrainian labor force would no longer be welcome in Russia if the EU Agreement with Ukraine went through (Hopf 2016, 245). Putin's chief spokesman on the Eurasian

---

[7] The sudden change in customs policy served as a warning that Russia was determined to invoke the clause in the 2011 trade agreement regarding "the danger of harm to an industry," and increase tariffs.

Union, Sergei Glazyev, implied that the EU deal would violate a 1997 Russia–Ukraine treaty, and that "Moscow could potentially cease to recognize Ukraine's current borders as legitimate" (Walker 2018, 126). Putin directly intervened in bilateral negotiations, holding three closed-door meetings with the Ukrainian president just before Yanukovych's surprising announcement that he was suspending the EU deal.

Violence on Maidan

The first few thousand protesters reacted within hours of Yanukovych's declaration, on November 21, 2013, that his government would not sign the EU–Ukraine trade deal. The first large crowds were comprised of students and young professionals. The main goal was pressuring the Ukrainian government into reconsidering its decision and signing the Agreement at the Vilnius Summit a week later. Suffused with Ukrainian and EU flags, the Maidan movement quickly adopted as its name a hashtag that had blown up on social media: #Euromaidan.

From the beginning, Europe was expressed as a "civilizational" ideal, grounded in perceptions of "modernity," social justice, and discomfort with subordination of Ukraine to the Kremlin (Baysha 2018, 132). Details regarding the economic aspects of the Agreement were pushed aside (Minakov 2015, 77). Maidan was partially a reaction to the lack of transparency or accountability in the abrupt reversal by the government on such an important issue (Portnov 2015, 7). Despite a spike in numbers on the first weekend, however, initial protests were small compared to the Orange Revolution of 2004. They appeared to have run their course after the failed Vilnius Summit. On November 29, the Euromaidan Organizing Committee announced its closure (*NV* 2017). Between 200 and 400 people decided to spend one final night on the square (Koshkina 2015, 30).

In the early hours of November 30, the riot police, known as Berkut, attacked the remaining protesters encamped on Maidan. Those attempting to flee were chased as far as a kilometer and beaten with truncheons. Seventy-nine people were injured, ten were hospitalized, and thirty-five were sent to the local police precinct (*Zn.ua* 2013). Over a hundred participants sought refuge in St. Michael's Golden Dome Monastery, just up the hill from Maidan.

The violence of this police attack shocked Ukrainian society. Surveys suggest a vast majority of the population, across regional and linguistic divides, expressed disapproval with police behavior.[8] In more than twenty years since Ukrainian independence, this was the first time that the police had used significant force against peaceful protesters.[9] Moreover, since the victims had been widely described as students, the imagery of a militarized police beating up defenseless "children" became a powerful trope. The EU and NATO both condemned the "excessive use of force" by police against "peaceful" protesters (European Commission 2013; NATO 2013). The White House added that "violence and intimidation should have no place in today's Ukraine" (*Euronews* 2013).

The Ukrainian government did recognize the violence as a fundamental transgression. Sixteen hours after the incident, Yanukovych declared himself "deeply outraged by the events," but also absolved the police of any responsibility, condemning "those who ... by their decisions and actions provoked a conflict on the Maidan" (*Ukrains'ka pravda* 2013b).[10] His interior minister, Vitaliy Zakharchenko, made it clear that the protesters were the "provocateurs" (Gorchinskaya 2013b). He claimed that the protesters had prevented city workers from accessing Maidan, and had thrown explosive packs, bottles, and other projectiles at the police, prompting a forceful response

---

[8] According to a survey conducted a few days later, 74 percent of the population disapproved of the police violence, with only 9 percent supporting it (*Slovodilo* 2013). Even in Eastern Ukraine (including the Donbas), where a majority of survey respondents supported the decision by Yanukovych not to sign the EU Association Agreement, 60 percent disapproved of the police violence, and only 26 percent reported believing that the police tactics were appropriate. The most gruesome scenes of protesters being beaten up had been shown without censorship on various oligarch-owned TV channels (Leshchenko and Nayyem 2013).

[9] All previous cases of police violence had involved the repression of radical right activists, and in no case had police-inflicted injuries been as widespread as on November 30. The most serious clashes with police had occurred in front of the Rada, in 2010 and 2012, when controversial laws were passed over the lease of the Russian Black Sea Fleet and the status of the Russian language. News reports suggested dozens of injuries (Center for Social and Labor Research 2013). The first substantial instance of political violence was in 2001, over allegations that President Leonid Kuchma had been implicated in the murder of a journalist. Hundreds were arrested, but no one was reportedly harmed (Isaienko 2016).

[10] Yanukovych claimed afterwards that he never ordered the breakup (*rozhin*) of Maidan, but an investigation by the General Procuracy later concluded that he had (*Ukrains'kyi tyzhden* 2015b). After learning that Maidan had been forcefully cleared, Yanukovych is reported to have said to his associates that "we showed them our strength and will show it again" (Zhartovskaia 2017).

(Zakharchenko 2016, 59). Russian television disseminated the Yanukovych administration's line (Leshchenko and Nayyem 2013). Though government spokespeople endlessly repeated the claim that protesters had instigated the clashes, evidence never surfaced to support this claim (Likhachev 2015, 264).[11] Meanwhile, the pro-government position was amplified by the State Duma (Russian parliament) which denounced the "pogroms" committed by protesters, and the "interference of foreign state actors in the internal affairs of sovereign Ukraine" (Gosudarstvennaia duma 2013).

On the following day, December 1, hundreds of thousands of people – possibly as many as half a million – converged on Maidan, defying court orders banning street protests in downtown Kyiv. This was the largest single-day demonstration since 2004. The previous day's police violence had broken a major psychological barrier.

Some protesters arrived ready for a fight. In the early afternoon, several hundred marched toward the Presidential Administration Building, on Bankova Street, fifteen minutes from the square. Brutal clashes ensued. Protesters approached a police cordon, armed with chains, rocks, Molotov cocktails, and even a tractor abandoned on Maidan by a city crew. The Berkut responded with even more vicious force. There were hundreds of injuries. Unlike the one-sided violence during the breakup of Maidan on the night of November 30, this time the authorities reported a nearly equal number of injured protesters (165) and policemen (140) (*Ukrains'ka pravda* 2013a; Koshkina 2015, 51).

The identity of those committing acts of violence against the police remains contested. Both the Yanukovych government and the Maidan supporters ascribed this explosive violent escalation to a "provocation," an omnipresent epithet in post-Soviet discourse meant to absolve a group of the responsibility of an outcome. Ukrainian authorities asserted that the police had been compelled, or provoked, to use force to defend themselves. The Maidan leaders' version of events is that the police had staged the attacks and infiltrated protests to engage in violence to discredit the popular movement. A notable eyewitness, Petro Poroshenko, the future president of Ukraine, amplified the view that police penetration of an otherwise peaceful movement explained

---

[11] Eyewitnesses remember a confusing and tense standoff with city workers, but claim it was quickly defused (Koshkina 2015, 32). There had been minor clashes on November 24, when the police used tear gas against rowdy protesters (Grytsenko 2013).

the escalation (Koshkina 2015, 49–51). Many subsequent accounts attested to this consensus storyline (Wilson 2014, 69; Chebotariova 2015, 344; Fedorenko, Rybiy, and Umland 2016, 620).

Assessing the veracity of contradictory details from different eyewitness accounts is difficult. On one hand, the police may indeed have infiltrated the protests. On the other hand, subgroups within the protest movement had violent intentions. Video evidence suggests that the bulk of the initial perpetrators of attacks on police belonged to one of two fringe groups operating outside the political mainstream (Shekhovtsov 2013b).[12] On November 30, the day before the major clash, some had been training for street confrontations near St. Michael's Monastery, where hundreds of Maidan protesters had taken refuge (Likhachev 2014, 100). The two groups – Tryzub and Patriot Ukraïny – had originated in Western Ukraine in the early 1990s. They operated as paramilitary branches of small parties that proudly claimed lineage from the World War II-era Organization of Ukrainian Nationalists (OUN) (Shekhovtsov 2011). The police knew these groups, and had even imprisoned the leaders of Patriot Ukraïny. Rather than having been fueled by agent provocateurs acting alone, it seems more likely that violence emerged from a social milieu resolutely hostile to the Yanukovych government. Social actors quick to dismiss the Party of Regions legitimacy as "an occupation regime" long before Maidan suddenly had a window of opportunity, a sympathetic cause, and a televised stage.

Days earlier, a new violent group – soon to become highly influential – emerged on Maidan, calling itself Pravyi sektor (Shekhovtsov 2013a; Rublevskii 2014). The group did not coordinate its actions with civic or political leaders on Maidan. The leaders of the three opposition parties represented in parliament – Arseniy Yatseniuk (Batkivshchyna, the party of the imprisoned Tymoshenko), Vitali Klitschko (Udar), and Oleh Tyahnybok (Svoboda) – called on the protesters to eschew violence. Even Tyahnybok, whose party identified with the OUN leader Stepan Bandera, forcefully berated a masked activist for employing

---

[12] The presence of Dmytro Korchynsky, widely suspected for years of being a police collaborator, added credence to the provocation thesis. The Ministry of Internal Affairs even claimed afterwards that 300 members of Korchynsky's own group, Bratstvo, had led the attacks against the police (*Kyiv Post* 2013b). Most militants, however, appeared to belong to other right-wing groups (Shekhovtsov 2013a), or to be under their influence. Ruzhelnyk (2021) writes that football fans (ultras), previously unaffiliated with the political extreme, were among the attackers.

what he called senseless violence (*VO Svoboda* 2013; Techynskyi Solodunov, and Stoykov 2014). The professional class of the political opposition, and the social media-savvy backbone of Maidan activists more generally, were adamant in their belief that the use of violence would weaken the moral authority of the protest movement.[13] But they did not control Maidan. Few Maidan participants, in fact, were mobilized by mainstream parties or social organizations.[14] If anything, a sense of broadly anti-elite, anti-institutional mistrust, directed at both the government and opposition parties, characterized Maidan from the outset (Onuch and Sasse 2016, 570).

The violent behavior of fringe groups on December 1 also brings up the fraught issue of descriptive categorization. What should academics call these groups? The consensus among those studying far-right movements in Western Europe has been to employ the concept of *radicalism*. Mudde (2007, 22–3) defines the *radical right* as nativist (protecting the native-born from "outsiders"), populist (appealing to the purity of "the people" against a corrupt elite), and authoritarian (unquestioned obedience to a leader). In this typology, *radical right* and *populist right* are synonymous with *far right*. The radical right is defined by its illiberal ideas, not by the use of violence, since it aspires to achieve its goals through electoral representation.[15] Democratic illiberalism, neutered of violence, is theoretically and empirically possible (Mounk 2018). Groups that privilege violence over electoral competition are called extremists (Mudde 1996, 231). Illiberal groups that do not engage in extra-parliamentary violence are radical.

The literature on terrorism, however, defines radicalism differently. Here *radicalization* denotes a path toward violence (della Porta 2008; Doosje et al. 2016). What matters are not political views per se, but a commitment to a path that legitimizes the commission of violent acts in

---

[13] For evidence supporting the theory, see Stephan and Chenoweth (2008), Chenoweth (2021).

[14] According to a survey conducted the first week of December 2013, only 2 percent of Maidan participants were affiliated with political parties, and 6 percent with social organizations, while 92 percent arrived independently (Kyiv International Institute of Sociology 2013a).

[15] Liberalism is defined here more broadly than in partisan politics, stressing the rule of law, the protection of individual and minority rights, and freedom of speech. Illiberalism attacks all three. Laruelle (2021, 23) notes that some illiberal leaders are not populist (whose conception of "the people" is divisive), but statist, emphasizing the might and legitimacy of the state.

order to achieve a political outcome.[16] We favor this approach in assessing the street violence during this critical juncture. When the government sent riot police to attack nonviolent protesters on Maidan, the regime radicalized. When a small subset of the Maidan protesters attacked the police and inflicted damage, the protest movement radicalized. Many of the radical protesters on December 1 belonged to groups that had engaged in unmistakably illiberal practices and opposed European integration (Hahn 2018, 182; Kudelia 2018, 508). Their violent actions generated support by Maidanites later on, too – not as an endorsement of their political platforms (always marginal), but rather because their violent tactics were gradually, grudgingly, recognized as having been effective. The radical right had been absent from the Orange Revolution. What was new on Maidan was that a critical mass of young men were ready to fight.[17] Moreover, the willingness by many of them to display World War II-related symbols offensive to many, was intended to distinguish them from the Maidan mainstream.[18] Russia media seized on these symbols to call the violent protesters fascists.[19]

[16] Conversely, *deradicalization* is not the renunciation of extreme views, but of violence as a legitimate means to achieve the goal. Violence is the dividing line. When individuals deliberately choose political violence – whether in order to violate taboos, in order to send a costly signal (to others, or to their future self) of seriousness and purpose, or for some other reason – they become radicals. The degree to which individuals are predisposed to violence before joining a group, or become socialized into using violence after they join a group remains a source of debate and controversy. Whether radical beliefs are deeply held or "cheap talk" to assist recruitment of young people too naïve to know the difference is also disputed.

[17] The football ultras did not have much of a political consciousness, but they were intensely hostile to the police and were experienced in street fights. In practice, many joined Pravyi sektor on Maidan (Ruzhelnyk 2021).

[18] The most alienating symbol was a variation of the infamous Nazi Wolfsangel, used by SS troops, including the Waffen-SS, which by 1943 had a "Galician" division. It was worn by members of Patriot Ukraïny, which joined Pravyi sektor during Maidan, and later created the volunteer battalion Azov. While it is claimed that the logo symbolizes the "idea of the nation" (with the runic letters "i" and "n") (Naureckas 2014), it unmistakably recalls Nazi symbolism. Another controversial symbol was the Pravyi sektor logo, which used the black and red colors of the flag of the OUN, active during World War II, itself inspired by the *blut und boden* ("blood and soil") trope of late nineteenth-century German nationalism, later coopted and racialized by the Nazi regime (Rossoliński-Liebe 2010, 89).

[19] While we consider radical right a more useful concept analytically, symbols and repertoires of contention matter. Fascism, stripped of Nazi connotations, remains a powerful, distinctly twentieth-century visual aesthetic. (Consider

Martyrs at the *Sich*

After the violence of November 30–December 1, Maidan became a permanent site of contestation. At least 5,000 activists were present around
the clock. On December 1, protesters seized two public buildings close to
the square – City Hall and the Trade Union Building. These became the
headquarters and improvised lodgings. As during the Orange Revolution,
a stage was erected on the square. A constant procession of speakers and
performers held forth. "Self-defense" groups were established to protect
the perimeter of Maidan from the police. Comprised of several dozen
activists, each group was symbolically dubbed a *sotnia* ("hundred"), following Cossack mythology. The unarmed civilian crowd milling about
on Maidan just thirty-six hours earlier gave way to disciplined groups of
men equipped with helmets, shields, and sticks. Maidan began to resemble a protected encampment. Barricades were erected.

The meaning of the protests evolved. There were fewer EU flags.
"Euromaidan" gradually morphed into the "Revolution of Dignity," a
broad affirmation that state officials ought to respect human and civil
rights (Gorchinskaya 2013a). The profile of the permanent protesters
also changed. Students were present, but were being crowded out by
older members of the middle class. The profile of the average activist
was a well-educated young professional, between thirty-five and forty-
five years old (Onuch 2014, 47; Paniotto 2014). Political grievances
extended to demands for the dismissal of the government and calls for
early elections.[20] Western leaders and diplomats called on Yanukovych
to defuse the conflict through political dialogue (European Commission
2013). Since Maidan activists vocally mistrusted establishment opposition parties that might have otherwise been brokers, the government
had no partner (yet) for substantive talks.

The following Sunday, December 8, another huge demonstration
took place (*Ukrinform* 2016b). In the early evening, a group of radical

---

the Galactic Empire in the *Star Wars* universe.) Writing in the 1930s, Walter
Benjamin explicitly theorized a combination of technologically enabled forms
of artistic reproduction, elemental drives, and primal symbols (Benjamin 2019,
173–6, 194–5).

[20] Regular presidential and parliamentary elections were scheduled for 2015.
Other demands included amnesty for all protesters arrested, an investigation
into the police assault on November 30, and constitutional amendments
returning more power to parliament (*Galinfo* 2013). A resolution regarding the
resignation of the prime minister was rejected by parliament on December 3.

right militants, many associated with Svoboda, toppled the last statue
of Lenin in downtown Kyiv, a short distance from Maidan (Pyvovarov
2018). The anti-Russia symbolism was palpable. The Ukrainian government responded with force. On December 11, in the early hours
of the night, Berkut policemen again deployed to clear the square,
this time enforcing a court order. They tried to dismantle barricades
and advance in columns to shove away protesters. Responding to an
appeal from the Maidan stage, St. Michael's Monastery rang its bell,
reportedly for the first time since the Mongol invasion. Thousands of
supporters gradually poured into Maidan, overwhelming the police
(Kobernik 2013; *Kyiv Post* 2013a). Forty-nine activists suffered injuries (*Mizhnarodnyi fond 'Vidrodzhennia''* 2015). The Maidan "self-
defense" forces had pushed back against the police with assistance
from civil society.

The government switched tactics. It first tried to just wait out the
protesters, letting the cold nights, the lack of tangible progress, and
the holidays snuff out the Maidan momentum. The protests endured,
albeit with depleted numbers, and by mid-January the Maidan
encampment remained defiant and active. The next step was to pass
repressive legislation. On January 16, the Ukrainian parliament
voted on a slate of ten laws identical to the harsh measures adopted
in Russia following the 2011–2012 mass demonstrations (Zygar
2016, 262).[21] These bills, which quickly became known as the "dictatorship laws," instituted high criminal liability for unauthorized
demonstrations, ill-defined "extremist" activities, and "defamation"
of public officials (Kotliar 2014; *Ukraïns'ka Hel'sins'ka spilka z prav
liudyny* 2014).[22]

On January 19, in the midst of a massive – and now illegal – Sunday
demonstration, hundreds of activists marched toward parliament on
Hrushevs'koho Street and encountered a police barricade. Opposition
leaders once again urged protesters not to succumb to "provocations,"

---

[21] For instance, amendments to existing laws requiring nongovernmental
organizations (NGOs) receiving international funding to register as "foreign
agents" were a literal translation – from Russian to Ukrainian – of a law
adopted in Russia in 2012 (Prezident Rossii 2012; *Zakonodavstvo Ukraïny*
2014c).

[22] The Party of Regions obtained the necessary majority, but the adoption of
these laws breached parliamentary protocols. There was no organized debate,
just a chaotic vote with a show of hands (*Civic Solidarity* 2014; Snyder 2014).

fearing that it would doom Maidan.[23] Protesters did not heed these warnings, hurling Molotov cocktails and slabs of pavement, using thick layers of smoke from burning tires as cover. The police escalated their countermeasures, throwing stun grenades laced with metal scraps, returning Molotov cocktails, and firing rubber bullets (Vitkine 2014a). Over two days, each side suffered a number of injuries much higher than on December 1 (195 among policemen, 213 among protesters) (*Bigmir. net* 2014a; *Mizhnarodnyi fond 'Vidrodzhennia''* 2015). Two protesters were shot dead at close range and a third died of his wounds a few days later (Coynash 2016a). Another was murdered after being kidnapped by *titushki* (Kozak 2020).[24] Maidan was now a movement with martyrs.[25]

In the early hours of the violence, the Ukrainian media circulated a statement from Pravyi sektor that the dictatorship laws "put an end to … a peaceful solution," and instead called for a "revolution" (*Banderivets'* 2014b). The group, still little known until then, openly took responsibility for inciting members to use violence against the police.[26] Pravyi sektor's repudiation of nonviolent protest as a tactic gained support.[27]

[23] Vitali Klitschko, leader of Udar and a former heavyweight boxing world champion, warned violent protesters that "what you are doing now is a great danger" (*Ukrains'ka pravda* 2014g). He was sprayed with a fire extinguisher. Arseniy Yatseniuk, leader of Batkivshchyna, said that "violence will not lead to anything other than bloodshed" (*Ukrains'ka pravda* 2014v). Oleh Tyahnybok, the Svoboda leader, reiterated the December claim that the government "want[ed] to destroy the Maidan with the help of provocateurs" (*Liga Novosti* 2014).

[24] The *titushki* were young men recruited from sports clubs by police officers to intimidate antiregime demonstrators (Salem and Stack 2014). The plural form *titushki* derives from the family name of one Vadym Titushko, who attacked a journalist during a demonstration in May 2013 (Mazanik 2014). In a case that attracted considerable attention, a group of *titushki* severely beat a well-known journalist, Tetiana Chornovol, in December 2013. The ringleader was sentenced to five years in jail in 2018 (*Hromads'ke radio* 2018).

[25] Maidan sympathizers attributed responsibility for the killings to the police. The Ministry of Internal Affairs claimed that the bullets came from rifles not used by the police (UNIAN 2015). The General Procuracy contradicted this assertion (Interfaks-Ukraina 2015). As of this writing, the cases had not proceeded to trial.

[26] There is a dispute as to whether the Maidan leadership knew in advance that nonviolence was about to be jettisoned. The leader of Pravyi sektor, Dmytro Yarosh, later made the uncorroborated claim that Andriy Parubiy, head of the "self-defense" groups in Maidan, had approved of the shift to violent measures (Kudelia 2018, 520).

[27] One of the authors recalls a conversation in the summer of 2014 with an articulate female upper-middle-class graduate student in her mid-twenties who, when describing her experience in Maidan, somewhat sheepishly admitted that

Other opposition leaders, taking the cue, began to reframe the violence of the protesters as self-defense and a necessary response to state coercion.[28] Intellectuals and professionals, while emphasizing their lack of sympathy toward "right-wing radical organizations," publicly declared their "solidarity with those who have been forced to use [violence]" (*Euromaidan PR* 2014). While most participants on Maidan continued to identify with "European values" (Onuch 2014, 48), violence was becoming legitimized.[29] "The protesting masses followed the nationalists," exulted Pravyi sektor, which was now receiving extensive domestic and international media coverage (*Banderivets'* 2014a). Maidan was no longer merely a "camp," but a "fortress" – a *sich*, in Cossack symbolism (Paniotto 2014).

The View from Outside Kyiv

Social unrest spread outside Kyiv as well. Despite the violence, public opinion surveys gave approximately twice as much support for the protests as for the government.[30] Violence seems to have become more legitimate in the eyes of many Ukrainians when the January 16 laws closed nonviolent avenues of political resolution.

As the radical right surged, the discourse of the state hardened. The Ukrainian prime minister vilified violent protesters as "extremists" bent on provoking the government to use force (*Government Portal*

---

she had volunteered for Pravyi sektor. Asked why, her response was disdain for the nonviolent alternatives: "It was clear to me they could *actually* get things done."

[28] For instance, Yatsenyuk now said that since the authorities had remained "deaf" to the claims of Maidan, "people had acquired the right to move from non-violent to violent means of protest" (*Ukrains'ka pravda* 2014w).

[29] "The most striking thing," noted *The Economist*, "was how willingly liberal, middle-class Ukrainians, who had hitherto been steadfastly insisting that the protests remain peaceful, rallied to the violence" (G. C. 2014).

[30] Many respondents were conflicted, confused, uncertain, or refused to state their opinions, as would be expected, but a public opinion survey, conducted in February 2014, before the final wave of violence (described in the following section) is revealing on this point. Forty percent of the population across Ukraine expressed "sympathy" toward the protesters, and only 23 percent for the government (Kyiv International Institute of Sociology 2014a). Comparisons with data from surveys conducted in December 2013 (*Hromads'kiy prostir* 2013; *Slovodilo* 2013) suggest that aggregate levels of social support for Maidan remained fairly steady before and after the January 2014 violence.

2014). Government-controlled news services in both Ukraine and Russia depicted them repeatedly as "fascists." Ukrainian government supporters, as a rule, appeared to believe that Maidan was a foreign conspiracy led by the United States, who had trained and paid protesters (Gorchinskaya 2014c).

Western powers noted protester violence critically. The US State Department found that Pravyi sektor was "inflaming conditions on the streets" (US Department of State 2014). The EU urged the opposition "to dissociate itself clearly from all those who make use of violence in pursuing their aims" (Delegation of the European Union to Ukraine 2014). The main interpretive disagreement between Russia and the West was about who should take responsibility for violence. The Russian government blamed the protesters and Western interference in Ukraine's "internal affairs" (Ofitsial'nyi internet-portal pravovoi informatsii 2014; Interfax-Ukraine 2014). The United States argued that "increased tensions" were the "direct consequence" of the refusal by the Ukrainian government to negotiate (US Department of State 2014).

While Maidan was clearly the focal point for national energy, the Kyiv violence also ignited a wave of unprecedented street disturbances in the regions. The vast majority (78 percent) of permanent protesters in the Kyiv Maidan were from the Central and Western oblasts (Kyiv International Institute of Sociology 2014b). This largely reflected the regional variation in public opinion. Support for the Maidan protests was much higher in the Ukrainian West than in the East.[31] Outside Kyiv, therefore, radical right activists seized the governors' buildings, symbols of state power, in eleven oblasts throughout Central and Western Ukraine. When they did, they rarely met resistance from the police (Rachkevych 2014c). The occupation of sites of state power seems to have been inspired by the attempt to storm the presidential administration building in Kyiv – and as we shall see in Chapters 6 and 7, this tactic would have far-reaching consequences months later in Eastern Ukraine. The idea of a Narodna Rada ("Popular Council"), a symbolic parallel government announced on Maidan, gained support in Western Ukraine. These regional parliaments had been under opposition control since 2012.

[31] A February 2014 survey asked: "On which side are your sympathies in the current conflict?" Among those favorable to Maidan, regional variation ranged from 51–80 percent in the Center-West to 8–20 percent in the Southeast. Support for the government, however, was below 40 percent in the Southeast (Kyiv International Institute of Sociology 2014a).

Even more ominously, unrest spread to several provinces in the Southeast. In January 2014, after sustained violence broke out in Kyiv, anti-Maidan activists in Kharkiv and Donetsk called for the creation of "self-defense" groups against allegedly incoming Pravyi sektor radicals (Platonova 2020, 233). In Zaporizhzhia, thousands of protesters attempted to storm the regional administration building but were rebuffed by riot police (Krivolapov 2014). Clashes were also reported in Dnipropetrovsk, Kharkiv, and Donetsk. Police intervention prevented the takeover of buildings. In Zaporizhzhia, Donetsk, and particularly in Kharkiv, pro-regime *titushki* violently clashed with demonstrators (Gorbachov 2014; Platonova 2020, 119). Pro-Maidan demonstrations were held in all nine Eastern oblasts (Gorbachov 2014). It bears emphasizing that prior to Maidan few analysts would have expected such agitation in these Eastern regions, since there had been no notable pro-Orange event there in 2004 (Arel 2008). In 2014, the numbers at pro-Maidan and anti-Maidan demonstrations seemed almost evenly matched everywhere in the Southeast except in Crimea and in the Donbas.[32]

The Last Days of the Old Regime

Though Maidan opposition leaders initially had a theory that resorting to violence would be political suicide, violent tactics were effective in breaking a two-month political impasse. Yanukovych met privately with one of the opposition leaders on January 19. A few days later, formal talks began with all three.[33] Negotiations addressed two sets of issues. First, the opposition demanded the release of hundreds of imprisoned protesters, a general amnesty, and the repeal of the

---

[32] According to a database of protest events compiled by the Center for Social and Labor Research in Kyiv, 14.7 percent of all pro-Maidan protests occurred in the Southeast (including Donbas and Crimea). Of these Southeast protests, 8.2 percent (or 45 out of 546) involved between 1,000 and 10,000 people (Ishchenko 2016, 458). While these are small numbers, the protests were nonetheless unexpected. The proportion of pro- and anti-Maidan events was even in the South (excluding Crimea), whereas the East (excluding Donbas) slightly favored pro-Maidan events. The number of anti-Maidan events was four to five times higher in Donbas and Crimea (Ishchenko 2015).

[33] Donbas oligarch Rinat Akhmetov, the main backer of the Party of Regions, issued a statement calling for the crisis to be solved peacefully. This was interpreted at the time as a rare signal that Yanukovych might be losing internal support from his Donbas base (*Metinvest* 2014; Olszański and Kononczuk 2014).

"dictatorship laws."[34] The January 16 anti-Maidan laws were voided, but a new law, adopted on January 28, granted the release of jailed protesters pending the evacuation of occupied buildings by February 17. On February 16, after a two-week lull in protests, Maidan activists relinquished City Hall, which had been occupied since December 1, as well regional administration buildings in Western Ukraine. A soft landing, with amnesty, had been set in motion.[35]

Far more contentious were negotiations over presidential power. Since December the opposition had been demanding the dismissal of government ministers. In late January, Yanukovych announced the resignation of Prime Minister Mykola Azarov. The decision was clearly not coordinated with the Russian government, since Moscow promptly suspended the second installment of a $15 billion loan that had been announced in December, pending clarification regarding cabinet composition (Gutterman and Balmforth 2014).[36] The opposition demanded a transitional "technocratic" cabinet, free from Yanukovych's direct control, until elections could be held.

More fundamentally, the opposition demanded a return to the 2004 Constitution – specifically to the constitutional amendments that had been agreed upon as a political compromise to end the Orange Revolution (Kurishko 2014b). After the election of Yanukovych in 2010, the Constitutional Court had overturned these amendments and reinstated the 1996 Constitution. The amendments transferred control over the four main ministry positions directing domestic state power – the prime minister, the Attorney General, the minister of internal affairs, and the head of the Security Service of Ukraine (SBU) – from the president to parliament. Some members of the

---

[34] The government wanted the amnesty to be linked to the emptying of all occupied buildings (in Kyiv and elsewhere). It seems dozens of Regions MPs initially backed unconditional amnesty if it would put the matter to rest. At this very moment, Russian custom officials increased delays in the shipping of Ukrainian goods to Russia. It took personal intervention (and threats) by Yanukovych to coerce its MPs back into line. Yanukovych reportedly told them that he had compromising information on "each one of [you]" (*Kyïvvlada* 2014).

[35] The Trade Union Building, adjacent to Maidan and also occupied since December 1, remained in the hands of protesters, as it was not officially considered a government building. Ostensibly, protesters "leased" the premises from the trade union authorities.

[36] There is circumstantial evidence that Russian economic aid came with political conditions, primarily the neutralization of Maidan (Snyder 2018, 134).

Maidan Coordinating Council were hopeful that their demonstration of massive popular support might have changed the political calculations of a sufficient number of Party of Regions MPs to reinstate the 2004 Constitution and create a new parliamentary majority (*Khartyia '97% 2014*). An empowered parliament could then dismiss the minister of internal affairs responsible for the special police units battling Maidan protesters, for instance, and appoint a new prime minister. Both moves would have been popular with the street. For the opposition, the hope was that this constitutional path could resolve the crisis.

For the Yanukovych government, however, an expedited return to the 2004 Constitution was one concession too many. After weeks of fruitless negotiations, the opposition insisted that a resolution on the reinstatement of the 2004 amendments be registered during a February 18 parliamentary session. The chairman of the parliament (Rada) refused on the grounds that this resolution lacked majority support (Kurishko 2014a). To pressure Party of Regions MPs, the opposition and Maidan civic leaders invited supporters to march to the Rada on the morning of February 18. The event was billed as a "peaceful offensive" (*mirnyi nastup*) (*Radio Svoboda* 2014).[37]

Tens of thousands of protesters answered the call. Early in the morning, all four streets leading to the Rada were filled with demonstrators. The threat of renewed violence was palpable. Thousands of Maidan "self-defense" activists, wearing masks and helmets and armed with clubs, batons, shields, and such, attended the march (Kudelia 2018, 153). Facing them were a roughly equal number of special police troops cordoning off parliament. Behind police lines, in Mariinskyi Park, a large park adjacent to the Rada, were hundreds of *titushki*, many wearing gear similar to that of frontline Maidan protesters.

Around 10am, when word came that the Rada chairman had refused to put the resolution on the agenda, violence exploded.[38]

---

[37] Two bodies sought to coordinate Maidan activities: the National Resistance Headquarters (Shtab natsional'noho sprotivu), which united the three opposition parties, and the Maidan People's Union (Narodne ob'ednannia "Maidan"), led by public figures mostly unaffiliated with political parties. The People's Union proposed the march, and the National Resistance supported the initiative. Neither of these two groupings nursed radical wings or had organized "self-defense" groups.

[38] Adding to the tension was the sudden announcement, the previous day, that Russia was resuming the payment of its December loan. The suspicion in

Maidan self-defense groups planned to encircle the parliament build-ing in order to prevent MPs from leaving without holding a vote on the constitutional amendments (*Tekhty*. n.d.). The tactical objec-tive was to secure a side entrance facing Mariinskyi Park. Frontline protesters burnt trucks blocking their path and attempted to enter the park, throwing small homemade bombs, fireworks, and rocks at the police. The police line responded with stun grenades, smoke bombs, and tear gas (Koshkina 2015, 123–4).[39] For the next three hours, with clashes all around the Rada, MPs were trapped inside. *Titushki* attacked protesters alongside the police (*Bigmir.net* 2014b; *Ukrains'ka pravda* 2014l). The nearby office of the Party of Regions was set on fire.

Gunshots were heard later in the morning. The authorities claimed that only protesters fired live bullets, injuring policemen. Many testi-monies and a later investigation blamed police.[40] By 2pm, three protest-ers were dead (*Jus Talionis* 2019). Pravyi sektor called on its followers to bring hunting rifles to the square (*Ukrains'ka pravda* 2014k). The opposition urged the government to avoid further casualties by having the police fall back to the perimeter, to allow protesters to return to the square, and for political negotiations to resume (Koshkina 2015, 127). Party of Regions officials rebuffed the offer, berating the opposition for inciting violence and attacking their party headquarters (*Ukrains'ka*

Maidan was that Yanukovych had agreed to conditions in return, such as appointing a prime minister close to Moscow (Jégo 2014) or clearing out Maidan (Recknagel 2014).

[39] The question of which side used violence first is hard to ascertain (Sidorenko and Radchuk 2014). One plausible story is that police first threw stun grenades at protesters to prevent them from advancing to the park in order to encircle parliament. What is clear is that the protesters were determined to confront the police.

[40] It was difficult for observers to determine the type of weapons employed, and which side used deadly weapons first. A reporter saw protesters using "what appeared to be hand guns," but could not determine if they were lethal (Olearchyk 2014). The minister of internal affairs claimed that the police were only using "traumatic" weapons, that is, nonlethal weapons, and shooting rubber bullets (*Istorychna pravda* 2015). A Berkut officer later testified that a number of policemen were handed pump guns with lead bullets, and that he witnessed their use during the clashes (*Tekhty* 2014b). The Procuracy established that protesters had been the first to suffer gunshot wounds (Haivanovych 2016). When the first deaths were announced, the Ministry of Internal Affairs alleged that the protesters had been killed by friendly fire (*Ukrains'ka pravda* 2014f).

pravda 2014x). The Ministry of Internal Affairs and SBU issued a joint ultimatum threatening to "restore order by all means provided by law" unless "atrocities (*bezchynstva*) cease" (*Ukrains'ka pravda* 2014p).

The police counteroffensive toward Maidan came next. Police units started out at the sites of prolonged battles around parliament, literally pushing their way down Institutka (the main street running downhill to Maidan Square) and Hrushevs'koho (the site of the January violence), beating anyone in their path (*Jus Talionis* 2019). They dismantled barricades as they went. By around 4pm, police forces were within 100 meters of Maidan Square. The death toll had reached eleven. Down to their last few dozen yards, Maidan defenders resorted to a technique used in the January clashes: burning tires and firewood to create a thick wall of smoke. A number of protesters used shotguns. By early evening, four policemen had been killed (*Jus Talionis* 2019).

A de facto state of emergency was implemented. The subway system was shut down, the main arteries were closed off, and a SBU elite force joined the riot police in an operation aimed at dismantling Maidan. The police action lasted all night. When the sun came up, "self-defense" activists still held the square.[41]

Why were the thousand-strong elite troops unable to crush Maidan with coercive force? Some blame Yanukovych personally for a lack of will (Trenin 2014b). The minister of internal affairs cited the sheer exhaustion of his troops and, as a practical matter, a shortage of stun grenades (Kudelia 2018, 514). The inability to extinguish huge bonfires was a major practical impediment (Quinn, Epstein, and Davidson 2014). A crucial and perhaps determining factor was the use of deadly weapons. Twenty-seven people died that night, including nine policemen (*Jus Talionis* 2019). All but four civilians were killed by guns (*Jus Talionis* 2019). Yuri Lutsenko, a Maidan leader and former minister of internal affairs, was categorical in his assessment of the situation: "Berkut stopped 50 meters from the Maidan stage ... because they found out we had weapons" (*Ukrains'ka pravda* 2014e). In just 20 hours after clashes around parliament, 36 people died and 509 were injured (*Ukraïns'kyi tyzhden'* 2015a).

---

41 Arkadii Babchenko, a well-known reporter who covered numerous post-Soviet wars, and witnessed the all-night assault on Maidan, wrote that "except for Chechnya ... this was the worst night on my life." He could not understand how the Maidan fighters were able to survive so many dizzying stun grenades and blows to their shields (*Tekhty* 2014a).

The violence in Kyiv had rippled through Western Ukraine and some Central oblasts. Protesters occupied regional administration buildings anew. This time activists stormed police institutions and often set them on fire. Offices of the Ministry of Internal Affairs (overseeing the special police troops in Kyiv) and of the SBU were attacked in eight oblasts. Police gunfire killed two civilians in Khmelnyts'kyi (Gal'chinskaia 2014; *LB.ua* 2014a). In Lviv, 10,000 protesters burned down buildings, including a Ministry of Internal Affairs installation (used for staging and training base troops) (*24L'viv* 2014).[42] Assaults were intended to prevent any further deployment of special police detachments from Lviv to reinforce government positions in Kyiv, and by February 19, this tactic had spread across Ukraine. Human chains encircled police academies, and improvised checkpoints sprouted up on the three major highways linking Kyiv to the West, South, and East. The roadblocks sought to prevent buses carrying *titushki* from reaching the capital (*Pid prytsilom* 2014; *Smotri.city* 2014). Groups of *titushki* violently assaulted protesters in Odesa and Kharkiv (*Tekhty* 2014a; *Tsenzor. net* 2014b). In at least two of the attacks on police facilities in Western Ukraine, protesters seized weapons. Central authorities feared that these weapons were headed to the Kyiv Maidan (Gorchinskaya 2014a).

Especially in Galicia, the police offered little to no resistance to these raids, in some cases announcing that they would side "with the people" (*24Kanal* 2014c).[43] In Poltava, on the road linking Kharkiv to the capital, local police and activists even manned checkpoints together (*Poltavshchyna* 2014). The central government in Kyiv was losing control of law enforcement bodies in a significant part of the country – but not much in the East. State authority never wavered in Donbas or Crimea.

---

[42] Most of the police officers deployed near Maidan came from two groups under the jurisdiction of the Ministry of Internal Affairs. The majority were Internal Troops, generally young army recruits reassigned to the task of protecting government facilities. The rest were elite Berkut units in charge of offensive operations. The military base attacked by Lviv protesters housed such troops.

[43] The central government was nearly paralyzed in Lviv, where virtually every major office under its jurisdiction was occupied, including the Procuracy, the Tax Administration, and even the traffic police station (Holovko and Mokryk 2014). In Rivne, also in Western Ukraine, in an incident widely broadcast in the Russian media, the Yanukovych-appointed governor was brought on stage, roughed up, tied to a pole, and forced to sign a letter of resignation (*Volyns'ki novyny* 2014a).

While a de facto truce was reached in Kyiv, Yanukovych signaled his intention to involve the military on February 19. The government officially launched an "antiterrorist operation" (ATO), which legally authorized the use of the army for domestic purposes. The chief of staff of the armed forces, Volodymyr Zamana, had reportedly been opposed to the use of troops (Woods 2014). He was fired on February 19. The Ministry of Defense announced that evening that its soldiers would engage in the operation (*Ukrains'ka pravda* 2014q). In the early morning of February 20, four brigades, totaling 2,500 troops, were dispatched to Kyiv from southern bases in Dnipropetrovsk and Mykolaiv.[44] Maidan activists prevented the Dnipropetrovsk brigade from proceeding by lying on railroad tracks (Bartkowski and Stephan 2014; *TSN* 2014b). Civilians also blockaded military facilities in Kyiv and Zhytomyr (*Gordon* 2014a; *Rupor Zhytomyura* 2014). No military units dispatched seem to have made it to Kyiv.

As events acquired momentum, the clash of Western and Russian geopolitical interests was becoming clearer. The Maidan protests as they were unfolding reinforced the view among Russian officials that antiregime social activism and democracy movements – since the "color revolutions" of the mid-2000s – were part of a strategic Western plan to buy geopolitical influence. The Russian Foreign Ministry blamed the West for refusing to recognize that "all responsibility" for the escalation of violence lay with the Ukrainian opposition (Ministerstvo inostrannykh del Rossiiskoi Federatsii 2014). Foreign Minister Sergei Lavrov spoke for the first time of an attempted *coup d'état* and seizure of power by force (Ministerstvo inostrannykh del Rossiiskoi Federatsii 2014b). The EU, however, condemned "the unjustified use of excessive force by the Ukrainian authorities" (European Council 2014b). German Chancellor Angela Merkel declared that "the convulsion of violence resulted from a deliberate delaying tactic … to avoid a compromise" (Myers 2014b), and her foreign minister added that the "responsibility to deescalate the conflict lies on … Yanukovych" (Pozdniakova 2014). Both the United States and the EU threatened Ukrainian officials with sanctions (Weaver, Owen, and Urquhart 2014).

---

[44] In an encrypted message sent to four southern brigades, the newly appointed Commander-in-Chief Yuri Il'in wrote that *radikal'no nalashtovanykh* ("radicalized") protesters were planning to use force to seize organs of state power and military installations (Bik 2014).

The Maidan Massacre

Despite the announcement of an ATO, the police gathered around Maidan refrained from any further attack that day. Negotiations resumed between Yanukovych and the opposition. The French, German, and Polish foreign ministers announced that they themselves would fly to Kyiv to mediate.

On February 20, shortly after 6am, armed Maidan militants on the roof of the Music Conservatory started shooting at the police (Chimiris 2014; Stack 2015; Gorchinskaia 2016; Siiak 2016).[45] Within an hour, these snipers had killed two policemen and injured a dozen more (Koshkina 2014). The police retreated up the Institutka Street hill, chased by hundreds of protesters from Maidan Square in an effort to regain territory lost in the previous days (Kramer and Higgins 2014). At some point, police snipers posted behind barricades began firing at advancing protesters. In less than an hour, the police shot thirty-nine protesters dead (*Jus Talionis* 2019). Nine more died over the rest of the day. In all, seventy-five protesters perished over the course of forty-eight hours.[46] This event became known as Bloody Thursday (Kryvavyi chetverh). It has spawned several conspiracy theories, and some facts remain contested. The Ministry of Internal Affairs acknowledged in real time that some police officers "used weapons (*zastosuvaly zbroiu*) … to give unarmed police officers an opportunity to get out from under fire" (*Ukrains'ka pravda* 2014r). The fact that two more policemen died during their retreat up Institutka Street supports the view that police were in danger. However, none of the forty-eight protesters who perished were armed. The evidence points to police snipers.[47]

---

[45] The Music Conservatory was located directly behind the front rows of policemen that were facing Maidan. This means many police officers would have understood that they were being fired on from above, and from a flanking position.

[46] By including a further seven deaths that occurred earlier in and around Maidan, the Procuracy investigated the deaths of eighty-two protesters (Roshchyna and Kariakina 2019). The official Ukrainian memory narrative refers to a "Heavenly Hundred" (*Nebesnia sotnia*) by adding deaths that occurred outside of Kyiv during and after Maidan. (Recall that *sotnia* was the term with which Maidan "self-defense" units referred to themselves). In including these additional deaths, the UN Human Rights Council counted 106 civilians (and 17 policemen) who died in events related to Maidan (UN Human Rights Council 2016, 10).

[47] Ukrainian prosecutors identified the snipers as members of a twenty-one-man Berkut unit, "Black Squadron" (Buckley and Olearchyk 2015). Most fled

The demographic profile of Maidan victims on the final day was symbolic of the East–West dynamics discussed in Chapter 3. During the violent clashes from the morning of February 18 to the early hours of February 19, two-thirds of the civilians killed were from greater Kyiv, and only four were from Western Ukraine. All but five were over the age of thirty, and only six reportedly belonged to self-defense units (*Jus Talionis* 2019; Nebesnia sotnia 2019). This suggests a pulse of violence against whoever attended the morning march and/or stood on Maidan in the evening during the assault. On the morning of February 20, however, over 60 percent of the victims in the first hour were from the five oblasts of Western Ukraine, mostly Lviv. Nearly 70 percent had arrived the day before. The youngest victim, seventeen-year-old Nazarii Voitovych, arrived only an hour before his death, after a night-long bus ride from Ternopil. These individuals responded to social media calls and arrived fresh, angry, and radicalized to reinforce the front lines.[48] Armed with shields and helmets, they chased retreating police troops. Remarkably, not a single one was associated with Pravyi sektor. The biographies of these latecomers indicate no prior affiliation with the radical right (*Jus Talionis* 2019; Nebesnia sotnia 2019). Among the forty or so who died in the first hour, only four came from the East, and only eight were from Kyiv or its suburbs. The violence initiated by radical right protesters months earlier had lit a flame that that had spread widely, especially in Western Ukraine.

Regime Failure

The mass shooting by police snipers set in motion the implosion of the Party of Regions. First came the mass defection of MPs in the Rada. The Party of Regions faction, along with its satellite Communist Party, controlled a majority of seats. The Party of Regions had

to Russia. As of 2022, the case had not gone to trial. A team of American social scientists developed a 3D virtual reconstruction of Institutka Street on February 20, using video footage from more than 400 sources. Based on the model, ballistic experts, looking at a sample of three Maidan civilians killed that morning, demonstrated that the shots most likely came from behind police positions (Beck-Hoffmann 2014; Schwartz 2018; SITU Research 2018).

48 Many seem to have left spontaneously on night buses without informing their families. Many had relatives who had fought in the Ukrainian Insurgent Army (Ukraïns'ka povstans'ka armiia, or UPA) or the Galician Division during World War II.

remained a monolith since the beginning of Maidan, with only five defections (three early on, two more on February 18 from MPs whose home districts experienced violence). Within hours of the killing on February 20, five Regions MPs from the Western Ukrainian oblast of Zakarpattia quit the party (*Ukrains'ka pravda* 2014j). The opposition demanded that parliament convene for a special session. Against the wishes of party leaders, the presence of thirty-five Regions MPs made quorum possible. These MPs then supported a resolution prohibiting "anti-terrorist operations," ordering special police units to cease the use of "any type of weapons" against protesters, and to return to their bases (*Zakonodavstvo Ukraïny* 2014e).

International pressure intensified. The US State Department "unequivocally condemn[ed] the use of force against civilians by security forces" (*The Guardian* 2014b), and the EU announced targeted sanctions against high-level Ukrainian officials "responsible for human rights violations, violence, and use of excessive force" (Council of the European Union 2014d).[49] Facing personal sanctions, Yanukovych finally caved and engaged with the demands he had refused to negotiate days before. Western diplomats, already on site, mediated talks between Yanukovych and the opposition that evening, after the Rada vote, in the presence of a Russian envoy.

The terms of the Agreement (Uhoda), were reached after an all-night session. The Agreement handed a near-complete victory to the opposition. The Rada would vote to reinstate the 2004 Constitution, ending the president's control of key domestic security institutions.[50] Early elections would be held, though the incumbent president could remain in post until December (*The Guardian* 2014a). The document reinforced the point that domestic repression was no longer government policy by stating that "the Government will use law enforcement

---

[49] The specific sanctions were announced on March 5 for people deemed "responsible for the misappropriation of state funds … and human rights violations." The actual charge levied at each of the eighteen former Ukrainian state officials targeted (including Yanukovych) was that of "embezzlement of state funds," with no reference to human rights violations. While the legal criteria for pressing the charge was corruption, it seems clear that what determined their inclusion on the list was the political determination of their responsibility for the use of "excessive force" against protesters (Council of the European Union 2014b).

[50] This was the key concession Yanukovych's administration had refused just three days earlier, triggering the violence.

forces exclusively for the physical protection of public buildings" (*The Guardian* 2014a). Normally, the State Guard (Upravlinnia derzhavnoï okhorony Ukraïny) is the special police unit entrusted with securing state facilities. During the mass disturbances of Maidan, the government quarter was reinforced with thousands of interior troops and elite forces (Berkut). The Agreement called for the internal troops and Berkut units to pull out. Unexpectedly, the State Guard withdrew as well (Sidorenko 2014).[51] By the time the Agreement was signed at 4pm, the Polish foreign minister, Radosław Sikorski, observed in wonder that the police had vanished. The units protecting the residence of Yanukovych at Mezhyhirya also abandoned their posts. Yanukovych and his cabinet were suddenly unprotected.[52]

In the early evening, at a huge Maidan rally that began as a public funeral for the dozens who had perished the day before, opposition leader Vitali Klitschko took the stage to defend the decision to allow Yanukovych to stay until a new presidential election at the end of the year. A Maidan combatant in homemade military gear shoved him aside. The speaker proclaimed that, if Yanukovych had not resigned by the following morning, he would lead an armed assault on the presidential compound (*Ukrains'ka pravda* 2014d).[53] Andriy Parubiy, an opposition MP who had become the de facto commandant of the Maidan "self-defense" forces, announced around the same time that the Kyiv garrison of internal troops now recognized the authority of

---

[51] The agreement called for the disarmament of Maidan militants within twenty-four hours of the passing of a special law, but the police evacuation left the State Guard – completely untrained in riot control – facing a possible confrontation with armed Maidan activists, if they refused to put their weapons down. Waves of defections of police units in the Central and Western oblasts compounded the issue. An armed contingent of the Lviv police arrived on the Kyiv Maidan on February 21 – not to reinforce state security, but to protect protesters (*24Kanal* 2014b).

[52] Remarkably, as an indication that the actors involved in the negotiations could not anticipate the collapse of the government mere hours before it occurred, guarantees regarding the personal safety of Yanukovych were not discussed (Sidorenko 2014). The dispersal of security forces took place without clear orders from the top. Vitaliy Zakharchenko, the minister of internal affairs, had disappeared sometime during the morning of February 21. The departure of troops required some coordination with self-defense units, who ensured that the buses transporting policemen could leave without incident (Higgins, Kramer, and Erlanger 2014).

[53] The combatant was Volodymyr Parasiuk who, early the previous morning, had been the leader of a group who shot at policemen from the Conservatory (Stack 2015).

Maidan (*24Kanal* 2014a).[54] Within hours, Parubiy declared all government buildings to be under the protection of "self-defense" forces (*Ukrains'ka pravda* 2014i).

What residual support for Yanukovych there was disintegrated in parliament, as well. The single-member districts of the Party of Regions are shown shaded in black in Maps 4.1, 4.2, and 4.3. When parliament reconvened, in the late afternoon of February 21, shortly after the official signing of the Agreement, fifty-three more MPs announced their defection from the Party of Regions. The Party had been in power since 2010.[55] Thirty-one of the thirty-five Party of Regions MPs who had voted for the landmark resolution against police violence on February 20 were from the Central and Western oblasts (by now in open rebellion).[56] In the following days, all but eleven (of sixty-nine) MPs from the Center-West defected. About half of those representing the South defected, too. Though waves of pro-Maidan demonstrations in late January had suggested that the Party of Regions was on shakier ground than previously believed, the cascade of post-February 20 defections was barely believable. The only regions in which MPs generally remained loyal to Yanukovych until the end were Crimea, Kharkiv, and Donetsk: precisely the parts of Ukraine where the proportion of self-declared ethnic Russians was the highest.[57]

On February 21, in compliance with the Agreement signed between Yanukovych and the opposition, the Rada voted, without any debates, to reinstate the 2004 constitutional amendments (*Zn.ua* 2014). The Rada exercised its newfound power in the next vote to dismiss Minister of Internal Affairs Vitaliy Zakharchenko, the official face of police misconduct. Zakharchenko – like most high-level cabinet members of the Party of Regions – was already on the run to Russia. Yanukovych

---

[54] In Lviv, as the police were retreating from the Kyiv Maidan, the four power ministries – Interior, SBU, Procuracy, and Army – published a joint document pledging their allegiance to Maidan (*iPress* 2014).

[55] Recall that in the 2010 presidential election, 78 percent had voted for Yanukovych in the Southern and Eastern provinces.

[56] Data was obtained by matching the roll call vote (*LiveJournal* 2014a) with public information on the oblast of affiliated MPs. Fifteen were elected on the national party list, and twenty in first-past-the-post individual ridings as independents who later joined the Party of Regions faction in parliament.

[57] During the vote to remove Yanukovych on February 22, an additional thirty MPs from the Party of Regions supported the motion without formally leaving the party (*Zakonodavstvo Ukraïny* 2014b).

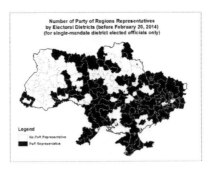

Map 4.1 Party of Regions single-member districts, February 19, 2014

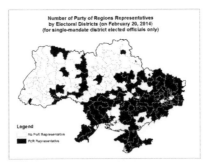

Map 4.2 Party of Regions single-member districts, February 20, 2014

Map 4.3 Party of Regions single-member districts, February 21, 2014

also fled, leaving by helicopter late on February 21, ostensibly to attend an anti-Maidan political event in Kharkiv, likely fearing for his freedom and his life (*Radio Svoboda* 2016). By the time parliament reconvened on Saturday, February 22, it was clear that a new majority had been formed. Oleksandr Turchynov, a veteran member of Yulia Tymoshenko's Batkivshchyna Party, became Speaker. The Rada first voted to symbolically nullify the article of the Criminal Code under which Tymoshenko had been convicted (Kalnysh 2014).[58]

The next order of business was the fate of Viktor Yanukovych. His whereabouts were officially unknown (Sidorenko 2014).[59] A procedure of impeachment, which would take months, could not address the urgent question of the executive power vacuum. The Rada settled on "self-removal" (*samousunennia*), an expedient term with no legal standing. A laconic resolution, passed by a constitutional majority, "established" that Yanukovych had "removed himself" from his duties (*Zakonodavstvo Ukraïny* 2014b).[60] As Rada Speaker, Turchynov was installed as interim president. Presidential elections were called for May 25.[61] An hour before his de facto impeachment, Yanukovych announced that he was "not going to leave the country" (Sidorenko 2014), but on February 23, with the help of the Russian Black Sea Fleet, Yanukovych left Ukraine for Russia for good (BBC News Russkaia sluzhba 2018).

After Regime Change

The next four chapters of our analytic narrative document the process of intra-Ukrainian bargaining that took place after this watershed event. The empirical material is presented in roughly chronological order, but

---

[58] Tymoshenko's release within hours was highly symbolic, since Maidan had begun over the abrupt decision by the Yanukovych government to suspend negotiations with the EU over an Association Agreement, and for a long time the main political obstacle for EU officials had been her imprisonment.

[59] Realizing that he left Kyiv without signing the law that reinstated the 2004 Constitution, as the Agreement stipulated, the Rada had to pass a second vote establishing that the 2004 Constitution was now in force, even without the presidential signature (*Ukrains'ka pravda* 2014n).

[60] The eighteen-word resolution stated: "To establish that the President of Ukraine V. Yanukovych has unconstitutionally removed himself from the exercise of constitutional authority and is not fulfilling his duties" (*Zakonodavstvo Ukraïny* 2014b).

[61] All but three of the forty-six Party of Regions MPs from Donetsk opted not to attend the session. A few later claimed they felt it would have been dangerous. The next day, the rump Party of Regions issued a statement denouncing Yanukovych for his "treason" and "criminal orders that led to human casualties," placing "all responsibility" on him and his personal entourage (*Holos Ukraïny* 2014).

the timeline will have to "double back" more than once. In different parts of Ukraine three simultaneous processes began to unfold, each according to somewhat different and independent cascading logics.

First, in the wee hours of February 23, Russian President Vladimir Putin decided to send military forces to Crimea. The intent, as he later put it, was to "return Crimea to Russia" (Zygar 2016, 275). This is where our narrative begins in Chapter 5.

Second, there was an abortive attempt, beginning on February 22, by Party of Regions officials in the Eastern oblasts to reorganize and coordinate an anti-Maidan countercoalition that would refuse to recognize the new government in Kyiv. The energy fizzled out within days. This is where our narrative begins in Chapter 6.

Third, on the afternoon of February 23, a majority in the Ukrainian parliament voted to repeal the 2012 language law. This was the Rada's first substantive decision post-Maidan. The vote occurred one day after Yanukovych's removal. The 2012 law, described in Chapter 3, had granted Russian status as a "regional language." The act of reversing it was widely interpreted as a symbolic attempt to "ban Russian." The political effect of the repeal – even if was later vetoed by Interim President Turchynov – was to encourage sedition in the East. Rebels continued to invoke this decision in their narrative as they seized buildings and took up arms.

Before we descend into our analytic narrative, with references to our model of bargaining between Russian-speaking communities and the center under conditions of uncertainty, it is useful to revisit and update the competing Russian and Ukrainian "master narratives" that introduced Chapter 3. Each of these three seminal events – the intervention into Crimea, the failed attempt by regional elites of the Party of Regions to mount a challenge to the new Maidan government, and the symbolic strike against the Russian language – can be nested within "master" narratives, useful for state officials and engaged publics. Both are relatively cohesive versions of events. The first version of events was orchestrated in Kyiv, dominant in the Ukrainian West and was largely adopted in the Western world in government, media, and academic circles. The other originated in Moscow and was broadcast on Russian television and media channels to an audience of Russian-speakers in Russia, in Ukraine, and internationally. At the time of this writing, as Russia has engaged in a full-scale invasion of Ukraine, these two master narratives have never been further apart.

Table 4.1 *The narratives diverge*

	Russian narrative	Western narrative
21 February Agreement	violated	overtaken by events
National Unity Cabinet	"of Victors"	no longer a priority
Yanukovych removal	coup	constitutional
Violence on Maidan	instigated by the West	failure to deescalate
Violence by police	heroic	disproportionate
Violence by protesters	fascist	tragic
Fate of Russian-speakers	imminent threat	[*downplayed*]

The Russian and Western narratives diverge on three basic issues: (1) the Agreement negotiated between Yanukovych and the opposition on February 22, (2) the transfer of power on February 23, and (3) the fate of Russian-speakers inside Ukraine. Table 4.1 succinctly summarizes the talking points on the Russian and Western narrative tracks.

The Agreement stipulated the adoption of constitutional amendments empowering parliament, the withdrawal of the riot police, the disarmament of protesters, the maintenance of Yanukovych in power until December elections, and the creation of a "national unity" government (*The Guardian* 2014a). Russia complained that the last three points were never implemented (*Regnum* 2014). Ukraine replied that Yanukovych had fled without signing the constitutional amendments into law (Sidorenko 2014), thereby reneging on these commitments, so the composition of the new cabinet did not need to reflect the defunct Agreement. In ignoring the "national unity" clause, the new government in effect deprived Eastern Ukraine of representation. Russia seized on the point in its public diplomacy, calling the post-Maidan ruling coalition an illegitimate "government of victors" (*LB. ua* 2014b).[62]

---

[62] The expression ("government of victors") is a wordplay on *S'ezd pobeditelei* ("Congress of victors"), which has a sinister connotation in Soviet history. It refers to the 1934 Congress of the Communist Party of the Soviet Union which celebrated the "victories" over collectivization, and the first five years of breakneck industrialization. The vast majority of Congress delegates were arrested and shot during the 1937 purges.

Both the Western and Russian narratives on the Agreement cloak inconsistencies. On the one hand, the Russian envoy who observed the talks had been instructed by Putin not to sign it and had publicly voiced doubts that it was enforceable even before Yanukovych fled (Hosaka 2018; *TASS* 2014). On the other hand, Western officials never strongly pressed the new Ukrainian authorities to build a cross-regional coalition (Legvold 2016, 138). In Russia's storyline, Western powers abandoned the Agreement as soon as it was convenient. In the Western storyline, the Agreement was overtaken by events and the subsequent sequence of votes in the Rada affirmed a legitimate, constitutional power transfer. The legality of the parliamentary vote that removed Yanukovych is critical here, since it was made possible only by the defection of a large number of Party of Regions MPs, including many from the East.

The second major divergence in Russian and Western narratives is over what to call this transfer of power. Russia calls it a coup.[63] The West prefers "Revolution of Dignity." The Russian narrative defends the use of force by the police (seen as heroic) and excoriates the violence of protesters as "fascist." The Russian narrative blind spot is that it sees Ukrainians as devoid of agency, at the command of their external patrons.[64]

The Western narrative, while deploring protest violence, stresses the political responsibility of government authorities in failing to deescalate the situation and the excessive (disproportionate) force used by the police against protesters. Support for democracy must include the right to protest, after all, and geopolitical self-determination must include the freedom to sign an Association Agreement with the EU, if a majority supports it. The Western narrative also insists that the role

---

[63] The Russian state had already described the first wave of violence on February 18–19 as "an attempt at a *gosudarstvenno perevorota* (coup d'état) and at seizing power through violent means" (Ministerstvo inostrannykh del Rossiiskoi Federatsii 2014b). From his temporary site of internal exile in Kharkiv on February 22, Yanukovych appropriated the term for himself, railing against the "banditism, vandalism, and coup" taking place in his country (Sidorenko 2014).

[64] This takes place in the form of political signals or directives, possibly put in place by United States Agency for International Development (USAID) contractors or European bureaucrats long ago. Often Western intelligence services and special forces are accused of having directly "trained" protesters (*Vesti.ru* 2014c; Belton 2020, 388–9).

of the far right should not be exaggerated. In this view, these events unfolded *largely nonviolently*, as the result of tens of thousands of small, brave choices, all made by domestic Ukrainian actors. In many ways, the most important moment of choice was the decision by Party of Regions representatives on February 22 that the sniper massacre crossed a line.

That being said, the Western narrative blind spot is its practical ambivalence toward protest violence. The dominant trope is the illegitimacy of excessive police force against peaceful protesters. The mainstream Maidan strategists were initially certain that violence would discredit their movement and that the Maidan protest had the moral upper hand only as long as it remained peaceful. Those talking points endured – but they turned out to be wrong. Violence "worked." The Western narrative treats the protest violence as the tragic consequence of government policy – which, ironically, also has the effect of depriving Ukrainian actors of agency. While there is no evidence that civic or political leaders on Maidan endorsed the use of violence, frontline activists did employ violence at three critical junctures – on January 19 after the dictatorship laws, on February 20 to force a vote on constitutional amendments, and on February 22 to break the police siege of the Maidan. All of this tends to be overlooked in the Western narrative, loathe to cede the "coup" talking point to Russia.

The third divergence is over the fate of Russian-speakers in Eastern Ukraine. In our model, the initiating crisis created fear in Russian-speaking communities that previous constitutional minority protections were being reneged upon. In late February, after an irregular transfer of power in the wake of significant violence, the trope of radical Maidan activists intent on threatening Russian-speakers in the East became omnipresent in the Russian media. The Western narrative emphasized that the transfer of power was orderly, that looting was rare, that cases of vigilantism were marginal, and that the government being ejected from power was grotesquely corrupt. There is little evidence that Western officials acknowledged the premise that Russian-speakers were relative losers in this moment of revolutionary change, or fully appreciated the political consequences of repealing the language law at the time. The same was not true in Russia, which seized on the optics. Russia's claim that Russians were under imminent threat resonated among a key segment of the Russian-speaking electorate: the concentrated ethnic Russian minority in Crimea.

5 | *Irredentist Annexation (Crimea)*

For years, the Kremlin had sent signals that it placed a high intrinsic value on Crimea, a defensible peninsula that can be isolated from mainland Ukraine by shutting down a narrow land bridge. This chapter documents strong early cues that Russia would assist local seditionists in seceding from Ukraine (parameter *a* in the model).[1] We now know that the Kremlin had laid some groundwork for the Crimea operation ahead of time, with contacts made with the Speaker of the Crimean parliament during the Kyiv Maidan (Matsuzato 2016, 240–1). The decision to send troops to Crimea occurred on February 23. Putin and four of his most trusted lieutenants – three of whom had begun their career, like Putin, in the Leningrad branch of the KGB – reportedly made the call.[2] Neither the Security Council nor the Foreign Ministry were involved (Myers 2014a). The irregular nature of the meeting, held mere hours after Yanukovych's removal, suggests a decision that was not fully premeditated. Once it was made, the two immediate imperatives were (1) to mask Russia's direct military intervention, and (2) to find local political allies in Crimea supportive of a Russian operation. As the nature of the crisis (and the Western response) became clearer, the Kremlin sent clearer and costlier signals of resolve.

---

[1] Following Fearon (1994, 1997), we signpost the chapter with a rough attempt to differentiate between ex ante and ex post signals of resolve.

[2] There is some uncertainty as to whether Putin decided to deploy special forces to Crimea immediately following the ousting of Yanukovych (February 23 in the very early morning) as he later claimed (RFE/RL 2015), or rather on February 20, the day when parliament broke with Yanukovych. Special operation forces were said to have received an order on February 20 for a "peace-keeping operation" (Treisman 2018, 287). Pictures of a Russian medal with the inscription "For the return of Crimea 20.02.14–03.18.14" were briefly posted on social media, then removed (Cathcart 2014). In an April 2014 law, the Ukrainian parliament established that the "temporary occupation of the territory of Ukraine" began on February 20 (*Zakonodavstvo Ukraïny* 2014d). No significant troop movements, however, were detected until after February 23.

The chapter also highlights two distinct mechanisms of Russian influence: television propaganda (vastly exaggerating the immediate physical threat to Russian communities post-Maidan to invoke existential zero-sum politics), and the use of unmarked soldiers to secure buildings and deter pro-Maidan street mobilization (lowering μ).[3] Specifying these mechanisms of influence contributes to the hybrid war literature without removing the agency of Russian-speaking community elites. Our account will go to some lengths, in fact, to demonstrate the importance of local calculations. The fact that Crimea was the only territory in Ukraine with constitutional autonomy lowered the costs of elite coordination, giving them special institutional resources that could be repurposed (Roeder 2007, 2018, 22–8, 123, 164–9). Since events moved so quickly in Crimea, the claim of "near unanimous" support for self-determination has become widespread. Our narrative refines and revises facets of that contention.

Initial Russian Signals

Russia's strategy seems to have been to begin sudden, large-scale troop exercises in the military districts closest to Ukraine in order to conceal the deployment of special forces to Crimea (Barabanov 2015, 192). Probing the willingness of Crimean elites to engage in sedition first required sending signals of Russian support (parameter a in the model) detectable by those elites.

Moscow sent Oleg Belaventsev, who had previously fulfilled a number of secret missions on behalf of Russian Defense Minister Sergei Shoigu (Zygar 2016, 276–7), to identify political allies in Crimea. The Party of Regions completely controlled Crimean politics (with 80 of the 100 seats in the regional parliament), but Russian authorities – even after three months of Maidan unrest – had only a "vague knowledge" of local dynamics (Matsuzato 2016, 242).

The two main figures of interest were Anatoliy Mohyliov, the prime minister of Crimea, and Vladimir Konstantinov, the Speaker of parliament. The two men were at loggerheads. Mohyliov was a product of the Donetsk political machine. When Yanukovych became president in 2010, the Donetsk elite not only captured the levers of national

---

[3] Recall that μ represents a threat of pro-Ukrainian vigilante violence against elites engaging in *sedition* if there is no safety in numbers.

power, but often of provincial networks as well. Since Mohyliov came with his Donbas retinue, the rule of Donbas "outsiders" was deeply resented by local Crimean officials, and the post-Maidan crisis became an opportunity for them to jettison the influence of both Kyiv *and* Donetsk (Matsuzato 2016, 227). Konstantinov was already known in Kremlin circles. In December 2013, while in Moscow, he met with Nikolai Patrushev, secretary of the Security Council (and one of the four officials present with Putin when the decision to invade Crimea was made). The following month, he hosted a Russian delegation attending a religious event. On each occasion, he reportedly signaled that a "subversion" of the Yanukovych government could push him toward secession (Matsuzato 2016, 240; Kozlov, Volkova, and Karpiak 2019). On February 20, back in Moscow at the height of Maidan violence, Konstantinov for the first time publicly invoked the specter of "separation" (*RIA Novosti* 2014).

The Russian envoy Belaventsev needed to find reliable partners in control of government and parliament. The current prime minister, Mohyliov, a Yanukovych man, was not deemed trustworthy. Perhaps as an indication of the improvised nature of the operation, Belaventsev first offered the job to someone – Communist Party leader Leonid Grach – who had long receded to the margins of real local power after a brief stint as Speaker in 1998–2002.

The decision caused an uproar among Crimean elites, causing him to rescind his offer (Treisman 2018, 289). He then turned to Sergei Aksyonov, who headed Russian Unity (Russkoe edinstvo), a small Russian nationalist party with only three seats in the Crimean parliament. Aksyonov had one major asset: he had established a militia days earlier. He also had the support of Konstantinov. Aksyonov and Konstantinov were the most powerful members of the local Crimean elite, determined to remove the outsider Mohyliov (Matsuzato 2016, 242).[4]

---

[4] Both Aksyonov and Konstantinov were born in Moldova but grew up as young adults in Crimea and are thus considered "locals." The Mohyliov group was transplanted to Crimea in 2010 from the Donetsk mining town of Makeevka. They were derisively nicknamed the "Macedonians" (*make-dontsy*, as in Makeevka, Donetsk). The marginal nature of Aksyonov's Russian party (4 percent of the vote in the 2012 Crimean election) is partly explained by the fact that the dominated Party of Regions did not allow open competition, including from Russian nationalists in Donbas and Crimea.

The first popular mobilization took place in Sevastopol. A port city hosting the Russian Black Sea Fleet, Sevastopol had a large majority of ethnic Russians (72 percent), and held a special place in the Russian national myth from the time of the 1853–1856 Crimean War (Plokhy 2000). A "National Will Rally against Fascism" took place on February 23, attracting an estimated 20,000 people, far exceeding expectations (Zhigulev, Sivtsova, and Skibitskaia 2017).[5] Speakers at the rally denounced what they saw as a coup in Kyiv, but also turned their ire against local officials and Yanukovych. Aleksei Chalyi, a Russian citizen and popular businessman who had launched a local television channel, was chosen as "people's mayor." As a military city, Sevastopol was directly subordinated to Kyiv, and the head of city administration was appointed by the Ukrainian capital. The appointment of a people's mayor was a direct symbolic challenge to the new government consolidating power in Kyiv. Chalyi saw February 23 as a turning point in the break with Ukraine: "At first, we wanted to join forces with the Southeast of Ukraine. But on the morning of February 23, the situation changed radically. The Southeast stopped resistance [and Yanukovych fled]. Had Yanukovych remained in Kharkov or Donetsk, united people there, it would have been a different matter" (Zhigulev, Sivtsova and Skibitskaia 2017). Chalyi was referring to a short-lived attempt in Kharkiv on February 22 to unite the Eastern oblasts in opposition to Kyiv (see Chapter 6). In the following days, Kyiv made a feeble attempt to arrest Chalyi, but protesters protected him.

On the same day as the Sevastopol rally, a "people's militia" organized by Aksyonov's Russian Unity Party gathered on the square facing the Crimean parliament in Simferopol (Ukrainian Helsinki Human Rights Union 2017). It was, in Aksyonov's words, "the mirror image of Maidan. If they can, then we can" (Volkov 2014). Like on Maidan, the militia branded itself as "self-defense" (*samooborony*), and organized into subgroups of 100-plus volunteers (called *sotni* in Kyiv, and *roty* in Simferopol).[6] As we saw in Chapter 4, during Maidan in Kyiv

---

[5] The protest coincided with Fatherland Day (Den' otechestvo), which celebrated the Soviet-era Red Army. The crowd was the largest Sevastopol had seen since the last years of the Soviet Union.

[6] The militia also called itself a *druzhina*, a term harking back to aristocratic armies in medieval Russia.

and Eastern Ukraine, *titushki* (irregular street enforcers set up by the Ministry of Internal Affairs) often attacked pro-Maidan protesters. Crimean *titushki* had clashed with a small group of pro-Maidan supporters in Simferopol on February 21 (*Ukrains'ka pravda* 2014t). Aksyonov's militia was different from those *titushki* in that the militia was not established by the Party of Regions or supported by the state. This would also occur in Donetsk (see Chapter 6).

Television Magnifies Local Threat Perceptions

What exactly was the danger that these militias were organizing against? The long-term threat to Russian-speaking communities was that they would find their status subordinated to Ukrainian-speakers from the Ukrainian West in a new social hierarchy. Even though the decision to immediately revisit the language law intensified these concerns, this was an abstract future threat. What stoked fear and focused minds was *real time* physical insecurity: the specter of vigilante violence coming from Kyiv.

Russian television alleged that hordes of Maidan radicals were poised to descend on the Crimean Peninsula to attack pro-Russian civilians (Volkov 2014).[7] The use of violence by protesters on the Kyiv Maidan was amplified with round-the-clock repetition, emphasizing the need for "self-defense." One incident in particular acted as catalyst. On February 24, Ihor Mosiychuk, a radical right activist from a group that eventually provided the backbone of Azov, made a boastful declaration on a television show in Kyiv. He opined that if the Ukrainian government was unable to stem separatist sentiment in Crimea, Pravyi sektor (the most visible radical group on Maidan) would send a "Friendship Train" of militants to Crimea to frighten "those people who are calling for the destruction of my country" (*StopFake* 2016).[8] On February 27, as Russian special forces were securing Crimea's

---

[7] As we saw in Chapter 4, this threat had earlier been expressed by anti-Maidan activists in Kharkiv and Donetsk.

[8] Mosiychuk invoked a 1992 event in which hundreds of members of a small Ukrainian radical right party boarded a chartered train to Sevastopol at a time when the status of the Black Sea Fleet was contested. The militants forced their way to the port city, removed Soviet and Russian flags, and brandished "Crimea for Ukrainians" posters. There was no violence (Kuzio 1997, 233–4).

parliament, Russian media fabricated the claim that a train carrying 1,500 Pravyi sektor activists to Simferopol had been intercepted and that a stockpile of weapons (wooden sticks, Molotov cocktails, guns, and ammunition) was found (*StopFake* 2016; Zeveleva 2019). There was no such train.[9]

A second incident was mostly played up retroactively on Russian media, weeks after the annexation, even though it had been reported in real time. On February 20, the last day of violence on Maidan, several buses with Crimean plates driving from Kyiv toward Crimea were stopped at an improvised checkpoint manned by pro-Maidan protesters in a town two hours south of Kyiv (Goncharova 2015). The day before, pro-Maidan checkpoints had appeared on all the major roads leading to Kyiv (from the West, East, and South), to prevent army or security troop reinforcements, as well as suspected *titushki*, from reaching Maidan (see Chapter 4). By February 20, checkpoint militants were now looking for *titushki* or anyone suspected of involvement in anti-Maidan activities) returning home from Kyiv.[10] According to Crimean Prime Minister Mohyliov, in a statement widely cited in Russian and Ukrainian media, "armed extremists" stopped several buses containing a total of 320 Crimean passengers. Physical force was used against some of them, three buses were burnt, and seven people were hospitalized (*Vesti.ru* 2014a). The propaganda in Russian retellings would later come to include the claim that passengers on that day were attacked with bats and shovels, doused with gasoline, and killed in gruesome ways – all claims that remain unsubstantiated, but fact-checking specifics in retrospect can distract from the propaganda's intent.[11] A critical mass of people in Crimea, Eastern

---

[9] Pravyi sektor announced on that same day that they were taking no action in Crimea, and that Mosiychuk himself was in Kyiv (*StopFake* 2016).

[10] The checkpoints were also aimed at police. On the night of February 21–22, a busload of Berkut officers on their way to Crimea was pelted with eggs, rocks, and fake blood (Shuster 2014b).

[11] In early April, the Crimean parliament held hearings on "victims of Maidan," and accused Maidan activists of murdering seven passengers (*RBK* 2014a). The claim was later included in a "White Book on Violations of Human Rights and the Rule of Law in Ukraine," released by the Russian Ministry of Foreign Affairs, and featured in a documentary extolling Vladimir Putin's role in the annexation of Crimea, broadcast on Russia's primary television channel in 2016 (Ministry of Foreign Affairs of the Russian Federation 2014b; *StopFake* 2016). In our reading of events, there was violent intimidation, but

Ukraine, and Russia, who were already unsettled by protester violence on Maidan, were inclined to believe the worst and seized on the event as evidence of an imminent threat.

The Cherkasy incident was believable because of the unprecedented sight of militias, often armed, that had operated with impunity in several Ukrainian provinces. In the pro-Maidan view, militias were defending civilians against abuse by the police, who had killed protesters on Maidan (often on camera). In the anti-Maidan view, vigilantes were threatening civilians suspected of having opposed Maidan (also often on camera). The Russian media thus constructed a narrative built on real incidents – the threat of a Pravyi sektor activist, the intimidation of bus passengers – to fabricate stories of killings, and thousands of armed militants in a train, that intensified fears in Crimea.[12] The heightened sense of threat was palpable, which led to numerous related rumors that spread like wildfire, such as the existence of "hit lists" of prominent pro-Russia Crimeans.[13] Focusing on the Russian television supply of communal threat narrative is only part of the equation. There was also a demand. Part of why these stories "took off" in Crimea more than elsewhere in Eastern Ukraine was its unique social milieu, one in which pro-Russian vigilantes had the run of the streets.

Polite Green Men Arrive

On February 25, approximately 400 pro-Russian protesters surrounded the parliament building, demanding a referendum on independence. Speaker Konstantinov soon announced that an

no evidence that anyone died. The top two Crimean officials, Konstantinov and Mohyliov, denied it in real time. The Cherkasy police stated that "such events [the killings, the egregious violence] did not take place," but admitted that two buses were burned (Goncharova 2015).

[12] Some Russian officials appeared to genuinely believe the stories. Mykola Malomuzh, then head of Ukrainian foreign intelligence, recounts how a Putin adviser, at the beginning of the Crimean events, told him about the "thousands of armed fascists and terrorists" who were on their way to Crimea by train and buses to seize property and attack civilians. Malomuzh asked him: "Is it really the position of the President of Russia, is he so disoriented?" (Volchek 2014).

[13] Zeveleva (2019), who asked local Crimeans about how they remembered the 2014 events, reports that some told her that "'Russian agents' and 'well-connected people' had shown them the hit lists." Lewis (2020, 43–59) provides a nuanced theoretical account of how information conveyed in rumors is important for antiregime seditious collective action.

extraordinary session would be held the following day (Ukrainian Helsinki Human Rights Union 2017). There was widespread sentiment that parliament would vote to separate from Ukraine. During Maidan, it had twice alluded to separation in formal resolutions. On January 22, Crimea's parliament warned that if protesters were able to force early elections through violence, "Crimeans will neither participate in illegitimate elections, nor recognize their results, nor live in 'Bandera' Ukraine!" (*Gosudarstvennyi soviet Respubliki Krym* 2014). On February 18, after excoriating the "unbridled bandits" (*raspoiasavshikhsia banditov*) who were igniting a "civil war" (*grazhdanskaia voina*), it threatened "to call on the residents of the autonomy to defend civil peace" (*Vgorode* 2014c). As Konstantinov promised, on February 26 an extraordinary session attempted to convene, but the suddenly high stakes brought out some 15,000 demonstrators in front of parliament. Eyewitness accounts suggest that about half of them opposed the referendum, while the other half demanded it.[14] It is possible that Russia planned for the Crimean parliament to first call for a referendum on Crimea's future, and then ask the Kremlin to send troops to protect Crimeans. If that had been the plan, street power had aborted it.[15]

The demographics and symbolism of these protests were very different from the Kyiv Maidan. The vast majority of the opponents were Crimean Tatars – Crimean Tatar flags outnumbered Ukrainian flags (RT 2014). This revealed some peculiar Crimean political dynamics. Slavic pro-Maidan groups (both Ukrainian and Russian) were very weak in Crimea, while Crimean Tatars had demonstrated that they could mobilize as much street power in Simferopol (but not in Sevastopol) as pro-Russian groups. It seems that Tatar groups only took steps to organize a self-defense militia after Russian special forces gained control of the streets (Gromenko 2018) (by which point it was too late, as we shall shortly see). Russian flags were also pervasive, as

---

[14] A report by nongovernmental organization (NGO) experts from four countries provided an estimated breakdown of protesters: 7,000 pro-Ukraine, 7,000 pro-Russia (including 500 "self-defense," 1,000 from Sevastopol, and 400 from nearby Yevpatoriya) (Ukrainian Helsinki Human Rights Union 2017).

[15] Russian envoy Belazhentsev left for Crimea on February 23, and was seen in Konstantinov's office on February 26, the day of the aborted extraordinary session. Coynash (2017b) mentions the Russian plan, but provides no direct evidence.

they had been in the Sevastopol demonstration on February 23. This was a notable symbolic departure from the anti-Maidan demonstrations in Kyiv, where presumably participants were deterred from waving the Russian flag.[16]

The two groups of protesters were separated from each other by only a few feet, with no riot police in sight, rendering the situation volatile.[17] Though Sergei Aksyonov, the Russian nationalist self-defense leader, and Refat Chubarov, the Crimean Tatar leader, worked in tandem to defuse the tension, a melee eventually broke out. The incident resulted in the killing of two civilians and injuries to several dozen more. Aksyonov blamed instigators on both sides, including his own. "Provocateurs" from Sevastopol, he said, "tried to convince people that somebody is coming here to slaughter someone. I went out to the people and said: 'There is no one. Do not stir up the situation, nobody is coming here, there are only Crimeans here'" (Ukrainian Helsinki Human Rights Union 2017).

The parliamentary session was eventually cancelled due to lack of quorum. Crimean Tatar deputies boycotted the session, but the empty seats primarily belonged to Party of Regions deputies who failed to register as present. The Party was in disarray nationally, and many Crimean party elites possibly feared retribution from the new

---

[16] Russian television distortions notwithstanding, in the language of the model, μ (the cost of engaging publicly in sedition) could defensibly be argued to be zero in Crimea. Since the end of the Kyiv Maidan on February 23, Crimea differed from most every other region of Ukraine in near-total absence of any pro-Maidan paramilitary militias or anti-Russia "self-defense" forces. On February 26, for instance, a single Pravyi sektor flag could be spotted, allegedly carried by a football hooligan itching for a fight (an "ultra") (Ukrainian Helsinki Human Rights Union 2017). Even before the seizure of high-profile locations by Russia, which sent a signal to the pro-Russia/anti-Maidan constituency that they could take to the streets without fear, there is little evidence that anti-Russia/pro-Maidan vigilantism was a threat. (Contrasted with the narrative to follow in Chapters 6, 7, and 8).

[17] The Crimean units of the Berkut riot police had returned to Crimea but were in Sevastopol. They were greeted as heroes on February 22 (*NV* 2014), in stark contrast to the hostile reception given to returning Berkut troops in Western Ukraine (see Chapter 4). On February 26, the Crimean units stayed in their barracks in Sevastopol (Matveeva 2018, 62). Berkut was disbanded on February 25 by the new government in Kyiv, and the Simferopol local authorities announced that the Crimean Berkut units would now be subordinated to the city council (Kanygin 2014).

authorities in Kyiv (see Chapter 6).[18] The immediate political future of Crimea was uncertain, but there is no evidence that these reluctant deputies knew that Russian military units would seize parliament the next day. A group of Crimean Tatar protesters broke the police cordon and entered parliament, only to find the legislative room empty. Crimean Tatar leaders claimed that Konstantinov had assured them that no session would be called in the foreseeable future (Galimova 2015), and so the Tatar protesters decided to leave the building and call off the demonstration. This proved to be the last day of Crimean autonomy within Ukraine.

The dispatching of Russian special forces to Crimea began very early in the morning of February 27. The Russian soldiers operated without insignia, but were armed with advanced weaponry unavailable to the Ukrainian army. In English-language parlance, they quickly became known as "Little Green Men."[19] The Russian government initially claimed that they were Crimean "self-defense" forces. A month after the annexation, the story changed. The Little Green Men were now acknowledged to be from the Russian military, acting in support of the Crimean self-defense movement (Yashin and Shorina 2015, 14). In a first anniversary documentary broadcast on Russian television, the story changed yet again, striking a celebratory tone: Putin had *personally* directed the military operation, and the local "self-defense" forces played only a supporting role (Toal 2017, 230–2; Shreck 2019).

The Russian military presence on February 27 consisted of two commando units of approximately thirty men each. These special forces, from the Pskov 76th Guards Air Assault Division, landed in Sevastopol, and then moved to secure parliament and the main government quarter in Simferopol (a ten-minute walk from each other) in Simferopol in the early morning (Zygar 2016, 277). The Crimean government was completely shut down, with ministers and personnel unable to reach their offices. This was the signal that a new government was about to

---

[18] Many deputies remained loyal to Mohyliov (the Donetsk outsider) and were wary of the power play to remove him. They stayed in their offices on that day (Matsuzato 2016, 247).

[19] While Russian media and blogs occasionally used the Russian equivalent (*zelyonnye chelovechki*), the preferred expression was by far *vezhlivye liudi* ("polite people") (Shiriaev 2014). We reproduce the English translation of that term in the main text.

be installed. The offices of the Crimean branch of the Party of Regions were also locked, never to reopen.

The Russian commandos encountered no resistance. Security forces under national jurisdiction – internal troops, army, police – received no instructions from Kyiv, and did not prevent deputies from entering parliament (Kozlov, Volkova, and Karpiak 2019). An unannounced extraordinary parliamentary session was held later that day.[20] The Speaker of parliament prefaced the session by denouncing the "unconstitutional seizure of power in Ukraine by radical nationalists," and the "rampant political extremism and violence" in the clashes the day before in Simferopol (Krym politicheskii 2015).

Two votes were taken. The first appointed Sergei Aksyonov as the new prime minister. The second called for a referendum on May 25, the same day as the Ukrainian presidential election. The referendum question did not mention independence (let alone annexation), and clearly indicated that Crimea was part of Ukraine. It read: "The Autonomous Republic of Crimea enjoys state self-rule (*gosudarstvennaia samostoiatel'nost'*) and is part of Ukraine on the basis of agreements and treaties."[21] The ambiguity of self-rule jarred, as many future critics would point out, with the reality of the presence of Russian special units in the building essentially forcing the vote. Parliament claimed that a slim majority of fifty-one deputies had voted for Aksyonov, and that sixty-one had supported the referendum, but there is evidence that, like the day before, quorum was not reached.[22]

---

[20] Historians will never know all of the details of this session, since it was conducted without television or stenographic recording of proceedings. (Ukrainian law stipulated that these were mandatory.)

[21] The question was a carbon copy of one proposed by the Crimean parliament in 1992, during a tense confrontation with Kyiv, but which was ultimately never put to a referendum vote (see Chapter 3). Some interpreted the wording in 1992 to mean Crimea and Kyiv were negotiating a treaty with each other as equals – like independent states, even though Crimea formally remained within Ukraine – but Ukraine's government never accepted this interpretation.

[22] An investigation by Norwegian journalists claimed that only thirty-six deputies were present for the vote. The journalists talked to a number of deputies who were registered as having voted, even though they did not attend the session (Ale and Espedal 2014). A Russian journalist claimed that the first vote was delayed by five hours for lack of quorum (Galimova 2015). One quarter did not vote, according to official results.

Speaker Konstantinov, now the main local Party of Regions official following the dismissal of Crimean Prime Minister Mohyliov, spearheaded the session.

More Russian Signals

The presence of highly trained special troops had the effect of dissuading street pushback. Pro-Russian militias took to the streets without fear. Under these conditions, the social tip to sedition on the part of Russian-speaking elites occurred quickly. On February 28, now with clear local elite support, the Russian operation accelerated, with hundreds (perhaps even thousands) of soldiers arriving (Beckhusen 2014). Russian troops seized the military airport in Sevastopol, the civilian airport in Simferopol, and the state television/radio complex, they severed telephone lines to the mainland, and blocked roads connecting continental Ukraine to Crimea (Weaver, Buckley, and Hille 2014). Russian attack helicopters and military transport planes crossed into Ukrainian airspace over Crimea, without asking permission, bringing with them as many as 1,500 special troops (Lavrov 2015b).[23]

A meeting of the National Security and Defense Council of Ukraine was held in Kyiv on February 28. The mood of participants was despondent (Shamanska 2016). Freshly appointed officials conceded that they barely had any reliable forces on the ground to mount resistance.[24] They were also convinced that the majority of Crimeans would side with Russia. Valentin Nalyvaichenko, head of the Security Service (SBU), was blunt: the local population "massively" supported Russia's actions. Interior Minister Avakov concurred: "The majority of the Crimean population is pro-Russian, anti-Ukrainian."[25] Most army troops were locals (a consequence of the autonomous

---

[23] The Russian government claimed that sending troops to the Sevastopol territory leased by Russia for its navy was allowed under the 1997 Russia–Ukraine Treaty regulating the Black Sea Fleet. The treaty required that Ukraine be notified in advance of large troop movements (Gorenburg 2014) and explicitly forbade Russian forces from "interfer[ing] in Ukraine's internal affairs" (Shreck 2019).

[24] With the exception of Arsen Avakov, named on February 22, the new government, including the defense minister, was appointed on February 27, the day Russian special forces seized the Crimean parliament.

[25] All the quotations in this paragraph are translated from the stenographic report of the meeting in the original Ukrainian (Shtorhin 2019).

status of Crimea within Ukraine) and, along with policemen, were from a social milieu sympathetic to the Russian version of events. Avakov announced that "very few" policemen had not defected, with the hopeful exception of a thousand uniforms who, "I hope, will be able to carry out orders." Nalyvaichenko said that the Berkut troops "and other law enforcement officers" had also immediately gone over to the Russian side. Acting Defense Minister Ihor Tenyukh unceremoniously stated: "Today we do not have an army." Though the Ukrainian army had more than 13,000 soldiers stationed in Crimea, he estimated that fewer than 2,000 were capable of fighting, which paled in comparison with the 20,000 troops that the Russian army had brought in under the auspices of the Black Sea Fleet. In the words of Prime Minister Arseniy Yatsenyuk: "We are not ready for a military operation, unfortunately. And the Russians know it." In the whole of Ukraine, only 5,000 troops were combat-ready.[26] The meeting concluded with the sobering realization that Ukraine was essentially on its own against the Russian military. "No country … is ready to help Ukraine right now," said Yatsenyuk. Officials from the United States and Germany cautioned Ukraine against the use of force.[27] At the meeting, only Turchynov voted in favor of declaring a state of emergency in Crimea.

The following day, March 1, the Russian Foreign Ministry released a short statement claiming that "armed people sent from Kyiv" had attempted to storm the building of the Crimean Ministry of Internal Affairs, resulting in several casualties. According to the Foreign Ministry, the attempt failed due to the "decisive actions of self-defense units" (Ministerstvo inostrannykh del Rossiiskoi Federatsii 2014c).

---

[26] Tenyukh ascribed the sorry state of the Ukrainian military to a conscious plan by Yanukovych and the Party of Regions to weaken state institutions. This stance, which became part of the standard Ukrainian government version of events in the following years, overlooked the simple fact that Ukrainian military officials, in the decades since independence, never planned seriously for a war with Russia – or indeed with anyone. The strongest elements of the army were trained in conjunction with NATO to serve in UN peacekeeping missions abroad, but this had no impact on domestic military readiness.

[27] The thinking was that military resistance would embolden Putin to expand his military intervention, as had occurred in 2008 during the war over Ossetia, when Russian forces entered two other Georgian provinces (Rogin and Lake 2015).

There is no evidence that these events occurred (Shuster 2014a). The statement also blamed "well-known political circles" in Kyiv for aiming to destabilize the situation in Crimea. The new Crimean Prime Minister Aksyonov then released a statement asserting that his security forces could not control the situation due to the presence of "unidentified armed groups" causing "riots" (*besporiadki*). He appealed to Putin to "assist in ensuring peace and tranquility in [Crimea]" (KIANews 2014).

Moscow used the political appeal from Aksyonov as the (retroactive) legal basis for a military intervention. The legal sequencing, in the Russian narrative, was straightforward: that same day, Putin sent an official appeal to the Russian Senate "to use the Armed Forces of the Russian Federation on the territory of Ukraine until the social and political situation in that country is normalized" (Prezident Rossii 2014b). The appeal implied that Ukraine was without a legitimate government, an anarchic situation which posed a great risk to the population (Trenin 2014a). The request was swiftly granted by the Senate. The resolution sent a powerful message to Russian-speakers in Eastern Ukraine that Russia was ready to intervene militarily anywhere in Ukraine to counter a threat, since it used the vague formulation "on the territory of Ukraine," instead of specifically Crimea. The threat was presented as armed aggression by Ukrainian militant nationalists seeking revenge against vulnerable Russian-speakers.

Two days later, Vitaly Churkin, Russia's Permanent Representative to the United Nations, submitted a document to the UN Security Council that purported to be a signed statement (*Zaiva*) by Viktor Yanukovych, from his exile in Russia, to Vladimir Putin. The document claimed that "the illegal seizure of power in Kyiv has brought Ukraine to the brink of civil war," and that "people's lives, safety and human rights are under threat." It appealed to Putin to "use the Armed Forces of the Russian Federation to restore legitimacy, peace, law and order, stability and protection of the Ukrainian population" (United Nations Security Council 2014).[28] In a press briefing on March

---

[28] When Yanukovych was later put on trial in Ukraine (*in absentia*, since he remained in exile in Russia) on charges of treason, his lawyers released a second, longer letter written by him to Putin on March 1, 2014, asking Russia to deploy a "police peacekeeping mission" on the basis of the 1997 Treaty of Friendship and Cooperation between Ukraine and the Russian Federation

4, Putin made it clear that he considered Yanukovych the "current legitimate president," and that his appeal for protection was "entirely legitimate" (Coynash 2018c). The argument held absolutely no water with any of the other members of the UN Security Council during an emergency meeting on March 3, however. All fourteen denounced Russia's claim to a right to military intervention. China insisted on the principle of "non-interference in the domestic affairs of a state" (Geneste 2014).

The Final Cascade

Events on the ground in Crimea proceeded at breakneck speed. On March 1, Aksyonov declared himself in charge of all security institutions (KIANews 2014). On March 2, merely three days after becoming prime minister, he swore in new acting heads of the Ministry of Internal Affairs, SBU, Emergency Service, and Border Service to serve "the people of Crimea" (*Russkoe edinstvo* 2014). In Sevastopol, Denis Berezovsky, appointed Commander of the Naval Forces of Ukraine the day before, defected to the Russian Black Sea Fleet (BBC 2014a).

The scope and swiftness of defection among Crimean officials was startling: Table 5.1 provides a breakdown of the 70 percent of security personnel, serving in various agencies, who went over to the new authorities (*Ukrinform* 2016a).[29] This included 85 percent of SBU officers, who went on to work for the Russian Federal Security Service (FSB), an event described as having "no parallel in the history of special services" (Shiriaev 2016). The scale of political defections was equally high. When the Crimean parliament declared "independence" (*nezavizimost'*) on March 11, nearly 80 percent (i.e., seventy-eight of the eighty-one MPs present – nineteen were absent) voted in favor.[30]

(Tsymbaliuk 2018; UNIAN 2018). Russia later claimed that it never formally received Yanukovych's letter (Coynash 2018c), despite the fact that it had been deposited in the UN digital archives (United Nations Security Council 2014). Yanukovych was convicted of treason by a Ukrainian court in 2019.

[29] For many, the choice was simply a practical one. They were locals, owned property, had no relatives on the mainland, and were offered better pay and perks (Lavrov 2015b, 179).

[30] This suggested that the several dozen deputies who either did not attend or were forced to attend the aborted February 26 session and the decisive one on February 27 had since rallied to the cause of separation from Ukraine.

Table 5.1 *Defections from Ukraine's state security services*

Types of security forces	Armed Forces of Ukraine	State Border Guard Service of Ukraine	National Guard of Ukraine	State security admin.	Security Service of Ukraine (uniforms/officers)	State Space Agency	Total
Soldiers present in Feb. 2014	13,468	1,870	2,560	1,614	527	247	20,286
Soldiers who did *not* defect to Russia	3,990 (30%)	519 (28%)	1,177 (46%)	20 (1%)	242 (46%)	61 (22%)	6,009 (30%)

Note: From Shiriaev (2016).

The Crimean branch of the Party of Regions, which had ceased to function as a distinct entity, organically merged with United Russia, the ruling party in Russia, after March 18, with the overwhelming majority of its officials keeping their positions (Loiko 2016).

On March 6, the Crimean parliament announced that the referendum would take place much earlier – on March 16 – and that the question was now one of "reunification" (*vossoedinenie*) with Russia. The initial call for a referendum, on February 27, merely a week earlier, had formally been for enhanced powers within Ukraine, even though the reality of the military takeover excluded any possible negotiations. By February 28, a draft law had been submitted to the Russian parliament allowing the Russian state to unilaterally annex a territory belonging to another state, instead of making it contingent on an agreement between those two states, as previous legislation had stipulated (Galimova 2015). It appears likely that the decision to annex Crimea was made in Moscow around March 3–4 (Galimova 2015), presumably after it became clear that Russian units would encounter no military or civilian resistance, and that Crimean political and security elites supported annexation.[31]

The referendum invited people to agree with one of two options presented in the form of questions. The first question asked whether voters were in favor of "reunification with Russia." The second was whether they supported the reinstatement of the 1992 Constitution of Crimea "as part of Ukraine" (Coynash 2016b). While the latter could have been interpreted as a vote against separation from Ukraine, the 1992 Constitution had granted the Crimean parliament complete "sovereign" powers, and the current parliament had already declared independence and expressed its preference for reunification with Russia on March 11 (Bialik 2014; BBC News Russkaia sluzhba 2014).[32] In other

---

[31] There is some evidence that the Crimean "self-defense" militia was strictly forbidden from speaking openly about reunification, or even using the Russian flag, until March 6 (Loiko 2016).

[32] There were actually two versions of the Crimean Constitution drafted in 1992: a more maximalist one, during a political confrontation with Kyiv, and another after the autonomous status was enhanced. The second option on the 2014 ballot did not specify which one would apply (Umland 2018). Our simple model prediction is not this nuanced, of course – we can only make much cruder sorts of statements (e.g., $a = 1$, $p + aC > 1$, $x^* = 1$, K accepted anyway).

words, the two options pointed to a single practical outcome. The referendum was held under conditions where no public debate was possible.[33] The Organization for Security and Co-operation in Europe (OSCE) electoral observation mission to Ukraine was also prevented entry into Crimea (*Gov.uk* 2014). The referendum appeared more like a plebiscite with a predetermined outcome.

To no one's surprise, the authorities announced a nearly unanimous vote (97 percent) in favor of reunification with Russia. These implausibly high results conflicted with the much lower estimates of a rapporteur of the Russian Presidential Human Rights Council.[34] Yet the die was cast. Within twenty-four hours Vladimir Putin welcomed Crimea as a new "subject" of the Russian Federation at a ceremonial event in Moscow (Prezident Rossii 2014a). Western powers and international bodies declared the referendum illegal on the grounds that it violated the territorial integrity of Ukraine. Russia vetoed a UN Security Council draft resolution to this effect on March 15 (with China abstaining), but a similar resolution was adopted by the General Assembly on March 27 (United Nations 2014; United Nations Meetings Coverage and Press Releases 2014). On March 17, the EU determined that the referendum was illegal, issuing sanctions against individuals and "entities or bodies associated with them" (e.g., companies of pro-Putin corporate oligarchs) that had taken actions "which undermine or threaten the territorial integrity, sovereignty and independence of Ukraine" (Council of the European Union 2014a).[35]

---

[33] Russian special forces seized the state-owned television channel, TRC Krym, on March 1. The largest independent channel, Chornomorska, was shut down on March 3. The national Ukrainian channels were disconnected on March 6 (Coynash 2014). The only television and radio channels that could be picked up on regular airwaves were under Russian or Crimean government control.

[34] In a report following a field investigation in Crimea, Yevgenyi Bobrov estimated the turnout during the referendum to be in the 30–50 percent range, and the support for reunification as between 50 and 60 percent (and up to 80 percent in Sevastopol). Later on, the Human Rights Council posted a statement calling into question the "objectivity" of the "personal" observations of the rapporteur (Bobrov 2014).

[35] On March 21, the Venice Commission, the legal advisory board of the Council of Europe, provided the full legal reasoning, which boiled down to the following: the Ukrainian Constitution did not allow the holding of a local

After the referendum, there were still pockets of loyal Ukrainian military forces, primarily confined to a few bases. A shooting on March 18 left two dead, and revealed the potential for further needless death. On March 19, the government of Ukraine announced that loyal units of the Ukrainian military would withdraw to safety through secured corridors. By March 26, these units had completed their retreat across the now-disputed border.

Conclusion

An authoritative strand of the literature argues that the annexation of Crimea was guided by a long-term geostrategic imperative: that it would be intolerable for Russia to lose access to a warm water port for its Black Sea Fleet if a Europe-oriented Ukraine were to be invited to join NATO (Ignatieff 2014; Lukyanov 2014; Mearsheimer 2014).[36] In this view, NATO expansion eastward, over the constant and bitter objections of Russia, had reached an unacceptable limit, and, when Putin felt he was losing Ukraine, "the spring snap[ped] back hard," as he himself put it (*Washington Post* 2014).

This is not the argument that Russians themselves made at the time, however. Once the Crimean referendum was a fait accompli, Putin's retelling of events in his March 18 speech celebrating Crimea's "homecoming" emphasized both the humanitarian nature of the intervention (including the invocation of familiar Responsibility to Protect arguments), and the defensive, reactive response to NATO expansion.[37]

---

referendum on secession, rendering the referendum unconstitutional (Venice Commission 2014). The United States and Canada also announced sanctions justified on nearly identical grounds. The behavior of the Bank of Russia immediately prior the Crimean independence referendum suggests that the Kremlin anticipated these sanctions (Johnson 2016, 256).

[36] Treisman (2018) holds a subtly different view: that Russia seized Crimea not because it necessarily feared that Ukraine would join NATO, but that a nationalist Ukrainian government would terminate the lease agreement over Sevastopol.

[37] Putin rhetorically asked what the prospects of Ukraine joining NATO "would have meant for Crimea and Sevastopol in the future? It would have meant that NATO's navy would be right there in this city of Russia's military glory and this would create not an illusory but a perfectly real threat to the whole of southern Russia" (*Washington Post* 2014). See also Toal (2017, 223–32).

During the month immediately preceding the Crimean referendum, the Kremlin's disciplined public diplomacy messaging had prepositioned arguments that would allow Russia to underscore the humanitarian nature of the intervention, notably the claim that residents of Ukraine were under threat from forces unleashed by Maidan. For Putin, the 2008 recognition of Kosovo had created a useful precedent. In his March 18 speech in the Kremlin on the annexation of Crimea, Putin quoted American diplomats, who argued in a 2009 submission to the International Court of Justice, that "declarations of independence may, and often do, violate domestic legislation. However, this does not make them violations of international law." Crimeans, Putin claimed, had that same unilateral right to demand protection from Russia, and to be annexed according to principles of self-determination (Dubinsky and Rutland 2019).

Did Crimea break with Kyiv on its own, and then ask Russia for help? Not exactly. After a mass demonstration prevented the Crimean parliament from enacting such a scenario, Russian special forces arrived the following morning. Meeting no resistance, they secured parliament, and installed a pro-Russia government. Within thirty-six hours, the new government issued the call for help. Elites in the Party of Regions, initially divided over the appropriateness of the operation, fell in line in short order. The vast majority of security personnel, including the Black Sea Fleet, defected. Elites from the collapsing Party of Regions then held a hastily organized voting exercise carried out under conditions approximating martial law. Afterwards, Russia declared the matter closed. It is unlikely that local coordination on sedition in Crimea would have occurred had it not been facilitated by Russian military activity. It is most unlikely that the claim of 97 percent support represents the legitimate "will of the people" living on the peninsula.

However, Crimea did not present a difficult operational environment for Russian special forces. They quickly identified high-status elites in the Party of Regions, the Black Sea Fleet, and Russian nationalist networks sympathetic to sedition. They found many willing and capable partners, and encountered very few heroic solo resisters. There were no riots, and just a few shots fired. Russian soldiers were not ambushed, humiliated, or attacked in the streets. Once community-level "tips" took place, and it was clear that there was no pro-Maidan street power, there was really nothing the government in Kyiv felt it could do. Crimea was not a site of civil war violence.

Nowhere else in Eastern Ukraine would the matter be resolved so neatly. The Russian government may have wanted to replicate the success of Crimea. Instead of legitimate partners among oligarchs and local officials, for the most part, the potential allies who came out of nowhere tended to be a mix of far-right Russian nationalists, unruly militiamen, soldiers of fortune, and biker gangs – anarchic outcomes that will be outlined in Chapter 6.

6 | "The Russian Spring" (Eastern Ukraine)

The salient question for Ukrainian territorial unity after Maidan, and especially after Crimea, was how Russian-speakers who were tempted to self-identify politically as Russians would interpret the events that had just occurred. The Russian media was providing a comprehensive script for Russian-speakers to perform in order to engage in *sedition*, and call for help – but who would heed the call? The purpose of this chapter is to document the numerous dogs that did not bark. Most Russian-speaking communities failed to tip toward sedition. These failed attempts at post-Maidan resistance should not be omitted from the dominant and narrow focus on Crimea and Donbas, and we hope the evidence in this chapter contributes to a more complete historical picture.

This chapter details how and why Russian-speaking elites gradually came to coordinate against sedition. Donbas is the part of Ukraine where, in the language of our model, elites did not coordinate on *sedition* in the first period, but pressure for sedition came from the street and proved stronger than elsewhere in Eastern Ukraine. To clarify: the "street" is not public opinion, but rather the capacity to mobilize and to engage using intimidation and violence. There is little evidence that Eastern Ukrainian public opinion was trending seditionist, but the street certainly did, at least in the early going – less so in Odesa and Kharkiv than in Donbas. The result was a costly standoff. Eventually, Russia intervened.

The current chapter describes the politics across the oblasts of continental Eastern Ukraine, including Donbas up to the start of the actual war. Coordinated sedition failed due to many complex factors, but we emphasize five: (1) mixed Russian signals about whether or where support for an insurgency would arrive; (2) the collapse of the institutional authority of the Party of Regions; (3) inconsistent behavior and resolve on the part of an unsteady new government in Kyiv, which resulted in some preventable policing failures but never in mass repression or police units firing into crowds; (4) fear of the consequences,

121

as everyone observed pitched battles on the streets of Eastern oblast capitals; and (5) uncertainty about what elites would do. The net effect was that *sedition* did not spread like a contagion.

This chapter focuses on the parts of Ukraine where Russian-speaking communities predominated. Pro-Russian activists were jockeying to emerge as dominant voices. The chapter describes a gradual testing of the waters but, ultimately, a decision against sedition almost everywhere. To build a tractable analytic model, in Appendix A we reduce the choice set to a binary decision (being against or for the post-Maidan state, *sedition* or against /*sedition*/). In so doing, we conflate a large repertoire of non-seditious acts. In lived experience, these behaviors would range from passive silence to active defense of the state, with many gradations between. Some anti-seditionist elites were fence-sitters, waiting for the dominos to fall on one side or the other. In different communities, anti-seditionist elites took to the streets and led from the front. Anti-seditionist coordination efforts could be subtle, like peaceful protests to memorialize police officers killed on Maidan, or overt, such as forming self-defense units or giving anti-Putin sermons.

Since the presence of these pro-Ukraine street groups deterred some performances of *sedition* (μ), there was likely preference falsification afterwards, too. This is true for both in communities that "tipped" (in the Donbas and Crimea) and the communities that did not. Once others' strategies are clarified, elites have incentives to pretend that they had been against /*sedition*/ (or for *sedition* in areas that tipped!) all along. This makes the exercise of retrospectively reconstructing events through the use of surveys or first-person accounts fraught. There are, however, sufficient credible observational accounts of the politics as they unfolded to anchor a causal narrative. We provide a variety of evidence in this chapter consistent with the claim that elites in Kyiv and Eastern Ukraine, as well as pro-Russian protesters and street fighters, second-guessed each other and Russia in the days and months after Yanukovych was removed. Uncertainty about what Russia would do in response to various moves and countermoves was central to strategic calculations.

In which areas was an uprising a practical concern? Essentially, in the South and East. Map 6.1 illustrates the geographical distribution of large-scale anti-Maidan protest activities that occurred during the period described in Chapters 7 and 8 (February 22 through early September).[1]

---

[1] The figure was constructed using raw data from Ishchenko et al. (2018).

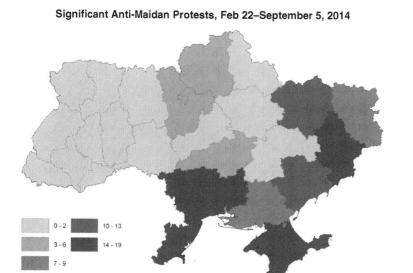

Significant Anti-Maidan Protests, Feb 22–September 5, 2014

0 - 2
3 - 6
7 - 9
10 - 13
14 - 19

Data Source: Ischenko et al (2018)

Map 6.1 East–West variation in views of post-Maidan regime legitimacy

It bears an eerie resemblance to Map 3.1, which provided a visualization of the proportion of ethnic Russians across Ukrainian oblasts. Observers at the time presented contested, sometimes misleading, interpretations of these demonstrations. We hope our account clarifies two contested historical points.

The first is the political goal of the anti-Maidan protesters. Many activists were putting pressure on their representatives to have their voices heard in the disorienting new post-Maidan reality. The most visible protest participants did wish to separate from the center violently – but not everyone. Separation was never a popular position among economic elites or the rump institutional Party of Regions. The crude slogans and performances of *sedition*, even when they were shouted on the street, contrast with the nuanced bargaining positions that emerged from elite factions, especially in Donetsk.

The second contested point is the role that Russian agents played in the protests. We could not find convincing evidence supporting the claim that Russia orchestrated these protests directly. Russian policy elites seem to have been banking on a scenario that did not come to pass: Ukraine splitting along regional/linguistic lines, with regional elites previously associated with the now-defunct Party of Regions retaining their local influence to provide Russia with an institutional agent on the ground. After the green light sent by Crimea, the Kremlin was probably surprised to see a rebellion originate in, and then be confined to, Eastern Donbas. Based on what we document in this chapter, it is hard to impute a carefully constructed plan for the Russian Spring. To provide warrants for this claim, we must wind the clock back from mid-March to February, and resume the narrative in Kyiv. The locus of action will shift quickly to Kharkiv, before the narrative expands to include the main squares of other Eastern urban centers.

The Failed Resuscitation of the Party of Regions

Viktor Yanukovych lost control of his government hours after the sniper massacre on February 20, 2014. About a fifth of Party of Regions MPs broke ranks that day, attending a parliamentary session halting the government effort to suppress Maidan. The party did not immediately disintegrate, however. On February 22, 73 percent of the remaining 134 MPs were not present for the vote removing Yanukovych as president. The following day, the rump fraction accused Yanukovych of treason, and declared itself in favor of a "united, strong, and independent Ukraine" (*Ukrains'ka pravda* 2014o).

In retrospect, the best chance for an elite-driven regional challenge to Kyiv would have been to keep pre-Maidan institutions intact to facilitate coordination. Yanukovych might have been a focal point for resistance: Residual regime loyalists in the state security service and the military, established crony networks, and a well-oiled favor economy based on the Party of Regions machinery would have been able to mobilize an insurgency that the Kremlin could have recognized and assisted as the legitimate Ukrainian government. Instead, at the end of February 21, with political defections multiplying, Yanukovych fled for Kharkiv by helicopter.[2]

Why Kharkiv? Ukraine's second largest city, near the Russian border, had a sizeable proportion of self-defining ethnic Russians (about 25 percent), and a majority of Russian-speakers. After violence broke out in Kyiv in January 2014, Kharkiv officials also revealed themselves

---

[2] As we saw in Chapter 4, the entire police force had abandoned all guard duties by this point (Higgins, Kramer, and Erlanger 2014). Yanukovych later claimed he feared for his life (*Ukrains'kyi tyzhden* 2018).

as the most outspokenly anti-Maidan community anywhere in Ukraine other than Crimea. On February 1, Governor Mykhailo Dobkin announced the formation of an anti-Maidan "Ukrainian Front." The Front called Maidan protesters "occupiers" who must be "cleansed from Ukrainian lands," and demanded their "unconditional withdrawal from public buildings and squares" across Ukraine (Kozachenko 2014b; *Gordon* 2014b). Its symbol was the Ribbon of Saint George, identified with the Soviet victory against Nazi Germany in World War II (Hudzik 2014), emphasizing commonality with Russia against the Western-oriented Euromaidan. On February 10, the Front announced the creation of a "national guard."[3] On February 20, the new movement issued a call for a "general mobilization" of the "guard" to "defend the Constitutional order" (Kozachenko 2014a). The "Ukrainian Front" was planning a "Congress of People's Deputies" from the Southeastern oblasts on February 22 in Kharkiv.

When the Yanukovych government suddenly fell, the planned Congress now became the best opportunity to coordinate resistance, repeating the script followed after the 2004 Orange Revolution (see Chapter 3). Russian TV broadcast the Congress live. The tone of speeches embraced the emerging Russian narrative that a coup was being orchestrated in Kyiv. After official speeches, a resolution, written in advance in Russian only and voted on without discussion, proclaimed that the Ukrainian parliament was working "in conditions of terror, under the threat of weapons and murder," raising doubts about the "legitimacy and legality" of its decisions. The resolution called for local and regional councils in the Southeast to cease to recognize the authority of the central government "until the reestablishment of the constitutional order" (*Mediaport* 2014a). Kharkiv officials seem to have believed that they were provoking a constitutional confrontation on their own terms.[4] What was taking shape was an ultimatum to the center launched from the periphery, just as our model assumes.

---

[3] In practice, this meant that civilians, working in conjunction with the police, were bussed in to intimidate and attack protesters in Kyiv (Butusov 2014). Street bullies hired by the state to harass and beat protesters were active during the Kyiv Maidan. Butusov claims many "street fighting men" who assisted the police were from this Kharkiv "national guard."

[4] A local observer noted that the resolution was actually not as radical as it could have been, since it avoided a direct demand of "federalization" (*Obozrevatel* 2014). As a declaration of intent to disobey orders from Kyiv, however, its purpose was clear (Shuster 2014b). Calling on nationally elected deputies to

Yet nothing was more striking at the Congress than Yanukovych's absence. He had, as everyone knew by then, fled to Kharkiv the night before. Yanukovych reportedly spent most of the night of February 21–22 at the residence of Kharkiv governor Dobkin. The governor apparently convinced Yanukovych not to attend the Congress – not due to security concerns, but because he feared a public shaming by the Party of Regions members about to be assembled (Koshkina 2015, 123). The Maidan killings, and the cumulative weight of months of inept response to opposition street power, had sapped party morale and cost Yanukovych the confidence of his own party's inner circle. Yanukovych then went into hiding. A few hours later, after announcing – by video from an undisclosed location – that he was staying in Ukraine (*Ukrains'ka pravda* 2014u), Yanukovych left for Donetsk, where he was prevented from boarding a flight to Russia. He was then driven by car to Crimea, met with officers from the Black Sea Fleet, and was smuggled into Russia.

Congress organizers attempted to proceed without Yanukovych's leadership, setting up an outdoor stage near the premises, with a plan to address thousands of supporters.[5] In the meantime, however, pro-Maidan crowds started to mobilize in the streets of Kharkiv. They congregated a single metro station away, and started a march toward the outdoor stage. Fearing a confrontation, Congress organizers cancelled the speeches, and were whisked away in official cars (Koshkina 2015, 124). The threat of spontaneously organized pro-Kyiv violence had disrupted elite coordination.

On the following day, the rump Party of Regions in Kyiv denounced Yanukovych, implicitly recognizing the legitimacy of the new governing coalition. The whereabouts of two important Kharkiv officials, Governor Dobkin and Mayor Hennadiy Kernes, remained unclear. On their return in the evening, they expressed their loyalty to the new Maidan government.[6] The Donetsk governor followed suit. In

---

return to their district, as the resolution did as well, would, minimally, have prevented the Rada from reaching a quorum, functionally paralyzing its work (Socor 2014b).

[5] Some supporters had cell phones and other devices ready to record and archive the event on social media. As a result, many videos remain on YouTube documenting a handful of pro-Congress people milling around an empty stage, as anti-Congress marchers shout.

[6] The appointment of Arsen Avakov, a former governor of Kharkiv, as the Maidan government's interior minister may have played a role in the political about-face of these Kharkiv elites. Dobkin resigned on February 26, replaced

Crimea, the wind was blowing in the other direction, but it seems the Crimean elite initially banked on a coordinated Southeastern rebellion, not secession. Crimea had sent a delegation to the Kharkiv Congress. Within twenty-four hours, with Yanukovych gone and the Kharkiv leaders backtracking, the situation "radically changed" and Crimean separation was suddenly on the agenda.[7] The Kharkiv plan for coordinated regional defiance against the new government appeared to be stillborn.

Into the Institutional Void

As it was becoming clear that Party of Regions elites were hesitant to engage in overt *sedition*, pro- and anti-Maidan forces began to clash. Politics spilled onto the streets. On February 23, pro-Maidan protesters in Kharkiv occupied the regional administration building (the Oblast State Administration, or ODA) on Freedom Square, demanding the resignation of the governor and mayor. The police offered no resistance. Across the square, pro-Russian activists set up a barricade around the Lenin statue.[8] Street fighting erupted on February 25, with the Kharkiv football ultras providing the muscle on the pro-Maidan side (Carroll 2014).

The street was also becoming active in Donetsk. A young entrepreneur, Pavel Gubarev, had attended the Kharkiv Congress as an observer. The "ridiculous spectacle" persuaded him that the Party of Regions elite was finished. Resistance to the Maidan regime change would have to occur outside official channels (Gubarev 2016, 81–5). Gubarev, who earlier in his life had flirted with radical right politics in Russia (Balmforth 2014), used his personal savings and contacts among graduates of the history faculty at Donetsk University to set up a "People's

---

by an associate of Avakov. Ukrainian oligarch Ihor Kolomoyskyi later claimed that he flew Kernes to his residence in Switzerland and convinced him to switch his allegiance to Maidan (Carroll 2015). The story has not been corroborated.

[7] The citation is from Mikhail Chalyi, brother of the Sevastopol well-known businessman and "people's mayor" Aleksei Chalyi who took over the reins of the City Council (Zhigulev, Sivtsova, and Skibitskaia 2017). See Chapter 5.

[8] A wave of Lenin statues being forcibly brought down (*Leninopad*) was picking up steam across Ukraine (Pshenychnykh 2020; Kutkina 2021). The pro-Russian militants were seeking to prevent that. The statue was eventually removed by the authorities in the fall.

Militia of Donbas" (Narodnoe opolchenie Donbassa).[9] Through social media, he boldly issued an "ultimatum" to the Donetsk City Council to implement the Kharkiv Congress resolution that refused to recognize the new government in Kyiv (*Za Donbass* 2014). Invited to speak at a session of the council on February 27, Gubarev warned party officials that, if they failed to oppose Kyiv, no one would defend them when Maidan radicals descended on Donetsk (Gubarev 2016, 92).

Donetsk Party of Regions local officials had never really had to justify themselves directly to people like Gubarev. Their legitimacy came from a promise that they could shape policy at the center to the benefit of their core voter constituents. In the past week, however, the Donetsk top brass had been abruptly and visibly ejected from power in Kyiv. Donetsk was soon to be completely shut out of power. There was no Donetsk representation at all in the new cabinet. The priority annulment of the 2012 language law had added symbolic power to what was seen as a looming political threat emanating from Kyiv. (The law, after all, had been a Donetsk creation.) Its repeal was interpreted by many in the East as a signal that hardline elements of Maidan were locking in their victory and bringing in "their" people by imposing the use of Ukrainian in state offices (see Chapter 3). There was also a major development: by the time Gubarev addressed the City Council, Russian special forces had seized the Crimean parliament.

On March 1, on the day that the Russian Senate granted Putin's official request to send Russian troops to Ukraine, massive demonstrations rocked both Kharkiv and Donetsk, as well as Odesa, Luhansk, and a slew of smaller towns in Eastern Ukraine. The most violent protest took place in Kharkiv. The governor's building (ODA) had by then been occupied by pro-Maidan activists for an entire week. On March 1, dozens of men, egged on by a crowd of a few thousands chanting "Thank you, Berkut," "Russia," and "Referendum," attacked the ODA with bats and stones. The Maidan occupiers were ejected as the police looked on (Sokolins'ka 2016). The pro-Maidan militants were pelted with garbage, forced to apologize on their knees, and beaten (Yurovskaia 2014).[10] The pro-Russian militants did not occupy the state building,

---

[9] Though the term *opolchenie* hails back to early seventeenth-century popular resistance during a Polish invasion of Russia, it was widely used in World War II to define ordinary people fighting German invaders.

[10] These acts of public humiliation were violent reenactments of rituals performed days earlier in several cities of Western Ukraine, and widely seen

however. They did not quite have the numbers to hold it. In the following days, the regional parliament refused to call an extraordinary session to address the demands by pro-Russian protesters (*Versii.com* 2014).

In Donetsk, the elite also found itself outflanked by the street. The local Party of Regions initially used "administrative resources" to organize a commemoration for the policemen killed on Maidan (Baranov 2018).[11] This was a symbolic challenge to the ceremonies, improvised memorial shrines, and open-air museums on the Kyiv Maidan honoring the victims of police violence. Contra the threatening street politics and explicit Russian symbols on display in Kharkiv, Donetsk elites were attempting to create and institutionalize a counterhegemonic interpretation of Maidan in a scripted and staged Soviet style. There were familiar speakers standing in front of familiar buildings. There were not yet Russian flags (this would quickly change.) A private security detail protected the stage, and the organizers would not allow the self-declared *opolchenie* (militia) leader Gubarev to speak. After he forced his way to the microphone, a scuffle ensued. Gubarev's supporters prevailed over the Party of Regions bodyguards.

The *opolchenie* had hijacked the rally.[12] Gubarev called for local officials to be dismissed, proclaimed himself "People's Governor," and denounced the Maidan "coup." The crowd chanted "Russia" (*Ros-si-ia*), and began to walk toward the governor's building (ODA), where other demonstrators had gathered. The assembly grew to as many as 10,000 people (*UAInfo* 2016).[13] The protesters' demands were simple: They

---

on TV and social media. In these incidents, officers of the special police unit Berkut, as they returned from the Kyiv Maidan, were brought on stage in front of thousands-strong crowds. In scenes replete with religious symbolism, the officers were asked to kneel in order to beg for forgiveness from the "Ukrainian people" (*TSN* 2014a; *Volyns'ki novyny* 2014b).

[11] Administrative resources (*adminresursy*) refers to the practice of using state assets for partisan advantage. A standard tool was to summon employees in state-owned enterprises to attend official events.

[12] The bodyguards were recruited from the same social milieu of subproletarian and uneducated enforcers that were employed as *titushki* by the regime in Kyiv to harass protesters just weeks earlier. In his private writings, the anti-Maidan Gubarev was just as contemptuous of these lower class *titushki* as Maidan protesters had been (Ishchenko 2014), framing his own followers as politically conscious, serious, and educated (Gubarev 2016, 83–92).

[13] This was a small fraction of the numbers at Maidan, and yet by far the largest demonstration in Donetsk (excepting strikes managed by the authorities) since Ukrainian independence.

wanted their regional government to defy Kyiv (overt *sedition*) and were symbolically identifying with Russia. They even succeeded in replacing the Ukrainian flag with the Russian flag atop the ODA building.

Under pressure, the Donetsk City Council met in an extraordinary session. At the end of the day, Donetsk mayor Oleksandr Lukyanchenko announced to the crowd that the council had heeded their demands. This was partially true. The council agreed to two demands: that Russian be granted official status (a longstanding Donetsk grievance) and that a "city militia" (modeled after "self-defense" groups) be created "to defend against nationalists." On the question of a referendum on independence, secession, or federation, however, the council hedged. While it declared support for "people's initiatives (*narodnye initsiativy*)," it merely appealed to the Donetsk Oblast Council (Oblrada – the regional parliament) "with a request to hold a referendum" whose content was left unspecified (*UAInfo* 2016).

With thousands of protesters outside the building, the Oblrada met two days later and adopted a resolution carefully written to stay within the bounds of the Ukrainian constitution.[14] The resolution requested the Verkhovna Rada in Kyiv to amend the law on local referendums to allow Donetsk to conduct one. This was a far cry from the behavior a week earlier in Simferopol when the Crimean parliament unilaterally voted to hold a referendum (contravening Ukrainian law). Gubarev was now explicitly calling for a referendum "to join Russia" (*RBK* 2014b) but the resolution would have none of it: "We condemn the secessionist statements (*raskol'nicheskie zaiavleniia*) or the calls for the separation of Donetsk oblast' from Ukraine!" (*Ostrov* 2014). Enraged by the refusal of the regional council to break with the post-Maidan government, protesters stormed the ODA on March 3 – and were cleared by the police in short order. When they tried again on March 5, Ukraine's State Security Service (SBU) arrested seventy of them, including Gubarev (*Vgorode* 2014a). For the most part, Donetsk officials held fast, using street pressure to demand more autonomy from Kyiv, but without engaging in open rebellion. Elites were trying to harness the energy of the street to gain leverage in their official bargaining with other elites at the center.[15]

---

[14] The resolution stated that "the decision was taken without discussion due to the fact that the work of the session was disrupted by Pavel Gubarev."

[15] An alternative reading is that in seeking to bargain with Kyiv, Donetsk elites gave impetus to street separatism. Matsuzato (2017, 190) wrote that "these generous compromises significantly helped the Novorussianists consolidate their position." Platonova (2020, 285) argues that the March 1 resolution (to request

Local elites also resisted street pressure in Odesa. March 1 saw parallel pro-Kyiv and pro-Russia demonstrations that remained peaceful (Tsiktor 2021). As in Kharkiv, the regional parliament (Oblsovet) held an extraordinary session on March 3. A crowd of more than 2,000 pro-Russian protesters gathered outside the regional government building (ODA), blocking the exits to prevent deputies from leaving until they acceded to their demands. Odesa governor Mykola Skoryk allowed the young pro-Russian protest leader Anton Davydchenko to address the council. The "Appeal to Odessans" that he read aloud was to break with Kyiv, take control of all security forces in the region, and announce a referendum (*Taimer* 2014) – echoing what had transpired in Crimea in the previous week. The parliament voted it down, with only 14 votes in favor out of 132 (Skorikov 2015). After several attempts, the deputies passed a resolution denouncing the entry of Russian troops in Crimea (Tsiktor 2021). They proved unable, however, to agree on a statement to be addressed to the Verkhovna Rada in Kyiv.

Unlike in Donetsk, pro-Russian street leaders opted not to storm Odesa's ODA building. Pro-Ukraine protesters arriving to match their rivals outside the building appeared to have been an important factor.[16] To deescalate the situation, Mykola Tyndiuk, the Oblrada Chair, and Davydchenko signed a statement establishing that a "coordinated council" would examine the protesters' demands, to be addressed at a new session of the regional parliament on March 6 (*Dumskaia* 2014). The Odesa governor was replaced with a Maidan loyalist on the following day. The March 6 session was cancelled and the Odesa parliament never formally voted on a resolution aimed at Kyiv. The pro-Russian protesters maintained a permanent tent city in a downtown park, eschewing street confrontations. Anton Davydchenko was arrested later in March.

In Luhansk, the smallest of the two provincial capitals in Donbas, a mass demonstration was also held on March 1, with protesters agitating for the same sort of radical anti-Maidan demands. The regional council held its own extraordinary session the following

---

the regional parliament to hold a referendum) "was clearly against the law." Our model assumes that regional elites for decades have used the Russia threat, implicitly or otherwise, in seeking to advance their position vis-à-vis the center.

[16] A pro-Russian protester claims that the pro-Ukraine camp came in full "Maidan self-defense" (shields, helmets, clubs, walked-in formation) while his camp was unprepared (Skorikov 2015). In other words, the street – understood here as those ready to engage in street fights – appeared to have been more pro-Ukraine than in the other major cities of the East.

day. As in Odesa, they were handed a resolution by protest leaders. This ambitious document called for a "radical transformation of the state," an "all-Union referendum" on the federalization of Ukraine, the disarming of "illegal military formations" (i.e., the Maidan "self-defense" groups), and the cessation of criminal investigations on the police "who fulfilled their duties" on Maidan (Lermontov 2014; *LiveJournal* 2014b). The council initially refused to consider this proposal, but demonstrators forcibly entered the gated territory of the ODA, blocked the entrances, and hoisted a Russian flag. Intimidated, the council adopted the resolution wholesale. The Luhansk Council became the only regional parliament in Eastern Ukraine to issue a formal challenge to the post-Maidan government in Kyiv.

There were some cross-regional trends in the anti-Maidan demonstrations that shook Eastern Ukrainian urban centers in early March 2014. All slogans were similar: referendum on the status of the region (sometimes couched as "federalization"), "self-defense" against "fascists," and official status for the Russian language. The chants of "Russia" (*Ro-ssi-ia*) and the ubiquitous presence of the Russian flag were difficult to misinterpret. Protesters usually demanded a special session of the regional parliament to address their demands, with differing degrees of success. Such sessions were held in Donetsk, Luhansk, and Odesa (not Kharkiv), with a menacing crowd outside and some protesters even getting inside.

Variation in compliance with radical street demands by elites that *did* convene special sessions is informative. Once they had established a quorum, the Odesa MPs refused to go along with what they had been handed. Those in Donetsk requested Kyiv *to allow them* to hold a referendum. In Luhansk, MPs caved and adopted the radical resolution, following in the seditious footsteps of Crimea. Everywhere else, local elites remained cautiously against sedition. Only Donetsk sought to openly engage in bargaining with the center. The street seemed to be tilting pro-Russian in many communities, and while the number of protesters paled in comparison to the Kyiv Maidan, this was an attempt to coordinate *sedition* that completely bypassed the Party of Regions as an institution. It was an ominous sign of what was to come in Donbas (see Chapter 7).

Returning to analytic narrative, we note three threads of the story arc that track the model. First, while the energy of the street was cacophonous, the elites that actually controlled the halls of regional government were adopting nuanced bargaining positions. Variation in these stances reflected variation in leverage. Luhansk, right on the

Russian border, was the single example of a community-level elite demand for extreme separation. Everywhere else, where p was lower, moderates proposed an intermediate bargain conspicuously short of full-throated *sedition*. Elites attempted to respond as they had before – to use street energy or the fear of disturbances to broker a better deal for their communities. They were now under street pressure, and the looming threat of a Russian invasion, but the playbook was the same.

Second, while there was tactical moderation of demands by strategic actors anxious about limiting violence, the stakes were understood to be existential and what was being bargained over was zero-sum (one side's gain was the other's loss). The grievances and slogans that motivated anti-Maidan activists to take to the streets had very little to do with trade policy. The threat was status reversals, the risk of reduced cultural autonomy for Russian-speaking communities, and "fascist" attacks from the Ukrainian core.

Third, in most localities, participants became aware that coordination on *sedition* was not forthcoming – and quite early on. Because the party institutions of cross-regional coordination had disintegrated, appeals were haphazard. The explosion of violence on the streets of some Russian-speaking communities was an emotional response by social forces who felt betrayed by the conservative (the phrase surely would have been "weak") behavior of "their" elites. Street forces appeared to be poised to bypass the institutions of the state on March 1–3. They did not, so a social tip to sedition did not occur anywhere – not yet. What followed instead was a rapid countermobilization by anti-*seditionist* militias, making sure the streets were contested. This contrasts with Crimea, where *seditious* elites could speak their minds assured by safety in numbers ($\mu=0$). The various displays of pro-Russia street energy uncorked on other Eastern Ukrainian streets did not go unchallenged ($\mu>0$). Neighborhood-level responses from self-organized pro-Maidan militia actors, particularly in Kharkiv and Odesa, were especially important.

Did Kremlin Agents Fail to Lead, or Did Locals Fail to Coordinate?

What role did Kremlin agents play in these early protests? Many claim the uprisings were orchestrated directly by subversive forces in Moscow's employ. If this is true, an analytic narrative emphasizing local agency rests on misleading assumptions, and the *real* action will require the opening of Russian state security archives. Certainly allegations that Russian military intelligence was pulling the strings of these pro-Russian street protests were (and remain) widespread. The initial claim was that many of the protesters were not really locals at all, but had been bussed in from nearby Russian oblasts (*Glavnoe* 2014; Kalinina 2014; Mykhailin and Vakulenko 2014; Roth 2014). A variation was that they were locals paid by Yanukovych operatives (Wilson 2016, 645). What is the evidence to support these claims?

In 2016, the SBU released edited intercepts of conversations between Russian officials and anti-Maidan activists in Ukraine held on the day of these multiple demonstrations – March 1, 2014 (Melkozerova 2016; *UA Position* 2016). Dubbed the "Glazyev tapes," after Russian government adviser Sergei Glazyev, who initiated the calls, they were touted as the smoking gun exposing a Russian plan to "manufacture" a war in Eastern Ukraine (Umland 2016; Whitmore 2016). Glazyev, on the tapes, is clearly hoping that members of local militias (he names Oplot in Kharkiv, Odesskaia druzhina in Odesa) will take the initiative, storm regional parliaments, force them to organize a referendum on regional autonomy, and then call for Russian help.

The calls only represent evidence that financial support from Moscow was on offer. Instead of unveiling a well-oiled Russian master plan to break up Ukraine, the content of the tapes reveals the *limits* of Russia's ability to control events on the ground.[17] Glazyev and other Muscovites on the calls were remote from the centers of power (Zygar 2016, 284). The Glazyev tapes contrast the professionalism of the Ministry of Defense in Crimea, revealing bumbling improvisations by minor political freelancers, trying to stoke urban unrest in another country by spreading around paltry sums of petty cash.[18] There was no logistical plan. As Konstantin Zatulin, Glazyev's partner and head of an institute dealing with the former Soviet republics, said on one of the calls: "We are not providing any operative management, just supporting them. Let's see what they can do on their own" (Shandra 2019a).[19]

---

[17] The exception being Crimea – except that even there Russian troops had to assist local militias in order to ensure that the parliament vote on a referendum unfolded smoothly. See Chapter 5.

[18] We are indebted to Fabian Burkhardt, a German scholar, for this interpretation. His insights appeared in a 2016 Facebook post.

[19] There was also an attempt by Kirill Frolov, from the Zatulin Institute, to have the local Russian Orthodox Church in Odesa come out denouncing Kyiv and asking for Russian help. This also failed (Hosaka 2019).

Considering that Donbas became the main front of violent insurgency a few weeks later, it is striking that no one from Donetsk was on the line for these calls from Moscow. The focus was virtually all on Kharkiv and Odesa. This probably reflects the thinking at the time in Moscow: banking on Kharkiv to lead the resistance against Kyiv, with a cascade of communities tipping in sequence. This strategy was laid out in a memorandum, leaked in 2015, that circulated in Kremlin circles in February 2014 (weeks before Yanukovych's flight). The document painted the Yanukovych government as "terminally bankrupt" and the Ukrainian state on the verge of regional disintegration. The document is treated as evidence that Russian intervention in Ukraine was planned before the Maidan events culminated (Lipskyi 2015; Snyder 2018, 136). Revealingly, the memorandum explicitly speculates that the "maximum integration" of Eastern provinces with Russia would not arise from Donetsk (where über-oligarch Rinat Akhmetov was seen as loyal to Kyiv), but rather from the "priority regions" of Kharkiv and Crimea. The memorandum writers, and the March 1 callers, all anticipated that Kharkiv, and secondarily Odesa, would drive the rebellion in Ukraine.

In light of this information, what "coordination" might have looked like, had everything gone according to plan from Moscow's perspective, is clearer. To maximize influence over Eastern Ukraine without resorting to costly occupation, Little Green Men needed freedom to act with the expectation of cooperation from local partners. The Kremlin would have needed someone like Vladimir Konstantinov or Sergei Aksyonov capable of strong-arming a majority of regional lawmakers into passing secessionist legislation, denouncing Kyiv, and making self-determination claims. No such leader could be found in Eastern Ukraine. Despite street pressure, elites resisted the temptation to take radical steps that would have destabilized Ukraine further.

An Aborted War in the Streets

Regional officials of the Party of Regions had issued a formal challenge to Kyiv at the Kharkiv Congress, but quickly folded. After this debacle, the Kremlin had to settle for second- and third-best options: hoping the pro-Russian street would force official institutions (regional parliaments) to hold referenda. This also failed most everywhere, the partial exception being Luhansk. Russia kept pushing the regional card, calling for the "federalization" of Ukraine, but lost control of events on the ground.[20] So did Kyiv, in many cases. For the next two months, street politics remained salient. The future of Eastern Ukraine was a drama played out in the streets. Linked political demonstrations, remembered in the Russian media as the "Russian Spring," reiterated the demands for a referendum on regional autonomy (Melnyk 2020).

These high-intensity public meetings were most frequent in Donetsk region. By one count eighty were held between late February and early April 2014, especially in the capital Donetsk and the port city of Mariupol (Platonova 2020, 137). Street violence was more frequent in Kharkiv, with some pro-Russian demonstrations featuring serious violence or destruction of property (Platonova 2020, 126). In mid-March, two of these clashes turned deadly. On March 13, pro-Ukraine demonstrators in Donetsk were attacked by a much larger pro-Russian contingent. The police failed to separate the groups, and one pro-Ukrainian participant was stabbed to death (*Vice News* 2014). The following evening, in Kharkiv, members of the pro-Russian Oplot fight club, which had previously sent *titushki* to the Kyiv Maidan, beat up Kharkiv Maidan activists (Kuzio 2017, 163) and attacked members of Patriot Ukraïny, a pro-Maidan Ukrainian far-right group that had barricaded itself in an office. The groups exchanged Molotov cocktails and gunshots, resulting in two deaths on the Oplot side (Khomenko 2015; Likhachev 2015). These events revealed new street dynamics. Pro-Ukrainian street fighters were virtually nonexistent in Crimea and outmatched in Donetsk, but not in Kharkiv.

The unwillingness of local police to neutralize violent anti-regime demonstrators enabled this slide toward anarchy. In part, this was an unintended consequence of Maidan. Institutional trust in the state was at an all-time low. Policemen, many from Eastern Ukraine, had been injured or killed by Maidan protesters only for survivors to ultimately be abandoned by lawmakers. The refusal to rein in violence was also partially a matter of practical confusion over lines of command and control. The legitimacy of the new government was being challenged and this affected police morale. The troubling realization that the

---

[20] On March 17, the day before the annexation of Crimea, the Russian Ministry of Foreign Affairs called for a referendum on a new "federal constitution" in Ukraine (Smolar 2014a) that would have dramatically reduced Kyiv's influence over its regions(Darden 2014).

loyalty of the local police was in question supercharged street politics. If a Russian-speaking community were to tip toward coordinated *sedition* what *could* the new Maidan government do? The national special police force tasked with containing street disorders, Berkut, had been disbanded by the Interior Ministry after Maidan. A plan to form a National Guard was announced on March 13 (*Ukrains'ka pravda* 2014m), but such a force was months away from becoming operational.

The empirical material that follows reveals the limits of the antiseptic game-theoretic language of "coordinated anti-seditionist strategies by elites" (see Appendix A) which does not really do justice to the drama. Violent tactics were improvised to keep pockets of *seditionists* from acquiring a territorial foothold or effectively coordinating. Analytically, there were two ideal-type interim strategies by which Kyiv reestablished control. First, it could rely on private vigilante groups willing to support the pro-Maidan government (μ). Second, it could reassign security forces from other parts of the country (c).

The first strategy succeeded and was exemplified by the case of Dnipropetrovsk. The oligarch Ihor Kolomoyskyi was appointed governor on March 1. He used his considerable private wealth to build militias to liquidate pro-Russian groups in short order (Carroll 2015). Nearby Mykolaiv followed a similar route. An anti-Maidan encampment had been present in the central square since February 25. Local entrepreneurs and businessmen funded a "self-defense" militia, which instituted checkpoints around the city, burned down the anti-Maidan tents, and scattered pro-Russian militants with tire irons and handguns (*Podrobytsi* 2014; Smolar 2014c). In Odesa, while we lack information on the involvement of businessmen, the decision by the pro-Russian camp to avoid direct confrontation appeared to have been a calculation that street fighters on either side were evenly matched. A few scuffles, as well as episodes of show of force and symbolic violence, proved the staying power of the pro-Ukrainian street in these three oblasts.

The second strategy, reassigning loyal troops, was a tactic of last resort when the street appeared on the brink of a tilt toward Russia.[21] On April 6, pro-Russian militants seized key government buildings in

---

[21] In the language of the model, this is an attempt to change elite strategies by clarifying the costs c associated with *repression*. When elites change strategies because attempts to coordinate are risky (local vigilante threats) that is μ. In a stag hunt, μ represents more intense hunger pangs for a hunter trying to catch a stag without enough help and c represents a thinner stag.

Kharkiv, Donetsk, and Luhansk. In each case, a "People's Republic" was declared. Local elites remained loyal to Kyiv, but could not count on the police to remove the intruders. This was so even in Kharkiv, despite the fact that two of the top security ministers in the new cabinet in Kyiv dispatched to Kharkiv – Arsen Avakov (Interior) and Stepan Poltorak (Defense) – had extensive connections in the Kharkiv police (Avakov as former governor of Kharkiv, Poltorak as former director of the Kharkiv Police Academy (Khomenko 2015). Fortuitously, a special police unit from Central Ukraine, trained to combat organized crime, was in the process of redeploying to Sloviansk, two hours southeast of Kharkiv, and ejected the militants from the Kharkiv ODA without casualties. The proclaimed republic lasted thirty-six hours (Khomenko 2015).

Yet it is worth noting that Kyiv had to rely on forces external to the oblast to defeat the Kharkiv insurrection. That strategy failed in Donetsk and Luhansk. One reason is that Kyiv did not have many elite police troops that it could deploy quickly to conduct high-risk counterinsurgency operations. Another major difference is that Donbas militants who took over government buildings, in both Donetsk and Luhansk, were armed with heavy weapons. The activists who stormed the Kharkiv ODA had no guns.

The weapons acquisition by Donbas militias provides a study in state breakdown. On April 6, a few thousand pro-Russian protesters gathered in central Donetsk intending to seize the ODA (*Vgorode* 2014b). This was the third such attempt by protesters but the first since March 5. Late at night, hundreds of masked individuals massed in front of the Donetsk SBU headquarters to commandeer firearms. After negotiations, SBU officials let them in. The militants refrained from using violence or vandalizing the premises, left with the weapons they had come for, and went on to storm the ODA (Gubarev 2016).[22]

The relatively orderly seizure of weapons contrasted with events of the same day in the neighboring Donbas oblast of Luhansk, where the SBU office was stormed by protesters demanding the release of anti-Maidan militants detained inside. In an attack that lasted six hours,

---

[22] A video shows a respectful, if surreal, encounter between masked men and an SBU employee trying to reach someone on the phone (*Zhitel UA* 2014). The masked men keep asking him for the key to the arms vault. The protesters initially claimed they had "seized" the SBU building (*Tsenzor.net* 2014a), but they eventually left.

stones were hurled, iron bars were used to break windows, and police officers were beaten. The more than 100 officers inside did not effectively resist. Imprisoned activists were freed. The attackers were given the key to the armory and obtained weapons (Dvali 2014).[23]

The official state response was to send high-profile government officials to Donetsk and Luhansk to attempt to defuse the situation.[24] These envoys arrived with a large retinue of over a thousand police, including elite SBU "Alpha" troops (*Tsenzor.net* 2014c; *Hromadske* 2016; *Obozrevatel* 2016). Kyiv's representative in Donetsk, Serhiy Taruta, who had been appointed governor on March 1, publicly came out against storming the building and in favor of negotiations, as did the oligarch Rinat Akhmetov (*Korrespondent.net* 2014; Guzhva and Korotkov 2015). After the fact, some in Kyiv blamed the responsibility for failing to retake control on police treason – they had allegedly refused to recapture the buildings (*Hromadske* 2016; *Obozrevatel* 2016). Ukrainian officials had in fact been ambivalent about using force once they failed to convince protesters to lay down their weapons through suasion (*RIA Novosti Ukraina* 2014). The strategy of clearing an occupied building with force was a last resort that worked best when the protesters were unarmed.

The armed seizure of government buildings in Donetsk and Luhansk was a qualitative change in the nature of the Russian Spring. In Donetsk, the insurgents sent an ultimatum to the regional parliament to meet at noon on the following day and adopt a resolution on a referendum to have Donetsk join Russia (*Ukrains'ka pravda* 2014c). The parliament did not meet and a "Donetsk People's Republic"

---

[23] Recall that the technique of storming offices of the SBU or of the police, with stones and Molotov cocktails, had actually first been implemented in seven oblasts of Central and Western Ukraine on February 19, after fifteen protesters were killed in clashes with the police in Kyiv (*24tv.ua* 2014; *Finance.ua* 2014; UNIAN 2014). In the Ukrainian West there are many more documented instances of rioters capturing weapons by either disarming policemen or raiding arms depots (see Chapter 4). SBU officials in the offices in Donetsk and Luhansk besieged on April 6 would surely have been aware of these events.

[24] Vitaliy Yarema, first deputy vice-premier, was sent to Donetsk. Andriy Parubiy, secretary of the National Security and Defense Council, was sent to Luhansk. Neither had ever served in government positions east of Kyiv. Even more awkwardly, Parubiy, in his younger days, had belonged to a far-right nationalist party, and had recently acted as a coordinator for Maidan "self-defense" units – precisely the groups that protesters in Donbas were most hostile toward.

was proclaimed (and a Luhansk People's Republic by the end of the month). The arrival, a week later, of an armed commando unit from Crimea, by way of Russia, headed by a murky Russian national (Igor Girkin, aka Strelkov) provoked a Ukrainian military response. This signaled the end of the Russian Spring in Donbas and the transition to war, and this is where our narrative picks up in Chapter 7.

In Kharkiv, the short-lived seizure of the ODA did not cauterize *sedition* or fully "tip" the community back toward political neutrality or loyalty to Kyiv. On April 13, street clashes left ten people injured (Leonard 2014b). A week later, pro-Russian militants tried to build a tent camp on the square facing the ODA. Police tore it down (Khomenko 2015). As a pro-Russian protest organizer confided later, they could not find enough people "who were ready to fight" (Platonova 2020, 259). On April 27, 4,000 football ultras from Kharkiv and Dnipropetrovsk held a march chanting "Ukraine is united!" Along with street fighters from the radical right (about to form the nucleus of the Azov battalion), they intimidated the pro-Russian camp out of holding a large May 1 event (Ruzhelnyk 2021, 222–3). Kharkiv's Russian Spring had fizzled out.

A similar fate awaited Odesa, but with a far more tragic and far-reaching outcome. Recall that for months, since the failed attempt to force a referendum in early March, an anti-Maidan tent city encampment had been holding ground in the Odesa city center. Contrary to Donbas and Kharkiv, despite street protests, there had been no attempt to storm the governor's building (ODA) on April 6. An "Odesa People's Republic" was declared on the Internet later in April, to little effect (*Ukrains'ka pravda* 2014h). Pro- and anti-Maidan "self-defense" groups had avoided clashing.

A May 2 football match between the Odesa and Kharkiv teams created the spark for a confrontation. Before the game, football ultras from both teams sought to replicate the march in favor of Ukrainian unity that had been successfully held in Kharkiv a week earlier.[25] Radical right elements were also marching, and the lines between the ultras and the radical right were increasingly blurred. A gunman from the anti-Maidan militia Odesskaia druzhina fired from behind police lines, killing a pro-Maidan demonstrator. A chaotic melee ensued and five more people were killed, four from the anti-Maidan camp (Hale,

---

[25] Another one was held in Dnipropetrovsk at about the same time.

Shevel, and Onuch 2018, 860). The anti-Maidan groups gradually lost the initiative, and were chased all the way to the tent city, taking refuge in the adjacent Trade Union Building. Pro-Maidan militants, incensed by the day's events, seem to have tried to burn down the tent city. Anti-Maidan protesters shot at them from the building. The two sides threw Molotov cocktails at each other. The building went up in flames. Forty-eight people died, all pro-Russian activists.[26]

Viewed in retrospect, what matters the most from an analytical point of view is that the facts of the event nested so neatly into *both* of the master geopolitical narratives (summarized at the end of Chapter 4) (Hale, Shevel, and Onuch 2018). There were two immediate consequences.

First, the incident signified the high-water mark for the Russian Spring as a potential insurgency. Putin had touted the *Novorossiya* concept, dating back to the late eighteenth century, that the Southeastern territories could be unified under Russian rule (Herszenhorn 2014b). It would turn out to be a project geographically limited to Donbas and Crimea, but the territory of this small oil spot would not expand to Odesa, Kharkiv, or anywhere else.

The second immediate effect added fuel to the fire – the emerging war – in the Donbas. Russian television depicted the Odesa events as a massacre (Coynash 2018b). There was now "incontrovertible evidence" that Ukrainian "fascists" intended to intimidate, humiliate, and indeed murder pro-Russian civilians (depicted simply as Russians or Russian-speakers) (Gaufman 2017, 119).[27] The systematic campaign of propaganda – in social media, through diplomatic channels, but especially on television – to delegitimize Ukraine's new government finally had the focal point it needed (Babak et al. 2017).

The use of the word fascist (*fashist*), strikes a deep chord in Russian (and post-Soviet) society. World War II – the defining moment in Russian historical memory – is remembered as the "victory over fascism"

---

[26] A proper government investigation was never completed (Council of Europe 2015). A group of citizens, calling themselves the 2 May Group, conducted an exhaustive inquiry, the main conclusion of which was that responsibility for the outbreak of the fire could not be ascribed to either side. It remains possible that anti-Maidan activists barricaded inside the building accidentally lit the fire (Coynash 2017a). The behavior of the police, passive if not complicit, was also controversial.

[27] For instance, the fire in Odesa was compared to the heavily memorialized massacre at Khatyn during World War II, when civilians were burnt alive in a building by German-led forces (Hale, Shevel, and Onuch 2018, 862–3).

(Tumarkin 2003; Volkov 2018). In the Russian lexicon, fascism is thus directly associated with a call to fight off an invasion (Laruelle 2021, 31).[28] When the Russian Foreign Ministry (and the Yanukovych government) began to call the Ukrainian radical right protesters on Maidan "fascist thugs" (*fashistvuiushiie molodichki*) (Ministerstvo inostrannykh del Rossiiskoi Federatsii 2014a), the implication was not just that they were fascists because they used violence. They were also in league with foreign enemies. The association of Maidan protesters to foreign interests became central to Russian propaganda. The violent ones (Pravyi sektor, Svoboda) symbolically identified with the Organization of Ukrainian Nationalists (Orhanizatsiia ukraïns'kykh natsionalistiv, or OUN) Bandera and were therefore "fascists." Peaceful protesters, meanwhile, were said to be following directives from Western powers, primarily the United States. "Fascism" began to blur with "Ukrainian nationalism," with the portrayal of nationalists as foreign agents. The storyline, to which the TV audience in Eastern Ukraine were particularly exposed, had a third component: The fascists (heirs to Bandera) conducted a coup (violently bringing down the president and his government) at the behest of the United States.

The formation of pro-Russian militias, often self-described as "self-defense" groups, must be understood in this context as a reaction to these fears. The language closely echoed the self-presentation of bands of protesters on Maidan who also called themselves self-defense groups (*samooborony*) whose stated aim was to protect Maidan against the police and state-paid vigilantes. The militias that formed in the East saw themselves as civil protection against the Maidan "self-defense" groups.[29] No law enforcement body was making arrests, so small vigilante armies across the Southeast took to the streets armed and prepared to face-off against each other. The vision of the Maidan government (and certainly of the Maidan street fighters) as fascist was largely shared in Russian public opinion (Laruelle 2021, 79), so even if

---

[28] The countless war monuments or plaques refer to fascists or invaders, almost never to Germans or Nazis. The *fascists* invaded, and were then heroically repulsed.

[29] This cycle of arms-racing by irregular light infantry units – all imagining themselves to be arming defensively, all unable to distinguish each other's intent, all acting in the shadow of military intervention from a third-party great power – has long been recognized as terribly dangerous, since "rescuers" often feel they have an incentive to "jump through any windows of opportunity that arise" (Posen 1993, 108–9).

it failed to capture the imagination of most Eastern Ukrainians, it was sufficient to convince some people to arm themselves in the Donbas and serve as a magnet for more patriotic volunteers as they arrived from Russia starting in April.

After Odesa, the floodgates opened.[30] These volunteers shared the political view that they were fighting to protect Russia – characterizing Donbas as part of *Novorossiya*, or *Russkii mir* – from fascists. Ideologically, they comprised an assortment of nationalist and religiously inspired groups.[31] They were motivated by a desire to stand bravely in defense of the threat faced by Russians "trapped behind the lines," destined to be humiliated, and vulnerable in a confidently nationalizing Ukrainian state. This depiction appears to have been a strong factor in convincing many Russian citizens to travel to Donbas to fight as volunteers.

Conclusion

The Kremlin seems to have expected that elites in mainland Eastern Ukraine would break from Kyiv after the transfer of power in Kyiv. That did not happen. The expectation then became that pro-Russian protesters would force regional parliaments to unilaterally organize referenda on "federalization" designed to weaken Kyiv's control. That did not happen, either. What followed instead were periodic popular disturbances. Russian television encouraged these, expecting that they would gradually provoke anti-Kyiv uprisings supported by Russian-speakers across the Ukrainian East. This materialized only in parts of Donbas.

Through April, Kharkiv appeared to be in the balance, but the pro-Russian camp could not find enough members to form effective militias. Further south, time and again, when heads were actually counted in the street, pro-Ukraine militants chased away pro-Russian ones. Uncertainty about willingness to follow commands, inconsistent orders, mixed signals, uncertain lines of command and control, and overall organizational failure was characteristic of the response of demoralized police forces. This surely resulted in some preventable

---

[30] For testimony of Russian volunteers on how the Odesa events jolted them into action, see Turchenkova (2014), Luhn (2014b), and Nemtsova (2014c).
[31] This was blurred distinction, since Russian nationalists increasingly defined themselves by their Russian Orthodoxy. One militia flocking to Girkin's banner called itself the Russian Orthodox Army.

injuries and deaths. Yet there was no mass repression and no spectacle of Ukrainian police units firing into crowds of civilians flying
Russian flags. Odesa was as close as anything came. The notion that
Russian-speaking Ukrainians living in the East would identify more
with the new Russian geopolitical project of *Novorossiya* than with
the Ukrainian state in a crisis was taken for granted before 2014 in
Russia. Many Western scholars, some deferring to conventional wis-
dom or tropes popularized by Samuel Huntington, were also unsure.

Nothing like *Novorossiya* was established by a popular uprising in
2014. This speaks to the importance of local agency. The common narrative of Russian-speakers as marionettes whose strings are pulled by the
Kremlin, or crystal radios receiving Kremlin television transmissions, is
condescending. The claim that Russian infiltrators were responsible for
the bulk of the violence is also plainly false. Subsequent events made it
clear that the key players on the ground were Ukrainian citizens. Every
one of the forty-odd protesters who were removed from the Kharkiv
ODA building on April 8 had a Ukrainian passport (Khomenko 2015).
The head of the Luhansk SBU (the security police), appointed in March
by the interim government, plainly stated that those who attacked the
SBU building on April 6 were recognizable locals (Dvali 2014).[32] In
Odesa, every single one of the forty-eight pro-Russian activists who
perished in the fire were from the region (Amos 2015).

The grain of truth in the account is that Ukrainian state lost control
over some territory and Russian television celebrated it as it happened.
What followed, however, was a great deal of calculation by strategic
Russian-speakers. For the most part, the Maidan government was able
to gradually consolidate its control throughout Eastern Ukraine, after
a hiatus, due to the choices of Russian-speaking community elites to
abjure *sedition*. In some cases, this was out of loyalty. In others, it was
probably in reaction to, or in anticipation of, violence. Whatever the
mechanism, these critical choices were made by Ukrainians – not by
Moscow elites.

---

[32] He also claimed that the Russian special services organized the attack, but
provided no evidence thereof. Two Luhansk natives who took part in the
SBU attack – Aleksei Mozgovoi and Aleksandr Bednov, aka "Batman" – later
became pro-Russian battalion commanders during the war. On the Luhansk
warlords, see Sautreuil (2018).

7 | *The War and Russian Intervention (Donbas)*

Let us briefly recap our game. In the first stage, the strategic actors are high-status members of Russian-speaking communities. A crisis reveals temporary weakness of state institutions. The crisis forces prospective assessments of the possibility of institutionalized discrimination from the center. Russian-speaking community elites then have to choose strategies in the shadow of vigilante violence. These members face a choice. They can seek security by rejecting the legitimacy of the new government in Kyiv, activate a political Russian identity, and hope for Kremlin protection, or they can seek security in the guarantees of citizenship provided by the Ukrainian government.

If there is a coordinated decision to engage in *sedition*, the periphery takes the initiative in bargaining. In the next stage, community elites act together and bargain with Kyiv for political and cultural autonomy as a unified force. If there is no consensus, the divisions within the community manifest as a less-coherent bargaining position and a lower probability of military success, but, if members persist, they can drag their communities into war. Kyiv may choose to reject what it sees as an unacceptable offer and make arrests. If it does, in a final stage, Moscow can opt to intervene to protect "its" community. The upshot of the equilibrium analysis in Appendix A is that if everything goes according to plan, Russian-speaking community elites get their highest payoff by mobilizing, and *threatening* to secede – but then not following through. It is a risky strategy.

Communities can manipulate the risk, too. They can exploit Kyiv's uncertainty about Russia's intentions, or other parameters, in order to strike a better autonomy bargain with the center. To succeed in poker, to avoid being taken by an aggressive bluffing strategy, players must sometimes "call" and actually see what cards the other player holds. In the narrative that follows, "bluffing" and "calling" between the street and state security forces is a useful metaphor to understand escalation past the point of no return in Donbas.[1] To continue the analogy, Chapter 6 focused on places where the ante was never raised very far to begin with (since coordinated *sedition* never really got off the ground). As a result, street politics were often resolved with relatively few casualties. In Donbas, home of the largest ethnic Russian community after Crimea, to continue the casino analogy: some of the emergent rebel leaders raised the ante considerably, assuming that they would be able to take out a loan from the house. The geographic contours of the rebellion likely took Kremlin decision-makers by surprise, since they expected the center of insurgency to be Kharkiv or Odesa. Once these insurgents had proven the ability to hold urban territory, Moscow threw its support behind the secessionist cause. Eventually it even deployed its forces when it was clear that the insurgents were in danger of losing to the Ukrainian army.

It is important to emphasize that the uprising did not occur exactly according to the antiseptic equilibrium logic of our model's predictions. Coordination on *sedition* was not dominant in Donbas communities. What happened instead was a ragged coalition of new elites emerged gradually from the streets, bypassing traditional community elites (many of whom were struggling to avoid sedition). These new entrants directed events. Russia did not know the new faces of the rebel leadership, as they were largely unknown even to local political operatives in Donbas. Important groups of people publicly demonstrated their support for Maidan Ukraine in Donbas, but they were beaten back by militant pro-Russian street groups. Civilian populations were dragged into a war *not* by well-known institutional community elites, but by previously unknown actors who suddenly occupied center stage, cannibalized institutions, and established reputations as warlords. Most irregular volunteers encouraged by Russia arrived after these local militia captains had demonstrated an ability to seize and hold Ukrainian territory for weeks.

The narrative in this chapter contributes to a chain of evidence that the decision by Russia to perform a military intervention occurred after Ukrainian state authority collapsed in the urban areas of Donbas. We trace the process by which a proto-insurgency transmogrified, in fits and starts, into a full-blown internationalized war fought with conventional

---

[1] In the context we are describing, the analogy to "calling" is state repression by K, because state actors believe a unified R is bluffing, misrepresenting its strength (p) or assessments of Russian propensity to send assistance (a).

weapons. We document initial efforts by Kyiv to probe intent, to bargain, and to try to avoid massive bloodshed. The relatively disorganized Ukrainian security forces arriving from Kyiv were at first cautious and limited in their use of force. Soldiers were unprepared for counterinsurgency operations. The disposition began to change by late May, with the election of a new Ukrainian president and the appearance of Ukrainian volunteer battalions. This tracks with the sequence and logic of our model fairly well. There was first a failure of elite-led coordinated sedition, then improvised police responses from the center attempting to stem street disturbances, then bargaining between Kyiv and regional elites, and ultimately rejection of overtures by a few radical Donbas insurgents. At each stage, escalation processes were prone to accident, misperception, emotion, information cascades, and simple miscalculation.

The Anti-Terrorist Operation

A week after the seizure of key government buildings by armed protesters in Donetsk and Luhansk on April 6, a fifty-man commando unit arrived to reinforce insurgents. They chose as their target Sloviansk, a small town three hours north of Donetsk. With the assistance of local militias who had raided weapons from state storage lockers, the commando unit cordoned off the city. In response, the interim Ukrainian president declared an "anti-terrorist operation" (*Antyterorystychna operatsiia*, hereafter ATO) and gave orders for the army to deploy. Within days, the first servicemen were killed. Heavy weapons entered the theater, initiating high-intensity fighting. Fighting never fully deescalated. Ukraine descended into war.

The military commando group that surfaced on Sloviansk on April 12 displayed no insignia and appeared to be a carbon copy of the Little Green Men in Crimea. The suspicion among many was that Russia had sent special forces to destabilize Donbas. Within days, it became known that the group was led by one Igor Girkin (aka Strelkov), a Russian citizen. Ukrainian officials quickly identified Girkin as a Russian military counterintelligence (Glavnoe razvedyvatel'noe upravlenie, or GRU) officer (*Euractiv* 2014).[2] His followers were conspicuously

---

[2] When Girkin was personally targeted for economic sanctions later in the year, the EU also named him "a staff member of the Main Intelligence Directorate of the General Staff of the Armed Forces of the Russian Federation (GRU)" (Rettman 2015).

not Sloviansk locals. Many, if not most, seem to have been Ukrainian citizens from Crimea or mainland Ukraine who had joined militias in Crimea (Alexandrov 2019). The high-stakes question was whether Russian special forces (*spetsnaz*) had been sent in advance of a deployment by Russian regular troops, like the Little Green Men in Crimea. Ukrainian government officials believed they were being invaded. So did many observers (Lobkov 2014; Rachkevych 2014a). Kyiv did not want a repeat of Crimea, where Ukrainian forces offered no resistance.

Girkin's main contact in Moscow was Konstantin Malofeev, a Russian Orthodox nationalist and investment fund billionaire.[3] In January 2014, he brought precious Orthodox relics to Crimea, along with a delegation that included two security officials – and Girkin. Attempts were made to meet with local power brokers (Matsuzato 2016, 241). In February, he sent Girkin to Kyiv twice, ostensibly on business trips. After the second one, Girkin went straight to Crimea and became involved with the pro-Russian militias under the command of Sergei Aksyonov, who would become prime minister (Grozev 2014b). Aksyonov's men were equipped with weapons captured from Ukrainian military depots (Loiko 2016). Girkin reportedly led a group of them in the storming of the Ukrainian Cartographic Center in Simferopol, killing two people (Alexandrov 2019) – a rare instance of violence in the Crimean takeover. Aksyonov wanted to export the rebellion to the Southeastern oblasts and apparently asked Girkin to head to Donetsk with fifty-two of his men (Guzhva and Korotkov 2015; Lavrov 2015a, 204).

The Girkin unit may not have been *spetsnaz*, but they radiated military experience, contrasted with the armed protesters who had occupied the Donetsk Oblast Administrative Offices (ODA) (Patrikarakos 2014).[4] The Girkin commando team crossed the unpoliced border

---

[3] Malofeev was seen as the antithesis of George Soros, operating a shadowy international network that championed illiberal values ("tradition" over individual rights, intolerance to gay rights, etc.) (Belton 2020, 421). Malofeev became more directly political during Maidan. Girkin ostensibly resigned from a Federal Security Service (FSB) desk job in 2013, months before Maidan, to become head of security for Malofeev's investment firm (Grozev 2014a). A Russian national associated with the unit later claimed that Malofeev funded the Girkin expedition, even though he initially was opposed to them being dispatched to Donbas (Kazanskyi 2019).

[4] In the 1990s, Girkin fought in post-Soviet wars (Chechnya, Transnistria), as well as in Bosnia (Grozev 2014a).

between Rostov oblast in Russia and Donetsk oblast in Ukraine in the dead of night to meet Donetsk *opolchenie* members (Gubarev 2016, 170–4). Girkin felt that his detachment could have maximum impact in a midsized town. He selected Sloviansk, seemingly on the reported strength of local anti-Maidan sentiments (Prokhanov 2014). In Sloviansk, on April 12, his group captured the police, Security Service (SBU), and government buildings. Local militias seized weapons. They then fanned out, creating checkpoints.

The conflict had now escalated dramatically. Rather than specific government buildings seized in downtown areas of regional capitals, *an entire city* was now captured. The claim that territory had been seized "by the Russians" was made believable by the manner the Girkin men dressed and presented themselves (Lavrov 2015a, 205). Was Girkin *actually* taking orders from Russian security officials? Or could the Girkin commando unit have traveled incognito through Russian territory in order to reach the Donetsk–Rostov border (Guzhva and Korotkov 2015) on their own? After all, the commando squadron was quite small (small enough to fit in the back of just one or two large trucks, in fact).[5]

The evidence points unambiguously to Malofeev.[6] After the first deadly clash occurred within a day of the commando arrival, the Ukrainian SBU released an intercepted phone call with Girkin reporting to an unidentified interlocutor in Moscow. Ukrainian officials presented the intercept as "smoking gun" evidence that the commandos had been sent by the Kremlin (Sluzhba bezpeky Ukraïny 2014a).[7] Malofeev was identified as the man Girkin was talking to (Grozev 2014b). The exact role of Malofeev in the Kremlin

---

[5] Asked afterwards whether he received assistance in Russia on his way to Donetsk, Girkin said he could not comment (*The Insider* 2017).

[6] Girkin's private correspondence, hacked and released by Anonymous International, revealed that he had worked for the FSB, not the GRU (Kanygin 2016). He served in the FSB *spetsnaz* (special forces) in the Second Chechen War (Guzhva and Korotkov 2015). Evidence that he was under FSB control while in Donbas has not emerged.

[7] The SBU entitled the call "GRU Slaviansk," using the acronym of Russian military counterintelligence. Another intercepted call was between a Girkin militiaman and an FSB handler based in Crimea. The handler is highly critical of Girkin. It seems to us to be evidence that the FSB did not meaningfully control events on the ground through this agent (Sluzhba bezpeky Ukraïny 2014b).

constellation of intrigue and power remains opaque and a matter of speculation.[8]

What is clear in retrospect is that, contra Crimea, no evidence has emerged indicating a definite (or indeed a coherent) plan for military intervention in the Donbas in this early stage. In the words of a Russian volunteer who managed aid contributions to Girkin, it was "Go ahead, and we'll see" (Alexandrov 2019).[9] It is likely that decision-makers in Moscow were waiting to see if conditions were favorable before committing further. Our interpretation, consistent with the model, is that Russian decision-makers were very anxious about the prospect of sending troops into a situation where they were treated as an invading army, since the "liberator and protector" narrative played so well with their "self-determination" talking points. The optics of Russian military units engaging in urban pacification against Russian-speaking militias in Ukraine's East complicated the story (as became clearer and clearer in 2022, when Russia soldiers moved the lines of control and were *not* greeted as liberators). The plan seems to have been to deploy the military in order to impose costs (C) on Kyiv only after it was clear that those soldiers would be supporting self-organized Russian-speaking communities with institutional continuity.

Girkin's plan was to create those conditions by putting his finger on the scale and initiating a social tip. At first, it seemed to be working. Girkin's mid-April takeover of Sloviansk was quickly expanded to neighboring Kramatorsk. Towns began to fall like dominoes across

[8] It seems fairly clear that Malofeev is "connected," but what that really means is disputed. In late 2013, he met with Vladislav Surkov, soon to become the Russian curator to the Donetsk People's Republic, and Sergei Glazyev, initiator of the infamous phone calls to pro-Russian leaders in Kharkiv and Odesa on March 1 (see Chapter 6), ostensibly to strategize about Ukraine (Hosaka 2018, 361). Yet Zygar (2016, 226, 283) claims that Surkov and Glazyev were peripheral players with unsubstantiated ties to Russian military intelligence (Belton 2020, 427).

[9] This begs speculative question about chain of command specifics. Was Girkin even a *spetznatz* commando, or was it just theatrical? We cannot know, of course, but we are doubtful. The unit did not display any particularly advanced military training and did not bring enough ammunition (Butusov 2020). Our hunch is that Girkin was an enthusiastic freelancer: monitored, but not controlled or deputized by authorities in Moscow (Guzhva and Korotkov 2015; Walker 2016; Matveeva 2018, 106). He claimed afterwards, once he had returned to Moscow, that his plan had been to provoke an uprising in Donetsk and set the stage for a Russian military intervention. Arguably an intervention *did* materialize three months later (culminating in the Battle of Ilovaisk). By then Girkin had been forced to depart.

Donbas. Over the next fourteen days, government buildings, police stations, and television stations were captured in thirty-two cities (Zhukov 2014). Civilians, civil servants, and policemen who resisted were attacked by armed insurgents. In the mining town of Horlivka, just outside of Donetsk, a police chief was badly beaten after he fought back, and a city councilor was kidnapped and murdered after he attempted to take down a Russian flag (Luhn 2014a; *Reuters* 2014). Local militiamen may not have been able to seize Sloviansk without leadership from the Girkin group (Hauter 2021b, 14), but there remains no evidence that the assaults on any of the other sites of state power in any of these dozen towns outside Sloviansk were initiated by Russian agents. It is possible that some exceptions at the edges will come to light when future archives are opened, but it seems clear that the Ukrainian state lost control over local armed men who began coordinating on strategies of *sedition* when they received a credible signal that the Russian military was arriving. As Serhiy Kudelia (2014) observed, "Given the ... delegitimation (and ultimate collapse) of local political institutions, the cost of starting an insurrection in the Donbas was minimal."

The Ukrainian government in Kyiv realized that it needed to try to stop the dominoes, but that it could not trust local police institutions to remain loyal. Nor could it rely on intra-community social sanctions or anti-secessionist vigilante threats to deter the seditionist energy spilling onto the streets, since the uprisings had momentum, safety in numbers, and had (the illusion of) Russian military support. And so the day after the fall of Sloviansk, after insurgents attacked a SBU special forces unit, killing one officer, the Ukrainian government launched its ATO (*Ukrains'ka pravda* 2014s; *Informatsionnoe soprotivlenie* 2020).

Ukrainian law defines an ATO as a police operation spearheaded by the Ukrainian SBU, with the assistance of the army, against a looming or ongoing terrorist threat (*Zakonodavstvo Ukraïny* 2018). Such an operation had the political advantage of involving the army without declaring a war or a state of emergency and did not need parliamentary approval (Wynnyckyj 2014). Ukrainian law broadly defines terrorism as the use of violence to intimidate the population. The post-Maidan government argued that the presence of armed men met this definition (Sherr 2014).[10]

---

[10] Social science research often associates terrorism with indiscriminate violence against civilians in order to force political change (Valentino 2004, 84; Semelin 2007, 350–1), for example setting off a bomb in a densely populated area.

The decision to send in the army marked the first time that the post-Maidan government publicly indicated a determination to use deadly force, and was the first time since Ukrainian independence that the army deployed to quell domestic disturbances. No explicit order to use weapons in a civilian environment had been given, but uniformed and heavily armed government troops were dispatched into urban areas of Donbas. Chaotic clashes exposed an untrained army, disoriented and unprepared for urban counterinsurgency, to a mobilized population in streets that were broadly supportive of the rebels (Luhn 2014c). Conscripts of the first regiment sent to Sloviansk on April 16 were encircled by angry crowds and easily disarmed by militiamen (Kramer 2014c). The police were overrun. In some regions, stations defected en masse.

The Ukrainian state, in its hour of need, turned to volunteers. On April 13, on the same day that the ATO was set in motion, Minister of Internal Affairs Arsen Avakov announced the formation of "special units of civilians" (*spetspidrozdiliv z tsivil'nykh*) for "the fight against terrorists" (*Ukrains'ka pravda* 2014b). These units were deemed "a response to saboteurs (*diversanty*), Green Men and other gangs (*bandy*) aiming to attack the statehood and territorial integrity of Ukraine" (*Ukrains'ka pravda* 2014b). Their creation was a partial admission that the Ukrainian government was losing control. The battalions were planned first in the East, then in the Center/West (Seddon 2014). The ATO was an emergency measure to protect government buildings.

In conceiving these "special units," which were to become volunteer battalions, Avakov had in mind the social forces that had already demonstrated a willingness to fight. The pro-Maidan "self-defense" groups that had formed in Kyiv and Eastern Ukrainian cities were the most obvious templates. Those street fighters, whose strategic use of violence altered the course of Maidan and whose determination to

---

This is not how the Donbas insurgency began. The decision to call insurgents "terrorists" sent a message that the central government would respond to violent ultimatums in kind – in the language of the model, a willingness to impose costs on communities that rebelled, if necessary (model parameter *c*). The language also signaled that the central government had no intention of negotiating, and fit within the rhetorical framework established over the prior decade of US foreign policy. It is worth noting that Western and NATO officials did not adopt this categorization, and (to our knowledge) never called the armed men fighting the Ukrainian army "terrorists." Two months earlier, the Yanukovych government had also launched an "ATO" against the Maidan protesters, but army units never made it to the capital (see Chapter 4).

confront pro-Russian militants may have swung the balance in favor of the Ukrainian state in the East outside of Eastern Donbas, were now given the opportunity to receive official status from the state, tasked with maintaining social order. From an anti-Maidan perspective, the fear – expressed in Donetsk since as far back as January 2014 and amplified by Russian propaganda during the Crimea invasion – that Maidan radicals would descend on Russian-speakers was actually materializing. Self-organized militias, functionally deputized to serve the post-Maidan state, were now backed by the Ukrainian military.

Volunteer battalions rapidly proliferated. On March 17, the day after the Crimean referendum, a Ukrainian presidential decree ordered a partial mobilization of troops (*Zakonodavstvo Ukraïny* 2014f). This activated a previously secret decree (signed, ironically, under the Yanukovych administration), providing for the creation of "battalions of territorial defense" in every Ukrainian oblast to protect strategic infrastructure (power plants), channels of communication (railroad hubs, highways), and organs of the state (*Ternopil's'ka oblasna derzhavna administratsiia* 2014; *Uriadovyi portal* 2014). The formation of territorial battalions demonstrated Kyiv's concern that the Russian invasion of Crimea, and potential acts of sabotage, would extend to other oblasts. The territorial battalions were mostly made up of army call-ups, and were managed by military boards. Several of these battalions were sent to other oblasts to reinforce border guard units, protect facilities, or man checkpoints, and at least twenty-four were eventually deployed to Donbas.[11] They came to be included, in public discourse (though not in official state documents), in the broader category of "volunteer battalions," even if most members were not really volunteering. The true volunteer battalions, as we saw, were not a creation of the army, but rather of the police – specifically the Ministry of Internal Affairs. They were meant from the start to serve in Donbas.

Many Maidan frontline activists were among these new battalion's first recruits. Pravyi sektor created its own.[12] The first battalion of the newly created National Guard, set to replace the dismantled Berkut, was comprised of armed volunteers who had fought on Maidan

---

[11] The estimate of twenty-four came from our own count of individual territorial battalions deployed to Donbas (Chinchilla and Driscoll 2021). Malyarenko and Galbraith (2016) came up with a slightly higher number (twenty-eight).

[12] Since the name became more like a brand than an actual organization on Maidan, many of its adherents ended up joining other battalions.

(Gorchinskaya 2014b). Making them official was justified at the time by the state as an attempt to officially disarm them (Goncharenko 2014). Membership can be traced from the Maidan "self-defense" forces to some of the new battalions, which maintained the same call signs and insignia. This was also true for some of pro-Maidan self-defense groups that operated in Eastern Ukrainian cities. The Azov and Donbas battalions had their origins in the violent clashes that erupted in the streets of Kharkiv and Donetsk on March 13. There were other recruitment routes, as some battalions attracted larger or more competent cohorts. The Aidar battalion was formed of Afghan war veterans, mostly from Luhansk, which explains the battalion's affiliation with the army (Hunter 2018). The Dnipro battalion was created by the oligarch-turned-governor Kolomoyskyi in Dnipropetrovsk (Gorchinskaya 2014b). These militias were almost always Russian-speaking, but no less fiercely loyal to the Ukrainian state and the government in Kyiv because of the language they preferred to speak.

Following the model: Russian-speaking communities that remained loyal formed fighting groups on the front lines for self-protection. Their transformation into battalions legitimized a violent strategy of deterring *seditionist* mobilization and disrupting coordination. The volunteer battalions had a vague and broad mandate to keep *sedition* at bay. The model incorporates both individual fears by Russian-speakers concerned about the threat of government-backed vigilantism against their families (μ) as well as the wider calculation that Kyiv would not let additional territory go without a fight and could draw on a huge pool of volunteers (c).[13]

Pro-Russian battalions were also sprouting up in the contested territory near Girkin's base of operations. With the seizure of police stations and government offices accelerating across Donbas, many militias competed for territorial control. In Donetsk, two of the strongest militias formed prominent battalions, Vostok and Oplot.[14] In Luhansk oblast, a number of self-described Cossack militias appeared

---

[13] In the Model in Appendix A, these are two separate parameters μ and c : a short-term fear of being terrorized for attempting collective action (μ), and a dawning realization that, if bargaining failed, counterinsurgency would devastate their neighborhoods and shatter their communities (c). Both sources of fear would have changed strategic calculations and been difficult to tease apart empirically.

[14] Vostok was led by Aleksandr Khodakovskyi, the former head of the Donetsk SBU Alpha elite unit, who had seen action in the Kyiv Maidan. Oplot was led by Aleksandr Zakharchenko, a mechanic who later rose to become the main

in the southern regions of the oblast. Several other groups contended for power in the regional capital, until the battalion Zarya eventually swallowed or displaced the rest (Matveeva 2018, 104).[15] Subregional dynamics began to resemble warlordism, with soldiers swapping commanders depending on perceptions of whose fortunes were rising and whose falling. Some militia members were joining armed units out of an authentic desire to defend their homes from marauders (Avdeev 2014; Ennis 2014; Ioffe 2014). Others were engaging in more complex private commercial strategies or social performances.

First Diplomatic Intervention

With the conflict in Donbas on the brink of open warfare, the United States and the EU brokered a meeting in Geneva on April 17 with the foreign ministers of Ukraine and Russia. Rather than defuse the situation, the forum served as a preview of the next decade of bilateral diplomacy between the two parties.

A joint declaration called for "all illegal armed groups" to disarm, and all "illegally seized buildings" to be vacated (*New York Times* 2014). The two parties had diametrically opposed interpretations of these ambiguous clauses, however. For Russian diplomats, the illegal groups were those which had originated on Maidan, such as Pravyi sektor, while the seizure of government buildings in Donbas by armed men reflected the "legitimate indignation (*zakonnoe vozmushchenie*)" of "the people" (Ministry of Foreign Affairs of the Russian Federation 2014a). Ukrainian diplomats regarded these claims as absurd. Since the launching of the ATO a few days earlier, Kyiv was openly calling the insurgents "terrorists" (and therefore their formations illegal). This made the first step at conflict resolution a nonstarter. The only lasting contribution of this initial diplomatic meeting involving the conflicting parties was a decision to mandate the Organization for Security and Co-operation in Europe (OSCE) to establish a permanent monitoring mission in the conflict zone (Taylor 2014).

Donetsk rebel leader. The Donetsk Oplot had links with the Kharkiv Oplot, which sent *titushki* to the Kyiv Maidan, and attacked Ukrainian groups in Kharkiv that later formed the Azov battalion.

[15] Zarya was formed by a civil servant, Valerii Bolotov, later replaced by Igor Plotnitsky. For microdata on recruitment into these sorts of militias, see Kudelia (2019).

At the same time that Russian diplomats were agreeing to a bilateral involvement, Putin, at a televised town hall meeting, stated that the predominantly Russian-speaking oblasts of Ukraine – geographically half of Ukraine, from Kharkiv to Odesa – were historically *Novorossiya* (the "New Russia"). They had been "given to Ukraine" by the Bolsheviks at the creation of the Soviet Ukrainian Republic in the early 1920s for "God knows what" reasons (Herszenhorn 2014b).[16] This was the first time since the fall of the Soviet Union that a Russian president had explicitly called into question the legitimacy of Ukrainian interstate borders. The Russian military also signaled readiness. For weeks, tens of thousands of troops had been gathering at the Russian–Donbas border near Rostov, officially to conduct regularly scheduled exercises (Charap and Colton 2017, 132). Such large-scale operations along the Ukrainian border were a first since the fall of the Soviet Union.[17] After the military takeover of Crimea and the permission granted by the Russian Senate on March 1 to use Russian Armed Forces "on the territory of Ukraine," it appeared plausible to observers that Russia was on the brink of sending troops to Donbas. Donbas insurgents would surely have been using television coverage to update their assessments of Russia's military intentions.

Escalation

Within a day of their arrival in Sloviansk, Girkin's men killed a SBU officer in an ambush (*Ukrains'ka pravda* 2014a). Later in the month, after Ukrainian special police units displayed restraint and refused to storm

[16] Putin was putting forward the standard Russian nationalist view that the Ukrainian Southeastern provinces are Russian land because they were settled under the Russian Empire and the majority speak Russian. Putin's "only God knows" rhetorical flourish was disingenuous. With some exceptions having to do with economic resources, the Bolsheviks used nationality (the census ethnic category) to delineate the boundaries of Soviet republics and autonomous areas (Schwartz 1990). The nationality criteria was thus foundational in the creation of Soviet administrative boundaries. At the time, ethnic Ukrainians formed majorities in all Southeastern oblasts (Krawchenko 1985, 48). Areas that were ethnically disputed, such as the Kuban, typically ended up in the Russian Soviet Federative Socialist Republic (RSFSR) (Martin 2001, 274–91).

[17] Although the total number of Russian troops involved (40,000–50,000) in military exercises was perhaps not extraordinary, the troops' concentration along the Ukrainian border and widespread coverage on Russian media conveyed a clear message (Petrov and Makutina 2014).

Sloviansk (Butusov 2020), five thresholds of escalation were passed: the first military-on-military conflict, the first downing of an air vehicle, the first shelling of civilian populations with military munitions, the opening of the interstate border for patriotic volunteer recruits to enter the Donbas, and the deliberate targeting of civilians by military forces.

On April 20, a Pravyi sektor volunteer unit opened fire on an insurgent checkpoint. Pravyi sektor had been tasked by political leadership to destroy an electrical transformer allowing insurgents to use TV broadcasts (Bukkvoll 2017), but apparently decided to take revenge for the murder of three unarmed activists in previous days (Hahn 2018, 257; 6262 2020). The dangerous operation, conducted outside official military channels, killed a Ukrainian volunteer and enraged a general who shouted at Pravyi sektor leader Dmytro Yarosh: "You have destroyed the peace process; you have started a war with Russia!" (Bukkvoll 2019, 297). This was the war's first official conventional fatality. Urban violence, involving police and civilians, or inflicted on civilians by other civilians, had finally given way to formal encounters between conventional armed units.

The war crossed another important threshold on April 25. Insurgents destroyed an army helicopter at the Kramatorsk airport (likely with a rocket-propelled grenade) (Witte and Booth 2014). Three days later, and hours before violence erupted in Odesa, the army conducted its first aerial assault on insurgent checkpoints. Insurgents downed two of the army's attack helicopters with man-portable surface-to-air missiles, known as MANPADs (or SAMs). Five crew members were killed (Lavrov 2015a, 208).

The appearance of SAMs raised questions. Were the Girkin men being supplied by Russia? Perhaps. In this early part of the conflict, and probably until June, the SAMs could have come from Ukrainian military depots or disarmed Ukrainian units (Matveeva 2018, 128).[18] The surprising capacity of insurgents to rebuff military incursions could have been evidence of the implosion of the Ukrainian state in parts of Donbas, not evidence of Russian meddling. Still, the ability of insurgents to bring down low-flying helicopters shocked the Ukrainian military. With only a fraction of the air force in any condition to fly, and with pervasive fears that Russia could introduce more

[18] There is evidence that some may have originated from stocks seized by Russian soldiers in Georgia in 2008, suggesting a smuggling operation involving decommissioned Russian weapons (*The Interpreter* 2014c; Snyder 2018, 179).

sophisticated antiair weapons into the theater at any time, the army prioritized readiness for ground options (Abdullaev 2014). The military eschewed man-to-man combat, since its unprepared conscripts had never been tested against capable opponents in direct engagements. Most incoming fighters from voluntary battalions were greatly motivated, willing to kill and to die, but lacked military training.

The third escalation threshold was to use weapons that can kill large numbers of civilians from afar. If you cannot fight face-to-face, a tempting fallback option is to encircle insurrectionist positions and strike from a safe distance. The army began to fire heavy artillery at positions inside Sloviansk. The bombing inflicted casualties in the low hundreds, a significant toll for a small town (Leonard 2014a). Following occasional clashes at the outskirts, the army besieged Sloviansk (*The Interpreter* 2014a). The siege would last two months. Deaths from falling shells were a harbinger of more gruesome destruction to come, but at no time in the emerging war – with the possible exception of a handful of discrete murders – were civilians the *main* target.

The fourth escalation was the gradual opening of the Russian border. Recall from Chapter 6 that the Russian-language media coverage of the Odesa fire in early May induced thousands of young Russians to heed what many saw as a patriotic duty to come to the defense of their ethnic kin. The battlefields of Ukraine changed as a result. The emerging war attracted the socially *déclassé*, unemployed, former soldiers struggling to adjust to civilian life, individuals suspicious of the state, Russian nationalists, Cossacks, mercenaries, or simply those enticed by the lure of war (Ioffe 2014; Matusova 2014; Mitrokhin 2015; Coynash 2017a, Yudina and Verkhovsky 2019). By early May, state authority had completely broken down in Donbas, providing heady opportunities for people at the margins of society to reinvent themselves as militiamen. Some who made a name for themselves, with catchy *noms de guerre* ("Givi," "Motorola," "Babay"), came from Russia. With the infusion of Russian volunteers, the opposing actors were heading toward a chaotic militia-on-militia bloodbath. That the Kremlin officially denied any responsibility for the arrival of these Russian combatants confused matters, since logistical involvement of the Russian state was hard to hide.[19] The military assistance

---

[19] After the Odesa fire, Russian volunteers were recruited by civic groups, with the assistance of Russian military enrollment centers (Digital Forensic Research Lab 2017). Russian agents would meet volunteers in Rostov, provide some training

remained indirect at this stage, however. Russia did not yet send its army. The flow of weapons remained tightly restricted.

The fifth escalation threshold was civilian fatalities that appear to have been the deliberate result of military actions. The event took place in Mariupol. On May 9, a national holiday commemorating the Soviet triumph in World War II, insurgents armed with automatic weapons stormed the main police station. The goal seems to have been to replicate the Sloviansk scenario. They were rebuffed by members of territorial battalions dispatched from Dnipropetrovsk and Lviv, as well as fighters from the newly created Azov volunteer battalion. Four battalion men were killed (Butusov 2016). Whether the local police sided with the pro-Russia or pro-Ukraine armed men remains disputed (Radchenko 2014).

Hours later, many residents converged on the station after the annual parade. The demonstration quickly turned violent. Gunshots were fired. At least seven people were killed. Many more were injured (Neistat 2014). The police station was burned to the ground. Russian media called it a "punitive operation" and a "massacre" of innocent people (*Vesti. ru* 2014b) – the second in a week, after Odesa. Videos of the incident showed that some protesters were armed and shooting at battalion members (Fitzpatrick 2014). The incident also revealed the risks of employing volunteers without proper military training for counterinsurgency.

The lack of discipline of Ukrainian volunteer battalions was on display again a few days later, when members of the Dnipro battalion, traveling from neighboring Dnipropetrovsk, were filmed entering a small town in northwestern Donetsk that had been captured by rebels. Local officials were threatened, and two civilians were killed (Chazan and Weaver 2014). The perception that armed pro-Ukraine groups were engaging in brazen violence took hold among a subset of Russian-speakers.

In areas where sedition enjoyed broad support, rebel tactics also became bolder. On May 16, a detachment commanded by Horlivka warlord Igor Bezler ambushed a Ukrainian company, killing sixteen, the largest single death toll in the military theater up to that point (Matveeva 2018, 125). Days later, a battalion from Chechnya arrived

in a facility linked to a Russian military base, confiscate passports, and send the recruits across the border without weapons to avoid raising the suspicion of Ukrainian border guards (Kramer 2014a). Once in Ukraine, they were assigned to armed groups. Whole contingents departed from Russia with full local television coverage (Racheva 2015). Crucially, Russian authorities did not consider them mercenaries, a status banned under Russian law (Yashin and Shorina 2015, 27), but volunteers fighting in an ancestral Russian territory (*Novorossiya*).

in Donetsk. This was the first instance of fighters from Russia coming not as individuals but as an organized unit (Biggs 2014). By this point, militias roamed downtown with impunity, and some turned their weapons on shop owners and bank personnel, engaging in kidnapping, intimidation, and torture (Human Rights Watch 2014a; Kazanskyi 2014; Amnesty International 2014).

Poroshenko's Choice: Rejecting Rebel Demands

Violence escalated. Attempts at defusing the conflict back in Kyiv came to naught. Greatly complicating efforts at deescalation was the uncertain status of the regional government. The core of the institutional crisis was the hole left by the delegitimization of the Donetsk Party of Regions. This political machine had held uncontested power for nearly a generation. It held its last meeting in mid-April, a week after the seizure of the governor's building (ODA). The Party of Regions in Donetsk proclaimed its loyalty to Ukraine, and called for the rebels to disarm (Nemtsova 2014b; Guzhva and Korotkov 2015). It soon became clear that Region officials were losing power. By summer, the Party had ceased activities altogether.

Rinat Akhmetov, Ukraine's richest man, was regarded as the kingmaker of Donbas prior to the war. He turned down Kyiv's invitation, on March 2, to become governor of Donetsk. In April, he interposed himself as a mediator between Ukrainian authorities and the insurgents, avowedly to avoid bloodshed if Ukrainian security forces were to storm the occupied regional administration building. This raised suspicion that he was using the insurgency as leverage against Kyiv (Chazan and Olearchyk 2014a).[20] He did not control the insurgents, though. In fact, all key establishment elites in Donbas – the local Party of Regions leader Mykola Levchenko, the Donetsk mayor Oleksandr Lukyanchenko, Akhmetov, and even the Kyiv-appointed governor Serhiy Taruta – were trying to do the same thing. They were all seeking to bargain with Kyiv, each demanding similar concessions (economic decentralization, regional status of Russian, and control over security forces) in order to deescalate the conflict.[21] In late May, Akhmetov

---

[20] This behavior by an established elite broker would be consistent with our model, if he had actually had control over the streets and been able to coordinate other elites to work with him.

[21] Akhmetov had a strong economic incentive to support Ukraine: his steel industry depended on access to global markets (Zhukov 2016, 2). The television channels that he owned ("Ukraina," "Donbas") were highly

came out strongly against the rebels, calling them "savages" and "a bunch of impostors terrorizing Donbas." He sent his workers out as a militia to patrol the streets of Mariupol, the location of his steel plants, the jewel of his empire (Akhmetov 2014; *The Interpreter* 2014b).

The pro-Russian militias did not recognize any hierarchical authority among themselves, either. Ukrainian officials discovered that the plethora of armed groups in Donetsk had no common leader or set of coordinated demands. The authority of the nascent Donetsk People's Republic (DNR) did not extend to certain Donetsk neighborhoods, let alone other cities. Girkin was not even indigenous to Ukraine, and even if his ties to Moscow were (and remain) disputed he was quite clearly his own man (Rachkevych 2014b; Smolar 2014b). DNR officials were also comically inexperienced in political matters. Neither Akhmetov, nor Taruta, nor the Party of Regions insiders had heard of *any of them* before (Witte 2014). The dearth of political expertise was such that a fringe political operative from Moscow, Aleksandr Borodai, proclaimed himself DNR prime minister in mid-May, creating an absurd situation in which Ukrainian government officials would have to negotiate with a literal Muscovite on the status of a Ukrainian province. Leaked emails show that Girkin's patron, the Russian oligarch Konstantin Malofeev, recommended Borodai's nomination to Vladislav Surkov, a Kremlin advisor who had recently been tasked to manage Donbas (Toler and Haring 2017).

The practical result of a completely new cast of characters onstage was ambiguity, bordering on incoherence, in the bargaining position that might "purchase order" from these aggrieved streets.[22] Symbolic rejection of a turn toward Europe, skepticism of NATO, fears of Ukrainization, and emphasis on brotherly ties to Russia were widespread. There was no consensus on what policies Kyiv should implement to make up for the fact that the Party of Regions no longer existed and the coal-mining East was now completely excluded from power in Kyiv. Insurgent factions sometimes appeared to desire unification with Russia based on the Crimea model, but this was a rhetorical stance that was probably deeply held by only a minority of the population

critical of the rebels, and in favor of the unity of Ukraine (Kudelia 2014). An argument has been made that Akhmetov and local Regions elites could have prevented the implosion of security forces, but didn't (Kuzio 2017, 187). The evidence suggests that they had lost control by mid-April.

[22] This fits the model. A demand x from the community to the center requires coordination. Without coordination, the center sets $/x/$

before the war.[23] The Donetsk and Luhansk rebels organized a referendum on May 11 but, according to the Ukrainian government, less than a third of the population came to the polls in what were chaotic and unverifiable conditions (Sindelar 2014). The question on the ballot was also ambiguous.[24] The Ukrainian government had made plans to hold a national referendum on regional autonomy on May 25, the day of the presidential election, but the initiative was tabled by the Ukrainian parliament on May 6, five days before the unsanctioned referendum in Donetsk and Luhansk. Donetsk governor Taruta called the Rada decision "a betrayal." A statewide referendum, in his view, would have sent "a signal for a constructive dialogue about the future of the whole of Ukraine" (Pancevski 2014a).

The election of Petro Poroshenko, on May 25, as president of Ukraine also clarified the range of the possible in terms of autonomy bargaining. His campaign was stoically center right, promising to defend Ukrainian national interests from Russia's aggression. His won decisively with 55 percent of the vote. This was a portent of how the removal of Crimea and a large chunk of Donbas voters from the electorate would change political coalition calculations. Poroshenko obtained a majority or plurality in all but one of the 201 electoral districts of Ukraine where elections could be held (*Tsentral'na vyborcha komisiia Ukraïny* 2014b).[25]

---

[23] Public opinion polls taken in spring 2014 showed support for unification with Russia to be at between one-quarter and one-third of the population (Illarionov 2014; Kyiv International Institute of Sociology 2014b). Giuliano (2018) shows ethnic Russians held these views in higher proportion than ethnic Ukrainians, but argues that this was out of a sense of abandonment from Kyiv, rather than affection toward Russia.

[24] The text avoided any reference to Russia or even independence by settling on the word *samostoitel'nost'* (BBC 2014b), an old concept from the perestroika days vaguely understood as claiming more power from the center short of declaring independence. By contrast, voters in the Crimean referendum on March 17 were straightforwardly asked to support *vossoedinenie s Rossiiei* ("reunification with Russia"). The December 1991 referendum that had led to Ukrainian statehood used the word *nezalezhnost'* (in Russian – *nezavisimost'*).

[25] The election marked the first time in post-Soviet Ukrainian history that a presidential candidate carried both the Southeastern (East) and Central-Western (West) provinces, and the first time since the inaugural 1991 presidential election that only one round of voting was necessary. Turnout was substantially lower in the East than in the West, even excluding Donbas and Crimea. In 2010, by contrast, the two macroregions had been within 1 percentage point of each other in turnout. Calculated using data from *Tsentral'na vyborcha komisiia Ukraïny* (2010, 2014a).

The election was not marred by violence, either, and radical right candidates received only a small fraction of the vote cast.[26]

The political legitimacy brought about by this election had an immediate impact on military operations. On May 26, the day after the vote, the Chechen battalion tried to capture the Donetsk airport. Kyiv bombed the airport with fighter jets, surprising the fighters (Shakirov 2014).[27] A jet-fired missile also obliterated a transport of retreating Chechen gunmen, killing forty (Walker 2014). The bodies were repatriated to Russia in complete media silence. Chechnya refrained from sending any more troops (Sneider 2014; Yashin and Shorina 2015, 29). The incident prompted Russia to take measures to deny Ukraine the use of its air space.

Through all of this, there were still attempts ongoing to reach a bargain. Recall that the path of play in our model specifies that there if there is coordination failure in Russian-speaking communities (and thus no coordinated sedition) bargaining over cultural autonomy does not cease. Areas with large Russian-speaking populations are not stripped of all rights – it is just that the institutional setting in which bargaining takes place favors Kyiv. The result is an equilibrium bargain that yields less autonomy.

This matched the flow of events quite closely. Kyiv sought to channel the demands for greater regional autonomy with the somewhat vague counteroffer of "decentralization." This came in the form of promises to provide regional authorities with greater discretion in the allocation of budgetary funds (Herszenhorn 2014a; Kondratova 2014; Levitas 2014), while avoiding the core political issues (e.g., Russian language status, control of security forces, special autonomous status of the type that Crimea had before 2014) that would have brought Ukraine closer to an actual federal model. The Kyiv government held preliminary meetings with some regional officials over decentralization, but invitations were never extended to representatives from Donbas (Herszenhorn 2014c). In other words, center–regional bargaining was actually taking place post-Maidan, but with the agenda set by the center.

---

[26] Russian official state organs temporarily ceased repeating the claim that Ukraine's government was run by fascists. These claims would resurface, of course (see Chapter 8).

[27] The Chechens had apparently been told that the Ukrainian military would not resist. This pattern would repeat itself often in 2022.

Internationalized War Begins

The border between the Donetsk/Luhansk oblasts and Russia was huge and largely unmanned, so weapons and people had probably been smuggled since the early weeks of the conflict (Kramer 2014a; International Crisis Group 2014). Checkpoints on major roads were still policed by Ukrainian uniformed border guards as late as May. Ukrainian agents were responsible for writing customs reports, seizing contraband, and, occasionally, engaging in firefights. With the flow of weapons increasing, especially during the Siege of Sloviansk in May–June, military clashes involving Ukrainian troops became increasingly common along the border and at the Donetsk airport (a transport hub). By mid-June, Ukraine had lost control of several checkpoints. This facilitated the arrival of Russian "volunteers" in unprecedented numbers and also the inflow of heavy weaponry (Cullison, Gorchinskaya, and Alpert 2014; Nemtsova 2014c).[28]

Ukrainian-speaking and Russian-speaking elites had bargained and brokered for decades in order to avoid exactly the international conflict now breaking out. Our model draws a sharp analytic distinction between the payoffs for the government in a domestic police action and an internationalized war. The social and economic costs of fighting a sustained interstate war (at any level of intensity!) are substantial. Overt conflict between Moscow and Kyiv had not reached this level of hostility since World War I. Until now, with Crimea out of the polity and war beginning to escalate, Russia had been notably restrained. By the early summer, the gloves were beginning to come off.

It is at this juncture that sophisticated anti-aerial weapons began to appear in the hands of insurgents. Ukrainian planes and helicopters incurred severe losses that summer (Miller et al. 2015).[29] Insurgents downed transport cargos carrying Ukrainian troops if they flew too close to the Russian border. Kyiv's inability ability to use air support for its military operations had a leveling effect on the capabilities of government and anti-government forces. A successful strike in the Luhansk

---

[28] Ukraine protested at the time that the closure of some of its posts along the Russian border did not entail the closure of Russian posts on the other side, as stipulated by a 1994 border agreement between the two states (Felgenhauer 2014).

[29] The rebels destroyed thirteen planes and eight helicopters of the relatively small Ukrainian air force (Lavrov 2015a, 228). For a disaggregated map of heavy weapons and vehicles destroyed in the Donbas, culled via crowdsourcing analysis of public images, see Dzutsati (2021).

area in mid-June killed forty-nine (Roblin 2017). These planes were fly-ing at high altitude, requiring far more advanced missiles known as Buk. In this context, commercial flight MH17, of Malaysian Airlines, was hit on July 17. Nearly 300 people died. The Donbas insurgents had suffered losses from air attacks, and downed several planes in the weeks and days leading to the incident (Balaban et al. 2017, 36). Whoever manned the Buk launcher probably mistook the flight from Amsterdam for a Ukrainian military plane (Matthews 2014; Miranda 2015). A Dutch-led international commission of inquiry ruled that the missile had been launched from an area controlled by Donbas insurgents, and that the Buk transport originated from Russia (Birnbaum 2018).

The downing of the plane was a major international news event. The first Western economic sanctions against Russia followed. The first two waves of sanctions – after forty people were killed on Maidan on February 20, and after the annexation of Crimea on March 18 – had been geared toward individuals, often political actors or military officers, or their enterprises. Other Russian elites had largely been spared. This time, core players around Putin were sanctioned. Western governments targeted the banking and energy sectors, restricted debt refinancing, as well as invest-ments in oil fields, and named Russia as the party responsible for "desta-bilizing" Ukraine (Ewing and Baker 2014; European Council 2014a).[30]

Meanwhile, the Ukrainian state seemed to be gaining momentum, manifesting as operational military advantage over the insurgency. Girkin and his commandos ran out of ammunition and decided to leave Sloviansk and bolt to Donetsk in early July. The Ukrainian army quickly retook the city and neighboring Kramatorsk. Ukrainians next turned attention (for the first time) to the two major Donbas cities – Donetsk and Luhansk – home to the "People's Republics." The strategy was to cut the supply lines between them, and between each city and the nearby border (Spaulding 2015). Critical to the plan was the establishment of a buffer zone of several kilometers along the

---

[30] The Kremlin may have feared the imposition of far harsher economic sanctions, such as those that were applied against Iran in 2012 (which cut off Iranian banks from the SWIFT interbank payment system). The idea of harsher sanctions circulated in Western circles in summer 2014, and was advocated for by the British government, but was ultimately not included in the EU sanctions package applied in late July (Ashton 2015). Sanctions may have had a detrimental impact on Russian economic development (Korhonen 2019) and bilateral trade (Crozet and Hinz 2020), but whether any of this affected Kremlin decision-making is disputed.

border, so that anyone seeking to cross the border would encounter the Ukrainian army (*The Economist* 2014).

Once again, Russia reacted to a sudden Ukrainian military advantage with a relatively low-cost and plausibly deniable countermove: firing missiles from multiple rocket launcher systems (MLRS) at Ukrainian military encampments from within Rostov oblast across the border (Clem 2018). On July 11, in the most devastating of these attacks, a Ukrainian unit was nearly wiped out (Parfitt 2014). The scope of these cross-border attacks was poorly understood at the time, but it seems that Russian missiles were launched at least 149 times over several weeks (Case and Anders 2016). As a result, rebels could resupply at low risk.[31]

Russian artillery hassling failed to stem the Ukrainian offensive, however. Momentum was on the Ukrainian government's side. The military reconquered many small towns and villages, bringing the troops to the door of the two major regional capitals and of their satellite mining towns (*The Economist* 2014). The Ukrainian army then resorted to the same tactic used in the Siege of Sloviansk: artillery warfare. The weapon of choice, from the old Soviet arsenal, was the Grad multirocket launcher. The Grad was originally designed as a saturation weapon, able to fire forty missiles in quick succession in order to pierce a NATO frontline tank division. There is no easy way to limit collateral damage (Bateson 2014) so its use was bound to result in severe civilian harm (Korolkov 2014).

And so it did. This metamorphosed into a large-scale humanitarian crisis because the Ukrainian army felt it had no alternative than to punish the cities of Donetsk and Luhansk for their sedition (*c*). Hundreds of thousands of civilians fled. Roughly half fled toward Russia. The other half fled to adjacent Ukrainian oblasts (White, Dalton, and Gorchinskaya 2014). The number of civilian deaths began to rise substantially. It probably reached 1,000, the threshold for defining a civil war, sometime in early August (Nebehay 2014; Office of the United Nations High Commissioner for Human Rights 2015).

The two sides settled on a macabre ritual. The rebels, who had access to the same Grad technology as the Ukrainian army (albeit in lesser quantity) would roll their launchers into civilian areas to fire at the Ukrainian positions. A short time later, often after the rebels had

---

[31] Russia still denies that it engaged in cross-border shelling (which would have constituted an act of territorial aggression).

left the scene, a volley of missiles would descend on the neighborhood, hitting apartment buildings, public squares, and everything else (Kramer 2014b). The rebels would thereby rely on a time-tested insurgency tactic: hiding behind civilians, baiting the Ukrainian army into firing back, then waving the bloody shirt. International human rights organizations documented all of this in damning reports that very few people read (Human Rights Watch 2014b; Nemtsova 2014a).

Freezing the Conflict

In late June, a month after his election, Petro Poroshenko decided to engage in formal negotiations. He declared a unilateral ceasefire, accompanied by a simple proposal: insurgent disarmament, amnesty for all, and a vague decentralization plan sidestepping security issues. The ceasefire did not hold. The conflict escalated to a full war in July.

Why? Part of the answer must be that neither side actually wanted to stop fighting. The territory of Donbas was an object of bargaining. Civilians, if they could anticipate frontline shifts, fled. UN figures suggest more combatants perished than civilians, despite the crudity of weapons and the primitive radar/drone technology used by the 2014 Ukrainian army to pinpoint rebel positions.[32] The use of artillery fire may have been effective in weakening insurgent military capacity, but it was politically counterproductive. The number of recruits in the DNR army – or rather, in the concatenation of uncoordinated battalions fighting under a nominal DNR banner – began to swell noticeably after artillery shells started falling. Many were outraged that the Ukrainian army would bomb their own people and saw themselves as defending their home (Robinson 2016).

If Ukrainians recall the arrival of the Girkin commando unit as the true beginning of the war, Russians recall this artillery assault as an inflection point. Contrary to manufactured atrocity in Crimea and an exaggerated fire in Odesa, the threat to civilians in Donetsk and Luhansk was manifestly real. Russia significantly deepened its military involvement after the Ukrainian army began shelling cities.

Another part of the answer is that it was still *just* possible for actors in Kyiv to believe that Russia would not send the regular army, making a decisive military victory by Ukrainians possible.[33] By mid-August,

---

[32] These capabilities would quickly improve.
[33] In the language of the model: $0 < a < 1$.

the military tide had turned in Ukraine's favor (Chazan and Olearchyk 2014b). Despite the presence of thousands of Russian volunteers, all with military experience, Russia had not sent regular formations and there were signs of demoralization and panic among insurgents (Pancevski 2014b; Socor 2014a). On August 9, newly installed DNR leader Aleksandr Zakharchenko issued a plea for a ceasefire to stem the rising "humanitarian catastrophe" (*Vmeste s Rossiei* 2014). Kyiv ignored the offer.

Russia finally responded to this newfound Ukrainian military advantage by sending forces sufficient to stop – and humiliate – the Ukrainian army. This allowed insurgents to regain confidence. It froze the conflict, as well. Before deploying its soldiers across the border, Russia made a decision that changed the political face of the insurgency: it pressured Girkin to leave, installing two local figures as heads of the DNR and Luhansk People's Republic (LNR) (Kates 2014). With indigenous leadership, the interlocutors of a future peace conference were cosmetically Ukrainian, allegedly speaking on behalf of the Donbas Russian-speaking communities.

Russia began its direct military intervention on August 25. The Russian army crossed the Southern border near Mariupol. This was a diversionary tactic to give the impression that constructing an overland "bridge" between territorial Russia and Crimea was their objective (Kramer and Gordon 2014).[34] The true main objective was the control of Ilovaisk, a strategic railroad hub and a key communication line between the Donbas regional capitals of Donetsk and Luhansk, both under siege by the Ukrainian army. Ilovaisk had been the scene of fierce combat between entrenched insurgent forces and Ukrainian volunteer battalions, but Ukrainian soldiers had failed to capture the city (Sanders 2017). Newly arrived Russian soldiers and their advanced weaponry quickly overwhelmed and routed the Ukrainian troops. There were over 300 casualties.[35] Ukrainian fighters may have been hit by missiles from across the Russian border (Ukraine Crisis Media Center 2016). Multiple sources – witnesses from the international media, military analysts, geolocated pictures, satellite imagery – pointed to

[34] After insurgents failed to take over Mariupol on May 9, the city was in a power vacuum until Ukrainian forces established control in mid-June (Salem 2014). The city was defended only by the Azov volunteer battalion, without military support, and would have been at risk if attacked.

[35] Official figures place the number of Ukrainian military deaths at 366, with an additional 158 missing, suggesting an even higher toll (Coynash 2016c). Many

the presence of Russian soldiers near Ilovaisk, and other locations in Donbas (Oliphant 2014; Rezunkov 2014; Sutyagin 2015; *Bellingcat* 2016; Case and Anders 2016; Semenova 2019). Ukrainian forces captured nineteen active-duty Russian soldiers (Zoria 2019). Up until the February 2022 war, Russia still denied military involvement.

What could have been the outcome had Russia *not* intervened? The standard assumption is a repeat of the Sloviansk model. Encircled, with their supplies seriously disrupted, and no longer willing to suffer losses from the shelling, the insurgents (or at least their leaders) would have given up, fleeing to Russia. We have to remember, however, that Sloviansk was a small city. A single warlord, Girkin, commanding just a few hundred gunmen, was able to pin down the Ukrainian army for two months. The Donetsk–Luhansk conurbation was a huge area, covering a third of the two provinces combined. Dozens of local armed groups had emerged organically, reinforced and resupplied from across Russia's porous border.[36] A siege might have gone on and on with tremendous human costs.[37] Our suspicion is that, had Russia chosen not to intervene, the Ukrainian military would eventually have had to depend on poorly equipped volunteer battalions for urban pacification. Instead, a Russian military intervention prevented outright Ukrainian battlefield victory. This is where our narrative picks up in Chapter 8.

perished after a ceasefire, and an agreement to allow Ukrainian troops to withdraw (Judah 2014). Three volunteer battalions (Azov, Donbas, Dnipro), and one territorial battalion (Kryvbas) did most of the fighting, even though, as mentioned earlier and as a Western correspondent noted, "their original function was to police areas liberated by the army, not to take on a full-scale invasion" (Kim 2014). Azov left early to defend Mariupol. The Donbas battalion was almost completely decimated in the fighting.

[36] Many foreign journalists observed that most of the insurgents that they encountered were locals (Chivers and Snider 2014; Reid 2014; Tavernise 2014). In August 2014, the Ukrainian military analyst Dmytro Tymchuk estimated that only 40–45 percent of pro-Russian fighters were from Donbas, though he cited no evidence (Mitrokhin 2015, 239). The first credible statistical evidence that we are aware of came with the leak, on an activist pro-Ukraine website in May 2016, of a list that included dates of birth, passport numbers, and residential addresses of 1,543 "fighters and mercenaries recruited through military commissions on the occupied territories in Donetsk province" in summer–fall 2014 (*Mirotvorets'* 2016). Nearly 80 percent of these fighters were Ukrainian citizens, mostly from Donbas.

[37] By August, the Ukrainian army was estimated to have a nearly 3-to-1 advantage in manpower over armed rebels, specifically 30,000–12,000 (Miller 2014). Without air power, it may have needed as much as a 10-to-1 advantage to break through, at the cost of tremendous civilian casualties (Cabana 2014).

Conclusion

The Donbas war emerged after a failure of elite coordination. Fragmentation and breakdown of coordination characterized the old institutional elites. They were overrun by the street. It is difficult to look at the cast of characters that initially occupied territory in what would become the DNR/LNR, even when they were organizing sputtering referenda, and identify the elite community actors that our theory assumes. The charismatic elites "emerging from the street" were revealed to be important social forces by the momentum of events, but it may be more accurate to say that their influence became more visible because wartime violence unraveled institutions.

Our model clarifies the causal importance of uncertainty. To return to the poker analogy, the Ukrainian government eventually made a decision to go "all in" on military suppression and "call the bluff" of the seditionists. This was after many intermediate policies signaling a willingness to broker. The slide into full-scale war resulted from a collapse in bargaining during this extended standoff. Moreover, the bargaining failure reflected confusion and disagreement about the probability and extent of Russian assistance to secessionists (a). This contributed to coordination failure among institutionalized Russian-speaking elites (with a few supporting *sedition*, but most trying to avoid taking that step. When elites found themselves dragged into conflict anyway, they issued overambitious autonomy demands (especially in Luhansk). These demands were rejected by Kyiv as being tantamount to capitulation to Russian aggression. We see this as evidence that actors held different assessments of a key parameter (a).

Russian military intervention followed only once there was a local "call" that they could respond to from an institutionalized actor, so that the Russian government could "carry over" an artifact map as a diplomatic focal point. Insurgents, having bypassed Donbas elites and seized the levers of local power, seem to understand they had something to offer potential patrons in Moscow (even if they did not quite know how to ask for it) and were completely mistrustful of Kyiv's intentions. They employed aggressively secessionist language. Kyiv then answered those calls with violence that brought significant civilian casualties. As a result of all of this, elites claiming to speak on behalf of the populations of these territories carried a very different set of assumptions about history and state legitimacy than did the victorious coalition in Maidan.

8 | *A Frozen Conflict Thaws*

We are nearing the end of our analytic narrative. The final chapter of this book will describe politics since the Russian military intervention at Ilovaisk in summer 2014 up until Putin unexpectedly began to prepare for full-scale war with Ukraine. In this chapter, we will analyze how Ukrainian state-building adapted to the frozen front lines, and observe the beginning of "shadow state"-building processes inside the two unrecognized entities – the Donetsk People's Republic (DNR), and the Luhansk People's Republic (LNR).

We have emphasized throughout the book that our favored analogy is a one-shot game. No crisis analogous to Maidan since 2014 "restarted" the game until early 2022. Payoffs reflect the path of play. The government in Kyiv paid the costs of fighting a low-intensity internationalized war. The residents of the DNR/LNR paid the costs of social devastation after being on the receiving end of a brutal counterinsurgency campaign in 2014–2015. The first part of this chapter is devoted to describing these costs in some detail. Many paths could have been better than the grim war of attrition. There was no diplomatic resolution in sight, however, at the moment that Putin decided to wage war.

We next see how the model performs in terms on the distribution of preferences over zero-sum cultural issues valued by Western and Eastern Ukrainians after the Eastern Donbas population exited. Had the balance of power between social and political forces in Ukraine changed? Were Russian-speaking communities and the government in Kyiv able to reestablish politically sustainable arrangements over language choices or the curriculum for teaching Ukrainian history?

The answers to these questions are outputs predicted by the model we present in Appendix A: a social contract that is worse for Russian-speaking elites than before Maidan. In the 2015–2021 period, two model parameters were lower. First, the probability of a successful military campaign by a community trying to exit the Ukrainian state was lower because of a higher-capacity Ukrainian state (which engaged in a wartime military buildup) than before Maidan, and also because support for this option collapsed outside Eastern Donbas in 2014. Second, many believed that the probability of a Russian military intervention to assist Russian-speaking communities was also lower than before. Everyone had observed, in the aftermath of Maidan, that the Kremlin sent troops to occupy territory only where it expected little to no resistance. The model was built with the assumption that Russia would factor in the potential for greater resistance by the Ukrainian army. Astoundingly, Putin still expected little resistance when he launched a full-scale attack on Ukraine in February 2022.

The second part of this chapter is devoted to describing what has happened to the members of Russian-speaking communities who did not take part in anti-Maidan *sedition* in 2014. The evidence suggests that the model's core prediction has been borne out. Now that these communities have less bargaining leverage, a new political center has imposed more stringent language policies rather than treating Russian-speaking Ukrainians as cultural coequals.

Geopolitical Recap

At the end of Chapter 7, the Russian government deployed troops in a way that was barely deniable, clearly conscious of the optics. Girkin was forced to leave and local actors were proclaimed heads of the breakaway republics. Direct Russian military intervention forced a stabilization of the front lines (the initial achievement of the first Minsk Agreement, or Minsk I). After war resumed in early 2015, the front lines stabilized anew (Minsk II) and the conflict then mutated to low-grade static attrition warfare. To understand why this standoff could persist for such a long time, it is necessary to consider how the players adapted on both sides of the line of control. First, however, we must temporarily raise our vision from the streets and trenches to the geopolitical picture. This will necessitate a short departure from the book's analytic narrative.[1]

Both Ukraine and Russia, as well as Western governments, were unprepared for the carnage in Donbas. After initially showing diplomatic prudence by not recognizing the DNR/LNR as states, the

---

[1] Those interested can follow parameters in an alternative formal model in Appendix B.

Kremlin seems to have felt it had to escalate to match the unexpected ability of the Ukrainian army to confront insurgents. In this summer of hostilities, Ukraine faced this Russian escalation more or less alone. At no point was there serious talk of Western military assistance. Western involvement was almost entirely economic. Relatively feeble sanctions over Crimea gave way to joint American–European enhanced sanctions over Donbas, but only announced after the conflict produced Western victims (the MH17 passengers) in mid-July 2014. The de facto Russian military intervention of late summer 2014 produced additional sanctions, at the same time when the first Minsk Agreement was concluded (Baker and Higgins 2014).[2]

The Donbas insurgents, observing that NATO militaries were not anxious to rush to the front to assist Ukraine, expected more direct support from Russia from the outset than they ended up receiving. They probably anticipated at least the provision of weapons, and at most an invitation to join Russia, as happened in Crimea. Russia was slow to send weapons, however, and never seems to have taken seriously the idea of using the DNR/LNR territories as anything more than bargaining chips.

It appears that part of Russia's refusal to act was due to the legal discontinuity in the proclamation of the DNR and LNR. The insurgents improvised the creation of parallel state institutions (such as regional parliaments), having been unable to capture existing ones – in contrast to Crimea. The coordination failure by Russian-speaking community elites meant that there was no legitimate institutional face of insurgency for Russia to support. Russia could do some things that were essentially costless: full-throated diplomatic and media campaigns, round-the-clock coverage favorable to the insurgency and amplifying the threat that arriving Ukrainian troops would commit atrocities, and constant information warfare on social media – all hoping the domestic insurgency would gather more momentum than it did.

---

[2] The initial Donbas-related sanctions aimed at limiting foreign credits to Russian banks and energy companies. Those issued after the Russian military intervention targeted oil and shale exploration. The key words in presenting the rationale were *destabilization* and *aggression*. Russia was accused of "destabilizing eastern Ukraine," or of "aggressive actions against Ukraine," but never officially of having intervened militarily in Donbas (US Department of the Treasury 2014; Council of the European Union 2014c; US Department of State n.d.). The core concept in the earlier Crimea sanctions had been *territorial integrity*.

What Russia did *not* do, between 2015 and 2021, was anything that would count as a smoking gun for direct military intervention. Ukrainian government statements depicted the conflict as "Russian aggression" from the outset. As far as we can ascertain, after sending troops to Crimea the Russian military pretended that it might intervene in Eastern Ukraine in April–May 2014 by massing troops at the border, assisted Donbas insurgents rebels from afar between June and July, and only directly intervened in the latter part of August, as the Ukrainian army was closing in on the insurgent-held regional capitals of Donetsk and Luhansk. Kremlin escalatory steps were calibrated and gradual, giving ambiguous and deniable support to a free agent like Girkin with a wait-and-see attitude; firing rockets from across its own territory to shatter Ukraine's control of its border; supplying insurgents with artillery and anti-aerial weapons; and only at the end dispatching regular Russian troops when there were signs that insurgents were about to be cut off from resupply by the Ukrainian advance. The goal of all of this was to force Ukraine to the negotiating table while maintaining the illusion that Russia was not involved (part of why the term "civil war" remained so toxic in Ukraine). Russia eventually sent military advisers in an attempt to coordinate the multitude of insurgent formations, but it appears that the full integration of Donbas militias into a Russian command structure did not occur until after international negotiations yielded the first Minsk Agreement.

International Negotiations Stall

The debacle at Ilovaisk resulted in a phone call between Ukrainian President Poroshenko, and Russian President Putin (Vitkine 2014b), the first direct contact between them since Poroshenko's election in May. The conversation produced the Minsk Protocol, a document signed by members of the Trilateral Contact Group, a special negotiating track set up in early summer 2014 that acted as the only direct channel of communications between Ukraine and the Donbas insurgents.[3] The Protocol laid the foundation for a resolution around three

---

[3] According to the diplomatic language used in the Protocol, its members were "representatives of Ukraine, Russia, and the OSCE." The names of the DNR and LNR heads, Aleksandr Zakharchenko and Igor Plotnitsky, appeared without affiliation. The areas outside the control of Kyiv were referred to as "certain districts of Donetsk and Luhansk regions."

main poles: cease-fire, autonomy, and removal of "illegal military formations" (*Kyiv Post* 2014).

The cease-fire did not hold for very long, but the front lines did stabilize for about four months. One important change, even if not specifically addressed in the Protocol, is that Ukraine ceased to use military aircrafts (but not drones). On the political front, the Protocol called for "decentralization of power" and the adoption of a Ukrainian "Law on special status" as a precondition to hold local elections in Eastern Donbas. The law (on "special order of self-government") was adopted in short order, but with the proviso that it would come into force only after local elections recognized by Ukraine (*Zakonodavstvo Ukraïny* 2014a). The elections were never held. Predictably, the removal clause remained a dead letter, since, as had been made clear already in the April 2014 Geneva Accords, Russia and Ukraine did not agree on how to define "illegal" armed formations. The Kremlin position was that Ukrainian volunteer battalions fighting against Russia were irregulars. Kyiv wanted the definition to apply only to the anti-Maidan insurgent formations fighting in the Eastern Donbas. Complicating matters further, Russia did not acknowledge that it had sent regular troops to the front lines.

The front lines started to move again in January 2015. The insurgents went on the offensive and, still relying on Grad missiles, became reckless, shelling missile clusters at two cities and one checkpoint, killing thirty civilians in Mariupol alone (Toler 2015; Tufft 2015). The main prize was Debaltseve, a key railroad hub linking Donetsk and Luhansk, allowing for the transport of military vehicles (MacDonald 2015). The city was mercilessly pounded by artillery, supported by tank divisions from Russia, causing more than 500 combatant and civilian deaths (*ReliefWeb* 2015a). The Battle of Debaltseve lasted five weeks before the battered and demoralized Ukrainian forces retreated. The intensity of the battle, the barely disguised Russian military presence, and broader concerns that the stable front lines might collapse elsewhere in Donbas, induced an emergency summit in Minsk between the chancellor of Germany and the presidents of France, Russia, and Ukraine.

The second Minsk Agreement (colloquially "Minsk II") was far more specific in defining steps toward conflict resolution – particularly regarding military disengagement from the front lines, election and territorial autonomy, and the reestablishment of border control – but

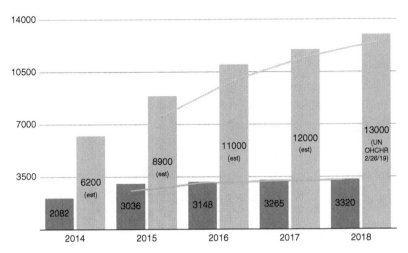

Figure 8.1 Civilian and military deaths in Donbas by year in light gray; Civilian deaths only in dark gray

its implementation never got past the first step, since no ceasefire held for any significant period of time. The Agreement, however, did lead to a long-term hardening of the front lines.[4] The basic territorial *ante* did not change much in 2015–2021. The Donbas conflict became defined by trench warfare, no-man's lands, drone flyovers, and artillery shelling. The use of military planes by Ukraine remained too dangerous, as the Donbas skies became "among the most heavily defended airspaces on Earth" (Peterson 2016).[5]

Though there were constant ceasefire violations, the Agreement saved lives. Figure 8.1 provides a time series of civilian and military deaths. In the first year of the war, when cities were under siege by artillery (in July–August 2014, mostly by Ukrainian forces; in January–February 2015, mostly by insurgent forces), we see the largest spikes of civilian deaths. After Debaltseve, with some exceptions,

---

[4] The Agreement was entitled "A Complex of Measures to Fulfill the Minsk Agreements." For simplicity, we will refer to it as the Minsk Agreement (in the singular) or Minsk II. The Minsk Agreement was signed by the same members of the Trilateral Contact Group as with Minsk I. In each case, the text was determined by heads of states.

[5] For a first-person observation of the improvised use of unmanned aerial vehicles (drones) for surveillance and targeting during this period, see Karber (2015, 12–21).

civilians could escape the line of fire. Combatant deaths were often the result of falling mortar shells, but also of snipers, exploding mines or ordnance, or noncombat causes.[6] The war, however, took a massive toll on civilian well-being. At least 1.5 million people, or approximately one quarter of the prewar Donbas population, fled to either Russia or Ukraine.[7] Those who stayed faced a tremendous decline in the standard of living, along with the destruction of infrastructure, the closing of factories, the wiping out of savings, and, until the onset of the COVID pandemic, the dangerous monthly trips across the front lines that retirees undertook to get their pension payments. All this even though the bombing of cities basically stopped by March 2015.

Minsk II was given additional international diplomatic weight by the action of the UN Security Council, which embedded the content of the agreement into a unanimous resolution (United Nations Peacemaker 2015). The two Minsk Accords did not mention Crimea at all, indicating that conflict resolution efforts formally separated Crimea (which Russia refused to discuss) from Donbas (which Russia was willing to discuss, but only on its own terms). This contrasted with statements from NATO which regularly linked the "illegal and illegitimate annexation of Crimea," and the "deliberate destabilization of eastern Ukraine caused by its military intervention and support for the militants" (NATO 2019).

Conversation among Western policy elites in 2015 revolved around whether it would be more prudent to give Russia diplomatic space, or rather attempt to deter additional acts of Russian military intervention. Around the time of Debaltseve and the Minsk Agreement, debate erupted on the issue of whether the United States should send lethal

---

[6] Nearly half of soldiers' deaths were not from enemy fire on the front lines, but from disease, road accidents, drugs or alcohol, or carelessness (Zhuk 2016). Injuries from the front lines are overwhelmingly fragmentation wounds, underscoring the conventional nature of the war (Gressel 2015).

[7] Over 1.3 million were officially registered as internally displaced persons (IDPs) in Ukraine (Office of the United Nations High Commissioner for Human Rights 2019), but approximately half these individuals did so in order to get a pension, and still lived in the unrecognized territories (Vikhrov 2019). Russia claimed in February 2015 that it had welcomed 900,000 refugees (Yekelchyk 2015, 151). IDPs become refugees when they cross an international border. At least 20,000 of the Ukrainian IDPs were from Crimea.

weapons to help Ukraine resist Russian aggression.[8] The United States eventually sent anti-tank missiles.[9]

Russia's Claim: A Humanitarian Intervention

The conventionalization of the war killed more combatants than civilians by a ratio of approximately three to one. These estimates are imperfect. The number of casualties among pro-Russian combatants remained a well-kept secret throughout the conflict. The DNR/LNR published no official figures, and Russia denied any military presence. In early 2019, the United Nations estimated that nearly 60 percent of combatant deaths since the beginning of the Donbas war – approximately 5,500 – were on the pro-Russian side (Ponomarenko 2019b). The estimate does not differentiate between local Donbas combatants, Russian volunteers, and Russian military personnel. Sources place the number of deaths among Russian soldiers in the 150–220 range (Czuperski et al. 2015, 17; Coynash 2016d). It appears likely that a huge majority of the others who perished were locals, that is, people who resided in Donbas before the war broke out.[10]

The Minsk Agreement was a humanitarian success in that it produced a significant decline in the aggregate number of casualties, both among combatants and civilians, but especially the latter. According to UN estimates, nearly 90 percent of civilian deaths related to the Donbas war occurred before March 2015 (e.g., up to and during the

---

[8] Those in favor argued that the weapons would deter a future offensive against Ukraine (Daalder et al. 2015; Kitfield 2015; Scales 2015). Opponents argued that the weapons could prompt Russia to double down in a theater where Russia is all-but-guaranteed to enjoy escalation dominance, ultimately increasing the odds of a more costly future offensive – with risks of nuclear use in the background (Hill and Gaddy 2015; Rumer 2015; Shapiro 2015).

[9] President Obama opted initially not to send these weapons at the time, fearing escalation. The Trump administration decided otherwise, announcing the first provision of lethal aid in April 2018 (Miller 2018; Eckel and Miller 2019). Javelin antitank missiles were not specifically prohibited in the Minsk Agreement (Lapaiev 2019). In the language of the model, we could say that the transfers were an example of how Western policy changed intra-Ukrainian bargaining parameters. Advanced anti-tank missiles made it more difficult for rebels to secede militarily and easier for Ukraine to sustain the war of attrition (lowering p, blunting C). Reciprocally, Russian support to strengthen the backs of the DNR/LNR fighting units was the other side of the ledger (raising p and C).

[10] There are reports of hundreds of unmarked graves in Donetsk, which might suggest that these deceased may not have been locals (Coynash 2016c).

Battle of Debaltseve). Military engagements across the disputed line of control steadily killed combatants afterwards, but in far lower numbers (estimated at close to 3,000 since Debaltseve). The ratio of civilian to combatant deaths decreased drastically from one to two (around 33 percent) before March 2015, to one to nine after and until end of 2021 (around 10 percent) (Office of the United Nations High Commissioner for Human Rights 2019).[11]

The fixed and conventional nature of the front lines had an overall positive effect on the level of civilian victimization (in the sense that far more combatants were killed, which is not the case in most civil wars). A great many civilians had the option of a safe exit, an option denied them in both irregular wars and zones of state failure like Somalia or Tajikistan (Kalyvas 2006; Kalyvas and Balcells 2010). Other mechanisms may have contributed to the comparatively low number of fatalities among civilians – mutual deterrence, cultural proximity – but the technology of warmaking seems to us to be the most compelling factor. When armies are fighting with conventional military tactics for *territory* – not fighting an irregular war for hearts and minds – civilians are not the resource being fought over. Civilians have a greater ability to just get out of the way. This is not to say that life near the front lines was comfortable. Social and economic devastation, isolation (reinforced by winter), lack of access to state resources, and constant ceasefire violations reinforced the costs of war for Donbas civilians. The claim is that irregular warfare would have had all these discomforts, plus additional agonies.

Before the front lines stabilized in early 2015, the war in Ukraine had been fought in an environment where it was very hard to hide atrocities committed against civilians. On the Ukrainian side, the dilapidated military found itself working hand-in-glove with civil society groups, activists, and nongovernmental organization (NGO) workers (Donnett 2015; Shapovalova and Burlyuk 2018; Stepaniuk 2018), as well as a panoply of volunteer battalions, including the paramilitary wings of radical right groups (Hunter 2018; Käihkö 2018; Bukkvoll 2019). The activities of volunteer battalions were

---

[11] Between April 2014 and early 2022, the Office of the United Nations High Commissioner for Human Rights (OHCHR) issued a thorough "Report on the Human Rights Situation in Ukraine" approximately every three months. It included data on civilian casualties, broken down by type: shelling, mines and explosive remnants, aerial attacks, and road incidents.

chronicled extensively on social media, giving the appearance of a Facebook- and Twitter-enabled *levée en masse*.[12] Additional clarifying facts came to light only gradually, as NATO member states' militaries commissioned outward-facing reports.[13]

On the pro-Russian side, the war also took place in the open, with international journalists and documentary filmmakers able to operate with a fairly wide degree of freedom in the first two years.[14] By 2016, however, access was severely restricted, and the two secessionist republics became relative information black holes. Governing institutions in the DNR/LNR no longer produced credible or transparent data of any kind. Local elections were not competitive, and it was difficult to decipher internal political dynamics. The one trend observable with clarity from a distance was the steady elimination of warlords. A wave of five high-profile murders first hit the LNR. The victims were reportedly all rivals of LNR leader Igor Plotnitsky (Olearchyk and Buckley 2016), who was later removed by a rival with Russian State Security (FSB) ties (*DFRLab* 2017). The trend carried over to the DNR, with some spectacular assassinations of volunteer battalion leaders who had developed reputations as heroes in Russia and war criminals in Ukraine, culminating in the killing of DNR chief (and Minsk I–II signatory) Aleksandr Zakharchenko in 2018 (*Kyiv Post* 2016; Kramer 2017; *DFRLab* 2018). Donbas insurgent leaders blamed Ukrainian authorities for the murders, but internecine competition for control of economic assets and illicit imports could also have explained their

---

[12] The open nature of social media data, among other things, creates new opportunities for researchers to observe war processes, and study war participants, from a safe distance (Käihkö 2020) The conflict zone can be visualized retroactively, through the reconstruction of maps of the zones controlled by militias (Zhukov 2016) or shared public attitudes (Driscoll and Steinert-Threlkeld 2020).

[13] A nonclassified synthesis of these reports can be found in Angevine et al. (2019). See also United States Army Special Operations Command (2016). The competitively edited Wikipedia page "War in Donbas (2014–2022)," as of August 2022, contained 645 footnotes, and a mine of open-source descriptive information (https://bit.ly/3P3szcx).

[14] For journalists representing Ukrainian media, or independent Russian media, covering the war became dangerous early on in 2014 (Young 2017). This explains why the number of Ukrainian and Russian on-the-ground sources in this chapter is lower than in Chapters 4–7. Two high-quality documentary films on the war, *DIY Country* (Butts 2016) and *Oleg's Choice* (Volochine and Keogh 2016), were shot in Donetsk in 2014–2015 by foreign filmmakers.

elimination. Because access was rare, and since actors feared prosecution and assassination, there was scant reliable data (Losh 2016).

International Negotiations Freeze

The sequencing of play of how actors *arrived at* this stalemate is specified in Appendix A. The sequencing of bargaining steps that might have extracted players from the stalemate is not specified. Both Kyiv and Donbas elites could observe the situation, and see that the conflict was tragic and inefficient, but they could not agree on (or credibly commit to) a division of the peace dividend that would have ended the war. Why?

The settlement problem resembled an intertemporal commitment problem. The classic statement on commitment problems in war settlement is that one actor fears that the other will take advantage of a post-negotiation window of peace to increase its power, then restart negotiations (or even war) at greater advantage (Fearon 1995b, 401–9).[15]

Imagine that the Donbas war were resolved, with a government in Kyiv agreeing to a package of rights protections allowing it to control the DNR/LNR territory in exchange for sparing locals the costs of militarized counterinsurgency. Let us further stipulate that Russian troops would have departed and the conflict would have ceased to be internationalized.

With Russia gone, however, the government in Kyiv might have been tempted to renege on the initial package of rights protections. Russian diplomats, foreseeing this possibility and bargaining on behalf of the Russian-speaking communities in the DNR/LNR, therefore demanded "renegotiation proof" policy concessions that would have "locked in" a set of social protections for the DNR/LNR populations in exchange for its disengagement from the conflict zone. Ukraine accepted these terms at the bargaining table in 2015 because of a fear that the costs of war might spill out of control. Since then, no Ukrainian government has been able or willing to incur the domestic political costs of implementing these terms. The peace dividend was therefore still being bargained over in early 2022. The final diplomatic negotiations over Minsk took place just a week before Russia attacked Ukraine.

The first point of the 2015 Minsk Agreement called for an "immediate and comprehensive ceasefire" (United Nations Peacemaker 2015).

---

[15] For applications of the commitment problem logic to civil wars and their settlements, see Walter (1997, 2002) and Fortna (2008, especially 82–5).

Despite numerous attempts over the years, no ceasefire ever became permanent. The second point prescribed the "withdrawal of heavy weapons by both sides on equal distances in order to create a security zone at least 50km wide." A process of disengagement was under way in 2015, but it collapsed, and heavy weapons reappeared at the front. Demilitarization failed because of an impasse over the Agreement's political components. The three contentious points were the conduct of elections, the reestablishment of border control by Ukraine, and autonomy for Eastern Donbas, which appeared in that order in the Agreement (points 4, 9, 11–12). A core substantive change from Minsk I is that autonomy ("special status") was defined as entailing official status to the Russian language ("right of linguistic self-determination"), control over local police, and consultation over the selection of judges and prosecutors. Contrary to Minsk I, the Agreement also called for the "[r]einstatement of full control of the state border" by Ukraine.

The main problem in implementation was agreeing on a sequence of steps. Border control was construed in the text as a process that began after the elections, but ended only after a "comprehensive political settlement" (consisting of elections and autonomy) was "finalized." This effectively placed the security component – Ukraine regaining control of its Donbas border with Russia – *at the end of the process*.[16] As its army and military proxies were moving the front line (at the Battle of Debaltseve), Russia pressured Ukraine to sign a document in which political steps (elections) preceded the reestablishment of border control. The text of Minsk II stipulated that Ukraine was to reacquire its territorial sovereignty only after granting autonomy to Eastern Donbas.

The process stalled from the beginning for lack of an agreement on how to conduct local elections in the disputed Donbas territories. After the Minsk Agreement was signed, Kyiv held that armed groups had to disarm or withdraw before local elections could take place, claiming that elections that meet international standards are incompatible with the presence of armed combatants roaming the streets (Carden 2016). The Minsk Agreement specified that elections could occur only once there is a cease-fire and verified removal of heavy weapons from the front lines (Scazzieri 2017). Russia, ceding no

---

[16] Close to half (44.3 percent) of the 923km land border between the Luhansk oblast or Donetsk oblast, and Russia was not under the control of Ukrainian border guards in 2014–2021 (Balaban et al. 2017, 8).

ground on this point, claimed that unconditional disarmament would *not* yield a free and fair election, but rather tempt Ukrainian forces to engage in mass arrests.[17] The fact that DNR/LNR actors continued to be regularly referred to as "terrorists" by Ukrainian actors reinforced this fear.

Complicating the matter was the identity of the combatants. The Minsk Agreement called for the "withdrawal of all foreign armed formations ... from the territory of Ukraine." When the Agreement was signed, in February 2015, the only such foreign forces were Russian (with the exception of a handful of foreign volunteers fighting on the Ukrainian side).[18] Western intelligence services knew that Russian forces had a significant presence in Eastern Donbas – in weaponry, military advisers, intelligence officers, and even regular soldiers during the Battle of Debaltseve. This reality could not be explicitly acknowledged in diplomatic documents (since Russia denied being involved and its role was essential for the Agreement).[19] The formulations in the Minsk Agreement reflected this ambiguity. Essentially, Ukraine's position was that Russia had to withdraw before legitimate elections could be held. Russia stubbornly denied that it had military personnel on the ground, and added that the Ukrainian unilateral modification of the sequence did not respect the text of the Minsk Agreement (Zinets and Balmforth 2015).

---

[17] Putin expressed the concern in hyperbolic terms in December 2019, when he warned of a "Srebrenica" massacre if Ukraine were to secure control of the Donbas–Russian border before elections could be held (*Polygraph* 2019). Between 2014 and 2017, courts operating in Ukrainian government-controlled Donbas territories convicted nearly 1,000 individuals of having supported the insurgency (Kudelia 2019).

[18] As we saw in Chapter 7, Russia has claimed that Russian citizens who fought in Donbas came entirely on their own initiative. The Organization for Security and Co-operation in Europe (OSCE), limited to two border checkpoints, could not effectively monitor the movement of Russian combatants across the border (Coynash 2018a).

[19] Since early in the conflict, the diplomatic necessity of allowing the Kremlin to maintain its official position of nonintervention has led to awkward phrasing in official statements. For instance, when the European Council declared that the economic sanctions imposed on Russia in the wake of the downing of the MH17 plane in July 2014 were "clearly linked to the complete implementation" of the Agreement (European Council 2015), but did not take the next step of stating that Russia was responsible. Knowledgeable military experts in the United States and NATO regularly made off-the-cuff statements to the effect that Russia had integrated various rebel battalions into a unified chain of command (e.g., Klapper and Dilanian 2015).

The Spoils of War

Behind the lines in the DNR/LNR, there were embattled militias ruling poverty-stricken populations, protected by heavy weapons supplied by Russia. The war had a devastating impact on the standard of living. In 2019, the average wage in the DNR was two and a half times less than in the part of Donetsk oblast under Ukrainian control (and three times less than across the Russian border in Rostov oblast). Pensions were nearly twice as high in Rostov and Ukrainian-controlled Donbas (von Twickel 2020, 95–6). Though reliable economic data from the conflict zone was limited, the scale of the economic contraction allowed it to be viewed from outer space – literally. Since the beginning of the conflict, examination of nighttime luminosity from satellite data suggested a huge drop in economic activity – by 38 percent in the DNR, and 51 percent in the LNR (Lasocki 2019).

Economic decline was aggravated in 2017 when DNR/LNR officials nationalized more than forty industrial plants after Ukraine imposed an embargo on trade, leading to an exodus of skilled workers and management (Neef 2017). Several officials continued to benefit from the conflict through asset seizure, smuggling, and misappropriation of Russian humanitarian aid (Alexandrov 2019), but conditions were bleak for most people. The DNR/LNR economy was heavily subsidized by Moscow by perhaps as much as $6 billion a year, according to Ukrainian government estimates (Havlik, Kochnev, and Pindyuk 2020, 21).[20]

We knew even less of public opinion and identity shift in the DNR/LNR population. It was virtually impossible to conduct valid surveys or engage in systematic academic observation in these unrecognized territories since 2015. One survey, conducted over the phone from across the line of control in Ukraine, reported that a quarter of the population (26 percent) felt "more Russian" and a fifth (20 percent) "both more Russian and Ukrainian" (Sasse and Lackner 2018, 145). Since Russian was already the hegemonic language of preference before Maidan, it was hard to speak of a real change in the day-to-day language of the region. What had observably changed was the attitude of authorities toward the use of the Ukrainian language, which moved from benign (if symbolic) tolerance to outright hostility.

[20] Russia provides no public information on its monetary transfers to Eastern Donbas (Zverev 2016). Secret subsidies were allegedly routed through a bank in the unrecognized state of South Ossetia (von Twickel 2017).

Before Maidan, most schools in Donbas were Russian-medium, but Ukrainian was taught as a second language. Ukrainian has since been removed from the school curriculum completely (Coynash 2019).

In some sense the reverse phenomenon could be observed in the rest of Ukraine. The idea that the Russian language represented a security threat to the territorial cohesion of the state became relatively mainstream in Ukrainian politics and served as the foundation of new language laws. Those institutional changes were seized upon by Putin as evidence of a desire to commit "genocide" against Russians and Russian-speakers (leaving, as always, the distinction between the two ambiguous). Yet outside of Eastern Donbas, language became in practice disconnected from loyalty to the Ukrainian state. Putin expected the mass of Russian-speakers in the Ukrainian East to side with Russia in a nationalist post-Maidan Ukraine. Most Russian-speakers instead sided with Ukraine. A critical mass *fought off* what they saw as a Russian invasion. The Donbas war, territorially frozen from 2015 to 2022, was depicted in Russian propaganda as a war against Ukrainian nationalists. This was profoundly misleading. The frozen conflict had a significant number of Russian-speakers on both sides and could actually be framed as an intra-*Russkii mir* (Russian World) civil war, between the eastern part of the Donbas and the rest of the Southeast (see Map 8.1).[21]

The *Russkii mir* war even included a large number of radical right paramilitary group members – the players so important to our narrative in Chapter 4 – who had previously taken it upon themselves to defend their nation-state in the streets of Eastern cities and were Russian-speakers. Most of them reconstituted as volunteer battalions to face down the Russian threat. After the Battle of Debaltseve (yielding Minsk II), the Ukrainian army began to rely on contract soldiers, former conscripts who agreed to stay on for a limited time. Many politically active veterans groups integrated into regular Ukrainian forces. Others maintained parastatal links to the army or the Ministry

---

[21] An indicator of Eastern Ukrainian involvement in the war (on the territories controlled by the Ukrainian government) was military deaths. Once adjusted for the loss of Crimea and of roughly half of the population of Donbas, the proportion of military deaths per region of birth was around 35 percent in the South/East (whose overall population was about 40 percent of the Ukrainian total in the last census), 43 percent in the Center (overall population around 37 percent), and 22 percent in Western Ukraine (about its demographic weight). Data calculated from Ukrains'kyi memorial, https://ukraine-memorial.org.

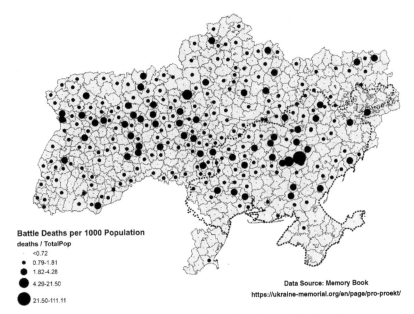

Battle Deaths per 1000 Population
deaths / TotalPop
·   <0.72
• 0.79-1.81
● 1.82-4.28
● 4.29-21.50
● 21.50-111.11

Data Source: Memory Book
https://ukraine-memorial.org/en/page/pro-proekt/

Map 8.1 Birthplaces of Ukrainian military dead per capita by *raion*

of Internal Affairs but remained ready to be called up if needed and retained their equipment as property (Kuzio 2017, 262). Two volunteer battalion "brands" in particular acquired outsized political visibility after the front stabilized: Pravyi sektor, for a while, but particularly Azov, which became the dominant radical right brand (Clapp 2016; Umland 2019).[22] Their effectiveness was not felt in parliament, but in the streets. Radical right groups used violence in August 2015 to prevent parliament from passing a constitutional amendment that

---

[22] Azov nested officially under the National Guard and maintained good relations with the National Police (Shekhovtsov 2015) and the Ministry of the Internal Affairs (Cohen 2018), even receiving some state funding for "national-patriotic education" projects (Kuzmenko and Colborne 2019). Pravyi sektor formally refused to be subordinated and maintained an ethos of confrontation with the post-Maidan government that proved self-defeating (Gorbach 2018). The radical right, prominent on Maidan, failed to make a dent in post-Maidan elections. A few of its candidates were elected in individual constituencies or to the party list of established parties (Fedorenko and Umland 2022), but no party or electoral bloc could get past the electoral threshold to get representation in parliament. In 2019, a coalition of Svoboda (which was in parliament before 2014), National Corps (the civilian face of Azov), and Pravyi sektor could only gather 2 percent of the national vote.

would have allowed autonomy for Eastern Donbas and facilitated implementation of the Minsk Accords (see "A New Equilibrium," below).[23] In 2017, veterans of the Donbas and Aidar voluntary battalions organized a railroad blockade to stop the coal trade that had persisted despite the war between the unrecognized Donbas entities and Ukraine (Grytsenko 2017; Kostanyan and Remizov 2017).[24] In each case, the government had been unwilling to confront the protesters – largely because they were armed, enjoyed a degree of military and political protection, and were savvy about timing their moments of public confrontation.[25]

A New Equilibrium: Language, Symbolic Politics, and Geopolitics Redux

Ukraine *did* become "more Ukrainian" after 2014. In losing control of Crimea and Eastern Donbas, the two areas with the highest density of ethnic Russians, Ukraine was suddenly deprived of at least 30 percent of all its Russians, decreasing the proportion of ethnic Russians from 17 percent to 12 percent. Surveys also suggested that the proportion of self-described Russians in government-controlled Ukraine had been declining steadily.[26] When former US Ambassador to Russia Michael McFaul famously likened taking Crimea, and losing Ukraine, to a "pawn for a queen" trade by Putin, this was the essence of his argument (Morrison 2014).

---

[23] The Ministry of Internal Affairs blamed Svoboda for the violence (Quinn 2015). Around 150 protesters in military gear wore volunteer battalion patches (*ReliefWeb* 2015b).

[24] The government objected, but then relented. Official trade never resumed.

[25] Azov/National Corps (and smaller groups like C-14) also supported urban street gangs that engaged in vigilantism (Shukan 2019). They framed their legitimacy narrowly, as a fight against crime and corruption, but people suspected of being "pro-Russian," "leftists," "fifth columnists," or outside acceptable morality (LGBTQ, Roma) were also frequently harassed (Shramovych 2017; Likhachev 2018). Recall that threats of violence meant to suppress free speech, and raising the cost of collective action for pro-Russian community leaders (μ), are important to our model.

[26] Kulyk (2018) estimated that the proportion could have decreased to 10 percent nationwide, hypothesizing that the decline is attributable to identity redefinition, not just outmigration. People who previously responded "Russian" to the question "what is your nationality?" are now more likely to declare themselves to be "Ukrainian." The trend had been observed before Maidan by Stebelsky (2009).

Adapting to the loss of Crimea and Eastern Donbas upended Ukrainian electoral math. The Russian-speaking East and the Ukrainian-speaking West had been voting as blocs that roughly balanced each other, seesawing with some regularity in and out of power. After Maidan the exclusion of the West could no longer be a viable path to electoral success (D'Anieri 2019a). In 2014, the party of President Petro Poroshenko, whose electoral base was in the Ukrainian West, obtained significant voter support in all Eastern oblasts.[27] Five years later, in 2019, the party of Dnipro-based President Volodymyr Zelensky in Eastern Ukraine obtained plurality or majority support throughout the East – and almost everywhere else in Ukraine, as well.

Just as disorienting, when out of power, the successor parties of the traditional pre-Maidan Eastern Ukrainian electorate no longer enjoyed anything like a veto on core political issues. In the seven years after Maidan, no opposition party emerged to aggregate the preferences of the Russian-speaking Eastern constituency and challenge the center.[28] Donetsk had been the headquarters of the Party of Regions. Without Donetsk, the East no longer spoke with one voice. The Opposition Platform remained an important political force in Ukrainian government-controlled Donbas, but it received just 9.7 percent of the vote nationally in 2014 (down from 30 percent two years before), and 7 percent of the seats in parliament.[29] No East-based party had the votes to successfully contest national power. Nothing could stop or slow legislation popular in the Ukrainian West.

The absence of a coordinated legislative advocate for Russian-speaking communities was felt most acutely in the debates over the autonomy of Eastern Donbas. Other areas of state policy became symbolic testing grounds and litmus tests for loyalty to the dominant Ukrainian bargaining position. Consider the matter of political decentralization. The Minsk Agreement explicitly called for the "special status" of contested territories to be given constitutional protection.

---

[27] Some noted at the time that turnout in the East that fall was much lower than in the West.

[28] The Donbas-based Communist Party of Ukraine, with 3.9 percent (down from 13.2 percent), failed to cross the minimal 5 percent threshold in 2014, and was banned altogether afterwards (Guz 2019).

[29] The coalition Opposition Platform – For Life got 13.1 percent of the vote (and 10 percent of the seats) in the 2019 elections (Herron, Thunberg, and Boyko 2015; *Ukrains'ka pravda* 2019).

In August 2015, the Poroshenko government sought to amend nine constitutional articles on self-government as part of a broad reform on "decentralization."[30] The very last clause made an exception for "certain districts of Donetsk and Luhansk oblasts" where the "peculiarities of self-government ... are determined by a separate law" (Verkhovna Rada Ukraïny 2015). The mere mention that the Eastern Donbas territories would be treated differently in the constitution, however, lit the fuse. After the amendments were adopted in a first reading (with a simple majority), MPs cried treason and seized the rostrum, forcing an end to the session (*Ukrains'ka pravda* 2015). Outside parliament, a demonstration turned violent. Protesters attacked the police with sticks, smoke bombs, and tear gas canisters, causing over 100 injuries. A live grenade killed three policemen (Quinn 2015). This was the worst violence outside of the war theater since February 2014 on Maidan. There was no further attempt to amend the constitution afterwards.[31]

Understanding the pushback against constitutional autonomy provisions requires understanding that, in the dominant Ukrainian discourse, the war in Donbas was a war against Russia. The Donbas fighters – who mostly resided in Donbas prior to the conflict – were seen as proxies. In a 2018 law, Russia was officially labeled the *derzhava-agresor* (aggressor-state), with no specific indication of when exactly the aggression began (Buderats'kyi 2018). Anyone advocating for autonomy became subject to charges of being a fifth columnist for Putin. In September 2019, an appeal by nearly 100 Ukrainian public figures, including two former foreign ministers who served under President Yushchenko, made the point explicitly: "The Ukrainian territories liberated from Russia cannot have any special status that would call into question the unitary structure of Ukraine" (*Tsenzor. net* 2019). The claim that Minsk implementation would "give Russia a veto" over Ukraine's future became a staple of mainstream political discourse (Ponomarenko 2019a; Shandra 2019b).[32]

---

[30] Decentralization is a broad-based reform giving more control to local units over their budget. The powers do not extend to the identity (language) or security (police) matters envisaged in the Minsk Agreement.

[31] A 2017 renewal of the (nonoperative) law on a hypothetical "special order" for the disputed Donbas territories created commotion in parliament when a radical nationalist deputy threw a smoke bomb (*RFE/RL* 2017).

[32] The text of the Minsk Agreement did not mention a veto over Ukraine joining NATO, though DNR/LNR leaders had lobbied for such language in February 2015 (*Zn.ua* 2015).

In 2015, the Ukrainian parliament passed a package of four "decom-munization laws."[33] Their passage accelerated a process of renaming streets and cities underway since Maidan.[34] The laws were criticized as vague and unenforceable, prohibiting "the public denial of the legiti-macy of the criminal nature of the (Soviet) regime," or the "falsification of history" (Shevel 2015) – but symbology was the more important goal. The laws clarified that the Ukrainian nation-state was associated with a single narrative, leaving no official space for a Russian/Eastern Ukrainian counternarrative of common descent between Ukrainians and Russians. The Holodomor was unambiguously a genocide. The war against Nazi Germany was to be named World War II (starting in 1939 with the destruction of Poland and the Soviet annexation of Western Ukraine), and *not* the Great Patriotic War (starting in 1941). The Organization of Ukrainian Nationalists (OUN) was proclaimed a national liberation movement, the Soviet Union a criminal totalitarian state.[35]

Religion also became a battleground. Historically, a staple of Ukrainian nationalist thought has been that the Orthodox Church in Ukraine should be independent (autocephalous) from the Orthodox Church in Russia. Attempts in the 1920s and 1940s to create a Ukrainian autocephalous Church were crushed (Denysenko 2018). In 1992 a Ukrainian Orthodox Church Kyiv Patriarchate was created, but most Orthodox believers stayed with the Moscow-affiliated Church – until Maidan. The Kyiv Church was not recognized by Constantinople, the "mother" church, until 2018 when the Ecumenical Patriarch of Constantinople announced that he would recognize the Ukrainian Church as autocephalous. This became official in January 2019. The Russian Orthodox Church (in Moscow and Kyiv) was vehemently

---

[33] Provocatively, the law banning Soviet symbols was named "On the Condemnation of the Communist and National Socialist (Nazi) Regimes, and Prohibition of Propaganda and their Symbols," placing the Soviet Union on the same moral plane as Nazi Germany (Ukrains'kyi institut natsional'noï pam'iati 2015a, 2015b).

[34] The laws institutionalized grassroots behavior. More than 500 monuments to Lenin had been removed from across the landscape by the time the laws were adopted (Shevel 2016). The exception being Galicia where such processes had unfolded already throughout the 1990s.

[35] Surveys suggested that the Holodomor-as-genocide interpretation has gained broad acceptance across most Ukrainian regions as a result of these new state policies, although the traditional East/West divide persisted over the heroization of the OUN-UPA, and the criminalization of the Soviet state (Sereda 2016).

opposed. The Russian government convened a meeting its Security Council to signal that it viewed these developments as a threat.[36]

Aspiration of geopolitical alignment with the West was symbolically locked in. The Ukrainian constitution was amended in 2019 to clarify that no future government of Ukraine could pass laws reversing Ukraine's status as a NATO aspirant. The United States and its Commonwealth allies (the United Kingdom, Canada, and Australia), while careful to insist that NATO membership was not on the table in the near term, began to train Ukrainian soldiers in Western Ukraine (Gorka 2017). Support for joining NATO increased substantially (59 percent in December 2021), but less so in the Southeast where voters were divided almost equally (Kyiv International Institute of Sociology 2021).

There were also substantial changes in language policy. In 2017, Ukraine passed an Education Law making Ukrainian the only language of instruction in high schools (*Zakonodavstvo Ukraïny* 2017).[37] The Opposition Bloc opposed the law, claiming that it violated "the right of citizens to use their native language," and was unconstitutional (*Radio Svoboda* 2019), but all other parties supported it. A 2019 language law reiterated the elimination of non-Ukrainian schools after the elementary level, pointedly declaring that granting official status to a non-Ukrainian language was unconstitutional (Vlasiuk 2019; *Zakonodavstvo Ukraïny* 2019).[38] By 2022, Russian schools were

---

[36] Although the Moscow Church predominates in the religious landscape of the East, most Russian Orthodox parishes are actually located in Central Ukraine, in an environment resolutely pro-Western (*Razumkov trentr* 2018).

[37] The Ukrainian law technically addresses classes, not schools. Officially, even in pre-Maidan legislation, all schools were Ukrainian, but classes could use another language, often Russian, as the main language of instruction, so long as Ukrainian was taught as a second language. The law elicited guarded criticism from Europe (Venice Commission 2017). Somewhat ironically, the law brought serious complications to the government *not* because it antagonized Russian-speakers (and mirrored the policy in Estonia – an EU member – regarding minority schooling), but rather because it eliminated *Hungarian* schools. Though Hungarians form just 0.003 percent of Ukraine's population, Hungary used its veto power to block talks on Ukrainian membership in NATO (Dunai 2019). The 2019 law therefore had to carve out a four-year delay for the implementation of Ukrainian-only schools for minority languages that are "official languages in the European Union," which excluded Russian (*Zakonodavstvo Ukraïny* 2019).

[38] The Constitutional Court ruled in 2018 that the 2012 language law had been unconstitutional (Ogarkova 2018). In the 2019 law, parliament granted itself the right to determine the question.

virtually gone. The main language of instruction in the great majority of high schools in Eastern Ukraine had in any case been Ukrainian by 2013, with the important exception of Donbas and Crimea (*MediaSapiens* 2015). The laws had clear implications for Russian-speakers living throughout the territory of Ukraine. There is a symbolic dimension, which we see as quite clearly meant to send a message to Ukrainian citizens living on territories Kyiv no longer controlled.[39]

A Full-Scale War

Though abandoning Minsk was not the official position of the Ukrainian government, it gradually became clear, between 2015 and 2021, that Russia and Ukraine were dug in. Ukraine wanted an outcome that looked something like in Cyprus: a permanent ceasefire, but without meaningful political concessions. Russia wanted Ukraine to implement the concessions agreed to at Minsk, namely, elections that in practice would have legitimized the DNR/LNR warlords and what amounted to autonomy on local security and language matters. Putin came to blame the West, and in particular the Americans, for the impasse. The Ukrainian negotiators dispatched from Kyiv, in this view, were merely the "messengers." Ukraine, for its part, blamed Russia for having fomented the war in the first place, the DNR/LNR elites puppets dancing on their strings. Russia, as became astoundingly clear in 2022, refused to treat Ukrainian actors as having any agency or legitimacy.

The reality is that Ukraine had been forced to sign Minsk at gunpoint – literally, the summit had been hastily called after Russia sent regular troops to assist DNR fighters in seize a key transportation hub (the Battle of Debaltseve). But the political components of the Agreement were not enforceable. France and Germany found themselves in the delicate position of seeking to move forward a framework premised on the diplomatic illusion that Russia was not directly involved in the conflict. In 2016, in an effort to break the deadlock, German Foreign

---

[39] The statement in the 2019 law that Ukrainian is the *yedinoï* ("only") *derzhava mova* (state language) – without exception – could be seen as a direct response to the Minsk Agreement, which invoked the "right of linguistic self-determination" in defining the "special status" of disputed territories. The 2019 language law emphasized the "unitary" constitutional status of the Ukrainian state established in the 1996 Constitution (which, incidentally, had also enshrined the "autonomous" status of Crimea).

Minister Frank-Walter Steinmeier proposed a formula which would make autonomy contingent upon the holding of elections. According to what become known as the Steinmeier Formula, a Ukrainian law granting autonomy to Eastern Donbas would come into force only once the OSCE certified that the local elections had followed international standards (*Hromadske* 2019). This was a sequence meant to acknowledge the Ukrainian position, while providing cover for Russia to "move last" on the withdrawal of heavy weapons from the theater. Political proxies in the far East would trade bullets for ballots, with warlords transforming themselves into regional governors.[40]

The Ukrainian government resisted endorsing the Formula, because it believed that the elections could not be open under the presence of Russian weapons and military advisers and would legitimize vassals of Moscow policy. In 2019, when the new Ukrainian president Volodymyr Zelensky wanted to reactivate negotiations over a permanent cease-fire, Russia made it a precondition that Ukraine formally accept the Formula. Under pressure from France, Germany, and the United States, Zelensky did so and immediately faced a substantial backlash from the Ukrainian center-right, which had rebranded itself as the "No to Capitulation Front" and fiercely opposed any idea of autonomy for Eastern Donbas. This view was widely shared in Ukrainian society.[41]

The concerns were twofold: First, that Russia was negotiating in bad faith, never planning to actually withdraw troops. Second, there was a serious concern that giving autonomy to Donbas would

---

[40] The memorable "bullets for ballots" alliteration is a nod to the empirical work of Matanock (2017) which shows that elections supported by nonmilitary third-party interventions can sometimes ameliorate this problem. Four practical difficulties would have been associated with buying peace. First, expectations of future aid rents can lead to a scramble for influence within local security forces (e.g., Driscoll 2015, 110; Staniland 2015). Second, the threat of individual-level extrajudicial retaliation for wartime behavior is hard to resolve in this part of the globe (see, e.g., Souleimanov and Siroky (2016), especially 696–9). Third, foreign aid is unlikely to be misspent by postwar governments if they can "game" the donor profile (e.g., Girod 2011). Fourth, post-socialist spoilers have access to a very potent symbol set (Petersen 2011) and the institutions to keep those symbols self-replicating (King 2001; Roeder 2018).

[41] In a survey conducted in October 2019 by the Razumkov Centre, 56 percent were against a special status for Donbas, with only 23 percent in favor (Razumkov tsentr 2019). While the survey did not provide a regional breakdown, the data suggests that Russian-speaking Eastern Ukraine was at best split on this issue.

sabotage Ukrainian sovereignty from the inside, forcing difficult parliamentary votes (such as having separate conversations for Crimea and the Donbas, for instance), perhaps even threatening once again regime change (Allen 2020). It is difficult to see how the millions of confident, aggrieved, and articulate Ukrainians could have been made to compromise on issues of national sovereignty. Russia's concern that Ukrainian leaders would drag their feet indefinitely on voting and autonomy for Eastern Donbas, whomever moved first, was valid. It was a stalemate with features of a classic commitment problem. Both Kyiv and Moscow believed that they would be worse off if they did their part, since the other would renege. By the end of 2021, Ukraine and Russia had been stuck at same impasse for more than six years.

This ends our analytic narrative. After Maidan, the equilibrium bargain was replaced by a new one, reflecting a different balance of power between contesting social forces. In the new equilibrium, Ukrainian voters became less receptive to cultural arguments that could be deemed pro-Russia in any form. Once bargains on cultural issues or language choices could be framed as concessions, the next step was usually to decide the concessions were not necessary. With uncertainty removed about whether or not Russia would intervene militarily (*a* close to 0, or so most commentators thought), radical right parties continuing to exercise visible street power (μ), and with foreign aid strengthening the power of the Ukrainian central government in Kyiv (a lower p and C), the level of autonomy necessary to buy off Russian-speaking communities decreased. Ukraine was becoming more Ukrainian, regional and linguistic issues were no longer central to electoral strategy. All of this was justified politically as Ukrainians resisting an unjust resolution of the Donbas war on Russia's terms.

Ceasefires could not hold, because Russia considered it in its interest to keep the war hot to pressure Ukrainians to concede on the political front. Some in Moscow hoped that Zelensky's election over Petro Poroshenko would open space for new negotiations, but it quickly became clear that there was not much daylight between the Zelensky position and the Poroshenko position. Ukraine would not budge. In 2021, although it was not apparent at the time, Putin appears to have concluded that the stalemate could no longer be solved diplomatically. A new strategy was necessary.

An early indication that something was afoot was the strange posting, in July 2021, of a lengthy essay attributed to Putin on the Russian presidential website entitled "On the Historical Unity of Russians and Ukrainians" (Putin 2021b) (see Chapter 3). The basic argument was that Russians and Ukrainians form the same people, that Ukrainian nationalism was a foreign creation, that Ukrainian nationalists are fascists because they collaborated during World War II, and – therefore – the post-Maidan pro-Europe and pro-NATO Ukrainian state was both (a) not real, and (b) intrinsically threatening to Russia. Little of that was new, and even the new bits were fairly on par with the standard Russian nationalist narrative toward Ukraine. Still, it was curious to observers at the time that Putin felt necessary to issue his statement in the form of a historical essay.

Beginning in October, Russia began to mass a considerable number of military personnel and equipment at the Ukrainian border under the guise of military exercises. That border now included Belarus, which had been vassalized in the previous year after Belarusian President Alexander Lukashenko requested Russian assistance to prop his regime following an illegitimate reelection. In December 2021, the Russian Ministry of Foreign Affairs issued a document, called a draft "treaty," between the United States and Russia. The treaty was an ultimatum of maximalist demands including the complete withdrawal of NATO military personnel and infrastructure in former Soviet Bloc states and a return to the situation that prevailed in 1997 before NATO expanded eastward (Meduza 2021). As became clearer in subsequent statements by Russian officials, what was desired, first and foremost, was a binding legal guarantee that Ukraine would never become a member of NATO and that the NATO presence in Ukraine (training soldiers, providing weapons) would end. While the demands expressed in the draft treaty were unexpectedly extreme, Russian demands regarding the resolution of the Donbas war fell essentially within the bounds of the Minsk process talking points from the past six years. But now Russia was overtly threatening war if the West did not respond.

The United States refused to engage with most of the premises of the "treaty" (and completely ignored the summer manifesto), countering with boilerplate proposals like transparency in troop movements and arms control (Aza and González 2022). Russian diplomats explained that this was nonresponsive (*TASS* 2022). Russia's official diplomatic tone gradually changed. Allegations of a Ukrainian "provocation" in Donbas became more frequent. Putin began to display open personal contempt for Ukrainian President Zelensky. Frantic diplomatic consultations took place while Russia's military buildup rose to 175,000 troops at the border. Neither NATO nor Ukraine budged from their core positions: (1) Ukraine had the sovereign right to seek NATO admission, even if the issue had not been and was not to be on the political agenda; (2) NATO was uninterested in withdrawing from Ukraine, let alone from the Central European member states; and (3) Ukraine refused to concede autonomy to the Donbas territories before the withdrawal of Russian troops and heavy weapons.

In the last week of February 2022, the new strategy revealed itself. On February 21, Putin convened an unscheduled meeting of his Security Council. The meeting was televised hours later (Prezident Rossii 2022). The purpose was to have every member on record recommending the recognition of the two self-proclaimed Donbas "republics" as independent states. Before signing the decree, he gave an hour-long public address on national television (President of Russia 2022a). The speech was in many respects an oral recitation of his summer essay, splicing together geopolitical and historical grievances. The tone was far more sinister, however. Ukrainians were again presented as a brotherly people, if not the same nation, but the emphasis was now on the malevolence of the government in Kyiv. Ukraine was perpetrating genocide in Donbas. Ukraine's government was a cabal of corrupt leeches, serving the interests of its foreign patrons, robbing its noble people blind. Ukraine was not a legitimate country. Ukraine had no sovereignty worthy of respect.

The recognition of the DNR and LNR signified the end of diplomacy, the end of Minsk. Rather than reintegrate Donbas, Russian policy was now to separate its territory completely – unilaterally altering Ukraine's borders for a second time since 2014. The full strategy was unveiled in the morning of February 24. Putin announced a "military operation for the protection of Donbas," allegedly because the Ukrainian army was attacking civilians and conducting "genocide" (President of Russia 2022b). Both were phenomenal lies. The entire Donbas war, since March 2015, had consisted of two armies occasionally shooting at each other, sparing civilians. Nothing had changed since, except that in the days immediately before the Putin announcement the armies in the DNR/LNR suddenly intensified the shelling of Ukrainian army positions (*Reuters* 2022).

In this bizarre logic, the "protection" of Donbas required officially sending the Russian army to invade Ukraine with a strike toward Kyiv. The expressed aims of the operation were to "demilitarize" "and

"denazify" Ukraine.[42] Putin had concluded that the ultimate way
tralize the security threat of a Ukraine one day joining NATC
eliminate the Ukrainian army in order to extinguish the state
nineteenth-century logic that no state can survive without an army; and
the national elite (who refuse to take orders from Moscow). This was the
new strategy: violently annihilating the actually existing state of Ukraine.

Throughout 2022, the world watched in horror as Russian soldiers dropped bombs and missiles on cities filled with predominantly
Russian-speakers – the very people that allegedly were persecuted
under a "fascist" government, allegedly members of Putin's fanta-
sized "Russian World." Unspeakable atrocities have been perpetrated
by the Russian army. The outcome of this war remains uncertain. In
seeking to forcibly bring back Ukraine through massive military force,
Russia may have lost Ukraine forever.

---

[42] We repeat the language of "denazification" here for historical purposes,
recognizing it is obscene to the victims of real Nazis. We believe Putin meant
the overthrow of the regime and the elimination of "nationalists" as a class.
This was an extreme version of the claim that Ukrainian nationalists are
foreign agents and act against the interest of the real Ukrainians.

Appendix A
Formalizing a Story of Strategic Ukrainian Adaptation

To ensure that our argument is internally consistent, and to be as clear as possible about how it works, we employ a simple formal model. One benefit of formalization is clarity about just what is being said. As scholars writing about a complicated period, we also found the discipline imposed by a model valuable.

A Game

Let us consider a formal model of a high-stakes game with $N + 2$ players. To keep things simple, we reduce our focus to the interaction between the capital city, which we call K, and a single Russian-speaking community, denoted by R.[1] The two players are bargaining over R's degree of political autonomy from K. Before this bargaining can take place, however, there must be coordination within the community R. R contains $N > 1$ community leaders, which we call i.

The game begins with institutional crisis. We have in mind a moment of discontinuous political change with implications for minority rights protections: an election that has been violently overturned, or an invasion that changes de facto borders (and thus alters demographics). State legitimacy is in question, and state capacity is in flux. Actors begin second-guessing each other's strategies and intentions. Following Jenne (2004, 734), the most dangerous kinds of crises are those which reveal something potentially disturbing about the intentions of the dominant group in the capital K toward minority communities R, or the intentions of a neighboring state with respect to K or R, or both.

The game is played in three stages.

---

[1] K is chosen for Kyiv in reference to the theory-generating Ukrainian case. The model could easily be applied to other countries sharing a border with a great power.

The first stage is one of coordination inside a Russian-speaking community R. In this stage, N individual community leaders i consider two possible actions, *sedition* or *neutrality*. Because the game is played against the backdrop of institutional breakdown, engaging in *sedition* may draw the attention of violent social forces, either state security or patriotic vigilantes.

Let $\mu \geq 0$ represent the costs imposed on each community leader i who plays *sedition*. These costs come in the form of pro-K intimidation and threats against leaders' family members. Following Kuran (1991), however, there can be safety in numbers. If many members of a community coordinate, and are *seditious* at the same time, the threat of pro-regime vigilante violence does not deter.

Call the number of elites playing *sedition* the *mobilizing elite group* or M. The order of play in the second stage depends on the degree of coordination taking place in the first stage. If and only if $M = N$, then *coordinated sedition* creates a leadership cadre in a community. The cadre seizes control of local institutions with legally recognized administrative resources, and attempts to bargain collectively on behalf of community R. Unanimity among elites also achieves safety in numbers, so if $M = N$, then $\mu = 0$.

With the community unified on a seditious posture, the game enters a second stage. R makes an autonomy demand to K, announced in the form of a take-it-or-leave-it offer to K. Since demands can be more or less extensive, represent the offer as a number x between 0 and 1. Arrangements more beneficial to K benefit R less. Larger demands correspond to more autonomy. $x = 1$ is a demand to completely exit the polity (e.g., full bore secession). $x = 0$ is a cosmetic demand for token accommodations that cost K nothing to concede (e.g., changing the mascot of a local sports team). Intermediate demands may include limited (or extensive) political autonomy, symbolic control over political rituals like parades, subsidies for public sector jobs (curating museums or working in educational administration), recognized cultural holidays, school curricula content, control of the language on local street signs (and their names), and especially control over the composition of police and security forces.[2]

If K accepts R's proposal x, then the situation deescalates. R receives a payoff of x, and K receives the remainder $(1 - x)$. If K rejects R's

---

[2] Cetinyan (2002, 649), Roeder (2007), and Petersen (2011, 54–5).

proposal, there is a violent escalation. Militias in seditious community R seize government buildings with the intent of provoking a militarized police action from K. Whether this community-led insurgency succeeds or fails is a costly probabilistic gamble. Either way, R pays violence costs $c > 0$.

The peripheral Russian-speaking community R and the state armed forces of K are not on equal footing if it comes to a fight. Fighting takes place around the homes of elites in R. Unless the conflict is internationalized, c is paid only by R, not K.

The end result of repressive action by K is uncertain. Success by R over K occurs with probability p.[3] Otherwise the insurgency fails, and K violently pacifies R with well-studied disciplinary and juridical tools. For both K and R, before subtracting the fighting costs, the utility of victory is 1 and the utility of losing is 0.

That is the path of play shown in Figure A.1. All of this assumes that $M = N$, with *coordinated sedition* in the first stage. If $M < N$, then there is no safety in numbers for elites who chose *sedition* in the first round.[4] Those elites will be subject to vigilante threats $(-\mu)$. There is also no successful formation of a leadership cadre capable of speaking on behalf of the whole community R. This creates an opportunity for elites in K to "buy off" one or more nonseditious community elites. The majority of elites may be neutral, or it may be a slim defection from unanimity (a "token face" of local legitimacy for the capital's centralization project). The presence of *neutrals* in the community facilitates attempts by K to rehabilitate the precrisis institutions in some form. The postcrisis regime will behave as if only the *neutral* elites in the community are the legitimate voices of the community to begin with, elevating their status as brokers to "buy off" a rebellion.

---

[3] Success can take many forms in Eurasia. Perhaps R survives as an unrecognized statelet like Abkhazia (see, e.g., Shesterinina (2016, 2021, 184–200)). Perhaps R is incorporated into Russia. Perhaps R holds out indefinitely in a peripheral political limbo, unrepresented and untaxed. With probability $1 - p$, the state disarms R.

[4] The need for unanimity is a stringent modeling assumption. Gelbach (2013), in his formalization of Kuran (1991), proposes analyzing the "tipping thresholds" of communities. This approach initially seemed promising to us, but we struggled with the question of how to empirically assess community thresholds ex ante (prior to seeing whether they "tipped" or not). Petersen (1999, 70–6, especially fn. 11; 2001, 294) argues that community-level anthropological observational data can address this problem in principle. In practice, we were stumped.

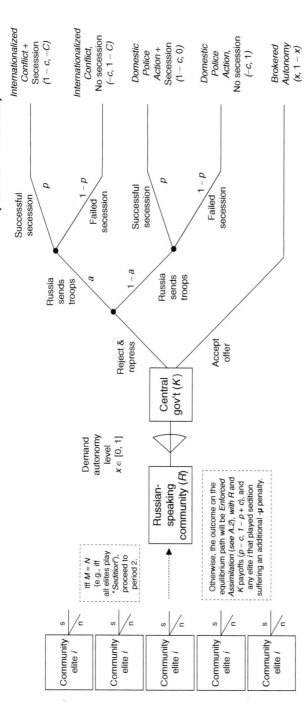

Figure A.1 The order of play if $M = N$ (*coordinated sedition*)

With this support for K inside a community, K sends military or police forces to protect loyal citizens and arrest (or deter) violent seditionists.

This means K can set the terms of the negotiation and dictate a division of x. Each elite i has to choose again between *sedition* and *acceptance (neutrality)*. *Sedition* in this second stage is a push for militarized resistance, hoping to invite police overreaction. Now that the community has shown itself to be fragmented, however, collective action will be riskier and thus more difficult. It is still possible that $M > 0$ and *sedition* persists, but i must attempt to secede without the whole community on board. p is lower. How much lower depends on the circumstances of coordination failure. If nearly the entire community remains *neutral* it is different than if most elites are *seditious* and just a few members of the elite are *neutral*. Call the community *fragmentation* penalty $f \geq 0$ (see Figure A.2).

If bargaining between R and K breaks down, there is an uprising and a police action. K sends armed forces to arrest seditious elites. The Kremlin may send military assistance to R, raising the costs of repression to K by C. Intervention occurs with probability a, modeled as a move by *Nature* after R and K commit to their strategies.[5]

To recap, the sequence of play is as follows:

Step 1. Each of N community elites simultaneously choose either *sedition* or *neutrality*. Use M to designate the number of elites mobilizing for *sedition*. If $M < N$, then all elites who played *sedition* may be targets of pro-regime vigilantism $-\mu$.

Step 2a. If $M = N$, treat the community as a unified player R. R articulates an autonomy proposal $x \in [0, 1]$. Capital elites K observe x, and either *acquiesce* and accept or *reject* the proposal. If K *accepts*, the game ends. If K *rejects*, *repression* and militarized counterinsurgency follow, imposing costs c on R, and the game proceeds to Step 3.

Step 2b. If $M < N$, then K will set the distribution x. Each elite i will observe x, and decide whether to continue pursuing *sedition*, or

---

[5] We considered simplifying the game further, "folding" the second and third moves together to entirely eliminate the move by *Nature*. This would let Russian intervention change both p and C. We did not, in order to draw attention to the distinction between a parameter composed of structural variables (e.g., community demography, distance to the Russian border, etc.) that are estimated the same way by all actors (p), and an unobservable, crisis-specific variable (a).

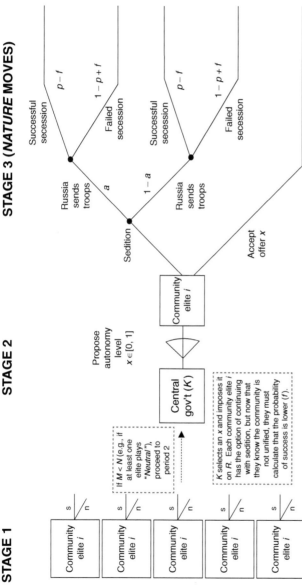

Figure A.2 The order of play if $M < N$ (*no coordinated sedition*)

accept. *Sedition* is a renewed attempt by i to incite a community to rebellion in Step 3 (now with a revealed noncoordination penalty $-f$). If all i choose *accept*, the game ends.

Step 3. If $M = N$ and K *rejects*, or if $M < N$ and at least one i plays *sedition* in the second round, *Nature* chooses *Russia Intervenes* (with probability a) or *Russia Does Not Intervene* (with probability $1 - a$). If Russia intervenes, then K pays costs C. *Secession* succeeds with probability p. The game ends.

Payoffs

Payoffs depend on the interactions of strategic choices.

What if $N = M$, R makes an offer x, and the offer is accepted by K? K receives $1 - x$ and every community leader i within R receives x. Call this outcome *Brokered Autonomy*.

What if $N = M$, R makes an offer x, and K rejects the offer? There will either be a *Domestic Police Action* or an *Internationalized Conflict*. Either way, payoffs for community elites' payoff calculations now include K's violent response to their *coordinated sedition* $(-c)$. The attempt to secede succeeds with probability p and fails with probability $1 - p$. The winner of the contest gets the whole pie, minus fighting costs. For K, those costs depend on *Nature* (Russia). A good outcome for K is a *Domestic Police Action* (*offer, repress, ~intervene*). In this case, the breakdown of bargaining imposes costs on the community R, but not on K. K's payoff in a *Domestic Police Action* is $1 - p$. K has a dominant advantage in the production of violence only if its sovereignty is respected by its larger neighbor. With probability a, its sovereignty is not respected. An *Internationalized Armed Conflict* occurs (*offer, repress, intervene*). K gets its worst payoff: $1 - p - C$.

The *Domestic Police Action* payoff for a community leader i is $p - c$. This payoff is the same for an *Internationalized Armed Conflict*. Russian military units, if they even come, cannot realistically arrive fast enough to prevent communal violence.

What if $N > M$ and at least some members of the Russian-speaking community remain *neutral*? Each of the M can expect threats from pro-K vigilantes $-\mu$. Next, a distribution x is selected by K. Each community elite i observes K's offer x. Each decides whether to *accept* it,

	Brokered Autonomy	International Armed Conflict	Domestic Police Action	Enforced Assimilation	Enforced Assimilation + Targeted Vigilantism
	$M = N$, i plays *sedition*, K accepts	$M = N$, i plays *sedition*, K rejects offer, Russia sends troops	$M = N$, i plays *sedition*, K rejects offer, Russia does not send troops	$M < N$, elite i plays *neutral* in stage 1 and *accept* in stage 2	$M < N$, elite i plays *sedition* in stage 1 and *accept* in stage 2
K	$1 - x^*$	$1 - p - C$	$1 - p$	$1 - p + c$	$1 - p + c$
Elite i	x^*	$p - C$	$p - C$	$p - C$	$p - c - \mu$

RANK-ORDERING OUTCOMES FOR CAPITAL CITY (K)	RANK-ORDERING OUTCOMES FOR RUSSIAN-SPEAKING COMMUNITY ELITE (i)
(1) **Enforced Assimilation** ($M < N$, *so* community remains neutral, $1 - p + c$) (2) **Domestic Police Action** (police action, no Russian intervention, $1 - p$) (3) **Brokered Autonomy** (accept equilibrium offer, $1 - x^*$) (4) **Internationalized Armed Conflict** (police action, Russian intervention): $1 - p - C$	(1) **Brokered Autonomy** (fully coordinated sedition as bargain offered to K: $x^* = p + aC$) (2) **Enforced Assimilation** (full-coordination neutrality, $p - c$) (3) All **Domestic Police Actions** and **International Armed Conflict** resulting from full coordination on *sedition* and the rejection of offer x by K ($p - c$) (4) **Enforced Assimilation + Targeted Vigilantism** coordination fails: others *neutral*, i plays *sedition* ($p - c - \mu$)

Figure A.3 Payoffs by strategy and rank-orderings of strategies by actor

or choose *sedition* (some for a second time). *Accepting* is a choice for political *neutrality*; *sedition* is an attempt to pull a community into rebellion. A choice must be made before knowing whether *sedition* will succeed (though i can estimate p, and also knows that *sedition* will provoke targeted police action by the state (imposing costs c) win or lose, even if the Russian military intervenes). If every i *accepts* x, and $M = 0$ in the second stage, the game ends. Call the outcome *Enforced Assimilation*.

For ease of reference, Figure A.3 shows the payoffs for K and a community member i for different strategy combinations and plays by *Nature*. (We have included a one-stop "cheat sheet," Figure A.4, which can be found at the end of this Appendix for readers having difficulty tracking all the model parameters.) *Nature* has no payoffs, nor are there payoffs for R (a corporate composite of many i payoffs). Payoffs for *Enforced Assimilation* assume no fragmentation penalty ($f = 0$) in the x from K if $M < N$.[6]

With the payoffs and structure of interaction defined, we can consider what should happen in the game under the assumption of strategic play.

---

[6] *Enforced Assimilation* payoffs in Figure A.3 could thus be even lower ($p - c - f$). With $f = 0$, K is already doing better in *Enforced Assimilation* that in any of the $M = N$ outcomes ($1 - p + c$), but it might be higher ($1 - p + c + f$) if $f > 0$.

Solving the Game by Backwards Induction

An appropriate solution concept for the game is a subgame perfect Nash equilibrium (SPNE), where no actor benefits from a change of strategies, and strategies form a Nash equilibrium whenever players make a decision on or off the equilibrium path.

Begin with the decision by K to *accept* an autonomy demand from a coordinated R threatening *secession*, or to *repress* the seditious community (the game shown in Figure A.1). The worst outcome for R is if K chooses *repress* ($p - c$). If R makes an offer, and K accepts, then K receives $1 - x$. If $1 - x \geq K$'s *repression* payoff, then K should choose *accept*.

The simple comparison of the offer x to its alternative is complicated by the fact that the *repression* payoff depends on *Nature*'s move. If Russia sends troops in response to *repression*, the payoff for K is $1 - p - C$. If Russia does *not* send troops, the payoff for K is $1 - p$. A strategic R should use the shadow of Russian power to extract concessions from the center to get as much as they can without crossing the threshold that provokes repression.

Lemma 1: If the game reaches stage two with R making an offer to K, the optimal offer from R to K is $x^* = p + aC$.

Proof: R chooses an x to make K indifferent between *repression* and *accepting*.[7] If $a = 1$, then K will reject any offer that nets it less than $1 - p - C$, but R gets to keep the remainder of the division, so x^* will be the lowest offer that fulfills the criterion $x^* = p + C$. If $a = 0$, then R and K are certain that Russia will *not* send military forces to defend a seditious community. To make K indifferent, elites in R now cannot exceed $x^* = p$. Comparative statics for x^* in intermediate cases with $1 < a < 0$ are straightforward, governed by $x^* = p + aC$. Any offer of more than x^* will be rejected by K, yielding the war payoff $p - c$ (worse for R). Any offer of *less* than x^* is weakly dominated by x^*. Since x^* cannot go higher or lower without making R or K worse off, x^* is a unique equilibrium offer.

Changing the order of offers changes the expected payoffs, so the game plays differently if $N > M$. Now K has the ability (and incentive!)

---

[7] A stickler may note that a token $+\varepsilon$ is necessary to overcome indifference, but we assume $\varepsilon = 0$ for a unique SPNE and to avoid notational clutter.

to select the lowest offer x that makes i indifferent between *sedition* and *acceptance* in the second stage. The offer that makes i indifferent is $x = p - c - f$. Even in a very permissive environment, with $f = 0$, an $x = p - c$ could be imposed on community R, yet no elite i would choose *sedition*. All would accept. Whichever player moves first in the game essentially make a proposal that "steals" the violence costs (c from R, or aC from K). Those costs are never realized on the equilibrium path, but they are "baked in" to a peaceful distribution of cultural goods.

Lemma 2: There is a pure-strategy SPNE that does not involve the play of weakly dominated strategies in which all elites play *sedition* in the first stage. Call this *coordinated sedition.*

Proof: If $M = N$, then the game continues to the second stage. R makes an offer. By Lemma 1, each elite i in the community should expect $x^* = p + aC$. If an elite i were to unilaterally alter her or his strategy, it would not improve i's payoff: defection would only mean that an elite transferring proposal power to K and penalizing her- or himself $(p - c - f < x^*)$.

Lemma 3: There is a pure-strategy SPNE that does not involve the play of weakly dominated strategies in which all elites play *neutral.* Call this *coordinated neutrality.*

Proof: If $M = 0$, i should expect to receive $p - c - f$. Even if $N = 2$, a change in strategy by i will not reach the higher x^* payoff; it just makes i a target for vigilantism $(p - c - f - \mu)$.

Proposition 1: There is a SPNE in which every elite i coordinates on sedition in the first stage, R offers K an x that fulfills the *equation* $x^* = p + aC$, and K accepts. Call this a *Brokered Autonomy SPNE.*

Proof: Consider defection by K. Playing *repress* nets K a payoff of $1 - p - C$ if Russia sends troops, and of $1 - p$ otherwise. Since the probability of Russia sending troops is a, if an offer $x^* = p + aC$ were presented, changing from *accept* to *repress* does not improve K's payoff. Next, consider defection by R. By Lemma 1, there is nothing to be gained by making a higher or lower offer x^*. Finally, consider defection by elite i. By Lemma 2, there is no gain to switching strategies from *sedition* to *neutrality*.

Proposition 2: There is a SPNE in which every elite i chooses neutrality in the first stage. Call this an *Enforced Assimilation SPNE*.

Proof: By Lemma 3, *coordinated neutrality* constitutes an equilibrium.

Brokered Autonomy and *Enforced Assimilation* are the only two pure-strategy SPNE that do not involve the play of weakly dominated strategies. The only logical alternative to these two equilibria would be an intermediate equilibrium, with only community elites playing *sedition* – but they will always wish to change strategies, either to avoid institutionalized discrimination ($p - c - f$), or to avoid vigilante threats ($-\mu$).

Summary, Key Results, and Comparative Statics

The model does not make predictions about war. War occurs only due to misplay (discussed shortly below). The model does make clear predictions about the relative levels of cultural autonomy for Russian-speaking communities based on their ability to *threaten* war, however. Nonviolent brokerage can short-circuit identity disputes and keep violence off the table, but the "missing" violence shapes the distribution of a zero-sum resource.

For i, the higher payoff of the two SPNE strategies is *Brokered Autonomy*. Achieving this outcome depends on *coordinated sedition* in the first stage. Following Laitin (2007, 143), our approach highlights "the political interactions *between* entrepreneurs and those whom they purport to represent, and *among* those who have coordinated beliefs of ethnic solidarity."

Since bargaining power for self-defined Russians depends on their ability to coordinate, it is not surprising that institutions – like the Party of Regions – emerged to facilitate that outcome. These institutions imploded after Maidan. They have been electorally noncompetitive ever since. The result is an *Enforced Assimilation* equilibrium observed in most of Ukraine (Chapter 8).

The exception to be explained is in the Donbas. The Luhansk Council became the only regional parliament in the Southeast to issue a challenge to the post-Maidan government in Kyiv. Elsewhere in the Donbas, what occurred resembled the sequence in Figure A.2: elites trying to keep their heads down and remain neutral, an offer from K to try to lure the communities back (sending police forces to create a perimeter around buildings but not storming them). Gradually, new social actors emerged from the streets that persisted with strategies of *sedition*. And eventually Russia arrived.

In our account, this war occurred as an outgrowth of uncertainty over what Russia would do (a). In the Donbas, neither local community elites nor Kyiv were certain how Russia would behave. In Crimea, certainty created quickly-brokered order. Most everywhere else, uncertainty led to coordination failure. Our account emphasizes miscalculation and asymmetric information.

Viewed from the perspective of many Russian-speaking communities R, the variable probability of Russian military intervention (a) was never satisfactorily resolved. From 1990 until 2014, communities with a high density of Russian-speaking populations had the opportunity to "activate" their Russian-ness as a crisis bargaining maneuver, acting as if they were poised to offer a safe military operating zone for Russian troops in order to extract bargaining concessions from Kyiv. Some engaged in these performances every few years in order to turn out votes.

To understand how this yielded war in 2014, return to Figure A.1 or A.2. Hold p and C constant. If $a = 0$ is "the floor," and $a = 1$ is "the ceiling," between these two is a range of bargaining outcomes that both R and K might prefer to war, and might both reasonably believe the other prefers to war, as well. This created room for local elites to bargain and to (try to) bluff. Our analytic narrative documents these elite machinations. Until late summer 2014, it was (just) possible for actors in Donbas to believe they could make extreme demands for autonomy from Kyiv, and that those demands would be accepted. It was also (just) possible for decision-makers in Kyiv to believe that Russia would actually stop at Crimea, and not send more troops, making decisive victory by Ukrainians over seditious communities possible. $0 < a \leq 1$. Some Donbas community actors behaved as if $a = 1$, seizing buildings and demanding amnesty. The analogy is an opening bid at $x = p + C$. This offer was rejected by K.

Figure A.3 clarifies a worst-case outcome for the seditious elites in the Donbas: *Enforced Assimilation*, accompanied by pro-K violent threats. That is what Donetsk People's Republic/Luhansk People's Republic (DNR/LNR) residents said they feared if Russia withdrew ($a = 0$) and they were forcibly disarmed. Russia demanded policy concessions that would "lock in" an equilibrium offer x^* in which $a = 1$ and $C > 0$ in exchange for a promise of future Russian military

FORMAL TERMINOLOGY PARAMETER REFERENCE

R = Russian-speaking communities
K = capital city
I = individual community elites
N = number of elites per community
M = number of elites playing "sedition"
μ = vigilante threats against *I*

x = autonomy offer proposed by **R** to *K*
p = probability of successful military secession by **R**
c = costs of attempted insurgency (repression of **R** by *K)*
a = probability that Russia intervenes militarily
C = costs imposed on *K* if Russia intervenes militarily
f = "failure penalty" to 2nd secession attempt by *I* if **M<N** in stage 1
x* = equilibrium offer by **R** that *K* should accept (= **p+aC**+ε)

Figure A.4 Reminder of parameter definitions (formal cheat sheet)

disengagement. At the moment Minsk was signed, some costs C were being imposed on the battlefield. Then there was a ragged ceasefire, the death count fell, Western governments blunted some of the pain of C with generous aid packages, the conflict froze, and Ukrainian politicians dragged their feet on implementing Minsk.

The Russian government never got what, in retrospect, it seems to have wanted very badly: an interpretation of Minsk that facilitated the emergence of a viable electoral base of influence in Ukrainian domestic politics. Meanwhile, the symbols and cultural policies of the Ukrainian polity adjusted to a new equilibrium, following our predictions: lower p, lower x^*. Putin wrote in the summer of 2021 that he would not tolerate the revised status quo. And so, in February 2022, Putin brutally raised costs C.

Appendix B
Formalizing a Story of Why Putin Chose War

This short appendix formalizes a familiar account of war in Ukraine as a result of geopolitical bargaining. The assumptions informing this model are not objectively true. They are defensible and seem (to us) to reflect Putin's beliefs based on his statements.

We begin by assuming a single policy dimension with utilities that are zero-sum. Russia's gain of influence in the Ukrainian polity is the West's loss, and vice versa. In international politics, unlike domestic politics, there is no third-party enforcement, so the only stable bargains that emerge have to be self-enforcing. Figure B.1 visualizes a range of possible bargaining outcomes. *R*, *W1*, and *W2* represent *ideal points*. Both *R (Russia)* and *W (the West)* prefer outcomes closer to their ideal to those further away.

Points closer to *R* represent limited Ukrainian freedom of action in foreign affairs and more deference to Russian preferences. Points further right represent greater Ukrainian freedom of action to make choices aligned with Western preferences. If a bargain is not reached that satisfies both Russia and the West, war occurs as Russia attempts to destroy Ukrainian institutions by force *(f)*. *f* is drawn closer to *R* than to *W1* (or *W2*).

f is not good from Russia's point of view, but it is preferable to any bargain right of Russia's break point. It is drawn at a point as far from *R* on the right as *f* is from *R* on the left. *f* is terrible for the West – worse, in this two-dimensional stylization, than "giving" Ukraine to Russia unambiguously. Why? Because Russia has decided that it has vital interests in Ukraine, and the West has decided it does not.[1]

---

[1] Following Schelling (1960, 187–203), we mean Russian leaders are more willing than their Western counterparts to endure huge risks over Ukraine-related specifics. Relative willingness to accept "not a small *bit* of retaliation, but a small *probability* of a massive war" (199) favors Russia. Figure B.1 makes it explicit that strategic stability between Russia and the West matters more to Western decision-makers than the fate of Ukraine-specific outcomes.

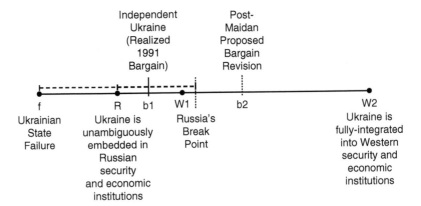

Figure B.1 Bargaining over Ukraine

R, the Russian ideal point, stays fixed in this stylization. Russia still desires what it has desired since 1990: a pliant Ukraine embedded in Russocentric security institutions. Western policy preferences do change over time in the stylization. *W1* was the West's ideal point in 1990. *W2* was the West's ideal point in 2013–2014. *W1* indicates more willingness to cede Ukraine to Russia as part of a geopolitical "sphere of influence." *W2* indicates changes in values or priorities – or perhaps just widely recognized shifts in relative power (both hard and soft power – see Chapter 1).[2]

Movement rightward from f to anywhere on the line segment between R and Russia's break point is at least a good for one party and no worse for the other (Pareto-improving). With many Pareto-improving bargains superior to f, and no supranational institutions to coordinate on (or enforce) a compromise, it is difficult to predict exactly which point on the $RW1$ segment or $RW2$ segment will be selected (Schelling 1960, 21–2, 54–74). All we can say with certainty is that it will not be to the right of Russia's break point, since any of those bargains would be worse than f from Russia's perspective.

To tell a serviceable story of postindependence Ukraine from the vantage point of Russia, begin with the geometric "fair" bargain $b1$, exactly between R and *W1*. Wind the clock forward twenty-five years. Replacing *W1* with *W2* visualizes gradual preference divergence

---

[2] This should not be decoded as our opinion of which actor is the "real" revisionist – but a gap widened between W and R on Ukraine-related issues over time.

between Russia and the West (described early in Chapter 4). Suffice to say that some components of a previously "fair" bargain of $b1$ came to feel like concessions to Russia for many Ukrainians, and also to diverse constituencies in the West. The row over the EU Trade Agreement and the Eurasian Economic Union was framed by Moscow's diplomats as formally locking-in aspects of the old bargain $b1$ (again, see Chapter 4). It was framed in Western capitals differently, as a coercive attempt to revise the bargain leftward, closer to R. None of this could be resolved peacefully – hence Maidan, Crimea, the Donetsk People's Republic/Luhansk People's Republic (DNR/LNR), Minsk, and all the rest (material in Chapters 4 – 8).

The growing gap also raised the problem of commitment. If Russia permitted a revision to the new "fair" bargain $b2$, already past Russia's break point, who could say that in the future there would be no $W3$ even further away (and a new demand $b3$)?[3] Elites in the Kremlin seem to have realized, at some point between 2018 and 2022, that they had "lost Ukraine." Rather than accept a shift to $b2$, the Kremlin response was to forcibly redraw the map (the end of Chapter 8).

The hope in Russia was that the occupation of Ukraine and forcible alteration of its institutions would be quick and easy. Western capitals hope that f will be a long, costly war for Russia, and less costly for the West over time. Perhaps attrition warfare, sanctions, and shunning will move f so far to the left that $b2$ or $W2$ is closer to R than f.

If the goal is developing a language to assist in brokering intra-Ukrainian compromise, a model in which Ukrainians themselves are not actors is the wrong place to start. It is foolish to assume that this conflict can be, or should be, settled "over the heads" of tens of millions of Ukrainians. This is why we anchor our book in a revisionist analytic narrative approach.

---

[3] For a formal treatment of arguments in this vein, with useful extensions, see Powell (2006).

References

24Kanal. 2014a. "Kievskii garnison vnutrennykh voisk pereshel na storonu Maidana – Parubiy." February 21. https://bit.ly/2TFungO

——— 2014b. "Lutsenko uzhe privez L'vovskuiu militsiiu na Maidan." February 21. https://bit.ly/2MpVlbq

——— 2014c. "U Ternopoli 'Berkut' pereishov na storonu narodu." February 19. https://bit.ly/2OXUHDQ

24L'viv. 2014. "Viys'kova chastyna u L'vovi napolovynu zhorila, popadaly perekryttia." February 19. https://bit.ly/2KqCD1d

24tv.ua. 2014. "U Ternopoli zakhopleno 8 derzhstruktur, dvi z nykh – pidpalyly." February 19. https://bit.ly/2FLqUZK

6262. 2020. "Richnytsia boiu 'Pravogo sektoru' u Slov'ians'ku abo 'vizytky Yarosha.'" April 20. https://bit.ly/3jz69ly

Abdullaev, Nabi. 2014. "New Book Tells How Russia Took Crimea So Easily." *Moscow Times*, August 28. https://bit.ly/2GrMItV

Akhmetov, Rinat. 2014. "Akhmetov Urges Donbas Residents to 'Fight, Fight, Fight.'" *Kyiv Post*, May 21. https://bit.ly/2GK7zrC

Ale, Per Kristian, and Jan T. Espedal. 2014. "Voting Fraud Secured pro-Russian Majority in Crimean Parliament." *Aftenposten* (Norway), March 9. https://bit.ly/3nTVinf

Alesina, Alberto, and Enrico Spolaore. 2003. *The Size of Nations*. Cambridge: MIT Press.

Alexandrov, Grigory. 2019. "Where Are They Now?" *Meduza*, May 31. https://bit.ly/2WEJBXa

Allen, Duncan. 2020. "The Minsk Conundrum: Western Policy and Russia's War in Eastern Ukraine." *Chatham House*, May 22. https://bit.ly/3JoH2xc

Allenova, Olga, Yelena Geda, and Vladimir Novikov. 2008. "Blok NATO razosholsia na blokpakety." *Kommersant*, April 7. http://bit.ly/2Eamzux

Amnesty International. 2014. "Ukraine: Mounting Evidence of War Crimes and Russian Involvement." September 7. https://bit.ly/2mKhmqf

Amos, Howard. 2015. "'There Was Heroism and Cruelty on Both Sides': The Truth Behind One of Ukraine's Deadliest Days." *The Guardian*, April 30. https://bit.ly/3rELd06

214

Amosov, Bogdan. 2018. "Maïdan. Nachalo – bol'shoi reportazh." *Novosti*, November 22. https://bit.ly/2I6Oh01

Angevine, Robert G., John K. Warden, Russell Keller, and Clark Frye. 2019. "Learning Lessons from the Ukraine Conflict." *Institute for Defense Analyses*, May. https://bit.ly/2sB8Ufx

Arel, Dominique. 2002a. "Interpreting 'Nationality' and 'Language' in the 2001 Ukrainian Census." *Post-Soviet Affairs* 18(3), 213–49.

— 2002b. "Language Categories in Censuses: Backward- or Forward-Looking?" In *Census and Identity: The Politics of Race, Ethnicity, and Language in National Censuses*. Edited by David I. Kertzer and Dominique Arel, 92–120. Cambridge: Cambridge University Press.

— 2008. "Orange Ukraine Chooses the West, but Without the East." In *Aspects of the Orange Revolution III: The Context and Dynamics of the 2004 Ukrainian Presidential Elections*. Edited by Ingmar Bredies, Andreas Umland, and Valentin Yakushik, 35–53. Stuttgart: ibidem-Verlag.

— 2014. "Double Talk: Why Ukrainians Fight Over Language," *Foreign Affairs*, March 18. https://fam.ag/2smOSFj

— 2017. "Language, Status, and State Loyalty in Ukraine." In *The Battle for Ukrainian: A Comparative Perspective*. Edited by Michael S. Flier and Andrea Graziosi, 271–308. Cambridge, MA: Harvard Ukrainian Research Institute. Distributed by Harvard University Press.

Arel, Dominique, and Andrew Wilson. 1994. "The Ukrainian Parliamentary Elections." *RFE/RL Research Report* 3(26), 6–17.

Arel, Dominique, and Valeri Khmelko. 1996. "The Russian Factor and Territorial Polarization in Ukraine." *The Harriman Review* 9(1–2), 81–91.

— 2005. "Regional Divisions in the 2004 Presidential Elections in Ukraine: The Role of Language and Ethnicity." Unpublished paper presented at the 2005 Danyliw Seminar on Ukraine, University of Ottawa.

Ashton, Gary. 2015. "Sanctions on SWIFT Could Hit Russia Where It Hurts Most." *Investopedia*, February 24. https://bit.ly/3bClBgK

Aslund, Anders. 2015. *Ukraine: What Went Wrong and How to Fix It*. Washington, DC: Peterson Institute for International Economics. Distributed by Columbia University Press.

Avdeev, Max. 2014. "The Soldiers of the Donetsk People's Republic: A Photo Gallery." *The New Republic*, June 17. https://bit.ly/2SP64Pi

Avgerinos, Katherine P. 2009. "Russia's Public Diplomacy Effort: What the Kremlin Is Doing and Why It's Not Working." *Journal of Public and International Affairs* 20, 115–32.

Aza, Hidai Arbide, and Miguel González. 2022. "US Offered Disarmament Measures to Russia in Exchange for Deescalation of Military Threat in Ukraine." *El Pais*, February 2. https://bit.ly/3IbYfZA

Babak, Artem, Tetiana Matychak, Vitaliy Moroz, Martha Puhach, Ruslan Minich, Vitaliy Rybak, and Volodymyr Yermolenko. 2017. "Words and Wars: Ukraine Facing Kremlin Propaganda." *Internews Ukraine.* https://bit.ly/2ucqiFl

Baker, Peter, and Andrew Higgings. 2014. "U.S. and European Sanctions Take Aim at Putin's Economic Efforts." *New York Times*, September 13. https://nyti.ms/3jWjlku

Balaban, Bohdan, Mykola Balaban, Christina Dobrovolska, Maksym Maiorov, and Olga Volyanyuk. 2017. "Donbas in Flames: Guide to the Conflict Zone." *Prometheus NGO*, April. https://bit .ly/2UZZYJm

Balch-Lindsay, Dylan, Andrew J. Enterline, and Kyle A. Joyce. 2008. "Third-Party Intervention and the Civil War Process." *Journal of Peace Research* 45(3), 345–63.

Balmforth, Tom. 2014. "Russia's Nationalist Fringe Takes Center Stage in Eastern Ukraine." *RFE/RL*, June 17. https://bit.ly/3wXbo30

Banderivets'. 2014a. "Zaiava 'Pravogo sektoru' shchodo potochnoï situatsiï v kraïni." January 20. https://bit.ly/2Z0H2MO

 2014b. "Zvernennia do Ukraïns'koho narodu." January 18. https://bit .ly/3gZeai1

Banerjee, Abhijit. 1992. "A Simple Model of Herd Behavior." *Quarterly Journal of Economics* 107(3), 797–817.

Barabanov, Mikhail. 2015. "Viewing the Action in Ukraine from the Kremlin's Windows." In *Brothers Armed: Military Aspects of the Crisis in Ukraine*, 2nd ed. Edited by Colby Howard and Ruslan Pukhov, 187–201. Minneapolis, MN: East View Press.

Baranov, Sergei. 2018. "Pervyi den' bedy. Kak na Donetsk obrushivalas' 'russkaia vesna.'" *DonPress*, March 1. https://bit.ly/2So5sgx

Barghoorn, Frederick C. 1964. *Soviet Foreign Propaganda*. Princeton, NJ: Princeton University Press.

Bartkowski, Maciej, and Maria J. Stephan. 2014. "How Ukraine Ousted an Autocrat: The Logic of Civil Resistance." *Atlantic Council*, June 1. https://bit.ly/31mNH50

Bartov, Omer. 2018. *Anatomy of Genocide: The Life and Death of a Town Called Buczacz*. New York: Simon & Schuster.

Bates, Robert H. 1998. *Analytic Narratives*. Princeton, NJ: Princeton University Press.

Bates, Robert H., Avner Greif, Margaret Levi, Jean-Laurent Rosenthal, and Barry Weingast. 2000. "The Analytic Narrative Project." *The American Political Science Review* 93(3), 696–702.

Bateson, Ian. 2014. "Will Donetsk Be the Next Grozny?" *Aljazeera America*, August 5. https://bit.ly/1pWk1Bj

Baysha, Olga. 2018. *Miscommunicating Social Change: Evidence from Russia and Ukraine*. Lanham, MD: Lexington Books.

BBC. 2014a. "New Head of Ukraine's Navy Defects in Crimea." March 2. https://bbc.in/2rrxa37

2014b. "Ukraine Crisis: Will the Donetsk Referendum Matter?" May 12. https://bbc.in/2TW0mbH

BBC News Russkaia sluzhba. 2014. "Parlament Kryma priznal Deklaratsiiu o nezavisimosti." March 11. https://bbc.in/3xVLtwZ

2018. "Telokhronitel' rasskazal sudu v Kieve, kak Yanukovych bezhal v Rossiiu." January 18. https://bbc.in/3BwoWpQ

Beck-Hoffman, John. 2014. "Maidan Massacre." YouTube video, October 20. https://bit.ly/2Vsxjwq

Beckhusen, Robert. 2014. "How Russia Invaded Crimea." *War is Boring*, March 1. https://bit.ly/2MP4ibO

Bellingcat. 2016. "Russia's War in Ukraine: The Medals and Treacherous Numbers." August 31. https://bit.ly/2bZwF6K

Belton, Catherine. 2020. *Putin's People: How the KGB Took Back Russia and Then Took on the West*. New York: Farrar, Straus and Giroux.

Benjamin, Walter. 2019. *Illuminations*. Translation by Harry Zohn (1968 reprint). New York: Mariner Books.

Berman, Eli and David A. Lake, eds. 2019. *Proxy Wars: Suppressing Violence through Local Agents*. Ithaca, NY: Cornell University Press.

Bialik, Carl. 2014. "Many Signs Pointed to Crimea Independence Vote – But Polls Didn't." *FiveThirthyEight.com*, March 17. https://53eig.ht/33IDIIt

Biddle, Stephen. 2021. *Nonstate Warfare*. Princeton, NJ: Princeton University Press.

Biggs, Claire. 2014. "Vostok Battalion, A Powerful New Player in Eastern Ukraine." *RFE/RL*, May 30. https://bit.ly/2ugfDsj

Bigmir.net. 2014a. "Maidan Online: khronika glavnykh sobytiy 22 ianvaria." January 22. https://bit.ly/32rOGSz

2014b. "Vooruzhenye titushki vmeste s militsiiei izbivaiut i streliaiut v mitinguiushchikh vozle Mariinskogo parka." February 20. https://bit.ly/2HcmvOI

Bik, Oleksiy. 2014. "Yanukovych kynuv armiiu proty narodu." *Glavkom*, February 24. https://bit.ly/2H6JZ7U

Bikhchandani, Sushil, David Hirschleifer, and Ivo Welch. 1992. "A Theory of Fads, Fashion, Custom, and Cultural Change as Informational Cascades." *Journal of Political Economy* 100(5), 992–1026.

Birnbaum, Michael. 2018. "Dutch-Led Investigators Say Russian Missile Shot Down Malaysia Airlines Flight 17 over Ukraine in 2014." *Washington Post*, May 24. https://wapo.st/3jCLqxp

Biuleten' 11. 1991. "Tretia sesiia Verkhovnoï Rady Ukraïny dvanadtsiatoho sklykannia." 12 February. Stenographic report. Verkhovna Rada.

Bobrov, Yevgenyi A. 2014. "Problemy zhitelei Kryma." *Sovet pri Prezidente Rossiiskoi Federatsii po razvitiiu grazhdanskogo obshchestva i pravam cheloveka*, April 22. https://bit.ly/2pw3ZuP

Böröcz, József. 2013. "Terms of Ukraine's EU-Dependency." *LeftEast*, December 3. https://bit.ly/2JARHsM

Brubaker, Rogers. 1995. "National Minorities, Nationalizing States, and the External National Homelands in the New Europe." *Daedalus* 124(2), 107–32.

——— 1996. *Nationalism Reframed*. Cambridge: Cambridge University Press.

Bruszt, László, and Julia Langbein. 2017. "Varieties of Dis-Embedded Liberalism: EU Integration Strategies in the Eastern Peripheries of Europe." *Journal of European Public Policy* 24(2), 297–315.

Buckley, Neil, and Roman Olearchyk. 2015. "No Justice One Year on for Those Killed in Kiev's Maidan Square." *Financial Times*, February 20. https://on.ft.com/2YSCDyV

Buderats'kyi, Yevhen. 2018. "Imenem Poroshenka. Yak zminyt' viynu zakon deokupatsiiu Donbasu." *Ukrains'ka pravda*, January 18. https://bit.ly/2mWWg7G

Bukkvoll, Tor. 2017. "Regular Forces and Pro-Government Militias: The Case of the Ukrainian Volunteer Battalions." Paper presented at the Danyliw Research Seminar on Contemporary Ukraine, Chair of Ukrainian Studies, University of Ottawa. https://bit.ly/2X3O1UH

——— 2019. "Fighting on Behalf of the State: The Issue of Progovernment Militia Autonomy in the Donbas War." *Post-Soviet Affairs* 35(4), 293–307.

Butts, Antony (dir.). 2016. *DIY Country*. Artline Films.

Butusov, Yuri. 2014. "22 liutogo 2014-go – proval putins'kogo planu rozkolu Ukraïny." *Tsenzor.net*, February 23. https://bit.ly/3ONozOl

——— 2016. "9 travnia 2014-go vony pershymy vstupyly v biy za ukraïns'kiy Mariupol'." *Tsenzor*, May 9. https://bit.ly/37q11uo

——— 2020. "Den' han'by sylovykh struktur Ukrainy: Yak zdavaly Slov'iansk." *Zik*, April 13.

Cabana, Brad. 2014. "The Mouse Trap-Battle of Ukraine." *Rock Solid Politics*, July 26. https://bit.ly/2XcVQHM

Carden, James. 2016. "Ukraine Peace Talks Stall While Divisions within the Country Deepen." *The Nation*, May 12. https://bit.ly/2S9tzBM

Carroll, Oliver. 2014. "Why Ukraine's Separatist Movement Failed in Kharkiv." *The New Republic*, June 22. https://bit.ly/3A8hbWf

——— 2015. "Star Wars in Ukraine: Poroshenko vs Kolomoisky." *Politico*, December 21. https://politi.co/2sbjpmE

Case, Sean, and Klement Anders. 2016. "Putin's Undeclared War: Summer 2014 – Russian Artillery Strikes against Ukraine." *Bellingcat*, December 21. https://bit.ly/2ifll5V

Cathcart, Will. 2014. "Putin's Crimean Medal of Honor, Forged before the War Even Began." *The Daily Beast*, April 25. https://bit.ly/2lukA0j

Cederman, Lars-Erik, Andreas Wimmer, and Brian Min. 2010. "Why Do Ethnic Groups Rebel? New Data and Analysis." *World Politics* 62(1), 87–119.

Cederman, Lars-Erik, Nils B. Weidmann, and Kristian Skrede Gleditsch. 2011. "Horizontal Inequalities and Ethnonationalist Civil War: A Global Comparison." *American Political Science Review* 105(3), 478–95.

Center for Social and Labor Research. 2013. "1 hrudnia sutychky pravykh radykaliv ta 'Berkutu' pryzvely do naikryvavishoho vulychnoho protystoiannia v istoriï nezalezhnoï Ukraïny." December 2. https://bit.ly/2ZDVqLa

Cetinyan, Rupen. 2002. "Ethnic Bargaining in the Shadow of Third-Party Intervention." *International Organization* 56(3), 645–77.

Charap, Samuel. 2015. "The Ghost of Hybrid War." *Survival* 57(6), 51–8.

Charap, Samuel, and Timothy J. Colton. 2017. *Everyone Loses: The Ukraine Crisis and the Ruinous Contest for Post-Soviet Eurasia.* New York: Routledge.

Chazan, Guy, and Courtney Weaver. 2014. "Ukraine Partisans Battling Separatists Raise Concerns." *Financial Times*, May 22. https://on.ft.com/2SCbxto

Chazan, Guy, and Roman Olearchyk. 2014a. "The Oligarch's Dilemma: Ukraine's Richest Man in East–West Bind." *Financial Times*, May 13. https://on.ft.com/2N8ZiyI

2014b. "Tide Turns for Ukraine Forces in Fight against Pro-Russia Rebels." *Financial Times*, August 1. https://on.ft.com/2BM0i7h

Chebotariova, Anna. 2015. "'Voices of Resistance and Hope': On the Motivations and Expectations of Euromaidaners." In *Ukraine's Euromaidan: Analyses of a Civil Revolution.* Edited by David R. Marples and Frederick V. Mills, 324–55. Stuttgart: ibidem.

Chenoweth, Erica. 2021. *Civil Resistance: What Everyone Needs to Know.* Oxford: Oxford University Press.

Chimiris, Margarita. 2014. "Kto i kak skryvaet pravdu o rasstreliakh na Maidane." *Vesti*, November 20. https://bit.ly/2YqoFR1

Chinchilla, Alexandra, and Jesse Driscoll. 2021. "Side-Switching as State-Building: The Case of Russian-Speaking Militias in Eastern Ukraine." *Studies in Conflict and Terrorism.* Published online, December 23.

Chivers, C. J., and Noah Sneider. 2014. "Behind the Masks in Ukraine, Many Faces of Rebellion." *New York Times*, May 4. https://nyti.ms/2twa6ht

Chivvis, Christopher S. 2017. *Understanding Russian "Hybrid Warfare" and What Can Be Done about It*. Testimony Presented before the House Armed Services Committee on March 22. Santa Monica, CA: RAND Corporation. https://bit.ly/2Vab7Jy

Civic Solidarity. 2014. "Brief Legal Analysis of 'Dictatorship Laws.'" January 20. https://bit.ly/31Chw2v

Clapp, Alexander. 2016. "How to Join a Ukrainian Militia." *The National Interest*, April 26. https://bit.ly/2sIZCOA

Clem, Ralph. 2018. "Clearing the Fog of War: Public versus Official Sources and Geopolitical Storylines in the Russia–Ukraine Conflict." *Eurasian Geography and Economics* 58(6), 592–612.

Cohen, Josh. 2017. "Point by Point, Russia's Violations of Budapest Memorandum." *Kyiv Post*, January 12. https://bit.ly/2XGHgcq

——— 2018. "Ukraine's Neo-Nazi Problem." *Reuters*, March 19. https://reut.rs/3pHl5zq

Conley, Heather A., James Mina, Ruslan Stefanov, and Martin Vladimirov. 2016. *The Kremlin Playbook: Understanding Russian Influence in Central and Eastern Europe*. Lanham, MD: Rowman & Littlefield.

Council of Europe. 2015. "IAP Report on Odesa Events." November 4. http://bit.ly/2hRygLQ

Council of the European Union. 2014a. "Council Decision of 17 March 2014 Concerning Restrictive Measures in Respect of Actions Undermining or Threatening the Integrity, Sovereignty and Independence of Ukraine." March 17. http://bit.ly/1qMcd8V

——— 2014b. "Council Regulation (EU) No 208/2014 of 5 March 2014 Concerning Restrictive Measures Directed Against Certain Persons, Entities and Bodies in View of the Situation in Ukraine." March 5. https://bit.ly/2WUoOxl

——— 2014c. "Council Regulation (EU) No 960/2014 of 8 September 2014 Amending Regulation (EU) No 833/2014 Concerning Restrictive Measures in View of Russia's Actions Destabilising the Situation in Ukraine." *EUR-Lex*, September 8. https://bit.ly/3z8tjpx

——— 2014d. "Main Results of the Council." February 20. https://bit.ly/2YQ75Kb

Coynash, Halya. 2014. "Crimean 'Referendum' a Grotesque Farce." *Kharkiv Human Rights Protection Group*, March 7. https://bit.ly/33AACWT

——— 2016a. "In Memory of the First Maidan Victims." *Kharkiv Human Rights Protection Group*, January 23. https://bit.ly/2Y2QOgm

——— 2016b. "Myth, 'Observers' and Victims of Russia's Fake Crimean Referendum." *Kharkiv Human Rights Protection Group*, March 16. https://bit.ly/2trORg1

2016c. "Remembering the Victims of Putin's Ilovaisk Treachery." *Kharkiv Human Rights Protection Group*, August 30. https://bit.ly/2V5KL9y

2016d. "Russia Refuses to Probe Sharp Rise in Soldiers' Deaths during War in Donbas." *Kharkiv Human Rights Protection Group*, February 12. https://bit.ly/2ychTWR

2017a. "Dramatic Acquittals in Trial over Odesa 2 May 2014 Riots." *Human Rights in Ukraine*, September 19. https://bit.ly/3p0sxra

2017b. "Russians Admit to Killing for Money – Ukrainians or Syrians, as Russia Demands." *Human Rights in Ukraine*, August 29. https://bit.ly/2yQUISc

2018a. "Russian Tanks Entering Ukraine that the OSCE is Mandated to Miss." *Kharkiv Human Rights Protection Group*, April 16. https://bit.ly/2I0idYd

2018b. "Ukrainian Journalist Loses Defamation Suit for Criticizing Moreira Propaganda Film on Ukraine." *Kharkiv Human Rights Protection Group*, April 13. https://bit.ly/2JXyZZK

2018c. "Yanukovych Switches Story about Letter Putin Used to Justify Russia's Military Aggression against Ukraine." *Kharkiv Human Rights Protection Group*, March 6. https://bit.ly/2t9CBBH

2019. "Russian-Controlled Donbas 'Republics' Remove Ukrainian Language and Everything Connected with Ukraine from Schools." *Kharkiv Human Rights Protection Group*, September 17. https://bit.ly/2m3LV9s

Crowley, Stephen. 1994. *Between Class and Nation: Worker Politics in the Post-Communist Ukraine*. Washington, DC: The National Council for Soviet and East European Research.

Crozet, Matthieu, and Julian Hinz. 2020. "Friendly Fire: The Trade Impact of the Russia Sanctions and Counter-Sanctions." *Economic Policy* 35(101), 97–146.

Cullison, Alan, Katya Gorchinskaya, and Lukas I. Alpert. 2014. "Ukraine Considering Martial Law in East." *Wall Street Journal*, June 4. https://on.wsj.com/2S6mcrb

Cunningham, David E., Kristian Skrede Gleditsch, and Idean Salehyan. 2009. "It Takes Two: A Dyadic Analysis of Civil War Duration and Outcome." *Journal of Conflict Resolution* 53(4), 570–97.

Czuperski, Maksymilian, John Herbst, Eliot Higgins, Alina Polyakova, and Damon Wilson. 2015. "Hiding in Plain Sight: Putin's War in Ukraine." *Atlantic Council*, October. https://bit.ly/2PBYbKw

D'Anieri, Paul. 2019a. "Gerrymandering Ukraine? Electoral Consequences of Occupation." *East European Politics and Societies* 33(1), 89–108.

2019b. *Ukraine and Russia: From Civilized Divorce to Uncivil War.* Cambridge: Cambridge University Press.

Daalder, Ivo, Michèle Flournoy, John Herbst, Jan Lodal, Admiral James Stavridis, General Charles Wald, Steven Pifer, and Strobe Talbott. 2015. "Preserving Ukraine's Independence, Resisting Russian Aggression: What the United States and NATO Must Do." *Brookings*, February 1. https://brook.gs/2mzOVuJ

Darden, Keith A. 2014. "How to Save Ukraine: Why Russia Is Not the Real Problem." *Foreign Affairs*, April 14.

Davenport, Christian. 2000. *Paths to State Repression: Human Rights Violations and Contentious Politics*. Lanham, MD: Rowman & Littlefield.

Davenport, Christian, Erik Melander, and Patrick M. Reagan. 2018. *The Peace Continuum: What It Is and How to Study It*. New York: Oxford University Press.

De Figueiredo, Rui, and Barry R. Weingast. 1999. "The Rationality of Fear: Political Opportunism and Ethnic Conflict." In *Civil Wars, Insecurity, and Intervention*. Edited by Barbara F. Walter and Jack Snyder, 261–302. New York: Columbia University Press.

Delegation of the European Union to Ukraine. 2014. "Local EU Statement on Recent Developments in Ukraine." January 27. https://bit.ly/2FtG5UM

della Porta, Donnatella. 2008. "Research on Social Movements and Political Violence." *Qualitative Sociology* 31(3), 221–30.

Denysenko, Nicholas E. 2018. *The Orthodox Church in Ukraine: A Century of Separation*. DeKalb: Northern Illinois University Press.

DFRLab. 2017. "Chaos in Luhansk, Explained." November 29. https://bit.ly/3b0QPLR

2018. "#MinskMonitor: New Details on Zakharchenko Assassination." September 10. https://bit.ly/2EtFhiM

Digital Forensic Research Lab. 2017. "Who Is Viktor Ageyev?" July 13. https://bit.ly/2tUxo1g

Donnett, Chris. 2015. "How Volunteers Created a 'Second State' Inside Ukraine." *Hromadske International*, January 30. https://bit.ly/2Z5c7jE

Doosje, Bertjan, Fathali M. Moghaddam, Arie W. Kruglanski, Arjan de Wolf, Liesbeth Mann, and Allard R. Feddes. 2016. "Terrorism, Radicalization and De-Radicalization." *Current Opinion in Psychology* 11, 79–84.

Dragneva, Rilka, and Kataryna Wolczuk. 2014. "The EU–Ukraine Association Agreement and the Challenges of Inter-Regionalism." *Review of Central and East European Law* 39(3–4), 213–44.

2015. *Ukraine between the EU and Russia: The Integration Challenge*. New York: Palgrave.

Dragojević, Mila. 2019. *Amoral Communities: Collective Crimes in Times of War*. Ithaca, NY: Cornell University Press.

Driscoll, Jesse. 2015. *Warlords and Coalition Politics in Post-Soviet States.* Cambridge: Cambridge University Press.

Driscoll, Jesse, and Zachary C. Steinert-Threlkeld. 2020. "Social Media and Russian Territorial Irredentism: Some Facts and a Conjecture." *Post-Soviet Affairs* 36(2), 101–21.

Dubinsky, Dasha, and Peter Rutland. 2019. "Russia's Legal Position on the Annexation of Crimea." *Journal of Soviet and Post-Soviet Politics and Society* 5(1), 45–80.

Dumskaia. 2014. "Protivostoianie pod OGA: gubernatora uvolili, a rossiiskii flag sniali." March 3. https://bit.ly/3BRUSp1

Dunai, Marton. 2019. "Hungary to Block Ukraine's NATO Membership over Language Law." *Reuters*, December 4. https://bit.ly/33QSO0V

Dvali, Nataliia. 2014. "Eks-nachal'nik SNU Petrulevich: Terroristicheskie hruppy GRU Rossii uzhe v Kieve i zhdut sihnala." *Gordon*, July 2. https://bit.ly/2RRLuhI

Dzutsati, Valery. 2021. "Geographies of Hybrid War: Rebellion and Foreign Intervention in Ukraine." *Small Wars & Insurgencies* 32(3), 441–68.

Eckel, Mike, and Christopher Miller. 2019. "Next Up for U.S. Weapons Supplies to Ukraine? Possibly Surface-to-Air Missiles." *RFE/RL*, June 11. https://bit.ly/2MUmJ2j

The Economist. 2014. "Closing In: How Far Will Vladimir Putin Go to Stave Off a Ukrainian Victory?" August 2. https://econ.st/2SEtMP4

Elster, Jon. 1989. *Nuts and Bolts for the Social Sciences.* Cambridge: Cambridge University Press.

1999. *Alchemies of the Mind: Rationality and the Emotions.* Cambridge: Cambridge University Press.

Ennis, Stephen. 2014. "UK Journalist Caught Up in Russia–Ukraine Media Battle." *BBC Blogs*, June 20. https://bbc.in/2SrQ2vi

Ernst, Douglas. 2015. "Vladimir Putin's Russia Threatens Poland with Hidden 'Hybrid War,' Senior General Says." *Washington Times*, March 25. https://bit.ly/2GcG6Q6

Euractiv. 2014. "Ukraine Submits Proof of Russian Covert Action." April 16. https://bit.ly/3jiG0Ya

Euromaidan PR. 2014. "We Are Not Extremists! Open Letter of the Ukrainian Scholars, Scientists, Artists, Doctors, Lawyers, Pedagogues and Journalists to their Fellow Citizens and to the International Community." January 25. https://bit.ly/2SkOkZm

Euronews. 2013. "The UN and Washington Condemn Violence in Ukraine." December 3. https://bit.ly/3vd37KY

European Commission. 2013. "Statement by High Representative Catherine Ashton and Commissioner Štefan Füle on Last Night's Events in Ukraine." November 30. https://bit.ly/2NjPkhQ

European Council. 2014a. "Statement by the President of the European Council Herman Van Rompuy and the President of the European Commission in the Name of the European Union on the Agreed Additional Restrictive Measures against Russia." July 29. https://bit.ly/2BBlxbN

2014b. "Statement on Behalf of the European Council on the Situation in Ukraine – The President of the European Council." February 19. https://bit.ly/2QJCRlD

2015. "European Council Conclusions on External Relations (19 March 2015)." March 19. https://bit.ly/2OWv1pd

Ewing, Jack, and Peter Baker. 2014. "U.S. and Europe Set to Toughen Russia Sanctions." *New York Times*, July 28. https://nyti.ms/2GSsKrL

Fearon, James D. 1994. "Signaling versus the Balance of Power and Interests: An Empirical Test of a Crisis Bargaining Model." *Journal of Conflict Resolution* 38(2), 236–69.

1995a. "Ethnic War as a Commitment Problem." Paper presented at the APSA Annual Meetings. https://bit.ly/2syWgNN

1995b. "Rationalist Explanations for War." *International Organization* 49(3), 379–414.

1997. "Signaling Foreign Policy Interests: Tying Hands versus Sinking Costs." *Journal of Conflict Resolution* 41(1), 68–90.

1998. "Commitment Problems and the Spread of Ethnic Conflict." In *The International Spread of Ethnic Conflict: Fear, Diffusion, and Escalation*. Edited by David A. Lake and Donald Rothchild, 107–26. Princeton, NJ: Princeton University Press.

2004. "Separatist Wars, Partition, and World Order." *Security Studies* 13(4), 394–415.

Fearon, James D., and David D. Laitin. 1996. "Explaining Interethnic Cooperation." *American Political Science Review* 90(4), 715–35.

2003. "Ethnicity, Insurgency, and Civil War." *American Political Science Review* 97(1), 75–90.

Fedorenko, Kostiantyn, and Andreas Umland. 2022. "Between Frontline and Parliament: Ukrainian Political Parties and Irregular Armed Groups in 2014–2019." *Nationalities Papers* 50(2), 237–61.

Fedorenko, Kostyantyn, Olena Rybiy, and Andreas Umland. 2016. "The Ukrainian Party System before and after the 2013–2014 Euromaidan." *Europe-Asia Studies* 68(4), 609–30.

Felgenhauer, Pavel. 2014. "Moscow's Dilemma: Finlandization of Ukraine or Occupation?" *Eurasia Daily Monitor*, June 12. https://bit.ly/2T0doYv

Finance.ua. 2014. "De i yak zakhoploiuiut' adminbudivli v Ukraïni. Inforhrafika." February 19. https://bit.ly/2Zfidhh

Fisher, Aleksandr. 2020. "Demonizing the Enemy: The Influence of Russian State-Sponsored Media on American Audiences." *Post-Soviet Affairs* 36(4), 281–96.

Fitzpatrick, Catherine. 2014. "A Reconstruction of the Tragic Shootings in Mariupol." *Minding Russia* (Blog), May 10. https://bit.ly/2KJRGDV

Fond demokratychni initsiatyvy. 2019. "Shliakhy dosiahnennia myru na Donbasi: suspil'ni nastroï, ochikuvannia, perestorohy – zahal'no natsional'ne opytuvannia." December 6. https://bit.ly/3hX3CAA

Fortna, Virginia Page. 2008. *Does Peacekeeping Work? Shaping Belligerents' Choices after Civil War*. Princeton, NJ: Princeton University Press.

Freedman, Lawrence. 2019. *Ukraine and the Art of Strategy*. Oxford: Oxford University Press.

Friedgut, Theodore H., and Lewis H. Siegelbaum. 1990. "The Soviet Miners' Strike, July 1989: Perestroika from Below." *The Carl Beck Papers in Russian and East European Studies* 804.

G. C. 2014. "A New and Dark Chapter." *The Economist*, January 22. https://econ.st/2JqJkzG

Galai, Yoav. 2019. "The Transnational Mythscape of the Second World War." *Memory Studies* 15(4), 842–57.

Gal'chinskaia, Ol'ga. 2014. "Gde i kak zakhvatyvaiut adminzdaniia po Ukraine." *Finance.ua*, February 20. https://bit.ly/2OHoel5

Galeotti, Mark. 2019. *Russian Political War: Moving beyond the Hybrid*. London: Routledge.

Galimova, Natal'ia. 2015. "My idem v Rossiiu. Kak – ne znaiu." *Gazeta.ru*, March 12. https://bit.ly/2YHjsV3

Galinfo. 2013. "Manifest Maidanu." December 19. https://bit.ly/2NxdWn1

Gartzke, Erik. 1999. "War Is in the Error Term." *International Organization* 53(3), 567–87.

Gartzke, Erik, and Jon R. Lindsay, eds. 2019. *Cross-Domain Deterrence: Strategy in an Era of Complexity*. Oxford: Oxford University Press.

Gaufman, Elizaveta. 2017. *Security, Threats, and Public Perception: Digital Russia and the Ukraine Crisis*. New York: Palgrave Macmillan.

Gehlbach, Scott. 2013. *Formal Models of Domestic Politics*. Cambridge: Cambridge University Press.

Geneste, Alexandra. 2014. "Moscou désavoué au Conseil de sécurité de l'ONU." *Le Monde*, March 4. https://bit.ly/2J5cvrg

Gentile, Michael. 2020. "Diabolical Suggestions: Disinformation and the Curious Scale of Nationalism in Ukrainian Geopolitical Fault-Line Cities." *Geopolitics*, November 1. https://bit.ly/3cdEoMm

Girod, Desha. 2011. "Effective Foreign Aid following Civil War: The Nonstrategic-Desperation Hypothesis." *American Journal of Political Science* 56(1), 188–201.

Giuliano, Elise. 2018. "Who Supported Separatism in Donbas? Ethnicity and Popular Opinion at the Start of the Ukraine Crisis." *Post-Soviet Affairs* 34(2–3), 158–78.

Glavnoe. 2014. "Russkoyazychnye pisateli Khar'kova: nam ne nuzhna zashchita Rossii." March 3. http://glavnoe.ua/news/n167796

Gleditsch, Kristian Skrede. 2007. "Transnational Dimensions of Civil War." *Journal of Peace Research* 44(3), 293–309.

Goncharenko, Roman. 2014. "Can the National Guard Save Ukraine?" *Deutsche Welle*, March 20. https://bit.ly/2N89Zla

Goncharova, Olena. 2015. "Debunking the Kremlin Myth about the 'Korsun Pogrom.'" *Kyiv Post*, March 18. http://bit.ly/2eUwIE2

Gorbach, Denys. 2018. "Entrepreneurs of Political Violence: The Varied Interests and Strategies of the Far-Right in Ukraine." *openDemocracy*, October 16. https://bit.ly/2LdCRvi

Gorbachov, Sergii. 2014. "Protests in Ukraine: Who Controls Local State Administrations." *Kyiv Post*, January 28. https://bit.ly/2V6bqUs

Gorchinskaya, Katya. 2013a. "Birth of a Nation." *Kyiv Post*, December 12. https://bit.ly/2E9jnir

2013b. "Interior Minister Justifies Police Attacks to EU, US Ambassadors." *Kyiv Post*, December 1. http://bit.ly/2vNCUko

2014a. "Fears of Conflict Escalation Grow as Police Report Numbers of Stolen Weapons." *Kyiv Post*, February 19. https://bit.ly/30gCvY1

2014b. "A Guide to Ukraine's Fighting Forces." *Kyiv Post*, July 10. https://bit.ly/2tlijVo

2014c. "The Ruling Party's View of EuroMaidan." *Kyiv Post*, January 29. https://bit.ly/2XVrfCP

2016. "He Killed for the Maidan." *Foreign Policy*, February 26. https://bit.ly/2Q83QGR

Gordon. 2014a. "Aktyvysty blokyruiut voinskuiu chast' na Vozdukhoflotskom prospekte v Kieve." February 20. https://bit.ly/31RnSuf

2014b. "V Khar'kove proshel slet storonnikov Partii regionov." February 1. https://bit.ly/2PNG02k

Gorenburg, Dmitry. 2014. "Crimea Taught Us a Lesson, But Not How the Russian Military Fights." *War on the Rocks*, May 19. https://bit.ly/2Yaqt1s

Gorka, Alex. 2017. "Canada Becomes Party to Ukraine's Conflict: Sells Lethal Weapons to Kiev Regime." *Global Research*, December 18. https://bit.ly/2kT7SIi

Gosudarstvennaia duma. 2013. "Gosduma priniala zaiavlenie o situatsii na Ukraine." December 10. https://bit.ly/2L6pVWK

Gosudarstvennyi soviet Respubliki Krym. 2014. "Zaiavlenie VR ARK. O politicheskoi situatsii." January 22. https://bit.ly/32tkSVk

Gov.uk. 2014. "Oral Statement to Parliament: Russia's Actions in Crimea." March 18. https://bit.ly/31vodSF

Government Portal. 2014. "Opening Statement of Prime Minister of Ukraine Mykola Azarov during Government's Meeting on January 22, 2014." January 22. https://bit.ly/2YMkj7n

Grabowicz, George. 2014. "Taras Shevchenko: The Making of the National Poet." *Revue des études slaves* 85(3), 421–39.

Gramsci, Antonio. 1987. *Selections from the Prison Notebooks of Antonio Gramsci.* Edited and Translated by Quintin Hoare and Geoffrey Nowell Smith. New York: International Publishers.

Gressel, Gustav. 2015. "Russian-Occupied Ukraine Is Consumed by Chaos." *Newsweek*, June 10. https://bit.ly/36LgHWS

Griffin, Sean. 2021. "Revolution, *Raskol*, and Rock 'n' Roll: The 1,020th Anniversary of the Day of the Baptism of Rus." *The Russian Review* 80(2), 183–208.

Gromenko, Sergei. 2018. "Rossiiskii 'Pearl-Harbor' v Krymu. Kak nachalas' real'naia okkupatsiia poluostrova." *Radio svoboda*, February 27. https://bit.ly/2sxcnvu

Grozev, Christo. 2014a. "The Orthodox Crusaders – Part 1." *Christo's Blog*, May 20. https://bit.ly/2LfIV6l

2014b. "The Orthodox Crusaders: Palm Sunday (Final Part III)." *Christo's Blog*, May 26. https://bit.ly/3CfFrqK

Grytsenko, Oksana. 2013. "Ukrainian Protesters Flood Kiev after President Pulls Out of EU Deal." *The Guardian*, November 24. https://bit.ly/2HMh1ry

2017. "Police, SBU Break Up a Railway Blockade in Donetsk Oblast." *Kyiv Post*, March 14. https://bit.ly/39XfUXp

The Guardian. 2014a. "Agreement on the Settlement of Crisis in Ukraine – Full Text." February 21. https://bit.ly/2JNY2BO

2014b. "US Piles Pressure on Yanukovych over Bloody Crackdown in Ukraine." February 20. https://bit.ly/2OTG2JW

Gubarev, Pavel. 2016. *Fakel Novorossii.* Moscow: Piter.

Guha-Sapir, Gebarati, Benjamin Schlüter, Jose Manuel Rodriguez-Llanes, Louis Lillywhite, and Madelyn Hsiao-Rei Hicks. 2018. "Patterns of Civilian and Child Deaths Due to War-Related Violence in Syria: A Comparative Analysis from the Violation Documentation Center Dataset, 2011–16." *The Lancet* 6, January, 103–10.

Gutterman, Steve, and Richard Balmforth. 2014. "Russia to Await New Ukraine Government before Fully Implementing Rescue – Putin." *Reuters*, January 29. https://reut.rs/3h4OoJ3

Guz, Serhiy. 2019. "Ukraine's Communists Were Banned, or So We Thought." *openDemocracy*, February 28. https://bit.ly/35z8YL5

Guzhva, Igor', and Dmitrii Korotkov. 2015. "Istoriia donetskoi boiny. Kak Donbas pogruzhali v voinu: rekonstruktsiia sobytii vesny – 2014." *Stena*, April 23. https://bit.ly/36TzFKN

Hahn, Gordon M. 2018. *Ukraine Over the Edge: Russia, the West and the "New Cold War."* Jefferson, NC: McFarland.

Haivanovych, Ivan. 2016. "Serhiy Horbatiuk: Ne mozhna buty odnobokym u 'spravi Maidanu.'" *Zbruc*, April 7. https://bit.ly/2lDWfVu

Hale, Henry, Oxana Shevel, and Olga Onuch. 2018. "Believing Facts in the Fog of War: Identity, Media and Hot Cognition in Ukraine's 2014 Odesa Tragedy." *Geopolitics* 23(4), 851–81.

Haran, Olexiy, and Mariia Zolkina. 2017. "The Demise of Ukraine's 'Eurasian Vector' and the Rise of Pro-NATO Sentiment." *PONARS Eurasia*, 458. https://bit.ly/36F4x1p

Hassner, Ron E. 2007. "The Path to Intractability: Time and the Entrenchment of Territorial Disputes." *International Security* 31(3), 107–38.

Hauter, Jakob. 2021a. "Conclusion: Making Sense of Multicausality." In *Civil War? Interstate War? Hybrid War? Dimensions and Interpretations of the Donbas Conflict in 2014–2020.* Edited by Jakob Hauter, 215–22. Soviet and Post-Soviet Politics and Society (SPPS). Stuttgart: ibidem-Verlag.

——— 2021b. "Forensic Conflict Studies: Making Sense of War in the Social Media Age." *Media, War & Conflict*. Published online, August 4.

Havlik, Peter, Artem Kochnev, and Olga Pindyuk. 2020. "Economic Challenges and Costs of Reintegrating the Donbas Region in Ukraine." The Vienna Institute for International Economic Studies, Research Report 447, June. https://bit.ly/2BQ5Ssx

Herron, Erik S., Michael E. Thunberg, and Nazar Boyko. 2015. "Crisis Management and Adaptation in Wartime Elections: Ukraine's 2014 Snap Presidential and Parliamentary Elections." *Electoral Studies* 40, 419–29.

Herszenhorn, David M. 2013. "Thousands Protest Ukraine's Rejection of Trade Pacts." *New York Times*, November 24. https://nyti.ms/2QFPyOh

——— 2014a. "At Center of Ukraine Talks, Degrees of Decentralizing." *New York Times*, May 13. https://nyti.ms/2S7c9SM

——— 2014b. "Away from Show of Diplomacy in Geneva, Putin Puts on a Show of His Own." *New York Times*, April 17. http://nyti.ms/2jOH7AH

——— 2014c. "Talks on Ukraine Crisis Open in Kiev without Representation for Separatists." *New York Times*, May 14. https://nyti.ms/2TQ8Dhi

Higgins, Andrew, Andrew E. Kramer, and Steven Erlanger. 2014. "As His Fortunes Fell in Ukraine, a President Clung to Illusions." *New York Times*, February 23. https://nyti.ms/2MnLVKn

Hill, Fiona, and Clifford Gaddy. 2015. "How Aiding the Ukrainian Military Could Push Putin into a Regional War." *Washington Post*, February 5. https://wapo.st/2LIuDH8

Himka, John Paul. 2006. "The Basic Historical Identity Formation in Ukraine: A Typology." *Harvard Ukrainian Studies* 28(1–4), 483–500.

Hirschman, Albert O. 1970. *Exit, Voice, and Loyalty*. Cambridge, MA: Harvard University Press.

Hobbes, Thomas. 1991 [1651]. *Leviathan*. New York: Penguin.

Holos Ukraïny. 2014. "Zaiava fraktsiï Partiï rehioniv." February 24. https://bit.ly/2KvsJv4

Holovatyi, Serhii. 1992. "'Indul'hentsiia' separatystam." *Literaturna Ukraïna*, May 14.

Holovko, Bohdan, and Danylo Mokryk. 2014. "Nich gnivu. Shcho stalosia u L'vovi v nich na 19 liutoho 2014 roku?" *Zakhid.net*, February 19. https://bit.ly/2MacuWy

Hopf, Ted. 2016. "'Crimea is Ours': A Discursive History." *International Relations* 30(2), 227–55.

Hosaka, Sanshiro. 2018. "The Kremlin's 'Active Measures' Failed in 2013: That's When Russia Remembered Its Last Resort – Crimea." *Demokratizatsiya* 26(3), 321–64.

2019. "Welcome to Surkov's Theater: Russian Political Technology in the Donbas War." *Nationalities Papers* 47(5), 750–73.

Hromadske. 2016. "Donetsk Spring: The Fight for the Homeland." May 9. Documentary. https://bit.ly/353tW6H

2019. "Steinmeier Formula and Why Ukraine Agreed to It." September 20. https://bit.ly/2moUQ5r

Hromads'ke radio. 2018. "Napadniku na Chornovol sud dav 5 rokiv, prokuratora zbiraiet'sia apeliuvaty." October 29. https://bit.ly/2LipUz7

Hromads'kiy prostir. 2013. "Suspil'no-politychna sytuatsiia v Ukraïni hruden' 2013." December 25. https://bit.ly/3naXdCy

Hudzik, James. 2014. "The St George Ribbon and Why Are They Wearing It?" *Euromaidan Press*, February 9. https://bit.ly/2S7d2vN

Human Rights Watch. 2014a. "Ukraine: End Politically Motivated Abuses." April 28. https://bit.ly/2UUMvCy

2014b. "Ukraine: Unguided Rockets Killing Civilians. Stop Use of Grads in Populated Areas." July 24. https://bit.ly/2EBUVKY

2016. "'You Don't Exist': Arbitrary Detentions, Enforced Disappearances, and Torture in Eastern Ukraine." July 21. https://bit.ly/2Y1XzAv

Hunter, Montana. 2018. "Crowdsourced War: The Political and Military Implications of Ukraine's Volunteer Battalions 2014–2015." *Journal of Military and Strategic Studies* 18(3). https://bit.ly/2SuYiLd

Huntington, Samuel. 1968. *Political Order in Changing Societies.* New Haven, CT: Yale University Press.

Ignatieff, Michael. 2014. "The New World Disorder." *New York Review of Books,* September 25. https://bit.ly/34ffJAd

Illarionov, Andrei. 2014. "Zhiteli Ukrainy ne uvlecheny separatizmom. Opros 16–30 marta 2014 g." *Radio Ekho Moskvy,* April 12. https://bit.ly/2S9GMqJ

Informatsionnoe soprotivlenie. 2020. "Shtepa prikryla Strelkova ot spetsnaza i dolzhna sidet': ofitser raskryl novye podrobnosti rasstrela 'Alfy.'" August 6. https://bit.ly/3xw737h

The Insider. 2017. "Igor' Girkin (Strelkov): 'K vlasti i v Donetskoi, i v Luhanskoi respublike Surkov privel banditov." December 8. http://bit.ly/2CqpheB

Interfax-Ukraine. 2014. "Statement: Russian Federation Council Concerned about Events in Ukraine." *Kyiv Post,* January 29. https://bit.ly/2JWpbAD

Interfaks-Ukraina. 2015. "Ubiitsy Nigoiana i Senika vo vremia Revoliutsii dostoinstva na dannoe vremia ne ustanovleny." November 26. https://bit.ly/2XBOWQd

International Committee of the Red Cross. 2014. "Ukraine Crisis: What the ICRC is Doing." August 14. https://bit.ly/2OWyKBX

International Crisis Group. 2014. "Ukraine: Running Out of Time." Europe Report No. 231, May 14. https://bit.ly/2IkZkEW

International Partnership for Human Rights. 2016. "Where Did the Shells Come From? Investigation of Cross-Border Attacks in Eastern Ukraine." July 11. https://bit.ly/29zfnMU

The Interpreter. 2014a. "Ukraine Liveblog Day 67: Will Russia Change Course?" April 25. https://bit.ly/2UWZDan

——— 2014b. "Ukraine Liveblog Day 88: Separatist Ultimatum for Ukrainian Government Forces to Withdraw Ends." May 16. https://bit.ly/2S5QSck

——— 2014c. "Ukraine Liveblog Day 91: Putin Orders Russian Forces to Withdraw from Ukrainian Border." May 19. https://bit.ly/2SA8T7D

Ioffe, Julia. 2014. "My Mind-Melting Week on the Battlefields of Ukraine." *The New Republic,* June 16. https://bit.ly/2Gn2uWL

iPress. 2014. "MVS, SBU, prokuratura i armiia, dislokovana na L'vivshchyni, staly na bik Maidanu, – dokument." February 20. https://bit.ly/2PdEP0u

Isaienko, Maksym. 2016. "Yak zrostalo politychne nasyl'stvo v Ukraïni. Khronolohiia." *Texty*, March 10. https://bit.ly/2RWyiF6

Ishchenko, Volodymyr. 2014. "Ukraine's Fractures: Interview." *New Left Review* 87 (May–June). https://bit.ly/3jg8IZK

—— 2015. "Beyond Strelkov and Motorola: Protest Event Analysis of Anti-Maidan Mobilization Preceding the War in Donbas." Paper presented at the Conference "Analyzing Violence in Ukraine," George Washington University.

—— 2016. "Far Right Participation in the Ukrainian Maidan Protests: An Attempt of Systematic Estimation." *European Politics and Society* 17(4), 453–72.

Ishchenko, Volodymyr, Andrii Hladun, Mykhailo Sluvkin, and Oleksii Viedrov. 2018. "Why Did Maidan Protests Radicalize?" Manuscript.

Istorychna pravda. 2015. "Mizh nevoleiu i nezalezhnistiu. 18–22 liutoho 2014 roku." February 18. https://bit.ly/2MiLZyb

Itzkowitz Shifrinson, Joshua R. 2016. "Deal or No Deal? The End of the Cold War and the U.S. Offer to Limit NATO Expansion." *International Security* 40(4), 7–44.

Jégo, Marie. 2014. "Crise ukrainienne: Moscou à la manœuvre sur tous les fronts." *Le Monde*, February 19. https://bit.ly/2WHogsP

Jenne, Erin. 2004. "A Bargaining Theory of Minority Demands: Explaining the Dog that Did Not Bite in 1990s Yugoslavia." *International Studies Quarterly* 48(4), 729–54.

Johnson, Juliet. 2016. *Priests of Prosperity: How Central Bankers Transformed the Postcommunist World*. Ithaca, NY: Cornell University Press.

Jones, Rodney W., Mark G. McDonough, Toby F. Dalton, and Gregory D. Koblentz. 1998. *Tracking Nuclear Proliferation: A Guide in Maps and Charts*. Carnegie Endowment for International Peace. Washington, DC: Brookings Institution Press.

Judah, Tim. 2014. "Ukraine: A Catastrophic Defeat." *New York Review of Books*, September 5. https://bit.ly/2ShBSrE

Jus Talionis. 2019. "Povnyi spysok vbytykh pid chas Yevromaidanu." https://bit.ly/2YQGsoV

Kahn, Jeff. 2000. "The Parade of Sovereignties: Establishing the Vocabulary of the New Russian Federalism." *Post-Soviet Affairs* 16(1), 58–89.

Käihkö, Illmari. 2018. "A Nation-in-the-Making, in Arms: Control of Force, Strategy and the Ukrainian Volunteer Battalions." *Defence Studies* 18(2), 147–66.

—— 2020. "Conflict Chatnography: Instant Messaging Apps, Social Media and Conflict Ethnography in Ukraine." *Ethnography* 21(1), 71–91.

Kalinina, Irina. 2014. "Busloads of People are Coming from across the Border of Russia, Armed with Bats [Donetsk Letter]." *The New Republic*, March 10. https://bit.ly/2KVVbE7

Kalnysh, Valerii. 2014. "Yuliia Tymoshenko stala svobodnoï." *Kommersant' Ukraina*, February 22. https://bit.ly/2Z4voUu

Kalyvas, Stathis. 2006. *The Logic of Violence in Civil War*. Cambridge: Cambridge University Press.

Kalyvas, Stathis, and Laia Balcells. 2010. "International System and Technologies of Rebellion: How the End of the Cold War Shaped Internal Conflict." *American Political Science Review* 104(3), 415–29.

  2014. "Does Warfare Matter? Severity, Duration, and Outcomes of Civil Wars." *Journal of Conflict Resolution* 58(8), 1390–418.

Kanygin, Pavel. 2014. "V Simferopole proizoshli stolknoveniia mezhdu prorossiiskimi aktivistami i krymskimi tatarami (Khronika)." *Novaia gazeta*, February 27. https://bit.ly/2BkiqVp

  2016. "Rasskazy Strelka prochitaiut v Gaage." *Novaia gazeta*, May 27. https://bit.ly/2MV5lXy

Karber, Philip A. 2015. "'Lessons Learned' from the Russo-Ukrainian War: Personal Observations." Paper presented at the Historical Lessons Learned Workshop, Johns Hopkins Applied Physics Laboratory and U.S. Army Capabilities Center. https://bit.ly/38YtNSy

Kates, Glenn. 2014. "Separatist Shuffle: Who's In, Who's Out among the Donbas Rebels." *RFE/RL*, August 15. https://bit.ly/2GUVoZh

Kazanskyi, Denis. 2014. "Everyday Life in the Donetsk Republic." *Euromaidan Press*, April 21. https://bit.ly/2DUjDDP

  2019. "Kniga '85 dnei Slavianska.' Yavka s povinnoi." *Blog Denisa Kazanskogo*, March 10. https://bit.ly/2HhPylt

Khartyia '97%. 2014. "232 deputata Verkhovnoï Rady trebuiut vozvrashcheniia Konstitutsii 2004 goda." February 6. https://bit.ly/2YcdEpT

Khomenko, Sviatoslav. 2015. "KhNR: Khar'kovskaia neudavshaiasia respublika." *BBC News Russkaia sluzhba*, April 8. https://bbc.in/2E4aqu1

KIANews. 2014. "Obrashchenie Predsedatelia Soveta ministrov ARK Sergeia Aksenova." March 1. https://bit.ly/30KuPwP

Kier, Giles. 2016. "Russia's 'New' Tools for Confronting the West: Continuity and Innovation in Moscow's Exercise of Power." Chatham House-Royal Institute of International Affairs, Research Paper. https://bit.ly/37cG05R

Kim, Lucian. 2014. "The Battle of Ilovaisk: Details of a Massacre Inside Rebel-Held Eastern Ukraine." *Newsweek*, November 4. https://bit.ly/2CoGRCj

King, Charles. 2001. "The Benefits of Ethnic War: Understanding Eurasia's Unrecognized States." *World Politics* 53(4), 524–52.

Kitfield, James. 2015. "How to Manage Putin: Russia's 'Escalation Dominance.'" *Breaking Defense*, February 5. https://bit.ly/2mw9sQB

Kivelson, Valerie A., and Ronald Grigor Suny. 2017. *Russia's Empires.* Oxford: Oxford University Press.

Klapper, Bradley, and Ken Dilanian. 2015. "US Commander: Russia Seems Set for New Offensive in Ukraine." *Associated Press*, April 30. https://bit.ly/36n9f3N

Kobernik, Katerina. 2013. "Как shturmovali Maidan. Reportazh." *Republic*, December 11. https://bit.ly/3EPizzX

Koliushko, Ihor, and Yaryna Zhurba. 2011. "Constitutionalism, or Mockery of the Constitution?" *Statutes and Decisions* 46(3), 11–15.

Kondratova, Valeriia. 2014. "Vmesto federalizatsii. Chto Kabmin Yatseniuka predlagaet regionam." *Liga novosti*, May 7. https://bit.ly/2tpol7v

Korhonen, Iikka. 2019. "Sanctions and Counter-Sanctions: What Are Their Economic Effects in Russia and Elsewhere?" *Zhurnal NEA* 3(43), 184–90. https://bit.ly/3s1C5D4

Korolkov, Alexander. 2014. "The Grad System: A Hot Hail of Cluster-Fired Rockets." *Russia beyond the Headlines*, August 25. https://bit.ly/2T1JcfG

Korrespondent.net. 2014. "Zakhvatchiki Donetskoi OGA ne khotiat v Rossiiu – Taruta." April 10. https://bit.ly/2RtBL0G

Koshkina, Sonia. 2014. "Vidrodzhennia Rady." *LB.ua*, February 22. https://bit.ly/2Hq41KW

2015. *Maidan: Nerasskazanaia istoriia.* Kyiv: Bright Star.

Kostanyan, Hrant, and Artem Remizov. 2017. "The Donbas Blockade: Another Blow to the Minsk Peace Process." CEPS Working Document 2017/08, June. https://bit.ly/2Mc5FC8

Kostyuk, Nadiya, and Yuri Zhukov. 2019. "Invisible Digital Front: Can Cyber Attacks Shape Battlefield Events?" *Journal of Conflict Resolution* 63(2), 317–47.

Kotkin, Stephen. 2008. *Armaggedon Averted: The Soviet Collapse, 1970–2000.* Oxford: Oxford University Press.

Kotliar, Dmytro. 2014. "Summary of Laws Adopted by the Ukrainian Parliament on 16 January 2014." *Voices of Ukraine*, January 17. https://bit.ly/2MRy9nn

Kovaleva, Elena. 2007. "Regional Politics in Ukraine's Transition: The Donetsk Elite." In *Re-Constructing the Post-Soviet Industrial Region: The Donbas in Transition.* Edited by Adam Swain, 62–77. London: Routledge.

Kovalov, Maksym. 2014. "Electoral Manipulations and Fraud in Parliamentary Elections: The Case of Ukraine." *East European Politics and Societies and Culture* 28(4), 781–807.

Kozachenko, Pavel. 2014a. "Itogi dnia v Khar'kove." *Redpost*, February 19. https://bit.ly/2CvW6K4

2014b. "V Khar'kove sozdali obshchestvennyi soiuz 'Ukrainskii front'. Podrobnosti." *Redpost*, February 1. https://bit.ly/2ENQopZ

Kozak, Tetiana. 2020. "Pershe pravylo 'Biytsivs'koho klubu'. Yak titushky zdavaly odyn odnoho v sudakh u spravakh Maidanu." *Hraty*, March 10. https://bit.ly/3aoNohG

Kozlov, Petr, Olesia Volkova, and Oleg Karpiak. 2019. "Khronika anneksi: 'Krymskaia vesna' v vospominaniiakh uchastnikov sobytii." *BBC News Russkaia sluzhba*, March 19. https://bbc.in/33xhSHf

Kramer, Andrew E. 2014a. "Russians Find Few Barriers to Joining Ukraine Battle." *New York Times*, June 9. https://nyti.ms/2SwnAbO

2014b. "A Ukraine City Under Siege, 'Just Terrified of the Bombing.'" *New York Times*, August 14. https://nyti.ms/2SesCVl

2014c. "Ukraine Push against Rebels Grinds to Halt." *New York Times*, April 16. https://nyti.ms/2MWh6Nq

2017. "Assassins Are Killing Ukraine's Rebel Chiefs, But on Whose Orders?" *New York Times*, February 8. https://nyti.ms/2lmvvax

Kramer, Andrew E., and Andrew Higgins. 2014. "Ukraine's Forces Escalate Attacks against Protesters." *New York Times*, February 20. https://nyti.ms/2Mev4wn

Kramer, Andrew E., and Michael R. Gordon. 2014. "Ukraine Reports Russian Invasion on a New Front." *New York Times*, August 27. https://nyti.ms/2T3ktHV

Krawchenko, Bohdan. 1985. *Social Change and National Consciousness in Twentieth-Century Ukraine*. Edmonton: Canadian Institute of Ukrainian Studies.

1993. "Ukraine: The Politics of Independence." In *Nations and Politics in the Soviet Successor States*. Edited by Ian Bremmer and Ray Taras, 75–98. Cambridge: Cambridge University Press.

Krivolapov, Mikhail. 2014. "Revoliutsiia po-zaporozhski: shturm OGA, 10 000-i miting i razgon Maidana." *061*, January 26. https://bit.ly/2YukiJd

Krym politicheskii. 2015. "Kratkaia khronika sobytii 'Krymskoi vesny' 2014 goda." June 17. https://bit.ly/2qZNW9x

Kudelia, Serhiy. 2010. "Betting on Society: Power Perceptions and Elite Games in Ukraine." In *Orange Revolution and Aftermath*. Edited by Paul d'Anieri, 160–89. Washington, DC: Woodrow Wilson Center Press.

2014. "Reply to Andreas Umland: The Donbas Insurgency Began at Home." *PONARS*, October 8. https://bit.ly/3y9TxXB

2018. "'When Numbers Are Not Enough: The Strategic Use of Violence in Ukraine's 2014 Revolution." *Comparative Politics* 50(4), 501–21.

2019. "How They Joined? Militants and Informers in the Armed Conflict in Donbas." *Small Wars & Insurgencies* 30(2), 279–306.

Kulyk, Volodymyr. 2010. "Nemynuchiy Bandera." *Krytyka* 14(3–4), 149–50.

2018. "Shedding Russianness, Recasting Ukrainianness: The Post-Euromaidan Dynamics of Ethnonational Identifications in Ukraine." *Post-Soviet Affairs* 34(2–3), 119–38.

Kupchan, Charles A. 2010. "NATO's Final Frontier." *Foreign Affairs* 99(3), 100–12.

Kuran, Timur. 1991. "Now Out of Never: The Element of Surprise in the East European Revolution of 1989." *World Politics* 44(1), 7–48.

Kurishko, Ol'ga. 2014a. "Vosstanovitel'nye protsedury." *Kommersant' Ukraina*, February 17. https://bit.ly/2SqZHz6

2014b. "V tome delo." *Kommersant' Ukraina*, February 4. https://bit.ly/2XSYyq1

Kuromiya, Hiroaki. 1994. "Ukraine and Russia in the 1930s." *Harvard Ukrainian Studies* 18(3–4), 327–41.

Kutkina, Anna. 2021. *Between Lenin and Bandera: Decommunization and Multivocality in Post-Euromaidan Ukraine*. Stuttgart: ibidem.

Kuzio, Taras. 1997. "Radical Nationalist Parties and Movements in Contemporary Ukraine before and after Independence: The Right and Its Politics, 1989–1994." *Nationalities Papers* 25(2), 211–42.

2017. *Putin's War against Ukraine*. Published in association with the Chair of Ukrainian Studies, University of Toronto.

Kuzmenko, Oleksiy, and Michael Colborne. 2019. "Ukrainian Far-Right Extremists Receive State Funds to Teach 'Patriotism.'" *Bellingcat*, July 16. https://bit.ly/3b8xSqy

Kyiv International Institute of Sociology. 2013a. "Maidan-2013: khto stoït', chomu i za shcho?" December 10. https://bit.ly/2FDtGyD

2013b. "Yakym shliakhom iti Ukraïni – do yakoho soiuzu priiednuvatys'? (preferentsiï naselennia za dva tizhni do Vil'nius'koho samitu)." November 26. https://bit.ly/2stIgF2

2014a. "Stavlennia v Ukraïni ta Rosiï do aktsiy protestu v Ukraïni." February 28. https://bit.ly/2XQ77kE

2014b. "Vid Maidanu-taboru do Maidanu-sichi: shcho zminylosia?" February 6. https://bit.ly/2XffS7C

2014c. "The Views and Opinions of South-Eastern Regions Residents of Ukraine: April 2014." April 20. https://bit.ly/2NcRbRC

2019. "Stavlennia ukraïntsiv do politikiv, otsinka dial'nosti orhaniv vlady ta aktual'nykh podiy." October 14. https://bit.ly/2Xv1B4Z

2021. "Stavlennia do vstupu Ukraïny do YeS i NATO." December 24. https://bit.ly/3Sy8OwD

Kyiv Post. 2013a. "EuroMaidan Rallies in Ukraine – Dec. 11 Coverage." December 12. https://bit.ly/2Yrtw4U

2013b. "Police Say Over 300 Radicals Led Attack on President's Office." December 2. https://bit.ly/2JjJABz

2014. "OSCE Releases the 12-Point Protocol Agreements Reached between Ukraine, Russia and Separatists in Minsk." September 8. https://bit.ly/2EiHTQR

2016. "Update: Russian Arseniy Pavlov, a.k.a. 'Motorola,' Killed in Donetsk Blast; Kremlin Separatists Blame Kyiv." October 16. https://bit.ly/2Z0ED5M

Kyïvvlada. 2014. "Yanukovych podavil bunt v Partii regionov." January 30. https://bit.ly/2YPCrQV

Lacina, Bethany. 2017. *Rival Claims: Ethnic Violence and Territorial Autonomy under Indian Federalism*. Ann Arbor: University of Michigan Press.

Laitin, David D. 1998. *Identity in Formation: The Russian-Speaking Populations in the Near Abroad*. Ithaca, NY: Cornell University Press.

2007. *Nations, States, and Violence*. Oxford: Oxford University Press.

2018. "Identity in Formation: A 20 Year Retrospective." Paper presented at the ASN Annual World Convention, Columbia University.

Lapaiev, Yuri. 2019. "Artillery Wars in Donbas Enter a New Stage." *Eurasia Daily Monitor*, March 18. https://bit.ly/2FpNa8X

Laruelle, Marlene. 2021. *Is Russia Fascist? Unraveling Propaganda East and West*. Ithaca, NY: Cornell University Press.

Lasocki, Janek. 2019. "The Cost of Five Years of War in Donbas." *New Eastern Europe*, September 24. https://bit.ly/2ocKoPA

Lavrov, Anton. 2015a. "Civil War in the East: How the Conflict Unfolded before Minsk I." In *Brothers Armed: Military Aspects of the Crisis in Ukraine*, 2nd ed. Edited by Colby Howard and Ruslan Pukhov, 202–27. Minneapolis, MN: East View Press.

2015b. "Russian Again: The Military Operation for Crimea." In *Brothers Armed: Military Aspects of the Crisis in Ukraine*, 2nd ed. Edited by Colby Howard and Ruslan Pushkov, 157–84. Minneapolis, MN: East View Press.

LB.ua. 2014a. "Hradus kypinnia. Khronika podiy 18–19 liutoho v oblastiakh." February 19. https://bit.ly/2GW79Oe

2014b. "Rossiiu oburylo nevykonannia kolyshn'oiu opozytsieiu domovlenostei iz Yanukovycha." February 27. https://bit.ly/33M3TPa

Lee, Melissa M. 2018. "The International Politics of Incomplete Sovereignty: How Hostile Neighbors Weaken the State." *International Organization* 72(2), 283–315.

Legvold, Robert. 2016. *Return to Cold War*. Malden, MA: Polity Press.

Leonard, Peter. 2014a. "Ukraine Death Toll Climbs, But Information Scant." *Associated Press*, July 11. https://bit.ly/2DFJu23

2014b. "Ukraine's Interim President Pledges 'Large-Scale' Anti-Terror Operation against Pro-Russia Forces." *Associated Press*, April 13. https://bit.ly/3rxdZ2B

Lermontov, Vladimir. 2014. "'Russkaia vesna' i osazhdennaia oblgosadministratsiia – v Luganske provodili Maclenitsu." *Paralel' media*, March 3. https://bit.ly/2QEfJan

Leshchenko, Sergii. 2013. "The Two Worlds of Viktor Yanukovych's Ukraine." *openDemocracy*, March 14. https://bit.ly/2JF2Iqc

Leshchenko, Sergii, and Mustafa Nayyem. 2013. "A Day and a Night of Viktor Yanukovych." *Ukraïns'ka pravda*, December 8. https://bit.ly/2DHYKgn

Levi, Margaret. 1999. "Producing an Analytic Narrative." In *Critical Comparisons in Politics and Culture*. Edited by John Richard Bowen and Roger D. Petersen, 152–72. Cambridge: Cambridge University Press.

Levitas, Tony. 2014. "Ukraine Should Decentralize, Not Federalize." *Global Post*, June 23. https://bit.ly/2Ihy9e7

Lewis, Janet. 2020. *How Rebellion Begins: Rebel Group Formation in Uganda and Beyond*. Cambridge: Cambridge University Press.

Liber, George O. 1992. *Soviet Nationality Policy, Urban Growth, and Identity Change in the Ukrainian SSR, 1923–1934*. Cambridge: Cambridge University Press.

Liga Novosti. 2014. "Pravyi sektor: Yak i chomu vybukhnuv Maidan." January 20. https://bit.ly/2JCc3S6

Likhachev, Viacheslav. 2014. "'Pravyi sektor' i drugie: natsional-radikaly i ukrainskii politicheskii krizis kontsa 2013 g.-nachala 2014 g." *Forum noveishei vostochnoevropeiskoi istorii i kultury*, 2, 75–116. https://bit.ly/2WULAYi

2015. "The 'Right Sector' and Others: The Behavior and Role of Radical Nationalists in the Ukrainian Political Crisis of Late 2013– Early 2014." *Communist and Post-Communist Studies* 48(2–3), 257–71.

2018. "Far-Right Extremism as a Threat to Ukrainian Democracy." *Freedom House*, June. https://bit.ly/2sMVmKY

Lipskyi, Andrei. 2015. "Predstavliaietsia pravil'nym initsiirovat' prisoedinenie vostochnykh oblastei Ukrainy k Rossii." *Novaia gazeta*, February 24, https://bit.ly/2wVvyRl

LiveJournal. 2014a. "Mraz', gnil' i predateli v Verkhovnoi Rade. Poimenno." *LiveJournal*, February 21. https://bit.ly/2yVJWXT

2014b. "Srochno molniia iz Luganska!" March 2. https://bit.ly/2RCnZVH

Lobkov, Pavel. 2014. "Zhurnalist Pavel Fel'gengauer: ispol'zovanie PZRK dokazyvaet, shto boevoe yadro v Slavianske – eto rossiskii spetsnaz." *Dozhd'*, May 2. https://bit.ly/3h1qBvl

Lohmann, Susanne. 1994. "The Dynamics of Informational Cascades: The Monday Demonstrations in Leipzig, East Germany, 1989–91." *World Politics* 47(1), 42–101.

Loiko, Sergei. 2016. "Ispoved' 'samooboronovtsa': kak v Krymu rossiane 'russkii mir' stroili." *Krym.realii*, May 30. https://bit.ly/2QuWXyq

Losh, Jack. 2016. "Is Russia Killing Off Eastern Ukraine's Warlords?" *Foreign Policy*, October 25. https://bit.ly/36ojcy1

Luhn, Alec. 2014a. "'Anti-Terrorist' Campaign in Peril as Kiev's Writ Fails to Reach Ukraine's East." *The Guardian*, April 14. https://bit.ly/2HTl4Y5

2014b. "Guns and Fighters Seep through Ukraine's Porous Russian Border." *The Guardian*, May 31. https://bit.ly/2UQENcC

2014c. "Troops Fire as Locals in Kramatorsk Confront Ukraine General Vasily Krutov." *The Guardian*, April 15. https://bit.ly/2MWZIYJ

Lukyanov, Fyodor. 2014. "Putin Has Stumbled in Ukraine." *Moscow Times*, August 10. https://bit.ly/2qG5vv6

Lustick, Ian. 1993. *Unsettled States, Disputed Lands: Britain and Ireland, France and Algeria, Israel and the West Bank-Gaza*. Ithaca, NY: Cornell University Press.

Macdonald, Euan. 2015. "Defeat in Debaltseve Invites More Attacks." *Kyiv Post*, February 21. https://bit.ly/2V4yySC

Maksymiuk, Jan. 2006. "Parliament Recognizes Soviet-Era Famine as Genocide." *RFE/RL*, November 29. https://bit.ly/2UOujNa.

Malyarenko, Tetyana, and David J. Galbreath. 2016. "Paramilitary Motivation in Ukraine: Beyond Integration and Abolition." *Southeast European and Black Sea Studies* 16(1), 113–38.

Marson, James, and Richard Boudreaux. 2010. "Brawl Marks Kiev's Approval of Fleet." *Wall Street Journal*, April 28. https://on.wsj.com/3olnPBX

Martin, Terry. 2001. *The Affirmative Action Empire: Nations and Nationalism in the Soviet Union, 1923–1939*. Ithaca, NY: Cornell University Press.

Matanock, Aila M. 2017. *Electing Peace: From Civil Conflict to Political Participation*. Cambridge: Cambridge University Press.

Matsuzato, Kimitaka. 2016. "Domestic Politics in Crimea, 2009–2015." *Demokratizatsiya* 24(2), 225–56.

2017. "The Donbass War: Outbreak and Deadlock." *Demokratizatsiya* 25(2), 175–200.

Matthews, Owen. 2014. "Vladimir Putin Paints Himself into a Corner." *Newsweek*, August 4. https://bit.ly/2TOGc3k

Matusova, Olena. 2014. "Belkovs'kyi: na Donbasi zbyraiut'sia marhinaly i vbyvtsi, yakykh vykorystovuvav Kreml' v ostanni roky." *Radio svoboda*, November 24. https://bit.ly/2kePKoi

Matveeva, Anna. 2018. *Through Times of Trouble: Conflict in Southeastern Ukraine Explained from Within*. Lanham, MD: Lexington Books.

Mazanik, Lesia. 2014. "The Titushki Generation." *SRB Podcast*, February 1. https://bit.ly/2YT5HTD

McFaul, Michael. 2020. "Putin, Putinism, and the Domestic Determinants of Russian Foreign Policy." *International Security*, 45(2): 95–139.

Mearsheimer, John J. 1993. "The Case for a Ukrainian Nuclear Deterrent." *Foreign Affairs* 72(3), 50–66.

2014. "Why the Ukraine Crisis is the West's Fault: The Liberal Delusions that Provoked Putin." *Foreign Affairs* 93(5), 77–89.

Mediaport. 2014. "S'ezd deputatov vsekh urovnei v Khar'kove. Tekstovaia translatsiia." February 22. https://bit.ly/2PLxPn7

MediaSapiens. 2015. "Stanovyshche ukraïns'koï movy v Ukraïni u 2014–15 rokakh: analitychnyi ohliad." Vseukrains'kyï komitet zakhystu ukraïns'koï movy, July 10. https://bit.ly/2Ii026v

Meduza. "Moscow's Terms." December 17, 2021. https://bit.ly/3IUjbWN

Melkozerova, Veronika. 2016. "Two Years Too Late, Lutsenko Releases Audio of Russian Plan that Ukrainians Already Suspected." *Kyiv Post*, August 27. https://bit.ly/2KS36Wb

Melnyk, Oleksandr. 2020. "From the 'Russian Spring' to the Armed Insurrection: Russia, Ukraine and Political Communities in the Donbas and Southern Ukraine." *The Soviet and Post-Soviet Review* 47(1), 3–38.

Metinvest. 2014. "Zaiavlenie kompanii SKM Rinata Akhmetova." January 25. https://bit.ly/2ZzQxDi

Miller, Christopher J. 2014. "Donetsk Faces Threat of Urban Warfare as Ukrainian Forces Move to Encircle City." *Kyiv Post*, August 4. https://bit.ly/2GUWjZu

2018. "U.S. Confirms Delivery of Javelin Antitank Missiles to Ukraine." *RFE/RL*, April 30. https://bit.ly/2kPVpVL

Miller, James, Pierre Vaux, Catherine A. Fitzpatrick, and Michael Weiss. 2015. "An Invasion by Any Other Name: The Kremlin's Dirty War in Ukraine." *The Interpreter*, Institute of Modern Russia. https://bit.ly/38QxCtC

Minakov, Mikhail. 2015. "Utopian Images of the West and Russia among Supporters and Opponents of the Euromaidan." *Russian Politics and Law* 53(3), 68–85.

Ministerstvo inostrannykh del Rossiiskoi Federatsii. 2014a. "O telefonnom razgovore S. V. Lavrova s Prezidentom Shveitsarii D. Burkkhal'terom." January 27. https://bit.ly/2Bdjhrr

2014b. "Otvet Ministra inostrannykh del Rossii S. V. Lavrova na vopros po situatsii na Ukraine." February 19. https://bit.ly/2AwKZPV

2014c. "Zaiavlenie MID Rossii po sobytiiami v Krymu." March 1. https://bit.ly/2Z8BsJm

2014d. "Zaiavlenie Ministerstva innostrannykh del Rossiiskoi Federatsii v sviazi s situatsiei na Ukraine." February 19. https://bit.ly/2OQach0

Ministry of Foreign Affairs of the Russian Federation. 2014a. "Kommentarii Departamenta informatsii i pechati MID Rossii v kontekste vstrechi v Geneve po ukrainskomu krizisu." April 18. https://bit.ly/2UYu8gi

2014b. "White Book on Violations of Human Rights and the Rule of Law in Ukraine (November 2013–March 2014)." April. https://bit.ly/2OoDrEB

Miranda, Charles. 2015. "Never-Before-Seen Footage Reveals Russian-Backed Rebels Arriving at the Wreckage of MH17." *News.com.ua*, July 17. https://bit.ly/2S67XTj

Mirotvorets'. 2016. "Spisok boevikov i naemnikov po Donetskoi obl. (leto-osen' 2014 goda)." May 2. https://bit.ly/2Xd6PRw

Mitrokhin, Nikolai. 2015. "Infiltration, Instruction, Invasion: Russia's War in the Donbass." *Journal of Soviet and Post-Soviet Politics and Society* 1(1), 219–50.

Mizhnarodnyi fond 'Vidrodzhennia''. 2015. "Tsina svobody: Zvit pravo-zakhysnykh orhanizatsiy pro zlochyny, skoieni pid chas Yevromaidanu." February 26. https://bit.ly/2NS8ATN

Morrison, Patt. 2014. "Michael McFaul – An Eye for Russia." *Los Angeles Times*, March 26. https://lat.ms/3qMXYES

Moser, Michael. 2013. *Language Policy and Discourse on Languages in Ukraine under President Viktor Yanukovych*. Stuttgart: ibidem.

Motyl, Alexander J., and Ksenya Kiebuzinski. 2016. *The Great West Ukrainian Massacre of 1941: A Sourcebook*. Amsterdam: Amsterdam University Press.

Mounk, Yascha. 2018. *The People vs. Democracy*. Cambridge, MA: Harvard University Press.

Mudde, Cas. 1996. "The War of Words Defining the Extreme Right Party Family." *West European Politics* 19(2), 225–48.

2007. *Populist Radical Right Parties in Europe*. Cambridge: Cambridge University Press.

Myagkov, Mikhail, Peter C. Ordeshook, and Dmitry Shakin. 2009. *The Forensics of Election Fraud: Russia and Ukraine*. Cambridge: Cambridge University Press.

Myers, Steven Lee. 2014a. "Russia's Move into Ukraine Said to Be Born in Shadows." *New York Times*, March 7. https://nyti.ms/2MQ5iMO

2014b. "Violence in Ukraine Creates Deepening Clash between East and West." *New York Times*, February 19. https://nyti.ms/2GX7Uqn

Mykhailin, Ihor, and Serhii Vakulenko. 2014. "Pro-Russian Fighters Beat Our Ukrainian Students with Bats." *The New Republic*, March 4. https://bit.ly/2VbIK0R

NATO. 2008. "Bucharest Summit Declaration." April 3. https://bit.ly/2VhAgRY

2013. "NATO Foreign Ministers' Statement on Ukraine." December 3. https://bit.ly/2XoyenA

2019. "Relations with Ukraine." November 4. https://bit.ly/2rRp9VD

Naureckas, Jim. 2014. "Denying the Far-Right Role in the Ukrainian Revolution." *FAIR*, March 7. https://bit.ly/2ZAzD7v

Nayyem, Mustafa. 2014. "Uprising in Ukraine: How It All Began." *Open Society Foundations*, April 4. https://osf.to/2uMPcww

Nebehay, Stephanie. 2014. "Ukraine Crisis Death Toll Doubles in Two Weeks to Aug. 10: UN." *Reuters*, August 13. https://reut.rs/2tygtk0

Nebesnia sotnia. 2019. https://bit.ly/3vM3ifT

Neef, Christian. 2017. "Pro-Russian Separatists Harden Split from Ukraine." *Spiegel Online*, July 28. http://bit.ly/2vfguvm

Neistat, Anna. 2014. "Dispatches: Truth a Casualty in Ukraine Conflict." *Human Rights Watch*, May 10. https://bit.ly/2BCYNs3

Nemtsova, Anna. 2014a. "Ukraine Denies Deadly Grad Rocket Attacks on Donetsk." *The Daily Beast*, July 22. https://bit.ly/2T1FfYt

2014b. "Ukrainian Troops Surrender to Unarmed Pro-Russian Protesters." *The Daily Beast*, 17 April. https://bit.ly/2TRpIaM

2014c. "Witness to a Ukraine Rebel Breakthrough." *The Daily Beast*, June 4. https://bit.ly/2IiMuXy

New York Times. 2014. "Text of Joint Diplomatic Statement on Ukraine." April 17. https://nyti.ms/2BwsZ8g

NV. 2014. "Vstrecha Berkuta v Sevastopole 22 fevralia 2014." YouTube video, February 22. https://bit.ly/341tHGL

2017. "Nichne poboïshche na Maidani: spohady ochevydtsiv." November 30. https://bit.ly/2QRSwis

Nye, Joseph S. 2004. *Soft Power: The Means to Succeed in World Politics*. New York: Public Affairs.

O'Loughlin, John, Gerard Toal, and Vladimir Kolosov. 2017. "The Rise and Fall of 'Novorossiya': Examining Support for a Separatist Geopolitical Imaginary in Southeast Ukraine." *Post-Soviet Affairs* 33(2), 124–44.

Obozrevatel. 2014. "Z'ïzd Dobkina priyniav rezolutsiiu bez radykal'nykh zaiav." February 22. https://bit.ly/2ScCUqm

——— 2016. "Ne pomogli i 1100 boitsov: nazvana prichina 'sdachi' Donetskoi OGA v 2014 godu." April 29. https://bit.ly/2HebZJ1

Office of the United Nations High Commissioner for Human Rights. 2015. "Report on the Human Rights Situation in Ukraine." February 15. https://bit.ly/2EkSTxC

——— 2019. "Report on the Human Rights Situation in Ukraine 16 November 2018 to 15 February 2019." March 12. https://bit.ly/34YlbuE

Ofitsial'nyi internet-portal pravovoi informatsii. 2014. "Ob obostrenii situatsii na Ukraine." January 22. https://bit.ly/2JAR1DH

Ogarkova, Tetyana. 2018. "The Truth Behind Ukraine's Language Policy." *Atlantic Council*, March 12. https://bit.ly/2L2EwDK

Olearchyk, Roman. 2014. "Riot Police Storm Ukraine Protest Camp." *Financial Times*, February 18. https://on.ft.com/315BfqK

Olearchyk, Roman, and Neil Buckley. 2016. "Mystery Surrounds Deaths of Pro-Russian Warlords." *Financial Times*, October 20. https://on.ft.com/34yshmF

Oliphant, Roland. 2014. "Russian Paratroopers Captured in Ukraine 'Accidentally Crossed Border.'" *The Telegraph*, August 26. https://bit.ly/2VbStiq

Olszański, Tadeusz A., and Wojciech Konończuk. 2014. "Crisis in Ukraine: The First Step Towards Compromise." *OSW*, January 29. https://bit.ly/2JHlVc7

Onuch, Olga. 2014. "The Maidan and Beyond: Who Were the Protesters?" *Journal of Democracy* 25(3), 44–51.

Onuch, Olga, and Gwendolyn Sasse. 2016. "The Maidan in Movement: Diversity and the Cycles of Protest." *Europe-Asia Studies* 68(4), 556–87.

Orenstein, Mitchell A. 2019. *The Lands in Between: Russia vs. the West and the New Politics of Hybrid War.* Oxford: Oxford University Press.

Ostrov. 2014. "Donetskii oblastnoi sovet progolosoval za provedenie referenduma o statuse Donetskoi oblasti." *Ostrov*, March 3. https://bit.ly/3i4m5g9

Ozhiganov, Edward. 1997. "The Republic of Moldova: Transdniester and the 14th Army." In *Managing Conflict in the Former Soviet Union: Russian and American Perspectives.* Edited by Alexei Arbatov, Abram Chayes, Antonia Hanfler Chayes, and Lara Olson, 145–210. Cambridge, MA: MIT Press.

Pancevski, Bojan. 2014a. "Kiev Lets Loose Men in Black." *The Times*, May 11. https://bit.ly/2V6TDf4

2014b. "Separatists' Defiance Wilts into Blubbering." *The Times*, August 17. https://bit.ly/2T7fSV5

Paniotto, Volodymyr. 2014. "Euromaidan: Profile of a Rebellion." *Global Dialogue*, March 9. https://bit.ly/31BQKHu

Parfitt, Tom. 2014. "Ukraine Promises 'Retribution' as at Least 19 Soldiers Killed in Rebel Rocket Attack." *Daily Telegraph*, July 11. https://bit.ly/2S902ob

Parkinson, Sarah. 2013. "Organizing Rebellion: Rethinking High-Risk Mobilization and Social Networks in War." *American Political Science Review* 107(3), 418–32.

Patrikarakos, David. 2014. "The Siege of Sloviansk." *Foreign Policy*, April 16. https://bit.ly/3flZzYK

Pauly, Matthew D. 2014. *Breaking the Tongue: Language, Education, and Power in Soviet Ukraine, 1923–1934*. Toronto: University of Toronto Press.

Petersen, Roger D. 1999. "Mechanisms and Structures in Comparisons." In *Critical Comparisons in Politics and Culture*. Edited by John Richard Bowen and Roger D. Petersen, 61–77. Cambridge: Cambridge University Press.

2001. *Resistance and Rebellion: Lessons from Eastern Europe*. Cambridge: Cambridge University Press.

2002. *Understanding Ethnic Violence: Fear, Hatred, and Resentment in Twentieth-Century Eastern Europe*. Cambridge: Cambridge University Press.

2011. *Western Intervention in the Balkans: The Strategic Use of Emotion in Conflict*. Cambridge: Cambridge University Press.

2017. "Emotions as the Residue of Lived Experience." *PS: Political Science & Politics* 50(4), 932–5.

Peterson, Nolan. 2016. "The Ukraine Front Line: The Somme Meets Normandy, Plus Drones." *Newsweek*, August 27. https://bit.ly/2YWdmS9

Petrov, Ivan, and Mariia Makutina. 2014. "Davlenie na granitsu: Rossiiskie voiska vernulis' v sosednie s Ukrainoi oblasti." *RBK*, June 19. https://bit.ly/2GEdPRH

Pid prytsilom. 2014. "Seliany vlashtuvaly propusknyi punkt: vidlovliuiut' 'titushok' ta paliat' avtobusy." February 20. https://bit.ly/2TJcrSr

Pifer, Steven. 2017. *The Eagle and the Trident: U.S.–Ukraine Relations in Turbulent Times*. Washington, DC: Brookings Institution Press.

Platonova, Daria. 2020. "Local Elites and the Donbas Conflict: A Comparative Case Study of Kharkiv City and Donets'k Region." PhD diss., King's College.

Plokhy, Serhii. 2000. "The City of Glory: Sevastopol in Russian Historical Mythology." *Journal of Contemporary History* 35(3), 369–83.

Podrobytsi. 2014. "Nikolaevskaia samooborona snesla palatochnyi lager' prorossiiskikh akitivistov." April 8. https://bit.ly/2BRJ5d2

Polian, Pavel. 2004. *Against Their Will: The History and Geography of Forced Migrations in the USSR.* Budapest: Central European University Press.

Poltavshchyna. 2014. "Militsiia Poltavshchyny pereishla na bik narodu." February 20, 18:53. https://bit.ly/2zc1FKZ

Polygraph. 2019. "Assessing Putin's Prediction of 'Srebrenica' in Donbas." December 17. https://bit.ly/2PCizey

Pomerantsev, Peter. 2019. *This Is Not Propaganda: Adventures in the War Against Reality.* New York: Hachette.

Ponomarenko, Illia. 2019a. "Ukraine Could Have Prevailed in Donbas, But Now is Doomed to Unjust Peace." *Kyiv Post*, October 7. https://bit.ly/2LTWNBb

2019b. "United Nations: 13,000 Killed, 30,000 Injured in Donbas since 2014." *Kyiv Post*, January 22. https://bit.ly/2WfJ8Yf

Popescu, Nicu. 2013. "The Russia–Ukraine Trade Spat." *European Union Institute for Security Studies Issue Alerts* 26, August. https://bit.ly/2t8pvE7

Popkin, Samuel L. 1979. *The Rational Peasant.* Berkeley: University of California Press.

Popova, Maria. 2013. "Authoritarian Learning and the Politicization of Justice: The Tymoshenko Case in Context." Updated version of a paper presented at the Danyliw Research Seminar on Contemporary Ukraine, University of Ottawa, 2012. https://bit.ly/2sP2cQm

Popovic, Milos. 2017. "Fragile Proxies: Explaining Rebel Defection against Their State Sponsors." *Terrorism and Political Violence* 29(5), 922–42.

Portnov, Andriy. 2013. "Memory Wars in Post-Soviet Ukraine (1991–2010)." In *Memory and Theory in Eastern Europe.* Edited by Uilleam Blacker, Alexander Etkind, and Julie Fedor, 233–54. New York: Palgrave Macmillan.

2015. "Ukraine's 'Eurorevolution.'" *Russian Politics and Law* 53(3), 6–27.

Posen, Barry R. 1991. *Inadvertent Escalation: Conventional War and Nuclear Risks.* Ithaca, NY: Cornell University Press.

1993. "The Security Dilemma and Ethnic Conflict." *Survival* 35(1), 27–47.

2014. Sixth Annual Kenneth N. Waltz Lecture, Presented at Columbia University. November 13. https://bit.ly/3n2GUJI

2016. "How to Think about Russia." *The National Interest*, November 29. https://bit.ly/2Oxku3S

Powell, Robert. 2006. "War as a Commitment Problem." *International Organization* 60(1), 169–203.

Pozdniakova, Natalia. 2014. "Glava MID FRG: Otkaz ot dialoga – bol'shaia oshibka Yanukovycha." *Deutsche Welle*, February 19. https://bit.ly/2W9qmRq

Pravozashchytnyi tsentr Memorial. 2015. "Mezhdu peremiriem i voinoi." February 16. https://bit.ly/2YFfayL

President of Russia. 2022a. "Address by the President of the Russian Federation." February 21. https://bit.ly/3HcLb5E

2022b. "Address by the President of the Russian Federation." February 24. https://tinyurl.com/2p8hr59w

Prezident Rossii. 2012. "Federal'nyi zakon o 25.07.2002 g. No. 114-F3 – O protivodeitsvii ekstremitskoi deiatel'nosti." July 25. https://bit.ly/2M11OcI

2014a. "Obrashchenie Prezidenta Rossiiskoi Federatsii." March 18. https://bit.ly/2J5SXDw

2014b. "Vladimir Putin vnes obrashchenie v Sovet Federatsii." March 1. https://bit.ly/2IteU0P

2022. "Zasedanie Soveta Bezopasnosti." February 21 [Transcript]. https://bit.ly/3s8Rq6y

Prokhanov, Aleksandr. 2014. "Kto ty, 'Strelok'?" *Zavtra*, November 20. https://bit.ly/2qDY3iB

Pshenychnykh, Anastasiya. 2020. "Leninfall: The Spectacle of Forgetting." *European Journal of Cultural Studies* 23(3), 393–414.

Putin, Vladimir. 2021a. "Ob istoricheskom edinstve russkikh i ukraintsev." *Prezident Rossii*, July 12. https://bit.ly/3DcnREB

2021b. "On the Historical Unity of Russians and Ukrainians." *President of Russia*, July 12. https://bit.ly/3myO76c

Pyvovarov, Serhiy. 2018. "P'iat' rokiv tomu v Kyievi na Bessarabtsi znesly pam'iatnyk Leninu." *Babel'*, December 8. https://bit.ly/328OHLj

Quinn, Allison. 2015. "Third Servicemen Dies from Rada Grenade Attack." *Kyiv Post*, September 1. https://bit.ly/2EyBoci

Quinn, Ben, Kayla Epstein, and Helen Davidson. 2014. "Ukraine Police Storm Kiev Protest Camp – As It Happened." *The Guardian*, February 19. https://bit.ly/2P2Ae0V

Racheva, Elena. 2015. "Poezd No. 336." *Novaia gazeta*, April 29. https://bit.ly/2SSyN5G

Rachkevych, Mark. 2014a. "Armed Pro-Russian Extremists Launch Coordinated Attacks in Donetsk Oblast, Seize Regional Police Headquarters, Set Up Checkpoints," *Kyiv Post*, April 12. https://bit.ly/38U9G8G

2014b. "Diplomats' Promise of De-Escalation Gets Skeptical Response." *Kyiv Post*, April 18. https://bit.ly/2BHe4bv

2014c. "Three More Gubernatorial Buildings Taken, Bringing Number to 11." *Kyiv Post*, January 25. https://bit.ly/2JytgMu

Radchenko, Ivan. 2014. "Mariupol' posle Dnia pobedy." *Ostrov*, May 13. https://bit.ly/3CtXPw1

Radio Svoboda. 2014. "Maidan ide u 'mirnyi nastup." I akshcho treba, znovy zakhopit' KMDA – opozytsiia." February 16. https://bit.ly/2KhmviG

 2016. "Dopyt Yanukovycha. Druha sproba." November 28. https://bit.ly/2KIyu7p

 2019. "51 deputat zvernuvsia do KSU shcho zakonu pro ukrains'ku movu." June 21. https://bit.ly/3oyRNTg

Radnitz, Scott. 2021. *Revealing Schemes: The Politics of Conspiracy in Russia and the Post-Soviet Region*. New York: Oxford University Press.

Razumkov trentr. 2018. "Osoblyvosti relihiynoho i tserkovno- relihiynoho samovyznachennia ukraïns'kykh hromadian: tendentsiï 2010–2018 rr." https://bit.ly/3ouWg9n

 2019. "Hromad'ska dumka pro situatsiiu na Donbasi ta shiakhy vidnovlennia suverenitetu Ukraïny nad okupovanymy terytoriiamy (sotsiolohiia)." October 11. https://bit.ly/3hXF1vg

RBK. 2014a. "Gossovet Kryma obvinil aktivistov Evromaidana v ubiistve semi krymchan." April 3. https://bit.ly/2r0ldS0

 2014b. "V Donetskoi oblasti ob'iavlen referendum o prisoedinenii k Rossii." March 3. https://bit.ly/3rB8396

Recknagel, Charles. 2014. "Explainer: How Ukraine Crisis Went from Compromise to Bloodshed in Just Hours." *RFE/RL*, February 19. https://bit.ly/2YTVINs

Regnum. 2014. "MID Rossii sdelal zaiavlenie po situatsii na Ukraine." February 24. https://bit.ly/2L9YMUi

Reid, Anna. 2014. "On the Ground with the Pro-Russian Separatists Suspected of Shooting Down MH17." *Newsweek*, July 18. https://bit.ly/2E0659O

Reisinger, Heidi, and Aleksandr Golts. 2014. "Russia's Hybrid Warfare: Waging War Below the Radar of Traditional Collective Defence." Research Paper No. 105. Rome: NATO Defense College, Research Division. November. https://bit.ly/3maruBP

Reiting. 2022. "The Fifth National Poll: Ukraine during the War (March 18, 2022)." March 20. https://bit.ly/37Ey6pH

ReliefWeb. 2015a. "Ukraine: Situation Report No. 29 as of 27 February 2015." UN Office for the Coordination of Humanitarian Affairs, February 27. https://bit.ly/2EmTcYP

 2015b. "Spot Report by the OSCE Special Monitoring Mission to Ukraine (SMM): Protest Outside National Parliament in Kyiv Turns Violent." August 31.

Remy, Johannes. 2016. *Brothers or Enemies: The Ukrainian National Movement and Russia, from the 1840s to the 1970s*. Toronto: University of Toronto Press.

Rettman, Andrew. 2015. "EU Breaks Taboo on 'Russian Forces in Ukraine.'" *EUObserver*, February 16. https://bit.ly/3prrmkC

Reuters. 2014. "'Murdered' Ukraine Politician Faced Hostile Mob, Video Shows." April 23. https://reut.rs/2JP2K2n

2022. "Ukraine, Russia-Backed Rebels Trade Accusations of Shelling across Front." February 17. https://reut.rs/3LGJK2X

Rezunkov, Viktor. 2014. "Gorod, kotoryi zhdet grobov." *Radio Svoboda*, September 7. https://bit.ly/2GyQ6mE

RFE/RL. 2015. "Putin Says He Decided to Take Crimea Just Hours after Yanukovych's Ouster." March 9. https://bit.ly/34DOhgL

2017. "Amid Scuffles and Smoke, Bills on East Ukraine Conflict Advance in Parliament." October 6. http://bit.ly/2y2Xu2u

RIA Novosti. 2010. "Yanukovych Reverses Ukraine's Position on Famine." April 27. https://bit.ly/2HqznEg

2014. "Krym podnimet vopros ob otdelenii pri smene legitimnoi vlasti Ukrainy." February 20. https://bit.ly/34Yxh7d

RIA Novosti Ukraina. 2014. "Mitinguiushe v Donetske poobeshchali slozhit's oruzhie, zaiavil Yarema." April 8. https://bit.ly/2mg9xVh

Robinson, Paul. 2016. "Explaining the Ukrainian Army's Defeat in Donbass in 2014." In *The Return of the Cold War: Ukraine, the West and Russia*. Edited by J. L. Black and Michael Johns, 108–26. New York: Routledge.

Roblin, Sebastien. 2017. "Airborne Fighting Vehicles Rolled through Hell in Eastern Ukraine." *Warisboring*, July 22. http://bit.ly/2h3kdXw

Roeder, Philip G. 2007. *Where Nation-States Come From: Institutional Change in the Age of Nationalism*. Princeton, NJ: Princeton University Press.

2009. "Ethnofederalism and the Mismanagement of Conflicting Nationalisms." *Regional & Federal Studies* 19(2), 203–19.

2018. *National Secessions: Persuasion and Violence in Independence Campaigns*. Ithaca, NY: Cornell University Press.

Roemer, John. 2019. *How We Cooperate: A Theory of Kantian Optimization*. New Haven, CT: Yale University Press.

Rogin, Josh, and Eli Lake. 2015. "U.S. told Ukraine to Stand Down on Crimea as Putin Invaded." *Bloomberg*, August 24. https://bloom.bg/37Rwjyb

Roshchyna, Victoria, and Angelina Kariakina. 2019. "How an Ex-Berkut Officer Tied to Euromaidan Crimes Ended Up in Ukraine's New Police." *Hromadske International*, February 1. https://bit.ly/2UXN0fg

Rossoliński-Liebe, Grzegorz. 2010. "The 'Ukrainian National Revolution' of 1941: Discourse and Practice of a Fascist Movement." *Kritika: Explorations in Russian and Eurasian History* 12(1), 83–114.

Roth, Andrew. 2014. "From Russia, 'Tourists' Stir the Protests." *New York Times*, March 4. https://nyti.ms/2XaezmT

Rowland, Richard. 2004. "National and Regional Population Trends in Ukraine: Results from the Most Recent Census." *Eurasian Geography and Economics* 45(7), 491–514.

Rozenas, Arturas, and Yuri M. Zhukov. 2019. "Mass Repression and Political Loyalty: Evidence from Stalin's 'Terror by Hunger.'" *American Political Science Review* 113(2), 569–83.

RT. 2014. "Video: Stones, Bottles and Shoes Thrown as Pro- and Anti-Russian Protesters Clash in Ukraine's Crimea." YouTube video, February 26. https://bit.ly/3JED9W0

Rublee, Maria Rost. 2015. "Fantasy Counterfactual: A Nuclear-Armed Ukraine." *Survival* 57(2), 145–56.

Rublevskii, Konstantin. 2014. "Chto takoe 'Pravyi sektor': fakty i domysly o radikal'noi organizatsii." *Voennoe obozrenie*, January 23. https://bit.ly/3vEYyrP

Rudnytskyi, Omelian, Nataliia Levchuk, Oleh Wolowyna, Pavlo Shevchuk, and Alla Kovbasiuk. 2015. "Demography of a Man-Made Human Catastrophe: The Case of Massive Famine in Ukraine 1932–1933." *Canadian Studies in Population* 42(1–2), 53–80.

Rumer, Eugene. 2015. "Arm Ukraine and You Risk Another Black Hawk Down." *Financial Times*, February 3. https://on.ft.com/34nWxAF

Rupor Zhytomyra. 2014. "Aktyvysty Zhytomyra blokuiut' vyïzdy z usikh viys'kovykh chastyny mista." February 20. https://bit.ly/2KS9oTP

Russkoe edinstvo. 2014. "Glavyi piati silovykh struktur Kryma prinesli prisiagu narodu." March 3. https://bit.ly/34tf4MQ

Ruzhelnyk, Olga. 2021. "Ultras du football ukrainien et reconfigurations politiques autour du Maïdan." PhD diss., Université Paris Nanterre.

Salehyan, Idean, Kristian Skrede Gleditsch, and David E. Cunningham. 2011. "Explaining External Support for Insurgent Groups." *International Organization* 65(4), 709–44.

Salem, Harriet. 2014. "Ukraine has Won Full Control over the Port City of Mariupol." *Vice News*, June 13. https://bit.ly/2VEmHAz

Salem, Harriet, and Graham Stack. 2014. "Streetfighting Men: Is Ukraine's Government Bankrolling a Secret Army of Adidas-Clad Thugs?" *Foreign Policy*, February 6. https://bit.ly/2YBOyO5

Sambanis, Nicholas. 2004. "What is Civil War? Conceptual and Empirical Complexities of an Operational Definition." *Journal of Conflict Resolution* 48(6), 814–58.

Sambanis, Nicholas, Stergios Skaperdas, and William Wohlforth. 2020. "External Intervention, Identity, and Civil War." *Comparative Political Studies* 53(14), 2155–82.

Sanders, Deborah. 2017. 'The War We Want; the War that We Get': Ukraine's Military Reform and the Conflict in the East." *Journal of Slavic Military Studies* 30(1), 30–49.

Sarotte, Mary Elise. 2014. "A Broken Promise?" *Foreign Affairs* 93(5), 90–7.

Sasse, Gwendolyn. 2007. *The Crimea Question: Identity, Transition, and Conflict.* Cambridge, MA: Harvard Ukrainian Research Institute. Distributed by Harvard University Press.

Sasse, Gwendolyn, and Alice Lackner. 2018. "War and Identity: The Case of the Donbas in Ukraine." *Post-Soviet Affairs* 34(2–3), 139–57.

Sautreuil, Pierre. 2018. *Les guerres perdues de Youri Belaiev.* Paris: Grasset.

Scales, Robert H. 2015. "The Firepower that Ukraine Needs." *Wall Street Journal*, February 21. https://on.wsj.com/38MmX2o

Scazzieri, Luigi. 2017. "Europe, Russia and the Ukraine Crisis: The Dynamics of Coercion." *Journal of Strategic Studies* 40(3), 392–416.

Scharpf, Fritz. 1990. "Game Real Actors Could Play." *Rationality and Society* 2(4), 471–94.

Schelling, Thomas. 1960. *The Strategy of Conflict.* Cambridge, MA: Harvard University Press.

Schram, Peter. 2021. "Hassling: How States Prevent a Preventative War." *American Journal of Political Science* 65(2), 294–308.

Schwartz, Lee. 1990. "Regional Population Redistribution and National Homelands in the USSR." In *Soviet Nationality Policies: Ruling Ethnic Groups in the USSR.* Edited by Henry Huttenbach, 121–61. London: Mansell.

Schwartz, Mattathias. 2018. "Who Killed the Kiev Protesters? A 3-D Model Holds the Clues." *New York Times Magazine*, May 31. https://nyti.ms/2IWqwtu

Seddon, Max. 2014. "Ukraine's New Government Has Lost Its Grip on East Ukraine." *BuzzFeed News*, April 14. https://bzfd.it/3wcTuci

Selznick, Philip. 1952. *The Organization Weapon: A Study of Bolshevik Strategy and Tactics.* New York: RAND Corporation.

Semelin, Jacques. 2007. *Purify and Destroy: The Political Uses of Massacre and Genocide.* New York: Columbia University Press.

Semenova, Aleksandra. 2019. "'Luchshe by etoi knigi ne bylo': vyshel sbornik 'Rossiia i Ukraina. Dni zatmeniia." *MBX Media*, February 4. https://bit.ly/2U52eiE

Sereda, Viktoriya. 2016. "Transformation of Identities and Historical Memories in Ukraine after the Euromaidan: National, Regional, Local Dimensions." Unpublished paper presented at the 2016 Danyliw Seminar on Ukraine, University of Ottawa. http://bit.ly/2uwEQwB

Seybolt, Taylor B., Jay D. Aronson, and Baruch Fischhoff, eds. 2013. *Counting Civilian Casualties: An Introduction to Recording and Estimating Nonmilitary Deaths in Conflict.* Oxford: Oxford University Press.

Shakirov, Mumin. 2014. "Interview: I was a Separatist Fighter in Ukraine." *RFE/RL*, July 13. https://bit.ly/34WIeWK

Shamanska, Anna. 2016. "Behind Closed Doors: Ukraine's Panicked Meeting Ahead of Crimean Seizure." *RFE/RL*, February 23. https://bit.ly/2rvy9up

Shandra, Alya. 2019a. "Glazyev Tapes, Continued: New Details of Russian Occupation of Crimea and Attempts to Dismember Ukraine." *Euromaidan Press*, May 16. https://bit.ly/2JrRrxi

2019b. "'Steinmeier's Formula' Seen as State Capitulation, Protested in Ukraine." *Euromaidan Press*, September 21. https://bit.ly/2mxRgWV

Shapiro, Jeremy. 2015. "Why Arming the Ukrainians is a Bad Idea." *Brookings*, February 3. https://brook.gs/2Pu65pe

Shaplak, David A., and Michael Johnson. 2016. "Reinforcing Deterrence on NATO's Eastern Flank: Wargaming the Defense of the Baltics." RAND Corporation. Research Report. https://bit.ly/3meRz2W

Shapovalova, Natalia, and Olga Burlyuk, eds. 2018. *Civil Society in Post-Euromaidan Ukraine: From Revolution to Consolidation*. Stuttgart: ibidem.

Shekhovtsov, Anton. 2011. "The Creeping Resurgence of the Ukrainian Radical Right? The Case of the Freedom Party." *Europe-Asia Studies* 63(2), 203–28.

2013a. "Provoking the Euromaidan." *openDemocracy*, December 3. https://bit.ly/2JLOqYI

2013b. "Ukrainian Extra-Parliamentary Extreme Right behind the Provocations at the President Administration." *Anton Shekhovtsov's Blog*, December 1. https://bit.ly/30RLezX

2015. "Whither the Ukrainian Far Right?" *Anton Shekhovtsov's Blog*, January 30. https://bit.ly/386e3OF

Sherr, James. 2014. "Ukraine's Fightback has Surprised the Kremlin." *Chatham House*, August 1. https://bit.ly/2BrMwXA

Shesterinina, Anastasia. 2016. "Collective Threat Framing and Mobilization in Civil War." *American Political Science Review* 110(3), 411–27.

2021. "Ethics, Empathy, and Fear in Research on Violent Conflict." *Journal of Peace Research* 56(2), 190–202.

Shevel, Oxana. 2011. "The Politics of Memory in a Divided Society: A Comparison of Post-Franco Spain and Post-Soviet Ukraine," *Slavic Review* 70(1), 135–62.

2015. "'De-Communization Laws' Need to Be Amended to Conform to European Standards." *VoxUkraine*, May 7. http://bit.ly/2mdXmbK

2016. "Decommunization in Post-Euromaidan Ukraine: Law and Practice." *PONARS Eurasia*, January. https://bit.ly/35Exg6F

Shiriaev, Valerii. 2014. "'Vezhlivye liudi' v Krymu: kak eto bylo." *Novaia gazeta*, April 17. https://bit.ly/2P9ARDU

2016. "Vosem' zhenshchin v dekretnom otpuske, moriak-geroi i real'naia agentura rossiiskikh spetsshlub. Kogo vkliuchili v spisok predatelei Ukrainy?" *Novaya gazeta*, March 29. https://bit.ly/2J2CxeS

Shramovych, V'iacheslav. 2017. "Група С14: khulihany, yaki lovliat' separatistiv." *BBC News Ukraïna*, July 4. https://bbc.in/37ZFkBm

Shreck, Carl. 2019. "From 'Not Us' to 'Why Hide It?': How Russia Denied Its Crimea Invasion, then Admitted It." *RFE/RL*, February 26. https://bit.ly/2M8bgvG

Shtorhin, Iryna. 2019. "Chomu ne vtrymaly Krym: stenohrama RNBO vid 28 liutoho 2014 roku." *Radio svoboda*, February 27. https://bit.ly/357UIuQ

Shukan, Ioulia. 2019. "Defending Ukraine at the Rear of the Armed Conflict in Donbas: Wartime Vigilantism in Odesa (2014–2018)." *Laboratorium: Russian Review of Social Research* 11(3), 71–104.

Shuster, Simon. 2014a. "Many Ukrainians Want Russia to Invade." *Time*, March 1. https://bit.ly/2W0OLKu

2014b. "The Russian Stronghold in Ukraine Preparing to Fight the Revolution." *Time*, February 23. https://ti.me/2wQdnww

Sidorenko, Sergei. 2014. "Ubyl v istoriiu." *Kommersant'*, February 24. https://bit.ly/2H3LDXT

Sidorenko, Sergei, and Aleksandr Radchuk. 2014. "S nimi boi." *Kommersant' Ukraina*, February 19. https://bit.ly/2xYjix8

Siiak, Ivan. 2016. "Maidan Activist Ivan Bubenchyk: It's True I Shot Them in the Back of the Head." *Bird in Flight*, February 19. https://bit.ly/2KIOBTI

Sindelar, Daisy. 2014. "Explainer: How Ukraine's Referendums Broke the Rules." *RFE/RL*, May 12. https://bit.ly/2V64beM

SITU Research. 2018. "Euromaidan Event Reconstruction." Center for Human Rights Science (CHRS) at Carnegie Mellon University, Jus Talionis Reconstruction Lab. https://bit.ly/2lH6cSd

Skorikov, Ivan. 2015. "Nerozhdionnaia respublika: ob oshibkakh 'Odesskoi vesny.'" *Institut stran SNG*, March 12. https://bit.ly/3rz32xJ

Skorkin, Konstantin. 2016. "25 let donbasskogo separatizma." *Realgazeta*, March 15. https://bit.ly/3pTFZeZ

Slovodilo. 2013. "Yak ukraïntsi spriinialy pryzupennia Asotsiatsiï z YeS ta rozhin Maïdanu?" December 23. https://bit.ly/2m5gaJq

Sluzhba bezpeky Ukraïny. 2014a. "GRU Slaviansk 14 04 14." YouTube video, April 14. https://bit.ly/3jiUVl4

2014b. "Rosiys'kymy spetssluzhbamy zdiysniuiut'sia zakhody po vyvedenniu do Krymu svoïkh spivrobitnikiv u sklady rozvid-dyversiynikh grup." YouTube video, August 14. https://bit.ly/2GBUVuy

Smolar, Piotr. 2014a. "Le fédéralisme, cheval de Troie de la stratégie russe en Ukraine." *Le Monde*, March 22. https://lemde.fr/2Ee8ZZW

2014b. "Le passé trouble de Denis Pouchiline, chef séparatiste de la 'république populaire de Donetsk.'" *Le Monde*, April 19. https://lemde .fr/2XdHwia

2014c. "Ukraine: aux armes, milliardaire!" *Le Monde*, June 9. https:// lemde.fr/2BS4FOy

Smotri.city. 2014. "Post v s. Man'kivka zupiniaie 'Titushok.'" February 20. https://bit.ly/2KGoxso

Sneider, Noah. 2014. "Pro-Russian Rebels in Ukraine Collect Their Dead and Ask, Where is Putin?" *Aljazeera America*, May 30. https://bit .ly/2TWBXme

Snyder, Timothy. 2014. "Ukraine: The New Dictatorship." *New York Review of Books NYR Daily*, January 18. https://bit.ly/30hbbrB

2018. *The Road to Unfreedom*. New York: Tim Duggan Books.

Socor, Vladimir. 2014a. "Donetsk 'Republic' Leaders' Morale Plummeting." *Eurasia Daily Monitor*, August 1. https://bit.ly/2GRmmAK

2014b. "Moscow Encourages Centrifugal Forces in South-Eastern Ukraine." *Eurasia Daily Monitor*, February 25. https://bit.ly/2rRtbJx

Sokolins'ka, Al'ona. 2016. "Chorne pershe bereznia 2014-go v Khar'kovi." *Den'*, March 1. https://bit.ly/2Pm5ZwK

Solzhenitsyn, Alexander. 1991. *Rebuilding Russia: Reflections and Tentative Proposals*. New York: Farrar, Straus, and Giroux.

Sorokin, Oleksiy. 2022. "Germany, France Ask Zelensky to Comply with Russia's Spin of Minsk Agreements." *Kyiv Independent*, February 15. https://bit.ly/3JtC6Hk

Souleimanov, Emil Aslan, and David S. Siroky. 2016. "Random or Retributive? Indiscriminate Violence in the Chechen Wars." *World Politics* 68(4), 677–712.

Spaulding, Hugo. 2015. "Putin's Next Objectives in the Ukraine Crisis." *Institute for the Study of War*, February 3. https://bit.ly/1Fetg9B

Stack, Graham. 2015. "Kyiv Blog: What Triggered the Maidan Massacre?" *BNE IntelliNews*, February 13. https://bit.ly/2YOe5rF

Staniland, Paul. 2015, "Armed Groups and Militarized Elections." *International Studies Quarterly* 59(4), 694–705.

Stebelsky, Ihor. 2009. "Ethnic Self-Identification in Ukraine, 1989–2001: Why More Ukrainians and Fewer Russians?" *Canadian Slavonic Papers* 51(1), 77–100.

Stepaniuk, Nataliia. 2018. "Lives Punctuated by War: Civilian Volunteers and Identity Formation amidst the Donbas War in Ukraine." PhD thesis, University of Ottawa.

Stephan, Maria J., and Erica Chenoweth. 2008. "Why Civil Resistance Works: The Strategic Logic of Nonviolent Conflict." *International Security* 33(1), 7–44.

Stone, Randall. 2002. *Lending Credibility*. Princeton, NJ: Princeton University Press.

StopFake. 2016. "Russian Crimea Annexation Documentary Filled with Lies and Errors." April 27. http://bit.ly/2v5cPk4

Sutyagin, Igor. 2015. "Russian Forces in Ukraine." Royal United Services Institute. Briefing Paper, March 9. https://bit.ly/3kplGFw

Taimer. 2014. "Shturm i natisk: protivostoiane pod Odesskoi OGA (khronika sobytii)." March 3. https://bit.ly/2BSnEc3

TASS. 2014. "Lukin: RF ne stala podpisyvat' ukrainskoe soglashenie iz-za prisutstvuiushchikh v nem neiasnostei." February 22. https://bit.ly/3AtE7Qh

2022. "Reaktsiia Rossii na otvet SshA po garantiiam bezopasnosti. Pol'nyi tekst." February 17. https://bit.ly/356RquI

Tavernise, Sabrina. 2014. "Whisked away for Tea with a Rebel in Ukraine." *New York Times*, July 16. https://nyti.ms/2V5NO1C

Taylor, Adam. 2014. "How the Obscure OSCE Ended Up at the Center of the MH17 Investigation." *Washington Post*, July 21. https://wapo.st/2WThnVQ

Taylor, Michael. 1982. *Community, Anarchy, and Liberty*. Cambridge: Cambridge University Press.

Techynskyi, Olexandr, Aleksey Solodunov, and Dmitry Stoykov (dirs.). 2014. *All Things Ablaze*. Journeyman Pictures.

Tekhty. n.d. "Try dni pered vesnoiu. Khto, koly i de zahynuv na Maidani 18–20 liutoho 2014 roku." https://bit.ly/31m3wZJ

2014a. "Antiterorystychna operatsiia ne mozhe provodytysia po sviy kraïni." February 19. https://bit.ly/2HeiboOY

2014b. "Eks-berkutivets: dlia rozstrilu Maidanu pidvozyly patrony zi svyntsem." October 7. https://bit.ly/2MMaWl2

Ternopil's'ka oblasna derzhavna administratsiia. 2014. "Rozporiadzhennia holovy oblasnoï derzhavnoï administratsiï. Pro proekt prohamy material'no-tekhnichnoho zabezpechennia 6-oho batal'ionu terytorial'noï oborony Ternopil's'koï oblasti." April 1. https://bit.ly/3BQjO2g

Toal, Gerard. 2017. *Near Abroad: Putin, the West, and the Contest over Ukraine and the Caucasus*. Oxford: Oxford University Press.

Toft, Monica Duffy. 2003. *The Geography of Ethnic Violence: Identity, Interests, and the Indivisibility of Territory*. Princeton, NJ: Princeton University Press.

Toft, Monica Duffy, and Yuri Zhukov. 2015. "Islamists and Nationalists: Rebel Motivation and Counterinsurgency in Russia's North Caucasus." *American Political Science Review* 109(2), 222–38.

Toler, Aric. 2015. "Unpicking the Donetsk People's Republic's Tangled Volnovakha Bus Massacre Narrative." *Bellingcat*, January 18. https://bit.ly/2T0EAqf

Toler, Aric, and Melinda Haring. 2017. "Russia Funds and Manages Conflict in Ukraine, Leaks Show." *Atlantic Council*, April 24. https://bit.ly/2Qm15lw

Treisman, Daniel S. 1997. "Russia's 'Ethnic Revival': The Separatist Activism of Regional Leaders in a Postcommunist Order." *World Politics* 49(2), 212–49.

———. 2001. *After the Deluge: Regional Crises and Political Consolidation in Russia*. Ann Arbor: University of Michigan Press.

———. 2018. "Crimea: Anatomy of a Decision." In *The New Autocracy: Information, Politics, and Policy in Putin's Russia*. Edited by Daniel S. Treisman, 277–97. Washington, DC: Brookings Institution Press.

Trenin, Dmitri. 2014a. "The Brink of War in Ukraine?" Carnegie Moscow Center, March 1. https://bit.ly/2J7Qjgn

———. 2014b. "The Crisis in Crimea Could Lead the World into a Second Cold War." *The Guardian*, March 2. https://bit.ly/2GTdqdC

———. 2017. "To Understand Ukraine." *Russia in Global Affairs*, December 27. https://bit.ly/34Y9YKr

Tsebelis, George. 1990. *Nested Games*. Berkeley: University of California Press.

Tsentral'na vyborcha komisiia Ukraïny. 2010. "Vybory Prezydenta Ukraïny: Khid holosuvannia po rehionakh Ukraïny." https://bit.ly/392d0y2

———. 2014a. "Vybory Prezydenta Ukraïny 2014: Khid holosuvannia – Vidomosti na zakinchennia holosuvannia." https://bit.ly/3BymdMj

———. 2014b. "Vybory Prezydenta Ukraïny 2014: Pidsumky holosuvannia v mezhakh rehioniv Ukraïny." https://bit.ly/3uXV6I0

Tsenzor.net. 2014a. "Separatisty zakhvatili SBU v Donetske." April 7. https://bit.ly/2UCksYs

———. 2014b. "'Titushki' Gepy iz 'Oplota' izbili bitami zhurnalistov i yevromaidanovtsev pod odesskoi OGA na glazakh u militsii." February 19. https://bit.ly/2P34KYA

———. 2014c. "V Donetsk pribylo spetspodrazdelenie SBU 'Al'fa', – soobshchestvo Evromaidan." April 7. https://bit.ly/2HQHGZf

———. 2019. "'Ne dopustymo kapituliatsiï': hromads'kist' zvernulasia do Zelens'koho z vidkrytym lystom." September 17. https://bit.ly/2kzUKaE

Tsiktor, Ol'ga. 2021. "Popytka gosudarstvennogo perevorota v Odesse 3 marta 2014 goda: Kak v gorode edva ne sozdali 'narodnuiu respubliku." *DepoOdessa*, March 3. https://bit.ly/3f09ZCW

TSN. 2014a. "'Berkut' na kolinakh poprosiv vybachennia pered l'viv'ianamy." February 25. https://bit.ly/2UjxD0X

———. 2014b. "Na Dnipropetrovshchyny aktyvisty zupynyly potiah iz desantnykamy, yakyi ïkhav do Kiieva – Svoboda." February 20. https://bit.ly/2lEdFS2

Tsymbaliuk, Roman. 2018. "Putin's Shadow." *UNIAN*, March 3. http://bit.ly/2FGsjjX

Tufft, Ben. 2015. "Russia Blocks UN Security Council Statement Condemning Shelling of Ukrainian City that Killed 30." *The Independent*, January 25. https://bit.ly/39IBwHe

Tumarkin, Nina. 2003. "The Great Patriotic War as Myth and Memory." *European Review* 11(4), 595–611.

Turchenkova, Maria. 2014. "Cargo 200." *Voices of Ukraine*, June 9. https://bit.ly/2RWpeyl

UAInfo. 2016. "Samyi massovyi prorossiiskii miting Donetska—kak eto bylo." March 24. https://bit.ly/3SybIBt

UA Position. 2016. "English Translation of Audio Evidence of Putin's Adviser Glazyev and Other Russian Politicians in War in Ukraine." August 29. https://bit.ly/2IEE5KP

Uehling, Greta. 2004. *Beyond Memory: The Crimean Tatars' Deportation and Return*. New York: Palgrave Macmillan.

Ukraine Crisis Media Center. 2016. "Le mois sanglant: Deux ans après la tragédie d'Ilovaysk." August 23. https://bit.ly/2ElrI5z

Ukrainian Helsinki Human Rights Union. 2017. "Report of the International Expert Group. '26 February Criminal Case.' Part 1. Reconstruction and Legal Analysis of the Events of 26 February 2014 Outside the Building of the Supreme Council of the Autonomous Republic of Crimea in Simferopol." March 15. http://bit.ly/2eV24dV

Ukraïns'ka Hel'sins'ka spilka z prav liudyny. 2014. "Yuridychnyi vysnovok TsPPR shchodo 'zakoniv' vid 16 sichnia 2014 roku." January 21. https://bit.ly/31hsc5G

Ukraïns'ka pravda. 2004. "Yanukovych pohrozhuie referendumom, yakshcho yoho ne vyznaiut'." November 28. https://bit.ly/2NSmlwv

——— 2013a. "Militsiia povidomyla, shcho gospitalizovano 75 ïï biytsiv." December 2. https://bit.ly/2Z6xVtU

——— 2013b. "Yanukovych zniav z sebe vidpovidal'nist' za rozhin Maidanu." November 30. https://bit.ly/2MW7ndu

——— 2014a. "ATO u Slov'ians'ku: vbyti i poraneni sylovyky ta separatysty." April 13. https://bit.ly/3xyhjMp

——— 2014b. "Avakov stvoriuie spetspidrozdily z patriotiv dlia borot'by z terorystamy." April 13. https://bit.ly/2I8IxB6

——— 2014c. "Donets'ki separatysty hotuiut'sia sformuvaty 'narodu oblradu' ta priednatysia do RF." *Ukraïns'ka pravda*, April 6. https://bit.ly/3ycCWCp

——— 2014d. "Liudy postavyly ul'tymatum: vidstavka Yanukovycha do ranku." February 21. https://bit.ly/OjFfOI

——— 2014e. "Lutsenko zbyraie u L'vovi pravookhorontsiv dlia zakhistu Maidanu." February 20. https://bit.ly/2lF721I

2014f. "Militsiia prydumala zruchnu versiiu: aktivisty sami vbybaiut' odne odnoho." February 19. https://bit.ly/32C8cfv

2014g. "Mitynhari shturmuiut' kordon okhorony do uriadovoho kvartalu." January 19. https://bit.ly/2JAX4I1

2014h. "Odes'ki separatysty v interneti oholosyly 'Odes'ku respubliku.'" April 16. https://bit.ly/2BB95Jd

2014i. "Parubiy: Maidan s'ohodni povnistiu kontroliuie Kyïv." February 22. https://bit.ly/2TvcIIC

2014j. "P'iat' nardepiv iz Zakarpattia vykhodiat' z Partiï rehioniv." February 20. https://bit.ly/31ADyBB

2014k. "Pravyi sektor zaklikaie liudei z vohnepal'nohoiu zbroieiu viyty na Maidan." February 18. https://bit.ly/2IbKQ6Z

2014l. "Prybichnyky rehionaliv hotuiut'sia do biyky z maidanivtsiamy." February 18. https://bit.ly/2HipOnt

2014m. "Rada stvoryla natsional'nu hvardiiu." March 13. https://bit.ly/2AuZ3bX

2014n. "Rada vidnovyla diiu Konstitutsiï – 2004." February 22. https://bit.ly/36UqZ9d

2014o. "Rehionaly zradyly Yanukovycha: 'mil'ionna partiia stala zaruchnykom odniieï korumpovanoï Sim'ï.'" February 23. https://bit.ly/2JPsWcQ

2014p. "SBU i MVS daly chas na prypynennia protystoiannia do 18.00, obitsiaiut' diiaty zhorstko." February 18. https://bit.ly/2y2UQec

2014q. "U Minoborony zaiavyly, shcho hotovi zatrymuvaty liudei." February 19. https://bit.ly/2XlfvF7

2014r. "U MVS vyznaly, shcho zastosovyvaly zbroiu na Maidani." February 20. https://bit.ly/2HdhFRt

2014s. "U Slov'ians'ku pochalasia Antyterorystychna operatsiia – Avakov." April 13. https://bit.ly/3ipB44r

2014t. "V Krymu viddilennia ne obhovoriuvaly, ale khochut' rozshirennia." February 21. https://bit.ly/32iFdN1

2014u. "Yanukovych: Ya ne zbyraiusia u vidstavku." February 22. https://bit.ly/2NWvMet

2014v. "Yatsenyuk: My zasudzhuiemo nasyl'stvo, yake vidbulosia. Tse ne nash plan." January 19. https://bit.ly/2LJTexU

2014w. "Yatsenyuk rozpoviv, choho opozytsiia chekaie vid Bankovoï." January 21. https://bit.ly/2XPTlyt

2014x. "Yefremov poperedyv opozytsiiu, shcho za Maidan dovedet'sia vidpovisty." February 18. https://bit.ly/2yMcCme

2015. "Rada ukhvalila zminy do konstitutsiï v pershomu chytanni." August 31. https://bit.ly/2JN1HS2

2019. "Vybory do Verkhovnoï Rady Ukraïny 2019. Rezul'taty pidrakhunku holosiv." July 21. https://bit.ly/36PshmJ

Ukrains'kyi tyzhden'. 2015a. "Pid chas rozgonu Maidanu protestuval'nykiv namahalysia vytisnyty na ozbroienykh 'titushok' dlia rozpravy." November 19. https://bit.ly/2LDO9sp

2015b. "Rishennia pro rozhin Yevromaidanu priyniav bezpeseredn'o Yanukovych – slidstvo GPU." November 17. https://bit.ly/37oP6Ob

2018. "Dobkin povidomyv pro zustrich z Yanukovychem u Khar'kovi v 2014 rotsi." *Ukrains'kyi Tyzhden*, April 18. https://bit.ly/2TBDpe6

Ukrains'kyi instytut natsional'noï pam'iati. 2015a. "On the Condemnation of the Communist and National Socialist (Nazi) Regimes, and Prohibition of Propaganda and their Symbols." April 9. https://bit.ly/35yN1Mx

2015b. "On the Legal Status and Honoring the Memory of Fighters for Ukraine's Independence in the Twentieth Century." April 9. https://bit.ly/37SEHdN

Ukrinform. 2016a. "Iz 20 tysiach ukraïns'kykh viys'kovykh z Krymu vyishly 6 tysiach – Matios." February 5. https://bit.ly/33UBy8P

2016b. "Marsh mil'iona. Yak tse bulo." December 8. https://bit.ly/2XOwint

Umland, Andreas. 2016. "Glazyev Tapes: What Moscow's Interference in Ukraine Means for the Minsk Agreements." *Raamop Rusland*, November 25. https://bit.ly/2qB2bx1

2018. "Whom Does Crimea Belong to?" *Vox Ukraine*, August 29. https://bit.ly/2XYIeB3

2019. "Irregular Militias and Radical Nationalism in Post-Euromaydan Ukraine: The Prehistory and Emergence of the 'Azov' Battalion in 2014." *Terrorism and Political Violence* 31(1), 105–31.

UN Human Rights Council. 2016. "Report of the Special Rapporteur on Extrajudicial, Summary or Arbitrary Executions on His Mission to Ukraine." May 4. https://bit.ly/2OSArDG

UNIAN. 2014. "U L'vovi horiat' viys'kovi sklady zi zbroieiu." February 19. https://bit.ly/2B4zfUp

2015. "Maidan Activists Nihoian and Zhiznevskiy 'Not Killed by Police.'" January 26. https://bit.ly/34Ga8Dv

2018. "Z'iavyvsia povnyi tekst zvernennia Yanukovycha do Putina pro vvedeniia viys'k v Ukraïnu." March 2, 2018. https://bit.ly/34oGmUf

United Nations. 2014. "General Assembly Adopts Resolution Calling Upon States Not to Recognize Changes in Status of Crimea Region." March 27. https://bit.ly/2wo64sB

United Nations Meetings Coverage and Press Releases. 2014. "Security Council Fails to Adopt Text Urging Member States Not to Recognize Planned 16 March Referendum in Ukraine's Crimea Region." March 15. https://bit.ly/2DTKmAR

United Nations Peacemaker. 2015. "Package of Measures for the Implementation of the Minsk Agreements." February 12. https://bit.ly/2H1oyC5

United Nations Security Council. 2014. "Letter Dated 3 March 2014 from the Permanent Representative of the Russian Federation to the United Nations Addressed to the Secretary-General." March 3. https://bit.ly/2w4rStj

United States Army Special Operations Command. 2016. "'Little Green Men': A Primer on Modern Russian Unconventional Warfare, Ukraine 2013–2014." https://bit.ly/2EtgoUf

Uriadovyi portal. 2014. "Minoborony: V oblastiakh stvoriuiut'sia batal'iony terytorial'noï oborony." April 30. https://bit.ly/2E4v50L

US Department of State. n.d. "Ukraine and Russia Sanctions." https://bit.ly/3CG3JdL

———. 2014. "Reported Deaths in Ukraine Street Clashes." January 22. https://bit.ly/2zxZC6f

US Department of the Treasury. 2014. "Announcement of Treasury Sanctions on Entities Within the Financial Services and Energy Sectors of Russia, against Arms or Related Materiel Entities, and those Undermining Ukraine's Sovereignty." July 16. https://bit.ly/3AEeJpX

Valentino, Benjamin A. 2004. *Final Solutions: Mass Killing and Genocide in the 20th Century.* Ithaca, NY: Cornell University Press.

Van Evera, Steve. 1997. "Hypotheses on Nationalism and War." In *Nationalism and Ethnic Conflict.* Edited by Michael Brown, Owen Cote, Sean Lynne-Jones, and Stephen Miller, 26–60. Cambridge: MIT Press.

Van Herpen, Marcel H. 2015. *Putin's Propaganda Machine: Soft Power and Russian Foreign Policy.* Lanham, MD: Rowman & Littlefield.

Van Houten, Pieter. 1998. "The Role of a Minority Reference State in Ethnic Relations." *Archives européenes de sociologie* 34(1), 110–46.

Venice Commission. 2014. "Opinion on 'Whether the Decision Taken by the Supreme Council of the Autonomous Republic of Crimea in Ukraine to Organise a Referendum on Becoming a Constituent Territory of the Russian Federation or Restoring Crimea's 1992 Constitution is Compatible with Constitutional Principles.'" Council of Europe, March 21. https://bit.ly/35BOMIZ

———. 2017. "Opinion on the Provisions of the Law on Education of 5 September 2017." Council of Europe, December 11. https://bit.ly/2PCCgDf

Verkhovna Rada Ukraïny. 2015. "Proekt Zakonu pro vnesennia zmin do Konstitutsiï Ukrainy (shchodo detsentralizatsiï vlady)." July 1. https://bit.ly/2JDDQ7E

———. 2021. "Pro korinni narody Ukraïny." July 1. https://bit.ly/3koBesA

Versii.com. 2014. "Khar'kovskii oblsovet otkazalsia naznachat' referendum." March 13. https://bit.ly/3iRlY6W

Vesti.ru. 2014a. "Avtobusy krymskykh propravitel'stvennykh aktivistov atakovali ekstremisty." February 21. https://bit.ly/2CZVHi4

2014b. "Litsenziia na ubiitsvo: natsgvardiia v Mariupole okhotilas' na liudei s videokamerami." May 10. https://bit.ly/2U37AQB

2014c. "Putin otvetil na voprosy po Ukraine: o vvode voisk, Yanukovyche i situatsii v Krymu." March 4. https://bit.ly/33w6mND

Vgorode. 2014a. "Khronika sobytii: chto proiskhodilo v Donetske s 3 po 6 marta." March 6. https://bit.ly/2zN9XcR

2014b. "Khronika sobytii s 17 marta po 9 aprelia: chto proiskhodilo v Donetske." April 9. https://bit.ly/2sX6zIE

2014c. "Parlament Kryma zaiavil o nachale grazhdanskoi voine." February 18. https://bit.ly/2rUuH1b

Vice News. 2014. "Protest Turns Fatal: Russian Roulette in Ukraine (Dispatch 9)." YouTube video, March 14. https://bit.ly/1o7cuV8

Vikhrov, Natalie. 2019. "In Ukraine's Donbas Region, Life Amid the Ravages of a Forgotten War." *World Politics Review*, February 12. https://bit.ly/2XgZtMS

Vitkine, Benoît. 2014a. "A Kiev, de l'autre côté des barricades, chez les terribles Berkout." *Le Monde*, February 1. https://bit.ly/2JnAUsK

2014b. "Après les revers de l'armée régulière, Kiev est contraint à un cessez-le-feu dans le Donbass." *Le Monde*, September 3. https://bit.ly/2W7lakZ

Vlasiuk, Vladyslav. 2019. "What Does the New Language Law Really Change?" *Kyiv Post*, May 10. https://bit.ly/2FiMnYp

Vmeste s Rossiei. 2014. "Srochnoe zaiavlenie prem'ier-ministra Donetskoi Narodnoi Respubliki Aleksandra Zakharchenko." August 9. https://bit.ly/355aS8e

VO Svoboda. 2013. "Oleh Tyahnybok zaklykaie liudei ne piddavatysia na provokatsiï vlady na Bankoviy." December 1. https://bit.ly/2RRWLeC

Volchek, Dmitrii. 2014. "Spetsoperatsii be provodiat cherez 'Facebook.'" *Radio svoboda*, May 23. https://bit.ly/2L5N2PX

Volkov, Denis. 2018. "What the Russian Public Thinks of Victory Day." *Moscow Times*, May 10. https://bit.ly/2Q7sZ3C

Volkov, Konstantin. 2014. "Nikto nikakikh rasporiazhenii maidana ne vypolniaiet." *Izvestiia*, February 24. https://bit.ly/2VUrY2O

Volochine, Elena, and James Keogh, dirs. 2016. *Oleg's Choice (Le choix d'Oleg).* Java Films.

Volyns'ki novyny. 2014a. "Gubernatora Volyni prykuvaly naruchnykamy do stsenii Yevromaidanu." YouTube video, February 19. https://bit.ly/2KBYpxJ

2014b. "Na kolinakh: Berkut v tsentri mista vibachaietsia pered luchanamy." February 23. https://bit.ly/2roLA0E

von Twickel, Nikolaus. 2017. "South Ossetia: A 'Little Switzerland' for Donbas?" *Eurasianet*, May 31. https://bit.ly/33MHS4e

2020. "The State of the Donbas: A Study of Eastern Ukraine's Separatist-Held Areas." In *Beyond Frozen Conflict: Scenarios for the Separatist Disputes of Eastern Europe*. Edited by Michael Emerson, 55–134. Center for European Policy Studies. London: Rowman & Littlefield.

Wagner, R. Harrison. 2000. "Bargaining and War." *American Journal of Political Science* 44(3), 469–84.

Walker, Shaun. 2014. "Ukraine Says It Controls Donetsk Airport after Fighting Leaves Dozens Dead." *The Guardian*, May 27. https://bit.ly/2V1lhdE

2016. "Russia's 'Valiant Hero' in Ukraine Turns His Fire on Vladimir Putin." *The Guardian*, June 5. https://bit.ly/2IpW1aY

2018. *The Long Hangover: Putin's New Russia and the Ghosts of the Past*. Oxford: Oxford University Press.

Walt, Stephen M. 2014. "No Contest." *Foreign Policy*, March 4. https://bit.ly/33C827f

2015. "What Putin Learned from Reagan." *Foreign Policy*, February 17. https://bit.ly/1vNrvdT

Walter, Barbara F. 1997. "The Critical Barrier to Civil War Settlement." *International Organization* 51(3), 335–64.

2002. *Committing to Peace: The Successful Settlement of Civil Wars*. Princeton, NJ: Princeton University Press.

2017. "The New Civil Wars." *Annual Review of Political Science* 20, 469–86.

Washington Post. 2014. "Transcript: Putin Says Russia Will Protect the Rights of Russians Abroad." March 18. https://wapo.st/2IYbhw4

Weaver, Courtney, Neil Buckley, and Kathrin Hille. 2014. "Obama Warns Moscow of 'Costs' over Ukraine." *Financial Times*, February 28. https://on.ft.com/2VQJZPp

Weaver, Matthew, Paul Owen, and Conal Urquhart. 2014. "Ukraine Crisis: US and EU Move to Impose Sanctions." *The Guardian*, February 19. https://bit.ly/2OOBzIA

Weiner, Amir. 2001. *Making Sense of War: The Second World War and the Fate of the Bolshevik Revolution*. Princeton, NJ: Princeton University Press.

Weingast, Barry R. 1997. "The Political Foundations of Democracy and the Rule of Law." *American Political Science Review* 91(2), 245–63.

White, Gregory L., Matthew Dalton, and Katya Gorchinskaya. 2014. "Russia to Join International Relief Effort as Ukraine Presses Fight." *Wall Street Journal*, August 11. https://on.wsj.com/2TWxznm

Whitmore, Brian. 2016. "How to Manufacture a War." *RFE/RL*, August 26. https://bit.ly/2SwbRp3

Williamson, Hugh. 2014. "Ukraine: Letter to President Poroshenko on Military Operations in Luhansk and Donetsk." *Human Rights Watch*, July 18. https://bit.ly/34FfRdi

Wilson, Andrew. 2005. *Ukraine's Orange Revolution*. New Haven, CT: Yale University Press.

2014. *Ukraine Crisis: What It Means for the West*. New Haven, CT: Yale University Press.

2016. "The Donbas in 2014: Explaining Civil Conflict Perhaps, but Not Civil War." *Europe-Asia Studies* 68(4), 631–52.

Wimmer, Andreas, Lars-Erik Cederman, and Brian Min. 2009. "Ethnic Politics and Armed Conflict: A Configurational Analysis of a New Global Data Set." *American Sociological Review* 74(2), 316–37.

Witte, Griff. 2014. "Pro-Russian Separatists in Eastern Ukraine Were 'Nobodies' – Until Now." *Washington Post*, April 30. https://wapo.st/2J29TI5

Witte, Griff, and William Booth. 2014. "As Russian Forces Escalate, Ukraine's Influence Waning." *Washington Post*, April 26. https://wapo.st/2GnQtR9

Wohlforth, William C. 1994. "Realism and the End of the Cold War." *International Security* 19(3), 91–129.

Wolczuk, Kataryna. 2001. *The Moulding of Ukraine: The Constitutional Politics of State Formation*. Budapest: Central European University Press.

Woods, Richard. 2014. "Special Report: Why Ukraine's Revolution Remains Unfinished." *Reuters*, November 3. https://reut.rs/2JSwTxk

Wylegala, Anna. 2017. "Managing the Difficult Past: Ukrainian Collective Memory and Public Debates on History." *Nationalities Papers* 45(5), 780–97.

Wylegala, Anna, and Margorzata Globawca-Grajper. 2020. *The Burden of the Past: History, Memory, and Identity in Contemporary Ukraine*. Bloomington: Indiana University Press.

Wynnyckyj, Mychailo. 2014. "Yanukovych Is Doomed to Fail: Mychailo Wynnyckyj's EuroMaidan Diary." *The Ukraine List (UKL)* No. 466, February 19.

Yashin, Ilya, and Olga Shorina. 2015. "Putin. War. Based on Materials from Boris Nemtsov." *Free Russia Foundation*. https://bit.ly/3kqrU80

Yekelchyk, Serhy. 2015. *The Conflict in Ukraine*. Oxford: Oxford University Press.

Young, Cathy. 2017. "Ukraine Journalists Still Enduring Brutal Kidnappings, Imprisonment, and Maybe Worse." *The Daily Beast*, July 12. https://bit.ly/38S1rZU

Yudina, Natalia, and Alexander Verkhovsky. 2019. "Russian Nationalist Veterans of the Donbas War." *Nationalities Papers*, 47(5), 734–49.

Yurovskaia, Daria. 2014. "Shturm obladministratsii v Khar'kove." *Mediaport*, March 1. https://bit.ly/2O9mSim

Za Donbass. 2014. "Ul'timatum Narodnogo opolchenie Donbassa deputatam Donets'kogo gorods'kogo soveta." YouTube video, March 9. https://bit.ly/2EGhOuV

Zakharchenko, Vitaliy. 2016. *Krovavyi Evromaidan – prestuplenie veka.* St. Petersburg: Piter.

Zakonodavstvo Ukraïny. 2014a. "Pro osoblyvyi poriadok mistsevoho samoriaduvannia v okremykh raionakh Donets'koï ta Luhans'koï oblastei." September 16. https://bit.ly/2mk30fF

2014b. "Pro samousunennia Prezydenta Ukraïny vid vykonannia konstitutsiynykh povnovazhen' ta pryznachennia pozacherhovykh vyboriv Prezydenta Ukraïny." February 22. https://bit.ly/2KzMAJP

2014c. "Pro vnesennia zmin do Zakonu Ukraïny 'Pro sudoustriy i status suddiv' ta protsesual'nykh zakoniv shchodo dodatkovykh zakhodiv zakhistu bezpeki hromadian." February 2. https://bit.ly/2T5lRY2

2014d. "Pro zabezpechennia prav i svobod hromadian ta pravovyi rezhym na tymchasovo okupovaniy terytoriï Ukraïny." April 15. https://bit.ly/2kSDsWq

2014e. "Pro zasudzhennia zastosuvannia nasyl'stva, shcho pryzvelo do zahybeli liudei." February 20. https://bit.ly/2Z20PL3

2014f. "Ukaz Prezydenta Ukraïny – Pro chastkovu mobilizatsiiu." March 17. https://bit.ly/2S0aXAt

2017. "Pro osvitu." September 5. https://bit.ly/2Z4TXOG

2018. "Zakon Ukraïny – Pro borot'bu z teroryzmom." November 11. https://bit.ly/2SAaQjL

2019. "Pro zabezpechennia funktsionuvannia ukraïns'koï movy yak derzhavnoï." April 25. https://bit.ly/2PX8Hes

Zanuda, Anastasiia. 2013. "Shparhalka 3x3: perevahy i ryzyky ekonomichnoï intehratsiï na Zakhid ta Skhid." *BBC News Ukraïna*, November 28. https://bbc.in/2EU9yYM

Zeveleva, Olga. 2019. "How Ordinary Crimeans Helped Russia Annex Their Home." *openDemocracy*, March 14. https://bit.ly/2TD07X0

Zhartovskaia, Mariia. 2017. "Po tu storonu Maidana. 'Lidery' revoliutsii i okruzhenie Yanukovycha rasskazyvaiut o zakulis'e pervykh dnei protestov." *TSN*, November 30. https://bit.ly/2KjSEqV

Zhigulev, Il'ia, Aleksandra Sivtsova, and Iuliana Skibitskaia. 2017. "'Nikto ne veril, chto eto vser'ez.' Kak prisoediniali Krym: vesna 2014-go glazami Moskvy, Kieva i Sevastopolia." *Meduza*, March 21. https://bit.ly/2qjOKpC

Zhitel UA. 2014. "Zakhvat SBU Donetsk 07.04.2014." YouTube video, April 8. https://bit.ly/3iTIYlO

Zhuk, Alyona. 2016. "Almost Half of Soldiers Killed in Donbas Are Non-Combat Losses." *Kyiv Post*, June 11. https://bit.ly/2sxtRIf

Zhukov, Yuri. 2014. "Rust Belt Rising: The Economics behind Eastern Ukraine's Upheaval." *Foreign Affairs*, June 11. https://fam.ag/3dnWnjX

2015. "Population Resettlement in War: Theory and Evidence from Soviet Archives." *Journal of Conflict Resolution* 59(7), 1155–85.

2016. "Trading Hard Hats for Combat Helmets: The Economics of Rebellion in Eastern Ukraine." *Journal of Comparative Economics* 44(1), 1–15.

Zinets, Natalia, and Richard Balmforth. 2015. "Ukraine Parliament Offers Special Status for Rebel East, Russia Criticizes." *Reuters*, March 17. https://reut.rs/2mwl8mj

Zn.ua. 2013. "Pri razgone Evromaidana v noch' na 30 noiabria postradali 79 chelovek." December 5. https://bit.ly/2WQRVUB

2014. "Rada vidnovyla diiu Konstitutsiï 2004 roku." February 21. https://bit.ly/2Tq6HNf

2015. "Predlozheniia 'DNR' i 'LNR' na peregovorakh v Minske: dokument." February 11. https://bit.ly/2Lwfx9j

Zoria, Yuri. 2019. "What We Know about Russia's Active Duty Soldiers Captured in Eastern Ukraine from 2014." *Euromaidan Press*, January 25. https://bit.ly/2MWhBqI

Zverev, Anton. 2016. "Moscow Is Bankrolling Ukraine Rebels: Ex-Separatist Official." *Reuters*, October 5. https://bit.ly/3mMbN4f

Zygar, Mikhail. 2016. *All the Kremlin's Men: Inside the Court of Vladimir Putin*. New York: Public Affairs.

Index

Made in the USA
Las Vegas, NV
03 October 2023

78505424R10157